LGBTQ+ Intimate Partner Violence

This book explores the unique issues involved in assessing, diagnosing, intervening, and treating intimate partner violence (IPV) in the LGBTQ+ population.

Currently, there is little to no instruction regarding this topic in training programs, and this volume is the culmination of an effort to remedy this deficit. The authors draw upon clinical examples and research from the IPV programs in their own organization as well as external research to provide a comprehensive overview. Chapters span topics that include definitions of IPV, its history, relevant issues within the LGBTQ+ community, the unique facets of LGBTQ+ IPV, and its assessment and diagnosis. Case examples indicate how an assessment should be carried out and how to develop appropriate and effective interventions and treatment plans.

This book will empower clinicians to assess for and treat LGBTQ+ IPV whenever and wherever they encounter it.

Susan Holt, PsyD, LMFT, CCDVC, has been a long-standing leader in the field of LGBTQ+ intimate partner violence. She founded the Los Angeles LGBT Center's Stop Violence Program, serves as its director, and was instrumental in the development of the Center's National Institute on LGBTQ Intimate Partner Violence.

Amir K. Ahuja, MD, is the director of psychiatry at the Los Angeles LGBT Center, president of AGLP: The Association of LGBTQ+ Psychiatrists, and president of the American Psychiatric Association LGBTQ Caucus. He also has a private practice in Beverly Hills, CA, USA.

"Thirty-five years ago I climbed out a window in my San Francisco apartment to escape my violent partner—who had locked the front door with threats to 'sort me out once and for all.' Back then, there were no books like this to help me. In fact, there's never been a book like this!

A monumental achievement by expert authors who don't shy away from the complexities of LGBTQ intimate partner violence: from intersections of race, class, gender identity, and HIV status, to the inherent challenges to the male–female abuse paradigm and the dearth of understanding within the broader queer community, it's all in here.

The duration and severity of intimate partner violence a queer person experiences, the authors say, is determined by the effectiveness of treatment they receive. This book is the key to that better treatment. If you're new to this topic or have been reading about such violence for years, this book will change what you think you know about it."

Patrick Letellier, *co-author of* Men Who Beat the Men Who Love Them

"Dr. Susan Holt and Dr. Amir Ahuja have written an indispensable volume for LGBTQ+ people who find themselves in the midst of intimate partner violence, as well as for people who care for them. Since LGBTQ+-affirming care is not readily available outside select major urban centers, this book has far-reaching impact that gives not only deep understanding and much-needed hope but also 'next steps' and very practical guidance to mental health clinicians across the globe."

Petros Levounis, MD, MA, *Professor and Chair, Department of Psychiatry, and Associate Dean, Rutgers New Jersey Medical School, USA*

"Holt and Ahuja's text is a detailed overview of a long-standing and long-misunderstood problem of intimate partner abuse/violence (IPV) in LGBTQ+ communities. Based on a comprehensive review of research and knowledge in this field, the authors effectively highlight the impact of homophobia and transphobia on the experience of IPV, and on clinical interventions to assist people facing the problem, whether they are aggressors or victims. This book is a valuable resource to support clinicians in their assessments and treatment plans."

Barrie Levy, MSW, LCSW, *UCLA School of Public Policy, Department of Social Welfare, psychotherapist, organizational consultant, and author of* In Love and in Danger: A Teen's Guide to Breaking Free of Abusive Relationships

LGBTQ+ Intimate Partner Violence

A Guide for Mental Health Practitioners

SUSAN HOLT AND AMIR AHUJA

Routledge
Taylor & Francis Group

NEW YORK AND LONDON

Designed cover image: © Getty Images / Viktoriia Melkisheva

First published 2025
by Routledge
605 Third Avenue, New York, NY 10158

and by Routledge
4 Park Square, Milton Park, Abingdon, Oxon, OX14 4RN

Routledge is an imprint of the Taylor & Francis Group, an informa business

ISBN: 978-0-367-14344-2 (hbk)
ISBN: 978-0-367-14345-9 (pbk)
ISBN: 978-0-429-03139-7 (ebk)

DOI: 10.4324/9780429031397

Typeset in Dante and Avenir
by MPS Limited, Dehradun

Contents

Foreword: A Conversation with Greg Louganis

No one who watched the 1988 Olympics on television will ever forget seeing Greg Louganis hit his head on the diving board during the ninth dive of the springboard preliminaries. Millions felt his pain and then held their breath as the two-time gold medalist returned to the board only minutes later, with four stitches and a waterproof patch, and executed what was perhaps the best dive of the 1988 Olympics.

(From *Breaking the Surface*, 1995)

Those who witnessed this event knew that Louganis was the personification of the Olympic spirit. What most did not know, however, was that Greg had tested positive for HIV just several months prior. They also didn't know that he was gay or that he had experienced domestic violence with a partner in 1980 and then again with another partner in 1984. He wrote about both experiences in his book because he thought it was important that others know what occurs in abusive relationships. His life story, including the domestic violence he experienced, was also portrayed in the 1997 television film *Breaking the Surface: The Greg Louganis Story*, which was based on his book.

We met Greg Louganis via Zoom. Settled in his office with a podcast-ready microphone, he had silver hair framing his face and reading glasses that made him look distinguished yet youthful. His frame still suggests the physique of someone who is not far removed from his life as a world-class athlete. Behind him, in the background, is a portrait of him with several of his dogs. This is a hint of his current life, which includes raising and training dogs. Despite the demands of this new journey, Greg still embraces his past and his community. He agreed to speak with us without hesitation when we indicated that we were writing this book. As you will see, he proved to be very honest, candid, and reflective about his experiences and never shied away from difficult or uncomfortable topics. For this, we are truly grateful.

Amir was only 5 years old when the infamous dive in which Greg hit his head on the diving board at the Olympics occurred. Susan was just beginning her career as a psychotherapist at the Los Angeles Gay & Lesbian Center (now the Los Angeles LGBT Center) and had several clients who were reporting domestic violence in their relationships. In 1988, however, information about either LGBTQ+ domestic violence or HIV was difficult to find—in fact, only one book about domestic violence (*Naming the Violence: Speaking Out about Lesbian Battering*), an anthology of stories of lesbian survivors, existed. It was also at this time that the *first* coordinated HIV/AIDS education campaign was launched by the U.S. surgeon general with its pamphlet entitled "Understanding AIDS."

Over time, as we learned more about Greg Louganis, he became an inspiration to us. It was with reverence for his life and story that we approached interviewing Greg for this book. We were hoping to learn about the unique and universal elements of his experience of intimate partner violence. We wanted to know what he felt he handled well, what he believed could have gone differently, and how he has since made peace with, and healed from, the trauma of domestic violence. This interview demonstrates all of these aspects.

The Transcript

Amir: How do you define intimate partner violence?

Greg: Intimate partner violence can truly be of varying degrees from fisticuffs, knock-down, drag-out, physical abuse to violent speech. Anything that diminishes somebody's self-worth is really an act of violence. It can take on various different forms, and we need to bring awareness to recognizing when you are in it, because, sometimes when you are in a relationship, you are not recognizing that. It is important to recognize if you feel diminished in any way, that it is not constructive communication, and that it does not bode well for a loving relationship.

Amir: Yes, when you are in a relationship, particularly when there is psychological and verbal abuse, people do not realize it is happening because they think you have to be hit for it to be abusive. So, in the relationships that you have publicly discussed, including the one with your former partner Jim, when did you realize that IPV was happening and that it was unhealthy?

Greg: In my relationship with Jim during the first year we were together, we were just dating at that time as far as I was concerned. However, he communicated to me that it was something far different than what I had in my own head. It turned violent, and I was raped. It was quite violent, and I can't remember if it was scissors or a knife held to my throat. You would think that after a confrontation like that, you would say "OK. That's it." That would be the healthy thing to do, but I stayed for 5–6 years. I think a lot of that is where we come from, what we are conditioned to believe is a normal relationship, and what we are conditioned to expect in a relationship. This is through seeing our parents' relationships. I convinced myself I deserved that treatment and was constantly making a "living amends" to my wrongdoings. It wasn't clear what those were … since looking back, it wasn't even clear what the relationship was.

That gave me a sense of confusion. The one thing that was a blessing for me was that I was training in Florida, and my home was in California, and that separation gave me strength to get to an equilibrium and to give me the realization that this treatment was tearing me down instead of building me up. After the 1988 Olympics, it led to me realizing I needed to make a change. It gave me the strength I needed to stand on my own two feet and stand up for myself. That is something that a lot of people don't have. Your mind says, "Who is going to touch me?" since it was 1988–1989 and I was HIV positive. HIV/AIDS was a death sentence, and I thought to myself, "Well, nobody else would touch me." So, I stayed. The breaking point happened once I got back home and I did some investigation and gathered some information about Jim mismanaging the finances. This really pushed me to make that confrontation of going to Jim and saying "OK, this is not working. You don't trust me, and I don't trust you, and I think that we are better off apart."

Susan: Abuse often escalates when the survivor attempts to leave the relationship or develops autonomy. Did Jim become increasingly abusive at that point because you were saying you wanted to be apart?

Greg: Well, he made threats and he said that, if I came back to the house, he was going to "blow my fucking brains out." He had purchased a gun. He said he would "take me to hell with him" and that he would come forward with my HIV diagnosis. He also said that "I killed him" because of the HIV and because I brought that into our relationship. You know, a lot of people like to point to Jim as having given me AIDS but I suspect I was probably HIV positive even before I was with him. My previous partner died of AIDS, so chances are, when we were together, me and my ex, we both seroconverted at that time. So, when people say, "Who gave it to who?" it really doesn't matter. It's just a virus. Viruses don't discriminate. You can't blame anybody, and it's just a fact of life. It is what I had to learn how to live with and navigate. That is the important thing, navigating through. That is why a book like this is so important—to help people navigate through a difficult situation. It is important to give people a perspective of what is right and what is wrong, because often when you are in an abusive relationship, that gets distorted. Your perception is distorted, so you don't recognize, you don't understand, you want to give someone the benefit of the doubt. You want to excuse their bad behavior by saying, "It was their upbringing" or something instead of seeing things for what they are.

Amir: Thank you for saying that. I think it is important to give therapists information so that they can assist LGBTQ+ people who are struggling with domestic violence. It is also important for there to be a face for this issue. It is good to see what we can do better in the future since we all learn and grow over time. You mentioned learning about relationships through your parents. Was that a situation that included domestic violence?

Greg: I remember standing in between my mother and my father and protecting my mother. Then, my mother instructed me to take my sister and go next door. Dad was an alcoholic. Sometimes he was a really pleasant drunk and sometimes he wasn't—"you don't approach him." That was one of the things my sister and I were thinking when we were making his martini at the end of the night: "Is it a day when I can ask him for a bike?" and it would be like "No, today is not that kind of day." So, we were walking on eggshells, which anyone knows who is dealing with addiction in the household. There are times when it is good times and times it is not such good times. When you are young, you think that is normal because you don't have any other gauge of what healthy relationships are. That is the reason there are so many dysfunctional families, because we just pass it from generation to generation.

In that way, you understood that that's how people deserve to be treated. It is like you were comfortable walking on eggshells. It was interesting because, as I was growing up, I lived with other families because I was in a particular athlete program so I had to travel to where the facilities were and where the coaching was. I left my family behind and moved in with other families and saw how those families operated. I stayed with one incredible family in Tucson, AZ—the Christensens—and they had bowling night and outings and they went camping together. That was eye-opening since that was far away from the way that I was raised. They had five kids and they all got along great. Of course, there were spats and disagreements, but I saw how they dealt with it, and they had better coping mechanisms to deal with adversity.

Susan: I was actually curious about the other families. Did you see anything similar to your own family with the others that you lived with?

Greg: A little bit when I lived with the Lees. There was a daughter who was older, and I was living in in her room since she was going away to college. They also had a son who was very close to my age, and it was challenging because here I'm taking his father away from him because of the diving. Overall, the lack of connection I saw was very similar to me and my dad. Fortunately, my dad and I had a beautiful reconciliation when he was diagnosed with cancer. That is when I came out to him early in 1989 about my HIV status, and then we had very important conversations about life. We were addressing some of the things that happened as I was growing up, and his interpretation of it. I also shared what I felt the experience was for me. So, we were able to see both experiences and really appreciate that and get to a place of forgiveness. You know, those were back in the days where kids were given spankings and were physically hit. Of course, the parent is saying "This is gonna hurt me more than it hurts you" but those were the only tools that they had. After all, that is what they grew up with, and that is

	what they knew how to do. They really thought they were being loving in disciplining that way.
Susan:	You speak articulately about it because you can see that it is intergenerational—and how it is can change in the next generation.
Greg:	Right. Too bad I don't have kids.
Susan:	It isn't all that important that you don't have kids. You speak out about it and have made your story public. That can have a significant impact on a lot of people.
Amir:	I want to ask you about being in a relationship with a man at that time and not being out. What impact did that have on you and on the IPV? I ask this because we know that it can be a huge reason to stay in an abusive relationship when you don't feel like you have anybody else or if there are threats of outing.
Greg:	That's a loaded question because I was out to my friends and family. Early on, people in diving knew my sexual identity. They had meetings on the international trips about "Who was going to room with the fag?" Often, I would qualify for two positions between the 3-meter springboard and 10-meter platform, so a lot of times I had my own room. However, other times there was usually one male person on the team that was secure enough in their own sexuality to room with me. A lot of people think that was very homophobic, but I believe it was more about envy than about true homophobia because I was winning. The whole coming out concept for me was in stages. I didn't come out publicly about my sexual identity until the 1994 gay games. Until then, it was my policy not to discuss my personal life with members of the media, and a part of that came from agents who were representing me. They said, "Greg, tone down the gay thing." So, what was kind of drilled into me was that I'm the ambassador for diving, so I can educate people. I made myself very much available to the reporters, and they were very grateful for that and out of respect they didn't really publish my personal life.

Actually, the fears of coming out and the idea of somebody knowing something about you were terrifying and scary, but that was more over the HIV, so that was a heavier burden. There was more stress and anxiety surrounding coming out about my HIV—with the book and Barbara Walters and Oprah interviews. That was more frightening to me.

Amir: I wanted to ask about the HIV because there are aspects of that that can be tough to navigate. This is, because you can feel guilty about partners having AIDS and having to leave them. There can also be restriction of access to HIV medication or to healthcare as a way of controlling people. There are also threats of outing, and other aspects to this that complicate things. How do you see that now with Jim and with past or future relationships?

Greg: We have a tendency of making the same mistake over and over again. You think, "OK I've learned my lesson," and then you are right back in the same relationship that you were in before. It takes time and grace to be able to recognize it and to say "Oh, shit, I did it again." You have to be forgiving of yourself and know that it did not work out last time and have the confidence to know it is not going to work out this time either. It's like what Oprah says, "When somebody reveals themselves, believe them the first time."

Amir: I wanted to ask about Jim since one of the things you brought up in the book was feeling guilty leaving him. He was sick at the time, and you said you didn't want him to be alone or have to die alone, and the feeling was mutual. Do you think that was one of the factors that led you to stay with him longer, or did that have nothing to do with it?

Greg: By the time I came back, and we had that conversation, it was done. There was really no looking back because I knew in my heart and in my body that the right thing to do was to step away. So, I think I was pretty strong at that time, but it did take those 3 years of separation to get on my feet. It was important to be around people who were more encouraging and more uplifting in order to gain confidence to stand on my own two feet and stand up for myself.

Susan: You said initially when we first started talking that the diminishment of self-esteem was devastating and that it was hard to recover from it.

Greg: Yes, it really is because, the more you think the thought, the more it becomes a belief. Then, then when it becomes a belief, it feels like it's hardwired. The trick is understanding and realizing that your belief is just a thought and that thoughts can change.

Amir: It strikes me as so interesting because you were in a position in the 80s and 90s where it's hard to get more external validation than you were actually getting and yet you were still feeling diminished in yourself. It just shows how powerful those beliefs are and that the validation really has to come from inside.

Greg: It is like Dr Wayne Dyer talks about, which is to be independent of the good opinion of others. So often we're just living for other people's validation when we should be looking inside in order to get the validation that is necessary. Another perspective is from Byron Katie's *Loving What Is* and that awareness of what your thoughts are and knowing what is true. It is important to be able to validate ourselves in a healthy way, to be able to stand on our own, and to not be so dependent on others for the validation we feel we need because that can come from within. It's also much more powerful when it's coming from within because you're standing in it. It's a part of you and it's something that isn't going to go away on a whim.

Amir: I think of the fuel for IPV being shame and secrecy as well as isolation. In the book, you detail the controlling aspects that Jim had, including controlling your day-to-day life and finances, and cutting you off socially from friends and family. How can people in relationships, including yourself, be able to safeguard against this?

Greg: The isolation and the cutting off of people often comes very gradually, and we don't even recognize it as it's happening. I allowed Jim to be my eyes to the world, and my life was lived through the lens of Jim. I was not investigating myself and saying "How do I feel about this? How does this sit with me?" You are getting skewed stories, and I was believing them. So, I think what I learned is to go to the source. If there's something that is reported to you, then don't take their word for it because it may have been misinterpreted. Go to the source that is in question to get into a peaceful place with that other individual rather than let it stay as a thought. As I said before, this can become a hardened belief as you think it more and more.

Amir: We see repeatedly how people are victims of this oppressive level of control from their partners. What changed your perspective on this? Was it something you just realized after going through it? Was it the therapy later?

Greg: Well, it is something that I went through several times. If you're going to make a mistake, then chances are you're going to make it again. The trick is not making it three times, but we still make those mistakes often more than three times. It is just bringing more awareness and confidence to yourself. It is one of those things I'm learning still today in taking more control of my finances, understanding what it is that I want, and standing up for myself.

Through therapy, I realized that my father said that I would never be able to handle my finances or that I was not smart enough to do it. In fact, I am pretty good at it when I have had to do it later in life. However, it was easier for me to hand it off to Jim and say, "Here. You handle this." It's a contention of stress for me, so a lot of times I will go into avoidance of that stress instead of getting more involved with it myself. Then, I could understand why certain things are done and the reasoning behind certain decisions. It really is a confidence thing for me. I am getting better, and we are all still a work in progress.

Susan: Was therapy helpful to you for the IPV that you experienced?

Greg: Therapy was very, very important in getting through this. It is never a "through" and it is never over as it is a continuing process. When I first got into therapy, there was such a stigma surrounding mental health. When I was 17 years old and I attempted suicide, they said I should go to a psychologist. My dad's response was, "You are not crazy," so I did not get therapy, but that also left an imprint on me that "Only crazy people get therapy." Once I got into therapy and started to work on myself, it was very beneficial, but I did have to go onto psychiatric medications. I was on some antidepressants to start the work. It helped me get going in order to continue on my own. Later, I no longer needed that, and it was important for me to feel the feelings and work through them. That is the only time I have ever been in rehab for my psychiatric medications. I was on such a regimen that I needed help to get off of them and to regulate without them. The medicines were good to a certain point, and then I needed to get off of them.

Amir: There are many ways that the community and individual practitioners can help with this. How was your experience with social workers, community resources, and/or police?

Greg: I had a support group going through the process. I had Debbie and Kathy Shaw, the nieces of Dr. Sammy Lee, the physician and diver. One is an attorney and one is a doctor. That is who was looking after me, and I moved into their place after I was "banned" from the house I was living in with my partner. That really helped stabilize me. When we did go up to the house to get my belongings, including my Olympic medals, we went there with a sheriff. That was quite stressful, and that was my experience of detachment from the physical house and my belongings and having to move on. It was helpful to know you have support.

Susan: Did you have any negative experiences with mental health providers or police?

Greg: The sheriff who showed up was like "What is this all about?" I think he was skeptical initially, but once we got in there and he heard the verbal exchange, he had a change of heart. He then appreciated the gravity of the situation, and we were thankful for his presence.

Amir: Was there any element of feeling that this was diminished in importance from the police officer?

Greg: There was not any disdain from the police officer, so that is good. There was skepticism, and a good cop, when they walk into a situation, should be skeptical. I don't think it could have been handled any differently. After all, you also don't want to feed into the drama, so approaching it this way was quite appropriate and kind.

Susan: Is there anything else you would want mental health practitioners, survivors of IPV, or people assisting survivors to know?

Greg: I think it is important to be patient. You go through stages in this process. Initially, you are a survivor. In this stage, you are still hanging on to a piece of that victim. Getting beyond survivor, you have to get to a place of forgiveness. It is not for them; it is for you. I had a difficult time with this, and I had a therapist say "In this difficult relationship, what was your part in it?" At first I balked at this, but I realized that my part in it was that I stayed. I have to take responsibility for that and get curious as to where that came from.

It was difficult to tell with Jim what was true and what wasn't since there were so many lies. However, he said his stepfather sexually abused him, and my suspicions are that this was probably true. As a young boy, he was so terrified being abused by his stepfather and all he was wanting was control. So, recognizing that was important. People don't hurt other people without being confused. So, to understand and acknowledge the confusion allows you to be in a healthier place and get close to forgiveness. Getting to that empathetic side allows me to realize that what happened was just events, and I am now grateful for them, as they allowed me to be more empathic to others who have gone through this. To forgive and to love is true healing. To forgive and to love, as it applies to Jim, in my mind's eye, I see this poor young boy who was molested by his stepfather and who was in tremendous pain. Can I forgive that boy and wrap my arms around that boy? Yes.

Amir: If we invest more in wrapping our arms around people at that age, we can prevent a lot of IPV, including what happened to you.

Greg: As long as you are hanging on to being a survivor, you are hanging on to a piece of being a victim. When I go to speaking engagements talking about domestic violence, I need time to recover. In speaking, you are reliving that experience and you are bringing those things into the present. It may not be representative of you anymore, but you are revisiting it. It took you all this time to dissect it and understand it so that it does not happen again, but, since you are going back to that space, you need to give yourself time to heal even just from the retelling of the story.

Amir: That summarizes what we are here to do. Our mission is to empower clinicians to help people examine this and overcome it. We appreciate you being vulnerable.

Susan: You talk about this so eloquently. Currently, many clinicians have no training about LGBTQ+ domestic violence. They are seeing people in crisis but may have never seen clients come out the other side of this like you have. So, thank you so much for giving us an example of someone who has overcome this.

Greg: Well, thank you for that. You just have to come to the point where you visit the past, but do not take up residency there. My way of viewing it is that I can visit an old house of mine but I don't live there. I live in a new house now, and it is much healthier.

Amir: Yes, I think our clients certainly need to be able to see that they can have a good outcome, but we as clinicians do too. Thank you for illustrating that healing is possible. When we are frustrated that clients are doing the same things over and over again, it can be helpful to see your example.

Greg: Yes, we all make those mistakes and learn in our own time. We all have to be patient with this process. I have learned not to be afraid of new relationships and new experiences. I also have learned to hold things with a light touch, which means that they are free to leave. This applies in relationships and with the thoughts that we have. If we hold on to them too strongly, they become hardened beliefs. It is better to hold them lightly and ask, "Is this still serving me?" If so, you can continue to have that thought. If not, you can discard it. This has worked for me throughout my healing process.

Amir and Susan: Thank you so much, Greg. You have been very generous with your time, and we wish you the best in all your future endeavors.

References

Naming the Violence: Speaking Out about Lesbian Battering. Kerry Lobel, Editor. 1986. National Coalition Against Domestic Violence. Seattle Press, Seattle, WA.

Breaking the Surface. Greg Louganis with Eric Marcus. 1995. Random House, New York, NY.

A Timeline of HIV and AIDS. HIV.gov. hiv.gov/hiv-basics/overview/history/hiv-and-aids-timeline. Retrieved July 30, 2022.

Acknowledgments

My gratitude and appreciation go to Routledge/Taylor & Francis Group and to Sarah Rae, Pragati Sharma, Nina Guttapalle, Olivia Powers, and Lillian Rand for their advice, patience, and assistance.

Thank you to Amir Ahuja, MD, for inviting me to co-author this book. I am grateful for the opportunity this partnership has given me.

My appreciation goes to the Los Angeles LGBT Center for its extraordinary commitment to the health and well-being of the LGBTQ+ community and LGBTQ+ people experiencing abuse and violence. Thanks as well to the staff of the National LGBTQ Institute on Intimate Partner Violence for their dedication and knowledge. I would be remiss if I did not thank Diane Kubrin, LMFT, Director of Mental Health Services, and Ward Carpenter, MD, Chief Health Officer, for their support of me throughout this process.

I extend my sincere appreciation and thanks to the staff members, previous and current, of the STOP Violence Program who have contributed to my development as a clinician and manager and have inspired me to expand and deepen my understanding of intimate partner violence.

I owe my never-ending appreciation to my clients throughout the years who have taught me so much about strength, resilience, and courage, and to my students who are a consistent source of inspiration.

Appreciation and thanks go to Barrie Levy, LCSW, for consistently sharing her knowledge and expertise about domestic violence with me and for her support and encouragement during the early years of my development as a clinician.

Significant thanks are due to Vallerie Coleman, PhD, for her pioneering work in intimate partner violence and for encouraging me to co-facilitate survivor and aggressor groups with her. You are, in large part, a reason why I work in this speciality.

A special thank you to Laureen Jacobs, LMFT. You are the personification of everything a LGBTQ+ affirmative therapist should be. Your influence is in the best of these pages, and I will be forever grateful.

On a personal note, thanks go to Leslie Podkin for her support and encouragement throughout the years and to the late Robert Harrison, LMFT, for his abiding friendship and insight.

I would especially like to acknowledge, express my gratitude to, and thank my parents, Faith and Robert Holt, for their consistent and unwavering support and for their patience and wisdom. It breaks my heart that you are no longer here to share in this accomplishment.

And finally, my extreme and heartfelt gratitude, thanks, and love go to my wife, Lynne, for her unwavering support, encouragement, knowledge, intelligence, love, and culinary skill. You are an inspiration to me.

I couldn't have done this without any of you!

Susan Holt

I am extremely grateful to Routledge publications for approaching me with the opportunity to write a book on LGBTQ+ mental health. They have always been very supportive, and I commend their efforts to expand the knowledge of clinicians in regards to treating the LGBTQ+ population.

In particular, I have to thank Lillian Rand, Olivia Powers, Nina Guttapalle, Sarah Rae, and Pragati Sharma. Thank you all for checking in with us and shepherding us along in this process.

I would like to thank Susan, of course, for her decades of work in this field and her expertise. She was a pleasure to work with on this book, and both of us juggled many other commitments to finish this, so I appreciate her dedication. In addition, the staff and patients of the STOP Violence Program and the new National Institute of LGBTQ+ Intimate Partner Violence have all been instrumental in increasing my own knowledge about this topic and helping me truly appreciate the gravity and breadth of this issue. Many of the patients have made themselves very vulnerable in telling their stories, and you will read some composite cases in this book. I thank them again for that and assure them that their stories will help others.

I would also like to thank the many people who helped me in my training and inspired me to write. They include April Fallon, MD, and

Donna Sudak, MD. Thank you both for the encouragement and the great example set by being true leaders in this field.

In addition, the Los Angeles LGBTQ Center leadership must be commended for their commitment to LGBTQ health and advocacy in general, and for their efforts to end LGBTQ intimate partner violence in particular. This would include our CEO, Joe Hollendoner, as well as Darrell Cummings, our former chief of staff, who was so supportive of this project from the beginning. I would also like to thank our medical director of research and education, Robert Bolan, MD, as well as the chief medical officer, Kaiyti Duffy, MD, and the chief health officer, Ward Carpenter, MD. Last, but not least, this project was greatly supported by our director of mental health, Diane Kubrin, LMFT.

On a personal note, I would like to thank my brother, Kabir, and his wife, Sofia, my sister, Nina, and my parents, Sudhir and Shamira. They always been my cheerleaders and, without their constant encouragement, I would not have accomplished anything in my career. I write this for them, and for my two nephews, Nikhil and Kai, who will hopefully grow up in a world with much less violence of any kind.

Amir Ahuja

In October of 1999, Amy Anderson, 34, shot and killed her 2-year-old daughter, Mikayla, then killed herself. Although neighbors claimed that they did not hear the shots, they did hear Mikayla's biological mother, Jennifer, age 26, screaming for help when she arrived home from work and found the bodies of her child and domestic partner. According to neighbors, the couple had been having problems and Jennifer was preparing to move out. Police indicated that Amy Anderson used a .357 magnum and left behind an angry note addressed to her lover. She was employed as a city animal control officer and often took care of Mikayla when Jennifer was at work. Sgt. Mike Long of the Van Nuys Division of the Los Angeles Police Department said the shootings appeared to have been the result of a lovers' quarrel. A young woman who visited the couple's home after the shooting and who identified herself as a friend of Jennifer's, told a Los Angeles Times reporter that "I had to come here to believe this was real."

(Sue Fox, *Los Angeles Times*, October 24, 1999)

Introduction and Terminology

1

An initial note about terminology and language: The term LGBTQ+ used throughout this publication is a common acronym encompassing self-identified lesbian, gay, bisexual, transgender, and queer/questioning persons. Other initials are also used to encompass a more complete range of sexual and gender identities, including, but not limited to, "I" for intersex persons and "A" for asexual or aromantic persons; the "+" sign incorporates all of these and other categories. Additional terms such as non-binary, pansexual, gender fluid, and genderqueer also exist, all of which are related to our growing understanding of the intricacy and complexity of gender and sexual identities. For simplicity, we have chosen to use the term LGBTQ+ in this book. However, this is in no way intended to deny, reduce, or lessen the importance of the full array of identities that make up the true reality of non-binary, non-heterosexual lives.

Lesbian, gay, bisexual, transgender, and queer/questioning (hereinafter referred to as LGBTQ+) intimate partner violence (also commonly known as "domestic violence") is a reality that, despite epidemic proportions, has remained relatively invisible. For more than one in three people in the LGBTQ+ community, however, intimate partner violence (IPV) is anything but invisible (L.A. Gay & Lesbian Center, 2011). In fact, according to the Centers for Disease Control and Prevention (CDC, 2013), individuals who identify as lesbian, gay, and bisexual (LGB) have an equal or greater likelihood of experiencing IPV, sexual violence, and stalking compared with self-identified heterosexuals. Prevalence rates for transgender individuals are also high and often greater than those of cisgender, heterosexual people (James et al., 2016). Furthermore, in the LGBTQ+ population, intimate partner violence is a civil

DOI: 10.4324/9780429031397-1

rights issue as well as one of the community's largest health problems (Island & Letellier, 1991), with attending physical health, mental health, and social consequences for its victims, their families, the LGBTQ+ community as a whole, and society at large (Houston & McKirnan, 2007).

Intimate partner violence, or IPV—a term that is used interchangeably with domestic violence—occurs when an individual's partner or former partner uses or threatens to use abusive, coercive, and/or violent behaviors, oppression, intimidation, and/or domination against the other to gain and maintain power and control.

Although it is rarely acknowledged, LGBTQ+ intimate partner violence has been a reality for centuries. A trial transcript documenting a case of lesbian violence in Germany in 1721 illustrates the court's focus on the "crime of lesbianism" rather than the frequent beatings of Catharina Muhlhahn by her female partner, Catharina Linck. Linck and Muhlhahn were on trial for "lesbianism" when the domestic violence was revealed. Linck was sentenced to death for the crime, and Muhlhahn was sentenced to 3 years of imprisonment followed by banishment (Robson, 1996).

Some 280 years later, in the United States, Wanda Jean Allen was sentenced to death for the murder of her lesbian partner, Gloria Leathers. Executed on January 11, 2001, Allen was the first African American woman executed in the United States since 1954, the first woman executed by the state of Oklahoma since statehood, and the sixth woman executed in the United States since the reinstatement of the death penalty by the Supreme Court in 1976. When urging the Pardon and Parole Board in Oklahoma City to grant Allen clemency, the American Civil Liberties Union (ACLU) documented Allen's history, which included head trauma as a child as well as the results of a psychological evaluation that revealed neurological deficiencies that were never treated despite recommendations to do so. Further, Allen's mental incapacities were never disclosed in court proceedings. These systemic deficiencies were coupled with "indications that race and sexual orientation may have been factors in Wanda Jean Allen's sentencing," and the ACLU maintained that the jury heard repeated references to Allen as an "aggressive, dominant, male-type figure who was, therefore, capable of committing murder" (Rust-Tierney, Bell, & Coles, 2001).

These cases illustrate the stigma of homosexuality, a reality that has not been eradicated in three centuries. Furthermore, they underscore the context in which LGBTQ+ intimate partner violence occurs. Like intimate partner violence in the non-LGBTQ+ population, LGBTQ+IPV includes various forms of verbal, psychological, physical, and/or sexual abuse and violence and, as mentioned previously, is generally perpetrated by a person to gain and maintain power and control over a current or former intimate partner. While non-LGBTQ+ domestic violence is believed to occur primarily within the context of sexism, misogyny, and the patriarchal structure of society, LGBTQ+IPV always occurs within the context of anti-LGBTQ+ oppression, discrimination, heterosexism, and homo/bi/transphobia—and, for LGBTQ+ people of color, it occurs within the context of racism as well—all effective power and control tactics.

"Domestic disputes" were historically considered to be private until the efforts of the women's movement in the 1970s were instrumental in transforming how our society responded to battered heterosexual women. Theories about intimate partner violence, and approaches to addressing it, developed within a gender-based, heteronormative framework and subsequently obscured LGBTQ+ domestic violence. Numerous misconceptions—including the misconceptions that partner violence is not as dangerous to LGBTQ+ victims as it is to those in the heterosexual community and/or that it is mutual—have increased its invisibility while potentially heightening harm to those experiencing it.

However, intimate partner violence is sufficiently widespread in both LGBTQ+ and non-LGBTQ+ populations to constitute a public health problem (Koop, 1987). No one—regardless of race, ethnicity, cultural background, nationality, socioeconomic class, age, ability, level of education, income, political affiliation, spirituality, religion, size, strength, gender identity, or sexual orientation—is safe from domestic violence (Holt, 2012). Abusers can be cisgender, non-binary, transgender, male or female, "butch" or "femme," large or small. So can victims.

According to the Williams Institute, an estimated 3.5% of adults in the United States identify as lesbian, gay, or bisexual, while another 0.3% identify as transgender. This translates to over 12.5 million LGBTQ+ Americans, a population larger than that of the state of Illinois, or of the countries of Finland and Denmark combined (Gates, 2011). However, the Human Rights Campaign Foundation more recently indicated that at least 20 million adults in the United States could be lesbian, gay, bisexual, or transgender, with more than 2 million identifying as transgender (Pitofsky, 2021) This data, from the Census Bureau's Household Pulse Survey, reflected more sophisticated research than previous data collection efforts.

Owing to nearly universal experiences of trauma, victimization, discrimination, stressors associated with the coming out process, or violence at some point in their lives, many of these LGBTQ+ people are vulnerable to domestic and intimate partner violence. While attempts to control, gain, and maintain power over an intimate partner take many forms—including verbal, emotional, psychological, physical, sexual, environmental, and/or financial control—they have in common the intense pain caused to, and pressure they place upon, victims and the difficult and, at times, overwhelming barriers they create to escaping abusive relationships.

While LGBTQ+IPV shares some similarities with domestic violence in the non-LGBTQ+ community, there are numerous and complex differences that complicate assessment, intervention, and treatment planning, as well as the safety and well-being of LGBTQ+ individuals experiencing it. Without an understanding of these differences, as well as the subject itself and appropriate responses to it, intervention is potentially damaging, oftentimes dangerous, and can increase risk for serious injury and death for the person(s) experiencing it and their family members, as it increases the risk of liability to service providers who attempt to intervene.

Despite these consequences, comparatively little is known about LGBTQ+ intimate partner violence, and comprehensive training on the subject is relatively rare. Few studies, and only a handful of books, have focused specifically on violence in gay and lesbian relationships (Coleman, 2002; Island & Letellier, 1991; NRCDV, 2007; Messinger, 2020), and fewer still have examined it in bisexual, transgender, non-binary, and other allied populations, compared with the hundreds of studies, books, and articles that have examined domestic violence in the non-LGBTQ+ community (Burke & Follingstad, 1999). Further, the LGBTQ+ community itself has often been reluctant to address battering (Lobel, 1986) for a variety of reasons (Island & Letellier, 1991). Nevertheless, prevalence studies have suggested that the frequency and severity of LGBTQ+ battering are, in fact, comparable to those in the non-LGBTQ+ population (Burke & Follingstad, 1999; Waldner-Haugrud, Gratch, & Magruder, 1997; GLBT Domestic Violence Coalition and Jane Doe, Inc., 2005; L.A. Gay & Lesbian Center, 2011), and it may be more prevalent (Walters, Chen & Breiding, 2013; CDC, 2013).

Although prevalence statistics vary, it is clear that IPV is a significant problem experienced by thousands in the LGBTQ+ population that is rarely addressed sufficiently, or effectively, thereby increasing risk for escalating levels of violence, injury, co-occurring problems, and lethality.

Mental health professionals have not received sufficient training and education in domestic violence, and this has very serious and significant ramifications for clients and providers alike. If you are a mental health practitioner, why should this topic be of primary importance to you?

- You will see it repeatedly throughout your career in mental health, regardless of where you practice or what type of practice you have.
- It causes significant injury and can be lethal without adequate intervention.

- It causes psychological and physical health problems, and existing psychological and physical health problems can be exacerbated by it.
- Without accurate assessment and effective intervention, it will usually increase in frequency and severity.
- If it is occurring but not effectively addressed, it will interfere with any and all therapeutic work you do with a client, and the client's prognosis—regardless of their presenting problems—will generally get worse rather than better.
- If you do not assess for it and/or intervene appropriately when it is present, it is a potential liability for you and the practice or agency where you are employed.
- LGBTQ+ clients will commonly seek assistance from mental health providers rather than traditional domestic violence services/programs and other forms of assistance.
- It is a civil rights issue for the LGBTQ+ community.
- It is always a treatment priority.

In this book, we will review existing literature focusing on intimate partner violence in both the LGBTQ+ and non-LGBTQ+ populations; compare and contrast LGBTQ+-affirmative approaches (Bieschke, Perez, & DeBord, 2007; Garnets et al., 2003; Chernin & Johnson, 2003; Holt, 2021) to the assessment of, intervention in, and treatment of intimate partner violence with traditional domestic violence theories and approaches (Walker, 1994; Wexler, 2000; Dutton & Sonkin, 2002; Harway & Hansen, 1994; LaViolette & Barnett, 2000); provide case studies of LGBTQ+ victims/survivors and abusers to illustrate proposed concepts and practices; discuss LGBTQ+-specific/focused domestic violence program development; and address the importance of a contextual approach when responding to intimate partner violence in the LGBTQ+ population. These factors will provide basic recommended beginnings for a blueprint for what is now essentially a non-existent standard of care when assessing for and intervening in cases of LGBTQ+ intimate partner violence.

Terminology and Key Supporting Concepts

A discussion of "domestic violence" or "intimate partner abuse/violence" in the lesbian, gay, bisexual, transgender, and queer/questioning communities cannot take place without first defining the population itself as well as pertinent basic factors about the subject. This section is not intended to be a simple glossary of terms. In addition to defining terms that will be used throughout the text, it also includes key and supporting concepts that further expand the definitions.

Universal agreement on terminology does not exist. Language and culture continually change and are subject to social changes as well as other factors such as geography. The terms explained here reflect this and are not static. For example, the term *homosexuality* has historically been associated with mental illness, criminal behavior, and deviance. Misunderstanding as well as negative stereotypes can be inadvertently perpetrated by outdated and biased language (APA, 1991). Today, the terms *gay* and *lesbian* are more commonly used than the term *homosexual*.

Broadly speaking, *gay men* and *lesbians* are individuals whose primary sexual and affectional orientation is toward persons of the same gender. Male homosexuals are typically referred to as *gay*; female homosexuals are commonly referred to as *lesbian*, although *gay* is often used to refer to the LGBTQ+ community as a whole. *Bisexuals* are persons whose intimate and/or sexual relationships are with others of the same or different genders; *transgender* refers to individuals who identify differently than their assigned gender at birth (U.S. Department of Health and Human Services, 2012). An *ally* is someone who advocates and supports a community other than their own.

Sexual orientation is a broader term that is commonly defined as an enduring emotional, romantic, affectional, and/or sexual attraction toward members of the same gender, different genders, or multiple genders. According to the APA (2008), it exists on a continuum, is not synonymous with sexual activity, and has not been conclusively found to be determined by any particular factor or factors. The term *sexual orientation* is preferred over the terms *sexual preference* and/or *lifestyle* because the latter suggest a degree of voluntary choice that is not necessarily reported by lesbians and gay men and has not been demonstrated in psychological research (APA, 1991). In contrast, *sexual orientation identity* involves self-labeling, such as gay, lesbian, bisexual, queer, or heterosexual (American Psychological Association Task Force on Appropriate Therapeutic Responses to Sexual Orientation, 2009).

Generally speaking, individuals identify themselves as *lesbian, gay, bisexual*, or *heterosexual* when referring to their sexual orientation but can also identify as *queer, pansexual*, and *asexual* (L.A. Gay & Lesbian Center, 2011). *Sexual minority* is another term that is sometimes used to encompass the above identifications. The terms *gay male* and *lesbian* refer primarily to identities as well as the culture and communities that have developed among people who share those identities and should be distinguished from sexual behavior, as some may have sex with others of their own gender but do not consider themselves to be gay or lesbian. In contrast, the terms *heterosexual* and *bisexual* are used to describe both identity and behavior (APA, 1991). *Queer* is a term used to describe a fluid range of sexual orientations and gender identities. Originally a slur, this term has been reclaimed by some LGBTQ+ community members while others find it derogatory (L.A. Gay & Lesbian Center, 2011). *MSM* are men of any sexual orientation who have sex with men, and, similarly, *WSW* refers to women of any orientation who have sex with women. *Pansexual* refers to a person who is sexually attracted to all gender expressions, while *polysexual* indicates attraction to multiple genders. *Polyamorous* is the practice of, or desire for, intimate relationships with more than one partner, with the accompanying consent of all involved partners. *Asexual* refers to an individual who is not sexually attracted to others or does not have a sexual orientation, while *aromantic* is defined as the lack of romantic attraction.

Gender identity is a psychological sense of one's gender and how one perceives oneself, whether male, female, a blend of both, or neither, while *gender expression* is the external presentation that usually expresses how the individual wants to be perceived. *Sex*, on the other hand, is a term that refers to hormonal, chromosomal, and genital characteristics that are generally observable. *Cisgender* is a term for those whose gender identity and expression are the same as their sex or gender assigned at birth, while *transgender* is used as an umbrella term encompassing people whose gender identity or expression differs from the cultural or societal expectations based on the sex or gender they were assigned at birth. Transgender persons may be gay, lesbian, bisexual, heterosexual, asexual, pansexual, and so on. *Genderqueer* and *gender non-conforming* refer to identities used by individuals who do not identify their gender within the gender binary, while *gender fluid* and *genderflux* are terms used to describe a changing or "fluid" gender identity. *Non-binary* is a term used to describe all genders other than the traditional binary while also describing the presentation of a cisgender or transgender person. *Demigender* is an umbrella term for non-binary identities that have a partial connection to a gender identity and can include terms such as demifluid, demimasculine, demifemme, demiboy, and demigirl.

Commonly used gender pronouns include *she/her/hers/herself; he/him/ his/himself; they/them/theirs/themselves;* and *ze/hir/zir/hirs/zirs/hirself/zirself.*

Femme and *butch* are identities or presentations that are associated with femininity and masculinity, respectively. *Butch* refers to those who identify themselves as masculine, whether the identification is physical, mental, or emotional. *Butch* is sometimes used as a derogatory term for lesbians, but it has also been claimed by some as an affirmative identity label. Similarly, *dyke* is a term used for lesbians and was commonly considered to be offensive, but has been redefined to describe a strongly assertive woman.

Transvestite, cross-dresser, and *androgynous* are terms that define presentations that are also often considered by societal norms to be outside the range of socially prescribed gender roles and behavior and/or represent other gender non-conforming people (U.S. Department of Health and Human Services, 2012). *Cross-dressing* is the act of dressing and presenting oneself as a different gender, while *drag* is a form of gender expression during which one cross-dresses; neither of them is necessarily indicative of one's sexual orientation or gender identity.

LGBTQ is an acronym that refers collectively to lesbian, gay, bisexual, transgender, and queer people. It encompasses a widely diverse population that includes all cultures, ethnicities, races, nationalities, socioeconomic classes, lifestyles, and so on. Variations of *LGBTQ* include *GLBT, LGBT,* and *LGBTQ,* with the *Q* representing *queer* or *questioning. Questioning* refers to the process during which an individual discovers their sexual orientation or gender identity. Another variation is *LGBTQI,* with the *I* representing *intersex,* or *difference of sex development* (DSD), which are terms that describe a range of conditions in which a person is born with chromosomes, genitals, reproductive organs, or hormone functions that were observed at birth to be different than the typical female or male binary and do not represent a gender identity (L.A. Gay & Lesbian Center, 2011). *LGBTQIA* stands for lesbian, gay, bisexual, transgender, queer, intersex, and asexual, while LGBTQIA2S includes Two Spirit identities. Yet another variation is *LGBTQH* or *LGBTQIH,* with the *H* representing *HIV-affected* individuals. *HIV-affected* is a term that describes HIV positive people, people living with AIDS, and includes partners, friends, lovers, family members, and the community of people who are impacted by HIV/AIDS (L.A. Gay & Lesbian Center, 2011). *LGBTQQIAPP+* refers to a collection of identities including lesbian, gay, bisexual, trans, queer, questioning, intersex, asexual, pansexual, and polysexual. *Rainbow communities* is a broad umbrella term that inclusively reflects the wide diversity of sexual orientation and gender identities and expressions.

Same-gender refers to relationships that are comprised of people who share the same gender and is a term that is sometimes preferred over *same-sex. Sexual minority* is an individual or group whose sexual identity, orientation, or practices differ from the majority of the surrounding society (Ullerstam, 1966). Initially, the term primarily referred to lesbians, gays, and bisexual people. In more recent years, the term *sexual minorities* has expanded to include numerous groups, regardless of sexual orientation or gender identity, and may include practitioners of kink, fetishists, BDSM, asexuals, swingers, polyamorists, people in non-monogamous relationships, and people who primarily prefer sex partners of a disparate age among others. *Kink* refers to sexual practices that fall outside of conventional beliefs and/or practices. *BDSM* is an abbreviation for bondage/discipline/sadism/masochism and refers to sexual role-play involving a power exchange between consensual participants (DeNeef et al., 2019). Usually, the term *sexual minority* is applied only to groups that practice consensual sex. For example, rapists are not considered to be sexual minority members.

Goffman (1963) defined *stigma* as an undesirable difference that discredits an individual or community. The stigma that defines sexual minorities was originally termed *sexual stigma* by Herek (2009) and consists of the negative regard, inferior status, and relative powerlessness that society accords to any non-heterosexual behavior, identity, relationship, or community. *Sexual orientation stigma* (Balsam & Mohr, 2007) is also a term for the same concept. *Minority stress* refers to the sexual stigma manifested as prejudice and discrimination directed at non-heterosexual sexual orientations and identities and/or the excess stress to which individuals from stigmatized social categories are exposed as a result of their social, often minority, position (American Psychological Association Task Force on Appropriate Therapeutic Responses to Sexual Orientation, 2009; Meyer, 2003).

Stereotype refers to a preconceived or oversimplified generalization about an entire group of people without regard for their individual differences. Although often negative, stereotypes can also be positive, but they may potentially have a negative impact because they involve broad generalizations that ignore individual realities (Green & Peterson, 2004). *Discrimination* is a combination of prejudice and power. It occurs when members of a more powerful social group behave unjustly or cruelly to members of a less powerful social group and can take many forms, including both individual acts of hatred or injustice and institutional denials of privileges normally accorded to other groups. Ongoing discrimination creates a climate of oppression for the affected group (Green & Peterson, 2004).

Sexual prejudice is defined as all negative attitudes based on sexual orientation, whether the target is homosexual, bisexual, or heterosexual (Herek, 2009). *Antigay harassment* was originally defined as verbal or physical behavior that injures, interferes with, or intimidates lesbian, gay, and bisexual individuals (Burn, Kadlec, & Rexer, 2005) and can be extended to all LGBTQ+ persons, while a hate crime is a criminal act in which the victim is targeted because of their actual or perceived race, color, religion, national origin, ethnicity, disability, sexual orientation, or gender identity (Anti-Defamation League, 2001). *Microaggressions* are brief and commonplace verbal, behavioral, or environmental indignities, whether intentional or unintentional, that communicate hostile, derogatory, or negative slights and insults toward people of minority status. Many times, those who inflict microaggressions are often unaware that they have done anything to harm another person (Sue et al., 2007).

Heteronormativity is the assumption, in individuals or institutions, that everyone is heterosexual, and that heterosexuality is superior to homosexuality and bisexuality. *Heterosexism* is an ideology that includes the cultural assumption that all people are, or would want to be, heterosexual and involves the belief that heterosexuality is the only normal model for romantic/sexual relationships (Iasenza, 1989). *Heterosexism* also refers to the prejudice against individuals and groups who display non-heterosexual behaviors and identities, combined with the majority power to impose such prejudice that is used to the advantage of the group in power. Conversely, *heterosexual privilege* refers to the benefits derived automatically by being heterosexual that are denied to LGBTQ+ people. It also refers to the benefits that LGBTQ+ people receive as a result of claiming heterosexual identity or denying LGBTQ+ identity (Green & Peterson, 2004).

Homophobia is generally considered to be the irrational fear or hatred of homosexuals, homosexuality, or any behavior or belief that does not conform to rigid and/or assumed sex role stereotypes. This fear enforces sexism as well as heterosexism (Weinberg, 1972; Green & Peterson, 2004), which may culminate in criminal victimization, commonly referred to as *hate crimes* or *bias crimes* (Klinger, 1995).

Hate violence, *anti-LGBTQ+ bias*, and *bias violence* are terms that describe acts against a person or property that are motivated by hatred for someone's actual or perceived identity, including sexual orientation, gender identity, gender expression, and/or HIV status (L.A. Gay & Lesbian Center, 2011). According to the U.S. Department of Justice, the term "hate" can be misleading because it refers not to rage, anger, or general dislike but rather to bias against people or groups with specific characteristics that are defined by the law. Hate crimes are generally violent and can include assault, murder, arson, vandalism, and threats to commit such crimes. At the federal level, hate crimes include crimes committed on the basis of the victim's perceived or actual race, color, religion, national origin, sexual orientation, gender, gender identity, or disability. The hate crime laws in most U.S. states include crimes committed on the basis of race, color, and religion but may or may not include crimes committed on the basis of sexual orientation, gender, gender identity, and disability. In contrast, a *bias* or *hate incident* is an act of prejudice that is not technically a crime and does not involve violence, threats, or property damage (U.S. Department of Justice, n.d.).

Internalized homophobia and *LGBTQ+ oppression* are terms that refer to the acceptance of and/or belief in the negative messages about sexual minority members that the dominant group in a society maintains or the process by which a member of an oppressed group comes to involuntarily accept the stereotypes, misconceptions, and myths that society has about them. This process commonly produces internalized self-hatred that sexual minorities often struggle with as a result of heterosexual prejudice (U.S. Department of Health and Human Services, 2012; Green & Peterson, 2004). *Heterosexual prejudice* is manifested in *institutionalized homophobia/biphobia/transphobia* or *institutionalized LGBTQ+ oppression*, which refers to the ways in which government, business, religious organizations, and other societal institutions discriminate against people on the basis of sexual orientation and subsequently benefit a group(s) at the expense of another group via language, media, education, religion, economics, and so on (Green & Peterson, 2004).

Conversion therapy or *reparative therapy* refers to a range of dangerous and discredited practices that falsely claim to change a person's sexual orientation, gender identity, or gender expression. This form of "therapy" can lead to depression, anxiety, drug use, homelessness, and suicide, among other problems. Every major medical and mental health organization in the United States has issued a statement condemning its use (HRC, 2021).

Coming out refers to the individual and personal process by which a person accepts his/her sexual minority status (U.S. Department of Health and Human Services, 2012). This term may also refer to the process by which one shares one's sexual or gender identity with others (Green & Peterson, 2004). The timing of the emergence, recognition, and expression of one's sexual orientation (or gender identity) varies among individuals (APA, 2008) and can be, for some, a continual, life-long process. *In the closet* refers to a LGBTQ+ individual who will not, or cannot, disclose their sex, sexuality, sexual orientation, or gender identity to their friends, family, co-workers, and/or society. There are varying degrees of being *in the closet*; for example, an individual can be out in their social life but *in the closet* at work or with their family. *In the closet* has been used interchangeably with *downlow* (Green & Peterson, 2004). *Out* and *out of the closet* are terms that refer to varying degrees of being open about one's sexual minority identification (U.S. Department of Health and Human Services, 2012).

Diversity embraces the richness inherent in race, ethnicity, socioeconomic status, gender, religion, sexual orientation, family identification, immigration status, functional ability, and age, while cultural diversity refers to the unique characteristics that distinguish people as individuals and as members within different groups (NAMI Star Center & University of Illinois at Chicago National Research and Training Center, 2010). *Cultural competency* is the ability to interact effectively and comfortably with people from different cultures.

People of color is a term used to describe those who identify as Arab/Middle Eastern, Asian/Pacific Islander, Black/African American, Hispanic/Latino(a)/

Latinx, Indigenous/First People, multiracial, South Asian, or any non-white racial or ethnic identity (L.A. Gay & Lesbian Center, 2011). *BIPOC* stands for Black, Indigenous, People of Color and acknowledges that not all people of color face equal levels of injustice while recognizing that Black and Indigenous people are severely impacted by systemic racial injustices.

Mainstream services and programs are those that have been designed primarily for heterosexuals. LGBTQ+-specific/focused services and programs are those that have been designed specifically and/or primarily for LGBTQ+ communities. Providers of LGBTQ+-specific/focused services specialize in working with LGBTQ+ individuals and families and have received extensive training in the subject. In contrast, *LGBTQ-sensitive/friendly/affirmative* services are those that welcome LGBTQ persons but have been designed primarily for members of the heterosexual community. Providers of these services receive varying amounts of training in LGBTQ+ issues (adapted from LGBTQ Sensitivity Model, U.S. Department of Health and Human Services, 2012; Neisen, 1997) or no training at all, and they may not receive any training in LGBTQ+ domestic violence itself. *LGBTQ sensitive*, *LGBTQ friendly*, and *LGBTQ affirmative* are oftentimes used interchangeably.

Note

Throughout this book, the term "violence" is used interchangeably with "abuse." "Violence" is a broad term with a wide spectrum of expression, from verbal insults and aggressive language to physical attacks, sexual assault, and even state oppression and terrorism (Whirry & Holt, 2020). "Domestic violence" or "DV" is used interchangeably with "intimate partner violence" or "IPV," "intimate partner abuse," "partner violence," "partner abuse," "interpersonal violence," and "spousal abuse," the latter often being a legal term. Unlike "intimate partner violence," "domestic violence" can, however, be problematic because it is frequently associated with heterosexual or non-LGBTQ+ IPV. Further, it is a broader term than IPV because it can encompass any violence in a household between various household and/or family members. To be more specific and inclusive, IPV is used to describe violence and abuse between intimate partners. While we prefer the terms "intimate partner violence" and "interpersonal violence," we use them interchangeably with "domestic violence" because of the latter's long-lasting and still common usage.

"LGBTQ+" is, on occasion, used interchangeably with "lesbian and/or gay." "LGB" is used when referring specifically to lesbians, gay men, and bisexual individuals of both (binary) genders. "Homo/bi/transphobia" is used interchangeably with "anti-LGBTQ+ bias." "Client" is used interchangeably with "patient," although use of the term "patient" is not intended to imply pathology. However, it is a term that is frequently used in clinical settings. The focus of this book is intimate partner violence/domestic violence that occurs with LGBTQ+ populations. The term "victim" is used interchangeably with "survivor." However, these terms can be problematic since "victim" may imply that a person is still enduring abuse or its consequences, while "survivor" can imply that they have recovered from the damaging effects of abuse. Further, "victim" is often used as a legal term. The term "battered woman" is problematic because it tends to indicate that violence is gender-specific. However, researchers and authors often prefer this term, and so it is used accordingly in this text. The term "abuser" is used interchangeably with "batterer," "perpetrator," "offender," "primary aggressor," and "person who harms." "Batterer" is often used as a legal term. The terms "primary victim," "primary survivor," "defending victim," "secondary aggressor," and "participant" are terms used for assessment purposes and are explained later in this text. The focus of this book is on intimate partner violence/domestic violence and does not include extensive information that is intended to apply to bisexual, transgender, asexual, intersex, pansexual, and so on, individuals unless specified, primarily because of the lack of research that exists with these populations.

Continuing Education Questions

1. According to the Williams Institute, what percentage of people identify as gay, lesbian, or bisexual?
   a. 2.5%
   b. 3%
   c. 3.5%
   d. 4.5%
2. An ally is someone who advocates for and supports a community other than their own.
   a. True
   b. False
3. Sexual orientation:
   a. Refers to enduring patterns of attraction
   b. Occurs along a continuum
   c. Is preferred as a term over "sexual preference"
   d. All of the above

4. Queer is an outdated term that no one in the sexual and gender minority communities uses anymore.
    a. True
    b. False
5. _____ is the psychological, internal sense of one's gender.
    a. Gender expression
    b. Sex
    c. Sexual orientation
    d. Gender identity

References

American Psychological Association (APA). (1991). Avoiding Heterosexual Bias in Language. *American Psychologist, 46*(9), 973, 974.

American Psychological Association (APA). (2008, October 29). Understanding Sexual Orientation and Homosexuality. www.apa.org/topics/lgbtq/orientation

American Psychological Association Task Force on Appropriate Therapeutic Responses to Sexual Orientation. (2009). *Report of the Task Force on Appropriate Therapeutic Responses to Sexual Orientation.* Washington, DC: American Psychological Association.

Anti-Defamation League. (2001). Hate Crime Laws. Retrieved October 1, 2009, from www.adl.org/sites/default/files/Introduction-to-Hate-Crime-Laws.pdf

Balsam, K.F., & Mohr, J.J. (2007). Adaptation to Sexual Orientation Stigma: A Comparison of Bisexual and Lesbian/Gay Adults. *Journal of Counseling Psychology, 54*, 306–319.

Bieschke, K.J., Perez, R.M., & DeBord, K.A. (Eds.). (2007). *Handbook of Counseling and Psychotherapy with Lesbian, Gay, Bisexual, and Transgender Clients* (2nd ed.). Washington, DC: American Psychological Association.

Burke, L.K., & Follingstad, E.R. (1999). Violence in Lesbian and Gay Relationships: Theory, Prevalence, and Correlational Factors. *Clinical Psychology Review, 5*, 487–512.

Burn, S.M., Kadlec, K., & Rexer, R. (2005). Effects of Subtle Heterosexism on Gays, Lesbians, and Bisexuals. *Journal of Homosexuality, 49*(2), 23–38.

Centers for Disease Control and Prevention (CDC). (2013). CDC Releases Data on Interpersonal and Sexual Violence by Sexual Orientation. Press Release. Retrieved July 4, 2022, from cdc.gov/media/release/2013/

Chernin, J.N., & Johnson, M.R. (2003). *Affirmative Psychotherapy and Counseling for Lesbians and Gay Men.* Thousand Oaks, CA: Sage.

Coleman, V.E. (2002). Treating the Lesbian Batterer: Theoretical and Clinical Considerations—A Contemporary Psychoanalytic Perspective. In D. Dutton & D.J. Sonkin (Eds.), *Intimate Violence: Contemporary Treatment Innovations* (pp. 159–205). New York: Routledge.

DeNeef, N., Coppens, V., Huys, W., & Morrens, M. (2019). Bondage-Discipline, Dominance-Submission and Sadomasochism from an Integrative Biopsychosocial Perspective: A Systemic Review. National Library of Medicine. PubMed.gov. Retrieved November 2, 2021, from pubmed.ncbi.nlm.nih.gov/30956128

Dutton, D., & Sonkin, D.J. (Eds.) (2002). *Intimate Violence: Contemporary Treatment Innovations.* Binghamton, NY: Haworth Press.

Garnets, L.D., Herek, G.M., Levy, B., & Kimmel, D.C. (2003). Violence and Victimization of Lesbians and Gay Men: Mental Health Consequences. In L.D. Garnets & D.C. Kimmel (Eds.), *Psychological Perspectives on Lesbian, Gay, and Bisexual Experiences* (pp. 188–206). (2nd ed.) New York, NY: Columbia University Press.

Gates, Gary J. (2011). *How Many People Are Lesbian, Gay, Bisexual, and Transgender?* Los Angeles: Williams Institute.

GLBT Domestic Violence Coalition & Jane Doe, Inc. (2005). *Shelter/Housing Needs for Gay, Lesbian, Bisexual and Transgender (GLBT) Victims of Domestic Violence: Analysis of Public Hearing Testimony.* Boston, MA: Authors.

Goffman, E. (1963). *Stigma: Notes on the Management of Spoiled Identity.* Englewood Cliffs, NJ: Prentice-Hall.

Green, E.R., & Peterson, E.N. (2004). LGVTQI Terminology. Retrieved September 14, 2011, from eli@trans-academics.org

Harway, M., & Hansen, M. (1994). *Spouse Abuse: Assessing and Treating Battered Women, Batterers, and Their Children.* Sarasota, FL: Professional Resource Press.

Herek, G.M. (2009). Sexual Stigma and Sexual Prejudice in the United States: A Conceptual Framework. In D. Hope (Ed.), *Nebraska Symposium on Motivation: Contemporary Perspectives on Lesbian, Gay, and Bisexual Identities* (pp. 65–111). New York, NY: Springer.

Houston, E., & McKirnan, D.J. (2007). Intimate Partner Abuse among Gay and Bisexual Men: Risk Correlates and Health Outcomes. *Journal of Urban Health, 84*(5), 681–690. Retrieved October 4, 2011.

Human Rights Campaign (HRC). (2021). The Lies and Danger of Efforts to Change Sexual Orientation or Gender Identity. Retrieved November 14, 2021, from hrc.org/resources/the-lies-and-danger-of-reparative-therapy

Iasenza, S. (1989). Some Challenges of Integrating Sexual Orientations into Counselor Training. *Journal of Counseling and Development, 68,* 73–76.

Island, D., & Letellier, P. (1991). *Men Who Beat the Men Who Love Them.* Binghamton, NY: Harrington Park Press.

James, S.E., Herman, J.L., Rankin, S., Keisling, M., Mottet, L., & Anafi, M. (2016). *The Report of the 2015 U.S. Transgender Survey.* Washington, DC: National Center for Transgender Equality.

Klinger, R.L. (1995). *Gay Violence. Journal of Gay & Lesbian Psychotherapy, 2*(3), 119–134.

Koop, C.E. (1987). *Healing Interpersonal Violence: Making Health a Full Partner.* Keynote address at the Surgeon General's Northwest Conference on Interpersonal Violence, Seattle, WA.

L.A. Gay & Lesbian Center. (2011). Bennett Bradley. In *Voices of Victims & Survivors: The 2010 Lesbian, Gay, Bisexual, Transgender, Queer & HIV-Affected Intimate Partner Violence Narratives.* New York, NY: NCAVP.

LaViolette, A.D., & Barnett, O.W. (2000). *It Could Happen to Anyone: Why Battered Women Stay* (2nd ed.). Thousand Oaks, CA: Sage.

Lobel, K. (Ed.) (1986). *Naming the Violence: Speaking Out about Lesbian Battering.* Seattle, WA: Seal Press.

Messinger, Adam M. (2020). *LGBTQ Intimate Partner Violence: Lessons for Policy, Practice, and Research.* Oakland, CA: University of California Press.

Meyer, I.H. (2003). Prejudice, Social Stress, and Mental Health in Lesbian, Gay, and Bisexual Populations: Conceptual Issues and Research Evidence. *Psychological Bulletin, 129*(5), 674–697. American Psychological Association.

NAMI Star Center & University of Illinois at Chicago National Research and Training Center. (2010). *Cultural Competency in Mental Health Peer-Run Programs and Self-Help Groups: A Tool to Assess and Enhance Yours Services*. Arlington, VA: Author.

National Resource Center on Domestic Violence (NRCDV). (2007). *Lesbian, Gay, Bisexual, and Trans (LGBTQ) Communities and Domestic Violence: Information and Resources*. Harrisburg, PA: Author. Retrieved October 17, 2004, from ncadv.org

Neisen, J.H. (1997). LGBTQ Sensitivity Model. In *Substance Abuse and Mental Health Services Administration: A Provider's Introduction to Substance Abuse Treatment for Lesbian, Gay, Bisexual, and Transgender Individuals* (p. 53). Rockville, MD: SAMHSA.

Pitofsky, M. (2021). There Could Be Twice as Many LGBT Adults in the US than Earlier Estimated, Report Says. *USA Today*. Retrieved from www.usatoday.com/story/news/nation/2021/12/09/more-lgbt-adults-in-united-states/6451887001

Robson, R. (1996). Lavendar Bruises: Intra-lesbian Violence, Law, and Lesbian Legal Theory. In D. Weisberg & H. Kelly (Eds.), *Applications of Feminist Legal Theory to Women's Lives: Sex, Violence, Work, and Reproduction*. Philadelphia, PA: Temple University Press.

Rust-Tierney, Diann, Bell, Joann, & Coles, Matt (2001). Wanda Jean Allen Clemency Letter, Jan. 3, 2001, American Civil Liberties Union. Retrieved August 24, 2010, from aclu.org/capital-punishment/wanda-jean-allen-clemency-letter

Staff Reports. (2016). Broadway Dancer Charged with Killing Boyfriend. *Washington Blade: LGBT News, Politics, LGBTQ Rights, Gay News*, August 24. Retrieved from washingtonblade.com/2016/08/24/broadway-dancer-charged-killing-boyfriend/

Sue, D.W., Capodilupo, C., Torino, G, Bucceri, J., Holder, A., Nadal, K., & Equin, M. (2007). Racial Microaggressions in Everyday Life: Implications for Clinical Practice. *The American Psychologist, 62*(4), 271–286.

Ullerstam, L. (1966). *The Erotic Minorities: A Swedish View*. New York, NY: Grove Press.

U.S. Department of Health and Human Services. (2012). *A Provider's Introduction to Substance Abuse Treatment for Lesbian, Gay, Bisexual, and Transgender Individuals*. Rockville, MD: Author. DHHS Publication # (SMA) 12-4104.

U.S. Department of Justice. (n.d.). Learn about Hate Crimes. Retrieved October 31, 2021, from justice.gov/hatecrimes/learn-about-hate-crimes

Waldner-Haugrud, L.D., Gratch, L.V., & Magruder, B. (1997). Victimization and Perpetration Rates of Violence in Gay and Lesbian Relationships: Gender Issues Explored. *Violence and Victims, 12*(2), 173–184.

Walker, L.E. (1994). *Abused Women and Survivor Therapy: A Practical Guide for the Psychotherapist*. Washington, DC: American Psychological Association.

Walters, M.L., Chen, J., & Breiding, M.J. (2013). *The National Intimate Partner & Sexual Violence Survey: 2010 Findings on Victimization by Sexual Orientation*. Atlanta, GA: National Center for Injury Prevention & Control, Centers for Disease Control & Prevention. Retrieved October 30, 2021, from cdc.gov/violenceprevention/pdf/nisvs_sofindings.pdf

Weinberg, G. (1972). *Society and the Healthy Homosexual*. New York, NY: St. Martin's.

Wexler, D.B. (2000). *Domestic Violence Group Leader's Manual: An Integrated Skills Program for Men*. New York, NY: W.W. Norton.

Whirry, R., & Holt, S. (2020). *Finding Safety: A Report about LGBTQ Domestic Violence and Sexual Assault*. Los Angeles, CA: Los Angeles LGBT Center.

Intimate Partner Violence Defined 2

To understand LGBTQ+ intimate partner violence fully, a discussion of it—regardless of the sexual orientation or gender identity of those involved—is a necessary first step. To note, the vast majority of non-population-specific domestic violence information refers to heterosexual and opposite-gender couples, or non-LGBTQ+ individuals.

Researchers throughout the world have not reached agreement about the definition of intimate partner violence and the characteristics of its various manifestations. While most family and domestic violence studies indicate that culture is not a significant factor in predicting or explaining violent behavior, the American Psychological Association (1996) notes that significant differences among individuals within minority or marginalized groups suggest that a person's cultural background may affect his or her *experience* of violence.

While "domestic violence" is often used interchangeably with "family violence," the latter refers to violence in family groupings and can include abuse between parent and child, siblings, and extended family members in addition to abuse between intimate partners (Wallace, 2005). "Intimate partner violence" is generally defined as violence directed toward an intimate partner.

Terms such as "family violence," "domestic violence," "dating or courtship violence," "spousal abuse," "marital violence," "interpersonal violence," "partner abuse and violence," "relational violence," and "intimate partner violence" have been used interchangeably but often mean different things in different contexts, with "domestic violence" being, arguably, the most common of these terms. Similarly, the terms "violence" and "abuse,"

DOI: 10.4324/9780429031397-2

while often used interchangeably, frequently mean different things to different people. For example, "violence" often includes the use of physical force or assault, while "abuse" may include emotional or psychological harm, and physical assault may or may not be part of the definition. Further, victims as well as perpetrators may have their own definitions of, or preferences for, these terms for various reasons.

Dragiewicz (2011) argues that the term "domestic violence" is not optimal since it obscures sex and gender differences and can contribute to a misleading impression that the dynamics of violence and abuse are the same for women and men. There is additional criticism of this term because it exposes some types of violence within the home but disregards larger violence such as state and racialized violence (Ristock, 2013). Still others have felt that, owing to the strong historical association of "domestic violence" with heterosexual relationships, the terms "relationship violence," "partnership violence," or "intimate partner violence" are more appropriate (Davis & Glass, 2013). Nevertheless, the term "domestic violence" endures and continues to be used regularly.

In the late 1990s, the Centers for Disease Control and Prevention (CDC) attempted to remedy this by creating a panel of experts who were charged with developing recommendations for consistency in research terminology (Goodman & Epstein, 2008). In 1999, the CDC published a set of guidelines that defined partner violence as encompassing threats of or actual physical and sexual violence and psychological and emotional abuse that occur in the context of prior physical or sexual violence (Saltzman et al., 1999). The CDC adopted the term "intimate partner violence" to describe this type of abuse because it was narrow enough to differentiate between partners and other family relationships yet expansive enough to include all partnerships, regardless of marital status or sexual orientation (McClennen, 2005). In 2015, the CDC updated the definition of the term "intimate partner violence" as the use of physical violence ("the use of physical force with the potential of harm"), sexual violence ("a sexual act that is committed or attempted by another person without freely given consent of the victim or against someone who is unable to consent or refuse"), stalking ("a pattern of repeated, unwanted attention and contact that causes fear or concern"), and psychological aggression ("the use of verbal and non-verbal communication with the intent to harm another person mentally or emotionally") by a current or former intimate partner (Longobardi & Badenes-Ribera, 2017).

Regardless of the abusive behaviors that are used, intimate partner violence is defined by the vast majority of theorists and practitioners as a systematic pattern of coercive and violent behavior used by one person in an intimate relationship to gain and maintain power and control over the other (Pence, 2005; NRCDV, 2007; NCADV, 2010; Fountain et al., 2009). The dyad of power and control is a dynamic in which one person uses their power and/or privilege to control their partner in a relationship (NCAVP, 2012). Intimate partners can include current and past spouses and non-marital domestic and dating partners. It is not necessary for the partners to be cohabitants, nor must the relationship involve sexual activities (Saltzman et al., 1999).

Although no single or universal definition of violence and abuse within families has been established and agreed to by those who study the subject (APA, 1996), the U.S. Surgeon General declared family violence to be a national epidemic. Since then, organizations such as the American Medical Association and the U.S. CDC have made similar declarations, agreeing that family violence is significantly underreported, and that large segments of the population are affected by it (APA, 1996).

According to the CDC, approximately one in four women and one in ten men have experienced physical violence, sexual violence, and/or stalking at the hands of an intimate partner during their lifetime and reported some form of IPV-related impact. Furthermore, over 43 million women and 38 million men have experienced psychological aggression from an intimate partner in their lifetime (CDC, 2020).

The National Violence Against Women Survey published by the U.S. Department of Justice/Office of Justice Programs in 2000 found that women living with female intimate partners experienced less IPV than those living with male intimate partners (11% versus 25% when comparing rape, physical assault, or stalking). Similarly, men living with female intimate partners also experienced less IPV than men living with male intimate partners (7.7% versus 15%, respectively) (Ristock, 2013).

A decade later, the CDC's National Intimate Partner and Sexual Violence Survey (National Center for Injury Prevention and Control/Centers for Disease Control and Prevention, 2010) revealed that most bisexual and heterosexual women (89.5% and 98.7%, respectively) reported only male perpetrators of IPV, while 67.4% of lesbians reported only female perpetrators of IPV. In the same survey, the majority of bisexual men (78.5%) and most heterosexual men (99.5%) reported only female perpetrators of IPV. The majority of gay male respondents (90.7%), however, reported having only male perpetrators of IPV (Walters, Chen, & Breiding, 2013).

In addition to causing psychological harm and/or physical injury, intimate partner violence can be lethal. In fact, 30–50% of female homicides and 12% of male homicides are committed by previous or current intimate partners (Lawson, 2013). There is a significant lack of data regarding intimate partner homicide (IPH), but the available data suggests approximately 42 confirmed cases of LGBTQ+ IPH per year. Proportionally, this is similar to the rates of IPH in heterosexual relationships. It tends to occur after an extended build-up of increasing violence and is more likely to be committed by men who have a history of highly controlling behaviors (Messinger, 2020). The proportion of male-perpetrated IPH is believed to be higher in LGBTQ+ couples (87–89%) than in heterosexual partners (62–77%). Available data suggests that its victims are more commonly gay men (80%) rather than lesbians (20%), and knives are used more commonly than guns (Messinger, 2020).

Domestic violence is believed to be traumatizing to most victims. Even a single act of violence by a family member or intimate partner may cause long-lasting trauma as well as immediate harm to a victim or an observer. In fact, repeated and severe violence can cause significant psychological distress and may result in post-traumatic stress disorder (PTSD), depression, dissociation, anxiety, mood disorders, substance abuse, suicidal feelings and attempts, among other problems (APA, 1996). The early literature attempted to understand why (heterosexual) women were victimized and concluded that victimization in childhood and adolescence was determined to be a factor, but later research concluded that battered women are no more likely to have been exposed to violence as children than non-battered women (Astin, Lawrence, & Foy, 1993; Bergman et al., 1988; Hamberger, 1991; Hotaling & Sugarman, 1990). However, studies indicate that individuals victimized earlier in life develop higher levels of fear than those who are victimized later (Kury & Ferdinand, 1997). In addition, research suggests that the effects of trauma are cumulative (Follette et al., 1996), and revictimization studies have indicated that childhood sexual abuse may put women at greater risk for a variety of victimization experiences at the hands of partners and other males in adulthood (Kingma, 1999; Sanders & Moore, 1999). Being exposed to domestic violence is also believed to have a significant effect on family members who are not directly involved as victims or victimizers, and secondary victimization may cause psychological symptoms similar to those experienced by the direct victims of violence (APA, 1996). To our knowledge, no research to date has studied risk factors for adult IPV associated with abuse and violence perpetrated against LGBTQ+ children, adolescents, and young adults, either within or outside families, owing to their sexual orientation or gender identity. The American Psychological Association (1996) suggests that domestic violence be understood from multiple perspectives, including those specific to sexual orientation, ethnic and cultural background, geographic location, family structure, social and economic position, and other individual characteristics, as well as physical, mental, and emotional abilities. Of these variables, however, sexual orientation is rarely included in discussions of family and domestic violence. Similarly, non-binary and fluid identities are often ignored in these discussions as well.

Physical abuse can include behaviors such as hitting, slapping, punching, choking, biting, shoving, burning, stabbing, and restraining. Sexual violence includes behaviors such as raping, refusing to practice safer sex, forcing prostitution, and using pornography, as well as other forms of sexual activity unwanted by the other (Davis et al., 2015). The National Intimate Partner and Sexual Violence Survey of 2010 defines emotional violence as expressive forms of aggression and coercive control (National Center for Injury Prevention and Control/Centers for Disease Control and Prevention, 2010). Others define it more broadly as a "range of verbal and mental methods designed to emotionally wound, coerce, control, intimidate, psychologically harm, and express anger." This can include behaviors such as humiliating the other, controlling what the other can and cannot do, undermining the other's self-esteem, withholding information, embarrassing the other, destroying the other's property, threatening abuse, forced isolation, induced debility-producing exhaustion, gaslighting, blackmailing, and denying the other access to resources and necessities (Woodyatt & Stephenson, 2016).

Stalking is generally considered to be a type of psychological intimidation, although the CDC puts it in its own category. It is defined by the National Institute of Justice (2007, p. 1) as "a course of conduct directed at a specific person that involves repeated visual or physical proximity, nonconsensual communication, or verbal, written, or implied threats that would cause a reasonable person fear." Cyberstalking, which is the use of technology to stalk victims, is included in this definition. Verbal abuse, which is the single variable most likely to predict intimate partner violence (Tjaden & Thoennes, 2000), includes name-calling, using profanity, and verbal degradation, while economic and financial abuse includes stealing money, creating credit card debt, refusing to allow the partner to work, preventing the other from finishing education, and withholding money. Furthermore, families and couples who live in poverty or have few financial resources may be more likely to experience intimate partner violence (Jewkes, 2002). Abuse related to status (e.g., class, race, level of education, ability, socioeconomics, residency or immigration status, religion, etc.) is also typically included among the abusive tactics used by the perpetrator in violent intimate partner relationships and has sometimes been defined as environmental abuse. In the LGBTQ+ community, abusive tactics are often designed by the perpetrator to address a part of the victim that is rejected by society, including their HIV status, coming out status, or transgender or non-binary identification.

Intimate partner violence is neither a spontaneous act of anger nor a one-time occurrence (CDC, 2006; Tjaden & Thoennes, 2000). Furthermore, it is not a "crime of passion," a "lover's quarrel," a "catfight," a "fair fight," or a "communication or relationship problem" (Holt, 2002). Rather than occurring because the abuser is out of control, violent behavior is believed to be intentional and deliberate, and numerous theorists and researchers agree that batterers choose to be violent (Letellier, 1996). In addition, IPV may or may not constitute a crime depending on the type of abuse, statutes, and other variables that are pertinent to the event.

Gender symmetry is a term that defines the belief that women perpetrate violence at roughly the same rate as men, while gender asymmetry indicates that men are more violent than women and are, most often, the abusers when intimate partner violence is present. While both victims and perpetrators can be male, female, transgender, or non-binary, the majority of assaults are believed to be committed by men against their female partners (Rennison, 2001). Further, it is also commonly believed that men's violence against women may be more serious than the violence committed by women against men because women are more likely to be injured, hospitalized, and/or killed by their male partners than the reverse (Dina & Langhinrichsen-Rohling, 1994). It is important to note that research has not been able to consistently show that either LGBTQ+ perpetrators or victims align with or utilize traditional binary gender roles, and so it in unknown how this information may or may not apply to LGBTQ+ populations.

In their study of severely violent couples, Jacobson and Gottman (1998) concluded that the frequency of violent acts is not as crucial as the impact of the violence and its function. More specifically, they indicate that the primary purpose of battering is to control and intimidate rather than to injure. Johnson (1995) argues that the forms and characteristics of violence vary, and that distinctions need to be made regarding the types of violence, the motivation of the perpetrator, and the social and cultural context. Further, it is argued that distinctions are not based on single incidents but on patterns across numerous incidents and perpetrator motives.

Johnson (1995) distinguishes between "common couple violence" or "situational couple violence" and "intimate terrorism." According to his belief, the former two categories are not typically related to general controlling behaviors but arise in a single argument where one or both partners lash out at the other. More specifically, in situational couple violence, conflicts occasionally escalate into relatively low-level violence, such as slapping or throwing an object at the partner. Unlike intimate terrorism, however, this type is not connected to a general pattern of power and control, but it can, nevertheless, be frequent and/or serious.

Intimate terrorism (originally known as "patriarchal terrorism"), on the other hand, includes a general pattern of control by one partner over the other. According to Johnson (1995), this type of violence is more common than the former among patients and those in domestic violence shelters, more likely to escalate over time, not as likely to appear to be mutual, and more likely to involve serious injury. Johnson also argues that the context for intimate terrorism is coercive control, while the context for situational couple violence is gender symmetry. Coercive control is present in situations where IPV not only is a series of violent incidents but occurs when "perpetrators of violence combine repeated physical abuse with intimidation, isolation, and control" (Goldenberg et al., 2016). While common couple violence is believed to be seen more commonly in overall population samples, intimate terrorism has been based on research from women's shelter populations (Wexler, 2000). Victims of intimate terrorism exhibit more symptoms of post-traumatic stress and are more apt to leave their partners (Johnson & Leone, 2005). They are also more likely to be seen in the health, mental health, and justice systems (Lloyd & Taluc, 1999; Zweig, Burt, & Van Ness, 2003) and to access shelter. The majority of research has focused on intimate terrorism, and far less is known about patterns of situational couple violence. These studies have looked at heterosexual and non-LGBTQ+ couples rather than LGBTQ+ couples, and intimate terrorism was, in fact, initially believed to occur only in opposite-gender relationships. We argue that these two categories are not sufficient, particularly when we consider LGBTQ+ populations, and propose at least three categories, including situational violence, common couple violence, and intimate terrorism, with situational violence being violence that occurs as the result of a crisis in the relationship but does not occur again once the crisis has been resolved. Further, it would not be part of a pattern of violent and abusive behavior in the relationship. Common couple violence would be abusive or violent behavior that occurs periodically in response to an issue in the relationship over which one of the partners wants control—for example, one of the partners wants to maintain control over the couple's finances but nothing else. This type of abuse can occur within a pattern when an LGBTQ+ couple, for example, disagree about who they should be "out" to, and one or both fight for control of the issue. The pattern, however, does not exist for other issues over which the couple disagree. Intimate terrorism is a pervasive pattern of coercive control, and, generally, the perpetrator will attempt to gain control and power over the partner by using any means necessary. Clearly differentiating between the varying types of violence can assist in treatment planning. For example, safe housing options should be considered for people who are experiencing intimate terrorism.

LaViolette suggests that one way of conceptualizing partner abuse is to place it on a continuum, which emphasizes the fact that anyone can (and many people do) commit acts or limited acts of aggression, whereas very few become involved in escalating and/or chronic patterns of physical abuse and coercive control (LaViolette & Barnett, 2000). LaViolette argues that a continuum also incorporates the possibility that interpersonal violence normally occurring at a low level may erupt suddenly into severe violence with significant repercussions. Common couple aggression, which may include relatively infrequent, non-injurious behavior that may be mutual, does not tend to victimize the partners, and generally does not create fear, would be at the low end of LaViolette's continuum. Intimate terrorism, which may cluster around a pattern of assaultive, fear-producing, controlling behaviors that are both criminal (e.g., physical assaults, terrorist threats, stalking) and noncriminal (e.g., isolating the partner, jealous monitoring of partner's friends and activities, humiliating the partner), would be situated at the high end of LaViolette's continuum.

Neidig and Friedman (1984) differentiate between expressive and instrumental violence, with the former defined as violence that is the result of escalating emotions between partners, and the latter resulting from the motivation to control, intimidate, and/or punish the partner. They indicate that expressive intimate partner violence is often mutual, mild to moderate rather than severe, and infrequent, while instrumental violence is most often perpetrated by men and can be severe. Other types of violence include "violent resistance" or "self-defense," which is violence perpetrated by victims against their abusive partners, and "mutual violence," which is abuse that occurs when both partners act in a violent manner, battling for control. The majority of these concepts have focused on non-LGBTQ populations and do not include an analysis when applied to LGBTQ+ populations.

"Mutual violence," sometimes known as "mutual battering," has also been termed "bidirectional" or "reciprocal" violence. It is believed to be more common in same-gender rather than opposite-gender relationships, and both partners are believed to be equally responsible for the violence. Renzetti (1992) argues that mutual battering is a myth, and that there are important differences between initiating violence, using violence in self-defense, and retaliating against a violent partner. In Island and Letellier's (1991) exploration of gay male IPV, they indicate that, when victims respond aggressively, the imbalance of power in the relationship determines which person is being victimized rather than the acts of aggression themselves. These factors are often not considered by providers, responders, or members of the LGBTQ+ community. Renzetti (1992) found that lesbians who have been abused believed themselves to be mutually violent even if they were violent toward their partner only once and/or fought back in self-defense. Furthermore, Asherah (1990) and Renzetti (1992) argue that battered lesbians will sometimes forego seeking help because of the guilt they feel from having fought back or defended themselves against their partners. We have found that they will also indicate upon presentation, when describing self-defensive or retaliatory behaviors rather than acts of primary aggression, that they believe themselves to be provocative and therefore the abuser in the partnership.

Walker (1986) indicates that lesbians are more likely to fight back against an abusive partner than are heterosexual women. She hypothesized that this could result from several factors, including a smaller size differential. Lie et al. (1991) indicated that, in a study of lesbians who reported being both victims and perpetrators of violence, 30.3% perceived their aggression to be self-defensive, and 39.4% saw it as mutually aggressive. Messinger (2020) indicates that, in a similar study, 23% of LGBTQ+ partners used violence in self-defense, and 28% used it in retaliation.

These factors, coupled with the myth of mutual battering, can complicate assessment and make differentiation of victim and perpetrator challenging for providers and responders as well as victims and perpetrators themselves. Marrujo and Kreger (1996) propose utilizing three assessment categories—primary aggressor, primary victim, and participant—to facilitate adequate intervention with lesbian clients. Similarly, Holt (2017) proposes four categories—primary victim, defending victim, secondary aggressor or retaliating victim, and primary aggressor—to enhance assessment protocols and better ensure appropriate and safe intervention and treatment planning with members of the LGBTQ+ population.

While many theorists believe that the dynamics of LGBTQ+ intimate partner violence are similar to partner violence in the heterosexual population, there are numerous and significant differences between the two, as noted above. One significant difference that is often pointed out by researchers concerns threats or behaviors that reveal the sexual orientation or gender identity of a partner to a family member, employer, or others to cause harm ("outing" someone).

Because LGBTQ+ intimate partner violence has been relatively invisible, little agreement exists about it. While practitioners may assume, for example, that the types of violence outlined in this chapter apply similarly to LGBTQ+ individuals as they do to heterosexuals, it is not known if the etiology is the same. Furthermore, members of the LGBTQ+ community are themselves unsure about its variables or what, in fact, constitutes abuse. A 2013 survey of gay men revealed that, while over 90% of the respondents agreed that hitting, punching, kicking, raping, slapping, and/or damaging property were examples of abusive behaviors, there was less universal, but still majority, agreement about not wearing a condom during sex, preventing one's partner from seeing their family and friends, cheating, and calling another derogatory names. Less than a majority felt that reading email or text messages without a partner's knowledge, criticizing a partner's clothing, or demanding that a partner "act straight" around certain people constituted intimate partner violence (Stephenson et al., 2013). In fact, results from surveys conducted by the Los Angeles LGBT Center with LGBTQ+ participants at various community events indicated that, while 71% of the respondents knew other LGBTQ+ people who had experienced intimate partner violence, only 30% considered it to be a significant problem (Holt, 2020).

It has been typical in our society to ask why people stay in abusive relationships. Victims stay for any number of reasons, including the presence of traumatic bonding; their beliefs about relationships, love, divorce, or separation; the presence of children; joint ownership/finances or lack of finances; religious views; and so on. LGBTQ+ victims often stay for all of these reasons in addition to the lack of LGBTQ+ domestic violence services; fear of bringing shame upon the community; child custody challenges due to sexual orientation; not recognizing the presence of domestic violence because of heterosexual images of abuse and violence; the belief in "mutual abuse" and, hence, the belief that both individuals are to blame; traumatic bonding ("It's me and you against the world because of homo/bi/transphobia"); the fear of not finding another LGBTQ+ partner; and so on. Most importantly, victims—regardless of their sexual orientation or gender identity—often stay because leaving does not necessarily stop the violence, which can continue long after the victim attempts to end the partnership. Furthermore, the majority of domestic violence homicides occur when one partner gains autonomy and wants to end the relationship. According to Wendy Mahoney, the executive director of the Mississippi Coalition Against Domestic Violence, "Women [victims] in abusive relationships are about 500 time more at risk when they leave" (Mitchell, 2017).

Continuing Education Questions

1. Which of these is *not* a criticism of the term "domestic violence"?
   a. It obscures sex and gender differences
   b. It is associated historically with LGBTQ couples only
   c. It ignores other types of violence, such as state violence
   d. None of the above
2. Gender symmetry indicates that men are more violent than women and are, most often, the abusers when intimate partner violence is present.
   a. True
   b. False
3. Which of the following is *not* one of the CDC's 2015 IPV categories?
   a. Physical violence
   b. Stalking
   c. "Outing"
   d. Psychological aggression
4. Stalking is the single variable most likely to predict intimate partner violence.
   a. True
   b. False
5. When compared with "common couple violence," intimate terrorism is:
   a. More likely to escalate over time
   b. More likely to be mutual
   c. Less likely to involve serious injury
   d. All of the above

References

American Psychological Association (APA). (1996). *Violence and the Family: Report of the American Psychological Association Presidential Task Force on Violence and the Family.* Washington, DC: American Psychological Association.

Asherah, K.L. (1990). The Myth of Mutual Abuse. In P. Elliott (Ed.), *Confronting Lesbian Battering* (pp. 56–58). St. Paul, MN: Minnesota Coalition for Battered Women.

Astin, M.C., Lawrence, K.J., & Foy, D.W. (1993). Posttraumatic Stress Disorder among Battered Women: Risk and Resiliency Factors. *Violence and Victims, 8,* 17–28.

Bergman, B., Larsson, G., Brismar, B., & Klang, M. (1988). Aetiological and Precipitating Factors in Wife Battering. *Acta Psychiatric Scandinavia, 77,* 338–345.

Centers for Disease Control (CDC). (2006). Understanding Intimate Partner Violence [fact sheet]. Retrieved August 29, 2007, from cdc.gov/ncipc/dvp/ipv_factsheet.pdf

Centers for Disease Control (CDC). (2020). Fast Facts: Preventing Intimate Partner Violence. Retrieved April 29, 2022, from cdc.gov/violenceprevention/intimatepartnerviolence/fastfact.html

Davis, Alissa, Best, John, Wei, Chongyi, Luo, Juhua, Van Der Pol, Barbara, Meyerson, Beth, Dodge, Brian, Aalsma, Matthew, Tucker, Joseph, & Social Entrepreneurship for Sexual Health Research Group. (2015). Intimate Partner Violence and Correlates with Risk Behaviors and HIV/STI Diagnoses among Men Who Have Sex with Men and Men Who Have Sex with Men and Women in China. *Sexually Transmitted Diseases*, 42(7), 387–392. doi:10.1097/olq.0000000000000302

Davis, Kierrynn, and Nel Glass. (2013). Reframing the Heteronormative Constructions of Lesbian Partner Violence. In Janice Ristock (Ed.), *Intimate Partner Violence in LGBTQ Lives* (pp. 13–37). Routledge.

Dina, V., & Langhinrichsen-Rohling, J. (1994). Are Bi-directionality Violent Couples Mutually Victimized? A Gender-Sensitive Comparison. *Violence and Victims*, 9, 107–123.

Dragiewicz, M. (2011). *Equality with a Vengeance: Men's Rights Groups, Battered Women, and Antifeminist Backlash*. Boston: Northeastern University Press.

Follette, V.M., Polusny, M.A., Bechtle, A.E., & Naugle, A.E. (1996). Cumulative Trauma: The Impact of Child Sexual Abuse, Adult Sexual Assault, and Spouse Abuse. *Journal of Traumatic Stress*, 9, 25–35.

Fountain, K., Mitchell-Brody, M, Jones, S.A., and Nicols, K. (2009). *Lesbian, Gay, Bisexual, Transgender and Queer Domestic Violence in the United States in 2008*. New York, NY: National Coalition of Anti-Violence Programs.

Goldenberg, Tamar, Stephenson, Rob, Freeland, Ryan, Finneran, Catherine, & Hadley, Craig. (2016). "Struggling to Be the Alpha": Sources of Tension and Intimate Partner Violence in Same-Sex Relationships between Men. *Culture, Health & Sexuality*, 18(8), 875–889. doi:10.1080/13691058.2016.1144791

Goodman, L.A., & Epstein, D. (2008). *Listening to Battered Women: A Survivor-Centered Approach to Advocacy, Mental Health, and Justice*. Washington, DC: American Psychological Association.

Hamberger, L.K. (1991). *Research Concerning Wife Abuse: Implications for Training Physicians and Criminal Justice Personnel*. Paper presented at the Annual Meeting of the American Psychological Association, San Francisco.

Holt, S.L. (2002). LGBT Domestic Violence. *Arise Magazine*, 5, 38–40.

Holt, S.L. (June 21, 2017). Interview: California Health Report. In a Push for Fair Treatment, Los Angeles LGBT Center Creates New Categories for Relationship Violence. Hannah Guzik.

Holt, S.L. (2020). Lecture. Antioch University Los Angeles. Family Violence and Abuse in LGBTQIA Communities course.

Hotaling, G.T., & Sugarman, D.B. (1990). A Risk Marker Analysis of Assaulted Wives. *Journal of Family Violence*, 5, 1–13.

Island, D., & Letellier, P. (1991). *Men Who Beat the Men Who Love Them: Battered Gay Men and Domestic Violence*. Binghamton, NY: Haworth Press.

Jacobson, N.S., & Gottman, J.M. (1998). *When Men Batter Women: New Insights into Ending Abusive Relationships*. New York, NY: Simon & Schuster.

Jewkes, R. (2002). Intimate Partner Violence: Causes and Prevention. *Lancet, 359*(9315), 1423–1429.

Johnson, M. (1995). Patriarchal Terrorism and Common Couple Violence: Two Forms of Violence against Women. *Journal of Marriage and the Family, 57,* 283–294.

Johnson, M.P., & Leone, J.M. (2005). The Differential Effects of Intimate Terrorism and Situational Couple Violence. *Journal of Family Issues, 26*(3), 322–349.

Kingma, J. (1999). Repeat Victimization of Violence: A Retrospective Study from a Hospital Emergency Department for the Period 1971–1995. *Journal of Interpersonal Violence, 14,* 79–90.

Kury, H., & Ferdinand, T. (1997). The Victim's Experience and Fear of Crime. *International Review of Victimology, 5,* 93–140.

LaViolette, A.D., & Barnett, O.W. (2000). *It Could Happen to Anyone: Why Battered Women Stay* (2nd ed.). Thousand Oaks, CA: Sage.

Lawson, D.M. (2013). *Family Violence: Explanations and Evidence-Based Clinical Practice* (p. 61). Alexandria, VA: American Counseling Association.

Letellier, P. (1996). Twin Epidemics: Domestic Violence & HIV Infection among Gay and Bisexual Men. In Renzetti, C.M., & Miley, C.H. (Eds.), *Violence in Gay and Lesbian Domestic Partnerships* NY: Routledge (p. 71).

Lie, G.Y., Schilit, R., Bush, J., Montagne, M., Reyes, L. (1991). Lesbians in Currently Aggressive Relationships: How Frequently Do They Report Aggressive Past Relationships? *Violence and Victims, 6*(2), 121–135.

Lloyd, S., & Taluc, N. (1999). The Effects of Male Violence on Female Employment. *Violence Against Women, 5,* 370–392.

Longobardi, C., and Badenes-Ribera, L. (2017). Intimate Partner Violence in Same-Sex Relationships and the Role of Sexual Minority Stressors: A Systematic Review of the Past 10 Years. *Journal of Child and Family Studies, 26*(8), 2039–2049. doi:10.1007/s1082 6-017-0734-4

Marrujo, B., & Kreger, M. (1996). Definition of Roles in Abusive Lesbian Relationships. In C.M. Renzetti & C.H. Miley (Eds.), *Violence in Gay and Lesbian Partnerships.* Binghamton, NY: Haworth Press.

McClennen, J.C. (2005). Domestic Violence between Same Gender Partners: Recent Findings and Future Research. *Journal of Interpersonal Violence, 20,* 149–154.

Messinger, A.M. (2020). *LGBTQ Intimate Partner Violence: Lessons for Policy, Practice, and Research.* Oakland, CA: University of California Press.

Mitchell, J. (Jan. 28, 2017). Most Dangerous Time for Battered Women? When They Leave. *Clarion-Ledger.* Retrieved from Clarionledger.com/story/mews/2017/01/28/most-dangerous-time/96955552

National Center for Injury Prevention and Control/Centers for Disease Control and Prevention. (2010). *2010 Findings on Victimization by Sexual Orientation.* Retrieved from cdc.gov/violenceprevention/pdf/nisvs_sofindings.pdf

National Coalition Against Domestic Violence (NCADV). (2010). *NCADV Domestic Violence Facts.* Washington, DC: Author.

National Coalition of Anti-Violence Programs (NCAVP). (2012). *Lesbian, Gay, Bisexual, Transgender, Queer, and HIV-Affected Intimate Partner Violence 2011: A Report from the National Coalition of Anti-Violence Programs.* New York, NY: New York City Anti-Violence Project.

National Institute of Justice. (2007, October 24). Overview of Stalking. Retrieved from https://nij.ojp.gov/topics/articles/overview-stalking

National Resource Center on Domestic Violence (NRCDV). (2007). *Lesbian, Gay, Bisexual, and Trans (LGBTQ) Communities and Domestic Violence: Information and Resources.* Harrisburg, PA: Author. Retrieved October 17, 2004, from ncadv.org

Neidig, P.H., & Friedman, D.H. (1984). *Spouse Abuse: A Treatment Program for Couples.* Champaign, IL: Research Press.

Pence, E. (2005). Women's Use of Violence in Intimate Relationships [Newsletter]. Duluth, MN: Advocates for Family Peace.

Rennison, C.M. (2001). *Intimate Partner Violence and Age of Victim, 1993–1999.* Bureau of Justice Statistics Special Report, Washington, DC: U.S. Dept. of Justice, NCJ # 187635.

Renzetti, C.M. (1992). *Violent Betrayal: Partner Abuse in Lesbian Relationships.* Newbury Park, CA: Sage.

Ristock, Janice L. (2013). Introduction. In Janice Ristock (Ed.), *Intimate Partner Violence in LGBTQ Lives* (pp. 1–13). Routledge.

Saltzman, L.E., Fanslow, J.L., McMahon, P.M., & Shelley, G.A. (1999). Intimate Partner Violence Surveillance: Uniform Definitions and Recommended Data Elements [fact sheet]. Atlanta, GA: National Center for Injury Prevention and Control, Centers for Disease Control and Prevention.

Sanders, B., & Moore, D.L. (1999). Childhood Maltreatment and Date Rape. *Journal of Interpersonal Violence, 14,* 115–124.

Stephenson, Rob, Hall, Casey D., Williams, Whitney, Sato, Kimi, & Finneran, Catherine. (2013). Towards the Development of an Intimate Partner Violence Screening Tool for Gay and Bisexual Men. *Western Journal of Emergency Medicine, 14*(4), 391–401. doi:10.5811/westjem.3.2013.15597

Tjaden, P., & Thoennes, N. (2000). *Extent, Nature, and Consequences of Intimate Partner Violence: Findings from the National Violence against Women Survey.* Washington, DC: U.S. Department of Justice. Retrieved May 19, 2009, from ojp.usdoj.gov/nij/pubs-sum/181867.htm

Walker, L. (1986). Battered Women's Shelters and Work with Battered Lesbians. In K. Lobel (Ed.), *Naming the Violence: Speaking Out about Lesbian Battering* (pp. 73–76). Seattle, WA: Seal Press.

Wallace, H. (2005). *Family Violence: Legal, Medical, and Social Perspectives* (4th ed.). Boston, MA: Pearson Education.

Walters, M.L., Chen, J., & Breiding, M.J. (2013). The National Intimate Partner and Sexual Violence Survey: Findings on Victimization by Sexual Orientation. Retrieved November 15, 2021, from https://www.cdc.gov/violenceprevention/pdf/nisvs_sofindings.pdf

Wexler, D.B. (2000). *Domestic Violence 2000 Group Leaders Manual: An Integrated Skills Program for Men.* New York, NY: W.W. Norton.

Woodyatt, Cory R., and Rob Stephenson. (2016). Emotional Intimate Partner Violence Experienced by Men in Same-Sex Relationships. *Culture, Health & Sexuality, 18*(10), 1137–1149. doi:10.1080/13691058.2016.1175027

Zweig, J.M., Burt, M.R., & Van Ness, A. (2003). *The Effects on Victims of Victim Service Programs Funded by the STOP Formula Grants Program.* Washington, DC: Urban Institute.

Myths, Misconceptions, Facts, and Statistics   **3**

For centuries, myths and misconceptions about domestic violence have flourished and have obscured its realities. A popular misconception about domestic violence for years involved the meaning of the term "rule of thumb." This term was believed to have originated in an English law that allowed a man to beat his wife with a stick no larger than the circumference of his thumb. In reality, the term had its origins in the 1600s, when measuring tools were not available and thumbs were used for measurement purposes. In the 19th century, American and English courts referred to the "rule of thumb" when outlawing wife beating. In 1976, Del Martin (author of *Battered Wives*) indicated a link between domestic violence and the term. Per Martin, "The common-law doctrine had been modified to allow the husband to whip his wife provided that he used a switch no bigger than a thumb—a rule of thumb so to speak." Many believed this to be a literal reference, and the term gained in popularity. Etymologists have since concluded that it originated instead from measuring practices rather than court rulings or law (sparkfiles.net, n.d.).

Other misconceptions about domestic violence/intimate partner violence include the following:

- Domestic violence is a "crime of passion."
- Intimate partner violence is a private family matter.
- Victims provoke the abuse and violence committed by an intimate partner or family member.

DOI: 10.4324/9780429031397-3

- Domestic violence is an anger management or impulse control problem.
- Domestic violence is caused by substance use and abuse.
- Intimate partner violence is a communication problem.
- Domestic violence is a codependency issue.
- Intimate partner violence occurs more frequently in certain races and cultures.
- Men are rarely victims of domestic violence.
- Both partners are responsible for the violence in their relationship. Domestic violence is often mutual.
- Domestic violence always includes physical abuse.
- Intimate partner violence is not all that common.
- Gender, physical size, and strength determine the partner more prone to behaving violently.
- If victims really want to leave an abusive relationship, it is easy enough to do so.
- The perpetrator of domestic violence is generally determined by gender.

Although these myths and misconceptions have been consistently applied to LGBTQ+ domestic violence, there are others that are specific when referring to IPV in the rainbow community. Some of the more popular misconceptions are included below:

- LGBTQ+ domestic violence is very similar to domestic violence in the non-LGBTQ+ community. There are no significant differences between the two.
- Intimate partner violence in the LGBTQ+ population does not happen as frequently as it does in the non-LGBTQ+ community.
- It is primarily heterosexual women with male partners who are most often battered.
- Violence in LGBTQ+ partnerships is often mutual.
- When LGBTQ+ couples fight, it tends to be a fair fight between equals or a "lover's quarrel."
- LGBTQ+ abusers are often the physically larger and stronger of the two people, while the victim is often more feminine, smaller in size, and weaker in strength.
- Abusers are butch, and victims are femme.
- Women are inherently not abusive and not apt to abuse their partners.
- Men are not victimized by other men.

- When violence exists in a female-to-female relationship, it's a cat fight.
- When violence exists in a male-to-male relationship, it's simply a version of boys being boys.
- LGBTQ+ intimate partner violence occurs primarily among individuals who are poor, people of color, and those who frequent bars and clubs.
- Since LGBTQ+ couples are more likely to be equal in size, the damage inflicted by the partner is typically less than that inflicted by a non-LGBTQ+ abuser.
- Violence occurs in LGBTQ+ communities because of the high(er) rates of drug and alcohol abuse.
- The popularity of methamphetamine in the gay community is a primary reason for the occurrence of intimate partner violence.
- The law does not protect LGBTQ+ victims of violence.
- Battered LGBTQ+ people are as likely to identify themselves as victims as are non-LGBTQ+ and/or heterosexual women.
- LGBTQ+ people are not as likely as non-LGBTQ+ individuals to have children and are less likely to need the same domestic violence resources and services.
- The sexual assault of a person by an individual of the same gender is not as traumatic to the victim as assault by someone of the opposite gender.
- The sexual assault of a lesbian by a woman is not as traumatic as assault of her by a male.

These myths and misconceptions have fostered a general lack of understanding of domestic violence in our larger culture and invisibility and minimization of LGBTQ+ intimate partner violence in particular. When working with clients impacted by domestic violence, it is important to assist them in identifying which myths and misconceptions about domestic violence they may have internalized and then provide accurate information to replace these fallacies.

Despite the number of misconceptions and the misinformation and lack of understanding they perpetuate, it is important to consider what we *do* know to be true about domestic violence. We know that it is a problem of epidemic proportions, and, while it is generally viewed through a heteronormative lens, it affects a significant portion of the LGBTQ+ population. We also know that it is a pervasive problem in all populations that has numerous negative effects, including poor mental and physical health outcomes, increased risk of substance use and further victimization, loss of ability to work effectively or sustain work over time, and a heightened chance of injuries and/or death. Unfortunately, this is compounded by the fact that sufferers rarely seek help, often do not know that help is available or where it can be found, and are frequently not assisted effectively and/or appropriately when they do seek help.

The study of domestic violence is young. Del Martin's 1976 book *Battered Wives* was the first book on the subject, although Dr. Richard Gelles is credited with the first systemic investigation of spousal abuse in 1974 (Seelye, 2020). The past five decades have produced numerous books, articles, and research studies that have broadened our understanding of this phenomenon. While our understanding of domestic violence is arguably in its early adulthood, however, the study of LGBTQ+ intimate partner violence is still in its infancy.

Despite the overall invisibility of LGBTQ+ domestic violence, there are numerous studies that suggest the significant magnitude of the larger problem overall (Tjaden & Thoennes, 1999), and there is debate about the accuracy of the data due, in part, to the lack of consensus on the definition of intimate partner violence, violence in general, who constitutes a victim, and so on. Multiple data sources, limitations of self-reported data, obstacles inherent in data collection, and social barriers, among other issues, are also the subject of debate (Saltzman et al., 1999; Culross, Fischer, & Bedair, 2010).

Johnson (2006) indicates that there are two major sources of data about domestic violence in general that exist at any given time and include (1) public agencies such as the police, courts, hospitals, and shelters and (2) random sample surveys that may claim to be more representative of reality than agency data. He argues that agency data is dominated by the types of violence defined as "intimate terrorism" and "violent resistance," because both forms are more likely to produce the fear that leads victims to turn to organizations for assistance. He indicates that researchers who work with this type of data also tend to see violence that primarily concerns male perpetrators.

According to Johnson (2006), surveys generally begin with representative samples, although 40% of the persons contacted refuse to participate in family violence surveys because this percentage often consists of intimate terrorists and their victims. Hence, the data is heavily dominated by situational couple violence, which involves as many women as men. Johnson concludes that the data, therefore, looks at two completely different phenomena (intimate terrorism and situational couple violence), but both are defined with the same term (domestic violence) to describe what they study.

The following section will summarize available data with the caveats above, which tend to explain many of the inconsistencies. This list is not comprehensive, and other sources may include similar data that may vary. The data about domestic violence is continually reviewed and updated by various sources. It is important to note that much of it is from general research unless otherwise noted and it *rarely* includes LGBTQ+ persons, and so it can be assumed that, while it may apply to LGBTQ+ people, it may also not apply to them. Similarly, this information is not pertinent to all IPV situations, regardless of the sexual orientation or gender identity of the individuals involved. It may or may not be present and may be modified by a wide variety of factors.

1. Prevalence rates suggest nothing less than an epidemic that has severe and tragic consequences:
    *   The CDC indicates that domestic violence affects over 10% of the U.S. population (Tjaden & Thoennes, 2000), and nearly one in four women in the United States report experiencing violence by a current or former spouse or boyfriend at some point in their life (CDC, 2008).
    *   The United Nations Development Fund for Women (2003) estimates that, globally, at least one in every three women will be beaten, raped, or otherwise abused during her lifetime (Sushma, 2000).
    *   The World Health Organization (WHO, 2021) indicates that violence against women is a public health problem that affects approximately one-third of women globally, while a study by UNICEF indicated that 20–50% of the female population of the world would be victims of domestic violence (Sushma, 2000). The World Health Organization also found that the proportion of partnered women who had experienced physical or sexual violence at the hands of an intimate partner ranged from 15% in Japan to 71% in Ethiopia (Garcia-Moreno et al., 2005).
    *   Every 9 seconds, a woman is assaulted or beaten in the United States (New Hope, 2022), and, on average, nearly 20 people per minute are physically abused by an intimate partner in the United States (Black et al., 2011). In fact, domestic violence accounts for 21% of all violent crime (Truman & Morgan, 2014).
    *   According to the U.S. Department of Justice, on average, more than three women a day are murdered by their husbands or boyfriends in the United States (Catalano, 2007).
    *   Out of all murder-suicides, 72% involve intimate partners, and 94% of the victims are female (Violence Policy Center, 2012).
    *   A study of intimate partner homicides found that 20% of victims were not the intimate partners themselves but family members, friends, neighbors, persons who intervened, law enforcement responders, or bystanders (Smith, Fowler, & Niolon, 2014).

- Nineteen percent of domestic violence incidents involve a weapon (Truman & Morgan, 2014).
- The presence of a gun in domestic violence situations increases the risk of homicide by 500% (Campbell et al., 2003).
- More than two-thirds of mass shootings are domestic violence incidents or are perpetrated by shooters with a history of domestic violence. (Mass shootings are defined as an incident with four or more fatalities by gunfire, not including the perpetrator.) Only one in six people survive a domestic violence-related mass shooting, compared with one in three people for non-domestic violence mass shootings (Geller, Booty, & Crifasi, 2021).
- In nearly half of all mass shootings, the perpetrator had previously shot an intimate partner or family member (Everytown for Gun Safety, 2023).
- States that restrict access to guns by people subject to active domestic violence restraining orders have seen a 13% reduction in intimate partner homicides involving firearms (Zeoli et al., 2018).
- Women ages 20–24 are at greatest risk of experiencing nonfatal intimate partner violence (Catalano, 2007).
- More than 15 (15.5) million children in the United States live in families in which partner violence occurred at least once in 2002, and 7 million live in families in which severe partner violence occurred (Whitfield et al., 2003).
- Difficult childhood experiences such as witnessing violence in the home are associated with an increased likelihood of intimate partner violence in adulthood (Mair, Cunradi, & Todd, 2012).
- Children who live in homes where domestic violence occurs are twice as likely to be abused as other children. Male children who witness their parents' domestic violence are twice as likely to abuse their partners in adulthood than male children of nonviolent parents (California Department of Public Health, 2007; Hotaling & Sugarman, 1986; Stith et al., 2000). Furthermore, boys who witness violence between parents demonstrate higher rates of bullying, psychiatric emergency room visits, alcohol and drug abuse, juvenile court appearances, and suicide (Baldry, 2003; Evans & Boothroyd, 2002; Shumaker & Prinz, 2000).
- Girls who witness violence at home are more likely to become victims of domestic violence (Mitchell & Finkelhor, 2001). In fact, children who witness domestic violence should not be treated as passive witnesses but rather as direct victims of domestic violence and, subsequently, child abuse (Callaghan et al., 2018)

- One in three adolescent girls in the United States is a victim of physical, emotional, or verbal abuse from a dating partner (Davis, 2008).
- Young people who witness domestic violence are more likely than others to commit sexual assault and engage in other forms of violence against strangers (Spaccarelli, Sandler & Roosa, 1994; Wolfe et al., 1995).
- Among women in domestic violence shelters, 71% report that their abuser threatened, injured, or killed a pet, and nearly half of victims stay in abusive situations rather than leave their pet(s) behind; 52% of survivors in shelters leave their pets with their abusers; and as many as 25% of survivors return to abusive situations because the abuser is using their pet as a means to get the victim back (Red Rover, 2013).
- Most domestic violence (77%) occurs at or near the victim's home (Truman & Morgan, 2014).
- Victims of domestic violence who are able to escape their abusers often deal with negative impacts long after reporting the abuse and leaving the relationship (Maddoux et al., 2018).
- Domestic violence is one of the most common causes of homelessness for women and their children (California Department of Public Health, 2007).
- On a typical day, there are more than 20,000 phone calls placed to domestic violence hotlines nationwide (NCADV, 2022).
- While only half of domestic violence incidents are reported to police (Greenfield, 1998), domestic violence calls constitute approximately half of all violent crime calls to law enforcement agencies (Cassidy, Nicholl, & Ross, 2001). Underreporting is common, and it is frequently the result of lack of confidence in police involvement and a disbelief that police involvement would make the situation better or safer (Philpart, Grant, & Guzman, 2019), in addition to fear of retaliation from the abuser. The inability of the family court system to protect domestic violence victims (for example, allowing abusers to file repeated court orders and forcing victims into mediation with their abusers) can cause deeper levels of traumatization (Coker, 2002; Douglas, 2018).
- Within the LGBTQ+ community, gay, lesbian, and bisexual persons report domestic violence victimization at rates 25% or more higher than non-LGBTQ+ communities. The transgender community reports a domestic violence rate of at least 50% (Brown & Herman, 2015).

- IPV is a major public safety issue and has been described as the third largest public health issue facing gay men. (Strasser et al., 2012).

2. There are numerous health and mental health consequences of domestic violence:
    - Domestic violence is the leading cause of injury to women, exceeding car accidents, muggings, and rapes combined (New Hope, 2022).
    - Only approximately one in five domestic violence victims with physical injuries seek professional medical treatment (Greenfield, 1998) although women experience 2 million injuries as a result of intimate partner violence each year (CDC, 2008).
    - Intimate partner violence results in injuries more often than violence perpetrated by immediate family members and other relatives (Truman & Morgan, 2014).
    - IPV results in physical injuries, most commonly to the head, neck, and face. Eve Valera, associate professor of psychiatry at Harvard University, estimates that there are 1.6 million survivors annually who suffer brain injuries because of domestic violence (Hillstrom, 2022).
    - IPV victims are more likely to have a range of negative outcomes, from increased suicide attempts and depression to increased use of cigarettes, alcohol, and illicit drugs, as well as increased risk of contracting HIV and practicing high-risk sexual behaviors. Sexual minority men (13–39%), sexual minority women (4–37%), and transgender people (10–13%) all have a substantial likelihood of being injured during abuse (Messinger, 2020).
    - Women who experience domestic violence are 80% more likely to have a stroke, 70% more likely to have heart disease, 60% more likely to have asthma, and 70% more likely to drink heavily than women who have not experienced it (CDC, 2008).
    - Chronic conditions such as heart disease and gastrointestinal disorders can be exacerbated owing to domestic violence (New Hope, 2022).
    - IPV frequently begins, or becomes more severe, during pregnancy and causes numerous complications for the pregnant woman and the unborn child (California Department of Public Health, 2007).
    - One out of six obstetrics patients are battered (Gelles & Straus, 1988), and pregnant victims have an inflated rate of preterm labor, infection, miscarriage, and fetal or neonatal death (Curry, Perrin, & Wall, 1998; Parker, McFarlane, & Soeken, 1994).
    - Women abused by their intimate partners are more vulnerable to contracting HIV and other STIs/STDs (World Health Organization,

2021), and sexual and domestic violence is linked to a wide range of reproductive health issues, including sexually transmitted disease and HIV transmission, miscarriages, risky sexual behavior, and more (Outlook, 2002). In fact, intimate partner violence is associated with a broad range of negative outcomes, including sexual risk behavior (Mittal, Senn, & Carey, 2011).

- Intimate partner violence among women with HIV or those at risk for HIV may be as high as 67%, a rate that is three to four times greater than among HIV negative women (Cobb, 2008; Brief, Vielhauer, & Keane, 2006).
- Serious mental health conditions resulting from domestic violence include depression (Arroyo et al., 2017), generalized anxiety disorder (Beck et al., 2014), and notably high rates of post-traumatic stress disorder (Kastello et al., 2016).
- One study found that children who witnessed domestic violence were 42–69% more likely to be developmentally compromised in their physical health, social competence, emotional maturity, cognitive skills, and communication skills (Orr et al., 2020).
- Teen victims of physical dating violence are more likely than their non-abused peers to smoke; use drugs; engage in unhealthy behaviors, including the use of diet pills, laxatives, or vomiting to lose weight; engage in risky sexual behaviors; and attempt or consider suicide (Silverman et al., 2001).

3. The societal costs of IPV are immense:
   - Domestic violence costs more than $37 billion a year in law enforcement involvement, legal costs, medical and mental health treatment, and lost productivity at work (New Hope, 2022).
   - Domestic violence may cause the victim to lose their job because of frequent absences, tardiness, or numerous phone calls from the abuser (California Department of Public Health, 2007). In fact, 21–60% of victims of IPV lose their jobs because of reasons stemming from the abuse (Rothman et al., 2007).
   - While some victims find it difficult to maintain employment because of the domestic violence, others are not able to obtain employment owing to their anxiety levels (Beck et al., 2014).
   - Overall, IPV victims lose nearly 8 million days of paid work every year, which is the equivalent of 32,000 full-time jobs. Women with a history of IPV also have a 19% higher total healthcare cost than those without IPV, which translates to $19.3 million per 100,000 women in the United States (Modi, Palmer, & Armstrong, 2014).

4. Much of the current data suggests that gender differences help us better understand IPV. This data, however, rarely takes LGBTQ+ individuals and families into account. Rather, while the findings help to explain domestic violence in non-LGBTQ+ relationships, they do not add to our knowledge about LGBTQ+ IPV.

   • Domestic violence has historically been thought of primarily as a crime against women, and, in fact, the vast majority of domestic assaults are committed by men (Rennison, 2001).

   • Of those murdered by their partners, 74% are women, and 26% are men (Rennison, 2001).

   • Women experience higher levels of fear than do men in domestic violence situations (Barnett, Lee, & Thelen, 1997; Foa et al., 2000; Jacobson, et al., 1994; Langhinrichsen-Rohling, Nedig, & Thorn, 1995; Morse, 1995).

   • Women in domestic violence situations are more likely than men to be injured and injured severely (Brush, 1990; Makepeace, 1986; Sorenson, Upchurch, & Shen, 1996; Zlotnick et al., 1998).

   • Although men are victimized by domestic violence, four out of five victims of domestic violence in the United States are women, with a higher incidence of domestic violence recorded for women of color and multiracial women than white women (Philpart et al., 2019).

   • Women experience 20 stalking victimizations per 1,000 females, while men experience 7 stalking victimization per 1,000 males (Baum et al., 2009).

   • Although many studies report that men and women use physical violence at equal rates within intimate relationships (Straus, 1999), these studies generally fail to take into account the nature of the violence and the level of fear and injury experienced by each person (Archer, 2000).

Continuing Education Questions

1. On average, nearly how many people per minute are physically abused by an intimate partner in the United States?

   a. 2

   b. 10

   c. 20

   d. 50

2. Domestic violence is the most common cause of homelessness for women and their children.
   a. True
   b. False
3. Boys who witness violence between parents demonstrate higher levels of
   a. Bullying
   b. Psychiatric emergency room visits
   c. Alcohol and drug abuse
   d. Suicide
   e. All of the above
4. About one in five domestic violence victims with physical injuries seek professional medical treatment.
   a. True
   b. False
5. Teen victims of physical dating violence are more likely than their non-abused peers to:
   a. Smoke or use drugs
   b. Use diet pills or laxatives to lose weight
   c. Attempt or commit suicide
   d. All of the above
   e. None of the above

References

Archer, J. (2000). Sex Differences in Aggression between Heterosexual Partners: A Meta-analytic Review. *Psychological Bulletin, 126,* 651–680.

Arroyo, K., Lundahl, B., Butters, R., Vanderloo, M., & Woo, D.S. (2017). Short-Term Interventions for Survivors of Intimate Partner Violence: A Systematic Review and Meta-analysis. *Trauma, Violence & Abuse, 18*(2), 155–171.

Baldry, A.C. (2003). Bullying in Schools and Exposure to Domestic Violence. *Child Abuse and Neglect, 27*(7), 713–732. doi:10.1016/s0145-2134(03)00114-5. PMID: 14627075

Beck, J.G., Clapp, J.D., Jacobs-Lentz, J., McNiff, J., Avery. M., & Olsen, S.A. (2014). The Association of Mental Health Conditions with Employment, Interpersonal, and Subjective Functioning after Intimate Partner Violence. *Violence against Women, 20*(11), 1321–1337.

Black, Michele C., Basile, Kathleen C., Breiding, Matthew J., Smith, Sharon G., Walters, Mikel L., Merrick, Melissa T., Chen, Jieru, & Stevens, Mark R. (2011). *The National Intimate Partner and Sexual Violence Survey: 2010 Summary Report.* Atlanta, GA:National Center for Injury Prevention and Control, Centers for Disease Control and Prevention.

Brown, T.N.T., & Herman, J.L. (2015). *Intimate Partner Violence and Sexual Abuse Among LGBT People.* The Williams Institute, UCLA School of Law, 1–32.

Barnett, O.W., Lee, C.Y., & Thelen, R.E. (1997). Gender Differences in Attributions of Self-defense and Control in Inter-partner Aggression. *Violence Against Women, 3,* 462–481.

Baum, K., Catalano, S., Rand, M., & Rose, K. (2009). *Stalking Victimization in the United States.* Washington, DC: U.S. Department of Justice, Bureau of Justice Statistics.

Brief, D., Vielhauer, M., & Keane, T. (2006). The Interface of HIV, Trauma, and Posttraumatic Stress Disorder. *Focus, 21*(4), 1–4.

Brush, L.D. (1990). Violent Acts and Injurious Outcomes in Married Couples. Methodological Issues in the National Survey of Families and Households. *Gender and Society, 4,* 56–67.

California Department of Public Health. (2007). *Genetic Disease Screening Program: Your Future Together ... Health Information You Need to Know.* Richmond, CA: Author.

Callaghan, J.E.M., Alexander, J.H., Sixsmith, J., & Fettlin, L.C. (2018). Beyond Witnessing: Children's Experiences of Coercive Control in Domestic Violence and Abuse. *Journal of Interpersonal Violence, 3*(1), 1551–1581.

Campbell, J.C., Webster, D., Koziol-McLain, J., et al. (2003). Risk Factors for Femicide in Abusive Relationships: Results from a Multisite Case Control Study. *American Journal of Public Health, 93*(7), 1089–1097.

Cassidy, M., Nicholl, C.G., & Ross, C.R. (2001). *Results of a Survey Conducted by the Metropolitan Police Department of Victims Who Reported Violence against Women.* Washington, DC: DC Metropolitan Police Department.

Catalano, S. (2007). *Intimate Partner Violence in the United States.* Washington, DC: U.S. Department of Justice/Bureau of Justice Statistics.

Centers for Disease Control and Prevention (CDC). (2008). *Adverse Health Conditions and Health Risk Behaviors Associated with Intimate Partner Violence, Morbidity, and Mortality Report [fact sheet].* Atlanta, GA: Author.

Cobb, A.J. (2008). *The Intersection: HIV/AIDS and Intimate Partner Violence.* Paper presented at Ryan White All-Grantee Meeting; August 25–28, 2008, Washington, DC.

Coker, D. (2002). Transformative Justice: Anti-subordination Processes in Cases of Domestic Violence. *Restorative Justice and Family Violence,* 128–152.

Culross, P.L., Fischer, K., & Bedair, D. (2010). *Los Angeles County Domestic Violence Data Sources, Injury & Violence Prevention Program [fact sheet].* Los Angeles, CA: L.A. County Department of Public Health.

Curry, M.A., Perrin, N., & Wall, E. (1998). Effects of Abuse on Maternal Complications and Birth Weight in Adult and Adolescent Women. *Obstetrics and Gynecology, 92*(4): 530–534. doi:10.1016/s0029-7844(98)00258-0

Davis, A. (2008). *Interpersonal and Physical Dating Violence among Teens.* Oakland, CA: National Council on Crime and Delinquency.

Douglas, H. (2018). Legal Systems Abuse and Coercive Control. *Criminology and Criminal Justice, 18*(1), 84–99.

Evans, M.E., & Boothroyd, R.A. (2002). A comparison of Youth Referred to Psychiatric Emergency Services: Police versus Other Sources. *Journal of the American Academy of Psychiatry and the Law, 30*(1), 74–80.

Everytown for Gun Safety. (2023). *Guns and Violence against Women: America's Uniquely Lethal Intimate Partner Violence Problem.* Retrieved May 26, 2023, from everytownresearch.org/report/guns-and-violence-against-women-uniquely-lethal-intimate-partner-violence-problem/

Foa, E.B., Cascardi, M., Zoellner, L.A., & Feeny, N.C. (2000). Psychological and Environmental Factors Associated with Partner Violence. *Trauma, Violence, & Abuse*, *1*, 67–91.

Garcia-Moreno, Claudia, Jansen, Henrica A.F.M., Ellsberg, M., & Heise, L. (2005). *WHO Multi-country Study on Women's Health and Domestic Violence against Women*. New York, NY: World Health Organization.

Geller, L.B., Booty, M., & Crifasi, C.K. (2021). The Role of Domestic Violence in Fatal Mass Shootings in the United States, 2014–2019. *Injury Epidemiology*, *8*, 38.

Gelles, R.J., & Straus, M.A. (1988). *Intimate Violence*. New York, NY: Simon & Schuster.

Greenfield, L.A. (1998). Violence by Intimates: Analysis of Data on Crimes by Current or Former Spouses, Boyfriends, and Girlfriends. In *Bureau of Justice Statistics Factbook*. Washington, DC: US Department of Justice. NCJ#167237.

Hillstrom, C. (March 1, 2022). The Hidden Epidemic of Brain Injuries from Domestic Violence. *New York Times Magazine*.

Hotaling, G., & Sugarman, D. (1986). An Analysis of Risk Markers in Husband to Wife Violence: The Current State of Knowledge. *Violence and Victims*, *1*, 101–124.

Jacobson, N.S., Gottman, J.M., Waltz, J., Rushe, R., Babcock, J., & Holtzworth-Munroe, A. (1994). Affect, Verbal Content, and Psychophysiology in the Arguments of Couples with a Violent Husband. *Journal of Consulting and Clinical Psychology*, *62*, 982–988.

Johnson, M.P. (2006). Gender Symmetry and Asymmetry. *Violence Against Women*, *12*(11), 1003–1016.

Kastello, J.C., Jacobsen, K.H., Gaffney, K.F., Kodadek. M.P., Bullock, L.C., & Sharps, P.W. (2016). Posttraumatic Stress Disorder among Low-Income Women Exposed to Perinatal Intimate Partner Violence. *Archives of Women's Mental Health*, *19*(3), 521–528.

Langhinrichsen-Rohling, J., Nedig, P., & Thorn, G. (1995). Violent Marriages: Gender Differences in Levels of Current Violence and Past Abuse. *Journal of Family Violence*, *10*, 159–176.

Maddoux, J., McFarlane, J., Symes, L., Fredland, N., & Feder, G. (2018). Using Baseline Data to Predict Chronic PTSD 48 Months after Mothers Report Intimate Partner Violence: Outcomes for Mothers and the Intergenerational Impact on Child Behavioral Functioning. *Archives of Psychiatric Nursing*, *32*(3), 475–482.

Mair, C, Cunradi, C.B., & Todd, M. (2012). Adverse Childhood Experiences and Intimate Partner Violence: Testing Psychosocial Mediational Pathways among Couples. *Annals of Epidemiology*, *22*(12), 832–839.

Makepeace, J.M. (1986). Gender Differences in Courtship Violence. *Family Relations*, *35*, 383–388.

Martin, D. (1981). *Battered Wives*. Volcano Press.

Messinger, Adam M. (2020). *LGBTQ Intimate Partner Violence: Lessons for Policy, Practice, and Research*. University of California Press.

Mitchell, K.J., & Finkelhor, D. (2001). Risk of Crime Victimization among Youth Exposed to Domestic Violence. *Journal of Interpersonal Violence*, *16*, 944–964.

Mittal, M., Senn, T.E., & Carey, M.P. (2011). Mediators of the Relation between Partner Violence and Sexual Risk Behavior among Women Attending a Sexually Transmitted Disease Clinic. *Sexually Transmitted Diseases*, *38*(6), 510–515. doi:10.1 097/OLQ.0b013e318207f59b

Modi, M.N., Palmer, S., & Armstrong, A. (2014). The Role of Violence Against Women Act in Addressing Intimate Partner Violence: A Public Health Issue. *Journal of Women's Health, 23*(3), 253–259. doi:10.1089/jwh.2013.4387

Morse, B.J. (1995). Beyond the Conflict Tactics Scale: Assessing Gender Differences in Partner Violence. *Violence and Victims, 10,* 251–272.

National Coalition Against Domestic Violence (NCADV). (2022).

New Hope. (2022). Facts about Domestic Violence. Retrieved from www.new-hope. org/facts-about-domestic-violence/#:~:text=Domestic%20violence%20is%20the %20leading,her%20current%20or%20former%20partner

Orr, C., Fisher, C., Glauert, R., Preen, D., & O'Donnell, M. (2020). The Impact of Family and Domestic Violence on Children's Early Developmental Outcomes. *International Journal of Population Data Science, 5*(5).

Outlook. (2002). Violence against Women: Effects on Reproductive Health. *Outlook, 20*(1), 5–9.

Parker, B., McFarlane, J., & Soeken, K. (1994). Abuse during Pregnancy: Effects on Maternal Complications and Birth Weight in Adult and Teenage Women. *Obstetrics and Gynecology, 84*(3), 323–328.

Philpart, M., Grant, S., & Guzman, J. (2019). *Healing Together: Shifting Approaches to End Intimate Partner Violence.* Policylink: Alliance for Boys and Men of Color.

Red Rover. (2013). redrover.org. Retrieved August 13, 2023.

Rennison, C.M. (2001). Intimate Partner Violence and Age of Victim, 1993–1999. Bureau of Justice Statistics Special Report. Washington, DC: U.S. Department of Justice, NCJ # 187635.

Rothman, E.F., Hathaway, J., Stidsen, A., & DeVries, H.F. (2007). How Employment Helps Female Victims of Intimate Partner Violence: A Qualitative Study. *Journal of Occupational Health Psychology, 12*(2), 136–143.

Saltzman, L.E., Fanslow, J.L., McMahon, P.M., & Shelley, G.A. (1999). *Intimate Partner Violence Surveillance: Uniform Definitions and Recommended Data Elements [fact sheet].* Atlanta, GA: National Center for Injury Prevention and Control, Centers for Disease Control and Prevention.

Shumaker, D.M., & Prinz, R.J. (2000). Children Who Murder: A Review. *Clinical Child and Family Psychology Review, 3*(2), 97–115. doi:10.1023/a:1009560602970

Seelye, K.Q. (July 25, 2020). Richard Gelles, Scholar of Family Violence, Is Dead at 73. *New York Times.*

Silverman, J.G., Raj, A., Mucci, L.A., & Hathaway, J.E. (2001). Dating Violence against Adolescent Girls and Associated Substance Use, Unhealthy Weight Control, Sexual Risk Behavior, Pregnancy, and Suicidality. *JAMA, 286,* 572–279.

Smith, S.G., Fowler, K.A., & Niolon, P. (2014). Intimate Partner Homicide and Corollary Victims in 16 States: National Violent Death Reporting System, 2003–2009. *American Journal of Public Health, 104,* 461–466. doi.org/10.2105/AJPH.2013.301582

Sorenson, S.B., Upchurch, D.M., & Shen, H. (1996). Violence and Injury in Marital Arguments: Risk Patterns and Gender Differences. *American Journal of Public Health, 86,* 35–40.

Spaccarelli, S., Sandler, I.N., & Roosa, M. (1994). History of Spouse Violence against Mother: Correlated Risks and Unique Effects in Child Mental Health. *Journal of Family Violence, 9,* 79–98.

Sparkfiles.net. (n.d.). "Rule of Thumb" Origin and Meaning (It's Not Wife-Beating). Retrieved July 18, 2023, from Sparkfiles.net/rule-thumbits-inch/

Stith, S.M., Rosen, K.H., Middleton, K.A., Busch, A.L., Lundeberg, K., & Carlton, R.P. (2000). The Intergenerational Transmission of Spouse Abuse: A Meta-analysis. *Journal of Marriage and the Family, 62,* 640–654.

Strasser, Sheryl M., Smith, Megan, Pendrick-Denney, Danielle, Boos-Beddington, Sarah, Chen, Ken, & McCarty, Frances. (2012). Feasibility Study of Social Media to Reduce Intimate Partner Violence among Gay Men in Metro Atlanta, Georgia. *Western Journal of Emergency Medicine, 13*(3), 298–304. doi:10.5811/westjem.2012.3.11783

Straus, M.A. (1999). The Controversy over Domestic Violence by Women: A Methodological, Theoretical, and Sociology of Science Analysis. In X. Arriage & S. Oskamp (Eds.), *Violence in Intimate Relationships* (pp. 17–44). Thousand Oaks, CA: Sage.

Sushma, K. (2000). *Domestic Violence against Women and Girls.* New York, NY: Innocenti Research Centre.

Tjaden, P., & Thoennes, N. (2000). *Extent, Nature, and Consequences of Intimate Partner Violence: Findings from the National Violence against Women Survey.* Washington, DC: U.S. Department of Justice. Retrieved May 19, 2009, from ojp.usdoj.gov/nij/pubs-sum/181867.htm

Tjaden, P., Thoennes, N., & Allison, C.J. (1999). Comparing Violence over the Life Span in Samples of Same-Sex and Opposite-Sex Cohabitants. *Violence and Victimization,* 14(4), 413–425.

Truman, J.L., & Morgan, R.E. (2014). *Nonfatal Domestic Violence 2003–2012.* U.S. Department of Justice.

United Nations Development Fund for Women. (2003). *Not a Minute More: Ending Violence against Women [fact sheet].* New York, NY: Author.

Violence Policy Center. (2012). *American Roulette: Murder-Suicide in the United States.*

Whitfield, C.L., Anda, R.F., Dube, S.R., & Felittle, V.J. (2003). Violent Childhood Experiences and the Risk of Intimate Partner Violence in Adults: Assessment in a Large Health Maintenance Organization. *Journal of Interpersonal Violence,* 18(2),166–185.

Wolfe, D.A., Wekerle, C., Reitzel, D., & Gough, R. (1995). Strategies to Address Violence in the Lives of High Risk Youth. In E. Peled, P.G. Jaffe, & J.L. Edleson (Eds.), *Ending the Cycle of Violence: Community Responses to Children of Battered Women* (pp. 255–274). New York, NY: Sage.

World Health Organization (WHO). (2021). *Violence against Women Prevalence Estimates, 2018: Global, Regional and National Prevalence Estimates for Intimate Partner Violence against Women and Global and Regional Prevalence Estimates for Non-partner Sexual Violence against Women.* Geneva, Licence: CC BY-NC-SA 3.0 IGO.

Zeoli,April M., McCourt, Alexander, Buggs, Shani, Frattaroli, Shannon, Lilley, David, & Webster, Daniel W. (2018). Analysis of the Strength of Legal Firearms Restrictions for Perpetrators of Domestic Violence and their Associations with Intimate Partner Homicide. *American Journal of Epidemiology, 187*(11), 2365–2371.

Zlotnick, C., Kohn, R., Peterson, J., & Pearlstein, T. (1998). Partner Physical Victimization in National Sample of American Families. *Journal of Interpersonal Violence, 13,* 156–166.

Historical Perspectives 4

From Roman times to the present, women in numerous countries throughout the world have been viewed as the property of their husbands, who were allowed to punish and discipline them using corporal punishment (Roberts, 2007). It wasn't until 1871 that two U.S. states, Alabama and Massachusetts, made wife beating illegal (Jacobson & Gottman, 1998).

In 1875, Martha McWhirter opened a shelter for battered women in Belton, Texas (Schechter, 1982), and, in 1885, the Chicago Protective Agency for Women was established to provide shelter and advocacy for women who had been physically abused by their husbands. Twenty-five other cities in the United States followed with the establishment of organizations for the protection of abused women (Pleck, 1987; Roberts, 1996). Further, many states regarded spousal abuse as grounds for divorce (Jacobson & Gottman, 1998). However, most advocates didn't yet conceptualize domestic violence as a result of sexism (Wilson, 2006) or the patriarchal structure of society, and, in fact, it wasn't until the second wave of feminism—otherwise known as the women's liberation movement, in the late 1960s and early 1970s—that domestic violence began to be identified as a significant social problem in the United States (Gamache, 1998).

In 1971, Erin Pizzey opened the first emergency shelter for battered women in West London, England. The following year, Haven House shelter in Pasadena, California, and Women's Advocates shelter in St. Paul, Minnesota, opened their doors (Roberts, 2007). Then, in 1976, *Battered Wives* by Del Martin was published. Martin identified as a lesbian and was one of the founders of the National Organization for Women. This first

DOI: 10.4324/9780429031397-4

book on domestic violence not only offered information about the subject but legitimized the concept that violence against women was deeply ingrained in societal sexism (Roberts, 2007; Schechter, 1982). In 1978, the Los Angeles city attorney established the nation's first Domestic Violence Prosecution Unit. Also in 1978, the National Coalition Against Domestic Violence (NCADV) was formed during the hearing of the U.S. Commission on Civil Rights, and the movement's focus shifted to include social change and political action in addition to the development of more social services (Wilson, 2006). In 1979, psychologist Lenore Walker, founder of the Domestic Violence Institute, wrote *The Battered Woman*, a book that won the Distinguished Media Award the same year it was published, and further defined the problem of domestic violence while identifying intervention strategies for it from a mental health perspective. Dr. Walker is also known for developing the concept of the cycle of abuse/violence. During these years, researchers and activists were attempting to determine the causes of spousal abuse and ultimately concluded that patriarchy, "wife chastisement" laws which justified a permissible level of physical abuse, and the belief in the privacy of family matters (Dobash & Dobash, 1978) underscored the problem. Also in the late 1970s, the Lesbian Task Force was founded and officially recognized by the NCADV.

During the 1980s, the U.S attorney general created a task force on family violence, held hearings on the subject, and released a report that addressed the epidemic proportions of the problem. Congress subsequently enacted the Family Violence Prevention and Services Act and the Victims of Crime Act (Wilson, 2006). In response, President Jimmy Carter established a White House office that offered technical assistance to start-up domestic violence programs. However, on President Ronald Reagan's first day in office in 1981, he closed the White House office on domestic violence, and the focus subsequently shifted to building state coalitions and passing legislation within the states (Wilson, 2006).

Although domestic violence had long been viewed as a private family matter, in 1985, the federal district court for the District of Connecticut held, in *Thurman v. City of Torrington*, that the police were liable for their negligence in failing to protect Tracy Thurman from severe and repeated injuries inflicted by her husband (Roberts, 2007).

In 1988, the Nussbaum–Steinberg case was one of the first trials to be televised and captured the attention of the nation (Russo, 1997). The previous year, Hedda Nussbaum, a children's book editor at Random House, and Joel Steinberg, an attorney, were arrested for the beating death of Lisa Steinberg, their 6-year-old daughter. Although both individuals were initially charged, the charges against Nussbaum were eventually dropped. The trial profiled a remarkably severe case of intimate terrorism and stirred up controversy among the public, media, press, and the feminist community itself about Nussbaum and her role in Lisa's death. *New York Times* writer Francine Russo wrote "Even feminists were split. Many figures joined Gloria Steinem's plea for understanding but others like Susan Brownmiller blasted her" and considered Nussbaum to be culpable in Lisa's death. Nussbaum became the image of a domestic violence victim—her distorted facial features, black eyes, bruises, and broken nose appeared in magazines, newspapers, and on television. Nussbaum later became an advocate for battered women and authored a book entitled *Surviving Intimate Terrorism* (2012).

In 1986, the NCADV's Lesbian Task Force published the first book that addressed lesbian battering entitled, *Naming the Violence: Speaking Out about Lesbian Battering*. This groundbreaking book was an outgrowth of "Violence in the Lesbian Community," a meeting in Washington, DC, in September of 1983. Sponsored by the NCADV and attended by over 100 participants, the meeting was the first opportunity that attendees had to discuss lesbian domestic violence outside the context of their local communities (Lobel, 1986).

Also during the same decade, the NCADV returned a grant awarded to it by the U.S. Department of Justice (DOJ) in protest at the DOJ's mandate that the term "battered people" be used in place of "battered women" in publications paid for with federal dollars, and that all references to lesbian battering be removed.

The decade of the 1990s brought heightened public awareness of, and advocacy for, survivors of domestic violence. Advocates working to establish federal legislation related to domestic violence formed the Domestic Violence Coalition on Public Policy in 1990 which, in turn, led to the establishment of the National Network to End Domestic Violence. In particular, the decade of the 1990s brought heightened public awareness of domestic violence as a result of the televised O.J. Simpson trial in 1994–1995, as well as the enactment of the Violence Against Women Act (VAWA) in 1994, the first federal legislation to strengthen the government response to crimes perpetrated against victims of domestic violence, sexual assault, and stalking. VAWA, authored by Senator Joe Biden, authorized financial support for state and local criminal justice and social service programs to assist battered women, as well as the creation of the National Domestic Violence Hotline, and included funding for the investigation and prosecution of violent crimes against women (Roberts, 2007; Wilson, 2006).

While the title of the Act refers to victims as women, the operative text is gender neutral and provides coverage for men as well.

Since VAWA was passed in 1994, reporting of violence has increased. The number of individuals killed by an intimate partner has decreased, as has the rate of nonfatal IPV. In its first 6 years alone, VAWA saved taxpayers at least $14.8 billion in net averted social costs, and states have passed more than 660 laws to combat domestic violence (Modi, Palmer, & Armstrong, 2014). By May of 2019, the National Domestic Violence Hotline had assisted more than 5 million callers. However, the majority of these facts and funding dollars have been applicable to non-LGBTQ populations rather than solidly inclusive of the LGBTQ+ community.

Initially, VAWA had bipartisan support. In 1995, however, House Republicans attempted to cut the Act's funding (Cooper, 1995). The Act was reauthorized by Congress in 2000 and 2005. The 2005 reauthorization defined which populations were underserved and covered under VAWA. Populations deemed to be underserved included racial and ethnic populations; those underserved because of special needs, including language barriers, disabilities, alienage status, age, or geographic location; and any population determined to be underserved by the attorney general or the secretary of health and human services, as appropriate. The LGBTQ+ population was not specifically included. VAWA expired in 2011, and the bill reauthorizing the Act in 2012 was, once again, opposed by conservative Republicans who objected to extending VAWA's protections to same-sex couples as well as battered undocumented immigrants. It was eventually reauthorized in 2013 by President Barack Obama, with protections extending to Native American women and LGBTQ people after a long legislative battle. However, even after its passage, 138 House Republicans voted against the version of the Act that became law, favoring a GOP-proposed alternative that did not contain provisions intended to protect gays, lesbians, transgender individuals, Native Americans, and undocumented immigrants (Bendery, 2013). As a result of the U.S. federal government shutdown of 2018–2019, VAWA expired in December 2018. It was temporarily reauthorized by a short-term spending bill in January of 2019 but expired again in February of the same year. On March 15, 2022, President Joe Biden signed the reauthorization of VAWA into law as part of the Consolidated Appropriations Act of 2022. This reauthorization had numerous enhancements to increase access to VAWA-funded programs and improve VAWA's responsiveness to survivors of domestic violence. Among those enhancements was the first ever federal standalone grant program for the LGBTQ community (White House, 2022; National LGBTQ Task Force, 2023).

Although only a handful of programs to assist heterosexual victims of battering existed in the mid-1970s, by 2001, more than 2,000 shelters, hotlines, and safe home networks existed nationwide (NCADV, 2004; Roberts, 2007). In 2000, U.S. Surgeon General C. Everett Koop declared that "Domestic violence is an overwhelming moral, economic, and public health burden that our society can no longer bear." His characterization of the problem as a public health concern—and not solely a criminal matter—led to the designation of state and federal healthcare dollars for domestic violence programs and gave the entire movement a new impetus (Rakowski, 2001). Now, 40 years later, what began as a grassroots movement is largely institutionalized (Almeida & Lockard, 2006). Throughout the years, activists have focused their energies on revolutionizing the terms of the debate, turned domestic violence into a widely condemned practice, and transformed societal response to this significant problem (Epstein, 2002). However, the LGBTQ+ community has essentially been left out of these achievements.

Ironically, lesbian feminists were among the first to advocate for and develop initial domestic violence services and resources for heterosexual women (Wilson, 2006). Similar to the way in which Del Martin's book, *Battered Wives*, initially provided information about battering in the heterosexual community, *Naming the Violence: Speaking Out about Lesbian Battering*, in 1986, broke the silence about battering in the lesbian community (Lobel, 1986).

The reality of lesbian battering has been difficult for lesbians and feminists to acknowledge because it threatens the gender-specific analysis of battering in which men and the patriarchy are believed to be the primary cause (Kelly, 1986). Early researchers and activists who acknowledged and studied the problem of violence in same-gender partnerships, however, focused almost exclusively on lesbian domestic violence, until the groundbreaking book by David Island and Patrick Letellier, *Men Who Beat the Men Who Love Them: Battered Gay Men and Domestic Violence*, was published in 1991 and challenged the mainstream conceptualization of intimate partner violence as a gender-based phenomenon grounded in societal patriarchy.

There is still little scholarly information about LGBTQ+ domestic violence. Most of the information that is available is, instead, the result of years of work and analysis primarily by survivors and advocates (NRCDV, 2007), most of them LGBTQ+ themselves. Indeed, only a handful of books have been published that deal exclusively with domestic violence in the LGBTQ+ population. Services designed to address the unique needs of the LGBTQ+ population exist in only the nation's largest cities and are significantly underfunded, if they are funded at all.

In fact, it wasn't until 1997 that the first national press release on the state of LGBTQ+ domestic violence was released as the result of collaboration between the leaders of California's LGBTQ+ domestic violence programs—Community United Against Violence (CUAV) in San Francisco and the L.A. Gay & Lesbian Center's STOP Domestic Violence Program in Los Angeles (Rakowski, 2001). CUAV, founded in 1979, developed services for survivors collaboratively with WOMAN, Inc. In 1987, the L.A. Gay & Lesbian Center, an agency that initially opened its doors in 1969, conducted the first national study that attempted to determine the prevalence of domestic violence in the broader gay and lesbian population and concurrently developed LGBTQ+-specific domestic violence services.

In the late 1990s, the issue of LGBTQ+IPV received attention from the press for the first time. Stories began to appear in mainstream newspapers, including the *New York Times* and the *Los Angeles Times*, as well as in the majority of the LGBTQ+ press and throughout the media in radio and television. Stories about LGBTQ+ domestic violence were included on the newsmagazine *Extra* on the NBC television network as well as on Univision, the American Spanish-language television network. Lentz (1999) indicates that the issue of domestic violence surfaces, fades, then resurfaces at different periods of time. Although the flurry of press and media attention focusing on LGBTQ domestic violence has, for the most part, subsided, the work has continued.

For example, California, a leader in the field of domestic violence prevention and intervention efforts, has been one of the states in the nation to address LGBTQ+ domestic violence through legislation. The state produced Senate Bill 564 (Speier) in 2004, Assembly Bill 2051 (Cohn) in 2007, and Assembly Bill 1003 (Perez) in 2009. Senate Bill 564 requires applicants for licensure as a psychologist; marriage and family therapist, or social worker, who began graduate study on or after January 1, 2004, to complete a minimum of 15 contact hours of coursework or training in spousal or partner abuse assessment, detection, and intervention strategies, *including same-gender abuse dynamics.* The bill also requires that persons licensed in these professions who began graduate study prior to January 1, 2004, take a continuing education course in spousal or partner abuse assessment, detection, and intervention strategies, including same-gender abuse dynamics (California Legislature, n.d.).

Assembly Bills 2051 (Cohn) and 1003 (Perez) established a continuously appropriated fund to support education and services that address the problem of domestic abuse among same-gender partners. Historically, persons applying for marriage licenses had been required to pay a $23 fee to fund various mainstream programs designed to prevent and mitigate the impact of domestic violence. This bill, entitled the Equality in Prevention and Services for Domestic Abuse Act, was enacted on January 1, 2007, and levies a similar fee on individuals registering as domestic partners. The funds generated from this legislation help to ensure that lesbian, gay, bisexual, and transgender people in abusive relationships have access to culturally appropriate services that encourage them to break the cycle of violence (California Legislature, n.d.).

Assembly Bill 1003 (Perez) made various changes to the law regarding the Equality in Prevention and Services for Domestic Abuse Fund. Specifically, the bill clarified that grants may be awarded to organizations that provide "any" rather than "all" of the domestic violence services specified in Assembly Bill 2051—the same services developed to assist battered heterosexual women in mainstream domestic violence shelters. These changes allowed the California Emergency Management Agency, which oversees the funding, the flexibility to issue more grants to support innovative program models that are proven most effective in serving LGBTQ+ survivors of violence, such as those being pioneered by LGBTQ+centers and LGBTQ+-specific organizations across the state.

This was a crucial and important change because, under Assembly Bill 2051, funding recipients were required to provide eight different services, some of which are not suitable for LGBTQ+ people to utilize. Further, organizations best equipped to develop or offer LGBTQ+-specific domestic violence services generally have not had sufficient financial or human resources to develop and/or maintain all eight required services, and so, until Assembly Bill 1003 was enacted, the only organizations in California that were able to secure funding were mainstream domestic violence shelters, which are generally not appropriate for many LGBTQ+ people to utilize.

Legislation like this is critical, as there is established evidence that LGBTQ+ people are disproportionately affected by IPV and are discriminated against in treatment and during intervention efforts. A 2010 study showed that nearly half of all LGBTQ+ survivors were turned away from domestic violence shelters, and more than 55% of survivors were denied orders of protection. Owing to the perception that they would be discriminated against, only 7% of LGBTQ+IPV survivors reported the crime to the police (Modi et al., 2014). Approximately 70% of respondents in one survey of IPV survivors who had sought assistance reported that they had experienced prejudice and/or negative responses to their gender or sexuality, ranging from service providers dismissing it altogether to shaming the client. In two cases, providers attempted to change the client's sexual orientation or gender identity (Whirry & Holt, 2020).

In April of 2010, the first LGBT Domestic Violence Whitehouse Roundtable convened to focus on the barriers facing LGBT victims of domestic violence, dating violence, sexual assault, and stalking. Among the many barriers discussed was the lack of overall knowledge and training of mental health practitioners who are among the first to be contacted by LGBTQ+ survivors when they are seeking assistance.

Today, two national organizations exist to specifically address LGBTQ+ IPV: First is the *National Coalition of Anti-Violence Programs* (NCAVP). This organization was founded in 1995 and is an organization dedicating to preventing, responding to, and ending, all forms of violence against and within LGBTQ+ communities. The coalition comprises multiple community-based anti-violence programs serving LGBTQ+ people throughout the country. It produces an annual report on LGBTQ+ intimate partner violence, which is the only national report of its kind, and documents the number of IPV cases reported to its member organizations while providing information about LGBTQ+IPV.

The *National Lesbian, Gay, Bisexual, Transgender, and Queer (LGBTQ) Institute on Intimate Partner Violence (IPV)* is a project of the Los Angeles LGBT Center—the nation's oldest and largest community-based LGBTQ+ service and support organization—in close collaboration with the NCAVP, and In Our Own Voices, Inc. Utilizing ongoing input from providers, experts, and consumers, the institute offers state-of-the-art training and technical assistance that significantly expand the capacity of public and private agencies to provide culturally relevant, survivor-centered LGBTQ+IPV intervention and prevention services, including to LGBTQ+ persons from racially and ethnically diverse communities. The institute also strives to enhance the visibility of LGBTQ-specific IPV needs, interventions, and strategies while conducting research to identify and disseminate evidence-informed interventions and overseeing policy initiatives that have a meaningful impact on the quality, scope, and accessibility of LGBTQ+IPV services nationwide. The overarching goal of the LGBTQ IPV Institute is to significantly enhance the safety, well-being, support, and health of LGBTQ+ intimate partner and domestic violence survivors throughout the United States.

In 2000, the *New York Times* published a story entitled, "Silence Ending About Abuse in Gay Relationships." It described multiple challenges faced by LGBTQ+ IPV survivors and ended with a quote that is as true today as it was more than two decades ago. When asked about the state of services for LGBTQ survivors, Susan Holt, director of the STOP Violence Program at the Los Angeles LGBT Center, remarked "Unfortunately, we're still 25 years behind the battered women's movement but at least we've gotten started" (Leland, 2000). We have indeed made progress throughout the past four decades, but we still have a very long way to go before LGBTQ+ survivors are afforded the same degree of safety and justice provided to non-LGBTQ victims.

Continuing Education Questions

1. Which were the first two states in the USA to declare wife beating illegal?
   a. Georgia and Florida
   b. New York and California
   c. Alabama and Massachusetts
   d. Rhode Island and Vermont
2. The Violence Against Women Act (VAWA) was initially passed in 2004 and has to be reauthorized every 5 years by the federal government.
   a. True
   b. False
3. The federal court case of *Thurman v. City of Torrington* found that
   a. Police do not have an obligation to address domestic violence
   b. Domestic violence abusers cannot be held liable for assault
   c. Domestic violence victims can be ignored by police with impunity
   d. Police departments can be held liable for negligence in regards to their handling of domestic violence calls and cases
4. California was the one of the first states in the United States to pass legislation specifically targeting LGBTQ IPV.
   a. True
   b. False
5. What percentage of LGBTQ IPV survivors report the crime to the police?
   a. 0%
   b. 7%
   c. 20%
   d. 50%

References

Almeida, R.V., & Lockard, J. (2006). The Cultural Context Model: A New Paradigm for Accountability, Empowerment, and the Development of Critical Consciousness against Domestic Violence. In N.J. Sokoloff (Ed.), *Domestic Violence at the Margins: Readings on Race, Class, Gender, and Culture* (pp. 301–320). Piscataway, NJ: Rutgers University Press.

Bendery, J. (March 7, 2013). *Violence Against Women Act Now Touted by Republicans Who Voted Against Bill. Huffington Post.*

California Legislature. (n.d.). California Legislative Information. https://leginfo.legislature.ca.gov/faces/billSearchClient.xhtml

Cooper, K. (July 15, 1995). House GOP Budget Cutters Try to Limit Domestic Violence Programs. *Washington Post.*

Dobash, R.E., & Dobash, R. (1978). Wives: The "Appropriate" Victims of Marital Violence. *Victimology, 2*(3–4), 426–442.

Epstein, D. (2002). Procedural Justice: Tempering the State's Response to Domestic Violence. *William & Mary Law Review, 43*(5): 1843–1904. In N.J. Sokoloff (Ed.), *Domestic Violence at the Margins: Readings on Race, Class, Gender, and Culture* (p. 293). New Brunswick, NJ: Rutgers University Press.

Gamache, D. (1998). Domination and Control: The Social Context of Dating Violence. In B. Levy (Ed.), *Dating Violence: Young Women in Danger* (2nd ed., pp. 69–83). Seattle, WA: Seal Press.

Island, D., & Letellier, P. (1991). *Men Who Beat the Men Who Love Them: Battered Gay Men and Domestic Violence.* Binghamton, NY: Harrington Park Press.

Jacobson, N.S., & Gottman, J.M. (1998). *When Men Batter Women: New Insights into Ending Abusive Relationships.* New York, NY: Simon & Schuster.

Kelly, L. (1986). National Coalition Against Domestic Violence Conference. *Off Our Backs, 16*(10), 1–5.

Leland, J. (2000). Silence Ending about Abuse in Gay Relationships. *New York Times National Report.*

Lentz, S.A. (1999). Revisiting the Rule of Thumb: An Overview of the History of Wife Abuse. In R. Feder (Ed.), *Women and Domestic Violence: An Interdisciplinary Approach* (pp. 29–36). Binghamton, NY: Haworth Press.

Lobel, K. (Ed.) (1986). *Naming the Violence: Speaking Out about Lesbian Battering.* Seattle, WA: Seal Press.

Martin, D. (1976). *Battered Wives.* San Francisco: Glide.

Modi, Monica N., Palmer, Sheallah, & Armstrong, Alicia. (2014). The Role of Violence Against Women Act in Addressing Intimate Partner Violence: A Public Health Issue. *Journal of Women's Health, 23*(3), 253–259. doi:10.1089/jwh.2013.4387

National Coalition Against Domestic Violence (NCADV). (2004).

National LGBTQ Task Force. (May 25, 2023). President Biden Signs Violence Against Women Reauthorization—National LGBTQ Task Force. www.thetaskforce.org/press-releases/president-biden-signs-violence-against-women-reauthorization/

National Resource Center on Domestic Violence (NRCDV). (2007). *Lesbian, Gay, Bisexual, and Trans (LGBTQ) Communities and Domestic Violence: Information and Resources.* Harrisburg, PA: Author. Retrieved October 17, 2004, from ncadv.org

Nussbaum, H., & Steinem, G. (2012). *Surviving Intimate Terrorism.* Hedda Nussbaum.

Pleck. E. (1987). *Domestic Tyranny: The Making of Social Policy against Family Violence from Colonial Times to the Present.* New York: Oxford University Press.

Rakowski, J. (2001). *Finding Our History—Carving Our Future.* San Francisco, CA: Community United Against Violence, unpublished paper.

Roberts, A.R. (1996). Introduction: Myths and Realities Regarding Battered Women. In A.R. Roberts (Ed.), *Helping Battered Women: New Perspectives and Remedies* (pp. 3–12). New York, NY: Oxford University Press.

Roberts, A.R. (2007). Battered Wives. In N. Jackson (Ed.), *Encyclopedia of Domestic Violence* (pp. 59–63). New York, NY: Routledge.

Russo, F. (1997, March 30). The Faces of Hedda Nussbaum. *The New York Times.* Retrieved from www.nytimes.com/1997/03/30/magazine/the-faces-of-hedda-nussbaum.html?auth=login-google1tap&login=google1tap

Schechter, S. (1982). *Women and Male Violence: The Visions and Struggles of the Battered Women's Movement.* Boston, MA: South End Press.

Walker, L.E. (1979). *The Battered Woman* (1st ed.). New York: Harper & Row.

Whirry, R., & Holt, S. (2020) *Finding Safety: A Report about LGBTQ Domestic Violence and Sexual Assault.* Los Angeles, CA: Los Angeles LGBT Center.

White House. (2022). Fact Sheet: Reauthorization of the Violence Against Women Act (VAWA). The White House. www.whitehouse.gov/briefing-room/statements-releases/2022/03/16/fact-sheet-reauthorization-of-the-violence-against-women-act-vawa/

Wilson, K.J. (2006). *When Violence Begins at Home: A Comprehensive Guide to Understanding and Ending Domestic Abuse* (2nd ed.). Alameda, CA: Hunter House.

Overview of the LGBTQ+ Community **5**

According to the Williams Institute, an estimated 3.5% of adults in the United States identify as lesbian, gay, or bisexual, while another 0.3% identify as transgender. This translates to over 12.5 million LGBTQ+ Americans, a population larger than that of the state of Illinois, or of the countries of Finland and Denmark combined (Gates, 2011). However, a report released in December of 2021 by the Human Rights Campaign Foundation, which analyzed data from the Census Bureau, revealed that at least 20 million adults in the United States could be lesbian, gay, bisexual, or transgender—a rate twice as high as earlier estimates (Pitofsky, 2021). The report also revealed that more than 2 million adults in the United States could identify as transgender, while bisexuals represented the largest contingent of the LGBTQ+ community. Roughly 2% of participants identified with a sexual orientation other than lesbian, gay, bisexual, or heterosexual (Pitofsky, 2021).

Sexual orientation is an enduring emotional, romantic, and/or sexual attraction toward men, women, and/or all genders. It occurs along a continuum and is generally discussed in terms of the traditional binary conceptualization which stipulates that individuals are either heterosexual (attraction to the opposite gender), homosexual (attraction to the same gender), or bisexual (attraction to both genders). Sexual orientation has not been conclusively found to be determined by any particular factor or factors, and the timing of the emergence, recognition, and expression of one's sexual orientation varies among individuals (Just the Facts Coalition, 2008). Sexual orientation is not synonymous with sexual activity, and individuals

DOI: 10.4324/9780429031397-5

may identify themselves as lesbian, gay, bisexual, pansexual, asexual, and so on, without having had any sexual experiences with others. In addition, others may have had sexual experiences with a person of the same gender but do not consider themselves to be lesbian, gay, bisexual, and so on (Just the Facts Coalition, 2008).

The broad LGBTQ+ population is highly diverse, and virtually every race, ethnicity, culture, age, language, level of education, socioeconomic status, physical ability, religious or spiritual affiliation, sexual orientation, affectional and gender identity, and so on, is represented within it. Furthermore, the acronym "LGBTQ+" can include numerous subpopulations including, but not limited to, individuals who have intimate relations and/or sex with members of the same gender but identify as heterosexual; lesbians and bisexual women who maintain intimate relationships with men; gay and bisexual men who maintain intimate relationships with women; children of LGBTQ+ parents; lesbians and gays whose previous relationships were with members of the opposite gender; intersex individuals; LGBTQ+ and heterosexual persons impacted by HIV/AIDS, and so on.

Each population within the broader LGBTQ+ population has its own specific needs, as well as varying and similar issues of diversity (California Department of Mental Health, 2012). Age, gender identity, gender assigned at birth, socioeconomic status, education, differences in abilities, religious or spiritual upbringing and practice, and ethnic and racial backgrounds all play a role in how an individual experiences their sexual orientation or gender identity (Wierzalis et al., 2006). A primary factor that LGBTQ+ individuals have in common is that they are seen as living outside the norm of expected heterosexual and assigned gender roles and behavior and, therefore, may, and often do, experience stigma, discrimination, and oppression from government, health systems, school systems, religious institutions, employers, family members, and society at large. Further, they represent essentially invisible populations whose existence is not accurately documented, and rarely acknowledged, in official bodies of data of any form (California Department of Mental Health, 2012).

Schulman (2009) asserts that there are two experiences that most homosexuals share: (1) "Coming out," a process defined by Schulman as self-interrogation in opposition to social expectation that has no parallel in heterosexual life and (2) substandard treatment by one's family of origin. Further, most LGBTQ+ people do not always share or have in common their sexual orientation with other family members, unlike other minority populations.

The process of growing up LGBTQ+ in a culture that often hates and/or fears homosexuals is, in itself, traumatizing (Schulman, 2009). According to Schulman (2009),

> It's the rare gay or lesbian person who has not been demeaned because of his or her sexual orientation, and this experience usually starts at home, among family members. Whether they are excluded from family love and approval, expected to accept second-class status for life, ignored by mainstream arts and entertainment, or abandoned when intervention would make all the difference, LGBTQ+ people are routinely subjected to forms of psychological and physical abuse unknown to many straight Americans.

Historians have commonly ignored this population, and researchers have produced research that has excluded the population altogether or contained a strong heterosexual bias. Overall, the LGBTQ+ population has been relatively invisible. To some degree, male homosexuals have been the exception and have generally been the focus of attention, while lesbians, bisexuals, non-binary, and transgender persons have been nearly unnoticeable in American society for much of the 20th century. Rich (2003) argues that lesbians, for example, have historically been deprived of a cultural and political existence through "inclusion" as female versions of male homosexuality and cannot be easily understood as a population if the population is grouped together with other stigmatized groups.

Lesbians occupy a double minority status, both as members of a sexual minority and as women, and are subjected to heterosexism, homophobia, and sexism. Further, lesbians of color face a "triple minority status" (DiPlacido, 1998). In addition, Koh and Ross (2006) found that lesbian and bisexual women experienced greater rates of discrimination than their non-lesbian/bisexual counterparts. Their lesbian and bisexual status has been used to deny variables such as custody or visitation with their children (Frederiksen-Goldsen & Erera, 2003). Furthermore, female same-gender couples earn 18–20% less on average compared with their married opposite-gender counterparts, and gay men earn as much as 27% less (Badgett, 2000).

Lesbians utilize mental health services at a higher rate than heterosexual women (Cochran, Sullivan, & Mays, 2003; Koh & Ross, 2006; Razzano et al., 2006; Ritter & Terndrup, 2002), and their usage rates for therapy have been found to be as high as 80% (Hughes & Eliason, 2002). Razzano et al. (2006) also found that lesbians reported use of mental health services at 3.5 times the rate of heterosexual women, and the effects of heterosexism, discrimination, stigma, and exposure to bias-related victimization have all been offered as explanations as to why lesbians seek out mental health services at such high rates (Koh & Ross, 2006; Razzano et al., 2006; Ritter & Terndrup, 2002).

The most common reason lesbians indicate that they seek psychotherapy is depression, and, according to Koh and Ross (2006), lesbians were 56% more likely than heterosexual women and 82% more likely than bisexual women to have received treatment for depression. Furthermore, the risk of alcohol dependence nearly doubles in co-occurrence with depression among this population (Bostwick, Hughes, & Johnson, 2005). It has been determined that lesbians are at greater risk for alcohol abuse, drug abuse, and dependency problems when compared with heterosexual women (Cochran & Mays, 2006; Corliss et al., 2006). They are also at higher risk for suicidality and suicide attempts (Koh & Ross, 2006). Further, lesbians who have not disclosed their sexual orientation to others are 90% more likely than heterosexual women to have attempted suicide.

Some research has indicated that lesbians may define sex differently than other populations. In fact, when allowed to define sex for themselves, 90% included hugging, cuddling, and kissing as sexual activities (Garnets & Peplau, 2006).

Phillips (2006) indicates that gay men often violate normative gender roles, which can come with severe consequences. Many gay men, especially those perceived to be effeminate, have been victims of anti-gay abuse since childhood, before they identified as gay (LaSala, 2006).

Having been socialized to have a strong emphasis on their sexuality, gay men do not always practice sexual exclusivity as a couple (Bettinger, 2004); however, studies indicate that relationship quality is not significantly different when monogamous and openly non-monogamous gay male couples are compared (Bettinger, 2004). In reality, gay male couples are second only to lesbians in forming emotionally close and connected relationships, while heterosexuals, in general, form the most disengaged partnerships (California Department of Mental Health, 2012).

The consequences of violence, discrimination, and stigma, as well as the internalization of societal homophobia, may all serve to jeopardize the mental health of gay men (LaSala, 2006). Men who are socialized to avoid appearing weak or vulnerable may remain silent about, or even repress, stigmatizing experiences (California Department of Mental Health, 2012). Often believed to be perverted, lonely, and dangerous to children (Boysen et al., 2006), gay and bisexual men seek out mental health services more frequently than their heterosexual counterparts. They suffer disproportionately from depression, anxiety, substance abuse, and panic disorder (Boysen et al., 2006; Cochran et al., 2003) and are at greater risk for eating disorders (Russel & Keel, 2002; Mills et al., 2004) as well as suicide (Cochran & Mays, 2006; de Graaf, Sandfort, & Tenhave, 2006; Paul et al., 2002). In fact, Skegg et al. (2003) found that men with even minor same-gender attraction were subject to greater risks of self-harm and self-induced injury than men who reported only opposite-gender attraction. Furthermore, HIV and AIDS may induce survivor's guilt, grief, anger, and depression (Wierzalis et al., 2006), and alcohol and drug abuse has been found to increase the likelihood that a gay or bisexual male will participate in unprotected sexual activities (Rosario, Schrimshaw, & Hunter, 2006; Shoptaw & Reback, 2007).

Bisexuality is often excluded from many sexual minority studies (California Department of Mental Health, 2012). Usage rates of mental health services for bisexual individuals are not known (Bieschke et al., 2000), although research suggests that bisexual individuals are at greater risk for psychological distress and mental health challenges than are gay men, lesbians, or heterosexual individuals (Miller et al., 2007). Koh and Ross (2006) found that bisexual women were more significantly closeted and experienced significantly more emotional stressors than lesbians and heterosexual women, and that those who were out to a majority of people were twice as likely as heterosexual women to have an eating disorder and to report suicidal ideation (California Department of Mental Health, 2012).

The shift that occurred in the mental health field which encouraged affirmative therapeutic approaches for gay men and lesbians did not generally include bisexuals (California Department of Mental Health, 2012). Page (2004) found that bisexual clients rated their mental health experiences lower than gay men and lesbians did, and Logie, Bridge, and Bridge (2007) found that mental health students had higher rates of bias toward bisexuals and transgender individuals than toward gay men and lesbians. According to the Centers for Disease Control and Prevention (CDC, 2013; Walters, Chen, & Breiding, 2013), bisexual populations make up the largest grouping of IPV cases.

Bisexuality is often viewed as a more deviant form of sexuality than homosexuality (California Department of Mental Health, 2012), and Miller et al. (2007) further indicate that heterosexuals rate bisexuals less favorably than a number of other stigmatized groups, including lesbians and people with AIDS. In addition, Israel and Mobr (2004) identified a perception in the gay and lesbian population, with accompanying feelings of resentment, that bisexuals are able to participate in the community without foregoing their heterosexual privilege.

Research suggests that bisexual identity development may be more complicated than sexual identity development for gay men or lesbians (Dworkin, 2006). Weinberg, Williams, and, Pryor (2001), in fact, suggest that there may be more commonalities shared between homosexuals and heterosexuals than either population shares with bisexuals.

Individuals with cross-gender and non-binary expression appear to be a stable minority among the human population, suggesting that gender variance is a natural part of human diversity (Lev, 2004). Gender-variant people may be heterosexual, gay, lesbian, bisexual, or asexual (Green, 2000), while some transgender individuals identify as pansexual rather than bisexual, as bisexual presumes two genders (Monro, 2000).

Transgender, non-binary, and queer individuals are also frequently excluded from studies, and there is a general lack of data regarding these groups. This is particularly true for queer people, who are very rarely a focus of research. Transgender people appear to be at higher risk for most mental health conditions. In fact, a multinational review found that the suicide rate for transgender people was between 32% and 50%, versus 1.6% for the general population (Virupaksha, Muralidhar, & Ramakrishna, 2016). Transgender people have higher rates of depression than their lesbian/gay/bisexual counterparts (Su et al., 2016), and, in some studies, over half of transgender respondents had a mental health diagnosis (Reisner et al., 2014).

The Study of Transition, Outcomes, and Gender (STRONG) points to a similar disparity among transgender youth. For transmasculine and transfeminine children, there was a lifetime prevalence of mental health conditions of over 70% and, in this population, a rate of mental illness three to four times higher when compared with matched non-transgender controls. Further, transgender youth had a higher incidence of every illness, including self-harm (Becerra-Culqui et al., 2018). A particular concern for individuals who are visibly gender non-conforming, as well as those who are out about their transgender status, is their vulnerability to transphobia and violence. This population has a very high risk for suicide (Grant et al., 2011) as well as substance abuse. Its rate for substance abuse is eight to ten times that of the general population in some studies (Cochran & Cauce, 2006; Keuroghlian et al., 2015), and gender non-conforming individuals often report using substances to cope with discrimination (Keuroghlian et al., 2015).

Some of the largest disparities are among transgender individuals of color, who are at very high risk for HIV, engaging in unsafe sex practices, and homelessness (Horvath et al., 2014; Flentje et al., 2016). Often targeted for violence and abuse by others, transgender individuals appear to be more likely to have annual incomes under $10,000, less likely to be employed, and less likely to have a higher education. This vulnerable population is at significant risk for a host of medical and mental health issues, including IPV (Su et al., 2016), in addition to societal and stranger violence.

Because mental health usage rates are so high in the LGBTQ+ population, as indicated in this chapter, it stands to reason that mental health practitioners are apt to see numerous queer clients who are experiencing domestic violence. In fact, community-based surveys conducted by the Los Angeles LGBT Center's STOP Violence Program annually since 2000 indicate that respondents are not apt to seek services commonly designed to assist victims such as shelters, the criminal justice system, family, and clergy, but would first and foremost seek individual counseling, couples counseling, support groups, and the help of friends, thereby underscoring the significant need for practitioners who have been trained to effectively assess and intervene with LGBTQ+ clients at risk for and experiencing domestic violence.

Continuing Education Questions

1. The sexual orientation that refers to being attracted to members of both genders (given the assumption of two exclusive genders) is:
   a. Homosexuality
   b. Bisexuality
   c. Heterosexuality
   d. Asexuality
2. Lesbians occupy a double minority status, both as members of a sexual minority and as women, and are subjected to heterosexism, homophobia, and sexism; lesbians of ethnic or racial minorities face a triple minority status.
   a. True
   b. False
3. According to Razzano et al. (2006), lesbians are how much more likely to use mental health services than their heterosexual counterparts?
   a. 2.5 times
   b. 3.5 times
   c. 4.5 times
   d. 5.5 times
4. Research suggests that there is a significant difference in the quality of monogamous versus non-monogamous relationships.
   a. True
   b. False

5. Which is true of the transgender and non-binary population?
   a. They are underrepresented in IPV studies
   b. They have a higher risk of almost every mental health condition
   c. They are more likely to suffer financially
   d. All of the above

References

Badgett, M.V.L. (2000). The Myth of Gay and Lesbian Affluence. *Gay & Lesbian Review*, *7*(2), 22–25.

Becerra-Culqui, Tracy A. et al. (2018). Mental Health of Transgender and Gender Nonconforming Youth Compared With Their Peers. *Pediatrics*, *141*(5). e20173845.

Bettinger, M. (2004). A Systems Approach to Sex Therapy with Gay Male Couples. In J.J. Bignere & J.L. Wetchler (Eds.), *Relationship Therapy with Same-Sex Couples* (pp. 65–74). New York, NY: Haworth Press.

Bieschke, K.J., McClanahan, M., Tozer, E., Grzegorek, J.L., & Park, J. (2000). Programmatic Research on the Treatment of Lesbian, Gay, and Bisexual Clients: The Past, the Present, and the Course for the Future. In R.M. Perez, K.A. DeBord, & K.J. Bieschke (Eds.), *Handbook of Counseling and Psychotherapy with Lesbian, Gay, and Bisexual Clients* (pp. 309–335). Washington, DC: American Psychological Association.

Bostwick, W.B., Hughes, T.L., & Johnson, T. (2005). The Co-occurrence of Depression and Alcohol Dependence Symptoms in a Community Sample of Lesbians. In E. Ettorre (Ed.), *Making Lesbians Visible in the Substance Use Field* (pp. 7–18). New York, NY: Harrington Park Press.

Boysen, G., Vogel, D., Madon, S., & Wester, S.R. (2006). Mental Health Stereotypes about Gay Men. *Sex Roles*, *54*(1/2), 69–82.

California Department of Mental Health. (2012). *First, Do No Harm: Reducing Disparities for Lesbian, Gay, Bisexual, Transgender, Queer and Questioning Populations in California*. Sacramento, CA: Author.

Centers for Disease Control and Prevention. (2013). CDC Releases Data on Interpersonal and Sexual Violence by Sexual Orientation. Press Release. Retrieved July 4, 2022, from cdc.gov/media/release/2013/

Cochran, B.N., & Cauce, A.M. (2006). Characteristics of Lesbian, Gay, Bisexual, and Transgender Individuals Entering Substance Abuse Treatment. *Journal of Substance Abuse Treatment*, *30*, 135–146.

Cochran, S.D., & Mays, V.M. (2006). Estimating Prevalence of Mental and Substance-Using Disorders among Lesbians and Gay Men from Existing National Health Data. In A.M. Omoto & H.S. Kurtzman (Eds.), *Sexual Orientation and Mental Health* (pp. 143–165). Washington, DC: American Psychological Association.

Cochran, S.D., Sullivan, J.G., & Mays, V.M. (2003). Prevalence of Mental Disorders, Psychological Distress, and Mental Health Services Use among Lesbian, Gay, and Bisexual Adults in the United States. *Journal of Counseling and Clinical Psychology*, *71*(1), 53–61.

Corliss, H.L., Grella, C.E., Mays, V.M., & Cochran, S.D. (2006). Drug Use, Drug Severity, and Help-Seeking Behaviors of Lesbian and Bisexual Women. *Journal of Women's Health, 15*(5), 556–568.

De Graaf, R., Sandfort, T.G.M., & Tenhave, M. (2006). Suicidality and Sexual Orientation: Differences between Men and Women in a General Population-Based Sample from the Netherlands. *Archives of Sexual Behavior, 35*(3), 253–262.

DiPlacido, J. (1998). Minority Stress among Lesbians, Gay Men, and Bisexuals: A Consequence of Heterosexism, Homophobia, and Stigmatization. In G.M. Herek (Ed.), *Psychological Perspectives on Lesbian and Gay Issues: Volume 4: Stigma and Sexual Orientation: Understanding Prejudice against Lesbians, Gay Men, and Bisexuals* (pp. 138–159). Thousand Oaks, CA: Sage.

Dworkin, S.H. (2006). The Aging Bisexual: The Invisible of the Invisible Minority. In K. Kimmel, T. Rose, & S. David (Eds.), *Lesbian, Gay, Bisexual, and Transgender Aging* (pp. 36–52). New York: Oxford University Press.

Flentje, Annesa, Leon, Armando, Carrico, Adam, Zheng, Debbie, & Dilley, James (2016). Mental and Physical Health among Homeless Sexual and Gender Minorities in a Major Urban US City. *Journal of Urban Health: Bulletin of the New York Academy of Medicine, 93*(6), 997–1009.

Frederiksen-Goldsen, K., & Erera, P.I. (2003). Lesbian-Headed Stepfamilies. In M.K. Sullivan (Ed.), *Sexual Minorities: Discrimination, Challenges, and Development in America*, (pp. 171 015–187). New York, NY: Haworth Social Work Practice Press.

Garnets, L., & Peplau, L.A. (2006). Sexuality in the Lives of Aging Lesbian and Bisexual Women. In K. Kimmel, T. Rose, & S. David (Eds.), *Lesbian, Gay, Bisexual, and Transgender Aging* (pp. 70–90). New York: Oxford University Press.

Gates, Gary J. (2011). *How Many People Are Lesbian, Gay, Bisexual, and Transgender?* Los Angeles, CA: Williams Institute.

Grant, Jaime M., Mottet, Lisa A., Tanis, Justin, Harrison, Jack, Herman, Jody L., & Keisling, Mara. (2011). *Injustice at Every Turn: A Report of the National Transgender Discrimination Survey*. Washington, DC: National Center for Transgender Equality and National Gay and Lesbian Task Force, 2011.

Green, R.J. (2000). Lesbians, Gay Men, and Their Parents: A Critique of LaSala and the Prevailing Clinical Wisdom. *Family Process, 39*(2), 257–266.

Horvath, Keith J., Iantaffi, Alex, Swinburner-Romine, Rebecca, & Bockting, Walter. (2014). A Comparison of Mental Health, Substance Use, and Sexual Risk Behaviors between Rural and Non-Rural Transgender Persons. *Journal of Homosexuality, 61*(8), 1117–1130.

Hughes, T.L., & Eliason, M. (2002). Substance Use and Abuse in Lesbian, Gay, Bisexual and Transgender Populations. *Journal of Primary Prevention, 22*(3), 263–298.

Israel, T., & Mobr, J.J. (2004). Attitudes toward Bisexual Women and Men: Current Research, Future Directions. In R.C. Fox (Ed.), *Current Research on Bisexuality* (pp. 117–134). New York, NY: Harrington Park Press.

Just the Facts Coalition. (2008). *Just the Facts about Sexual Orientation and Youth: A Primer for Principals, Educators, and School Personnel*. Washington, DC: American Psychological Association. Retrieved May 20, 2009, from apa.org/pi/lgbc/publications/justthefacts.html

Keuroghlian, Alex S., Reisner, Sari L., White, Jaclyn M., & Weiss, Roger D. (2015). Substance Use and Treatment of Substance Use Disorders in a Community Sample of Transgender Adults. *Drug and Alcohol Dependence, 152*, 139–146.

Koh, A.S., & Ross, L.K. (2006). Mental Health Issues: A Comparison of Lesbian, Bisexual, and Heterosexual Women. *Journal of Homosexuality, 51*(1), 33–57.

Lasala, M.C. (2006). Cognitive and Environmental Interventions for Gay Males: Addressing Stigma and Its Consequences. *Families in Society, 87*(2), 181–189.

Lev, A.I. (2004). *Transgender Emergence: Therapeutic Guidelines for Working with Gender-Variant People and Their Families.* New York, NY: Haworth Clinical Practice Press.

Logie, C., Bridge, T.J., & Bridge, P.D. (2007). Evaluating the Phobias, Attitudes, and Cultural Competence of Master of Social Work Students toward the LGBTQ Populations. *Journal of Homosexuality, 53*(4), 2018–2221.

Miller, M., Andre, A., Ebin, J., & Bessonova, L. (2007). *Bisexual Health: An Introduction and Model Practices for HIV/STI Prevention Programming.* New York, NY: National Gay and Lesbian Task Force Policy Institute, Fenway Institute at Fenway Community Health, and BiNet USA. Retrieved May 28, 2008, from thetaskforce.org/downloads/reports/reports/

Mills, T.C., Paul, J., Stall, R., Pollack, L., Canchola, J., Chang, Y.J. et al. (2004). Distress and Depression in Men Who Have Sex with Men: The Urban Men's Health Study. *American Journal of Psychiatry, 161*(2), 2788–2285.

Monro, S. (2000). Theorizing Transgender Diversity: Towards a Social Model of Health. *Sexual and Relationship Therapy, 15*(1), 338–245.

Page, E.H. (2004). Mental Health Services Experiences of Bisexual Women and Bisexual Men: An Empirical Study. In R.C. Fox (Ed.), *Current Research on Bisexuality* (pp. 1378–2160). New York, NY: Harrington Park Press.

Paul, J.P., Catania, J., Pollack, L., Moskowitz, J., Canchola, J., Mills, T. et al. (2002). Suicide Attempts among Gay and Bisexual Men: Lifetime Prevalence and Antecedents. *American Journal of Public Health, 92*(8), 13388–21345.

Phillips, D.A. (2006). Masculinity, Male Development, Gender, and Identity: Modern and Post Modern Meanings. *Issues in Mental Health Nursing, 27*(4), 4038–2423.

Pitofsky, M. (2021). There Could Be Twice as Many LGBT Adults in the U.S. than Earlier Estimated Report Says. *USA Today.* Retrieved July 3, 2022, from www.usatoday.com/story/news/nation/2021/12/09/more-lgbt-adults-in-united-states/6451887001

Razzano, L.A., Cook, J.A., Hamilton, M.M., Hughes, T.L., & Matthews, A.K. (2006). Predictors of Mental Health Services Use among Lesbian and Bisexual Women. *Psychiatric Rehabilitation Journal, 29*(4), 2898–2298.

Reisner, Sari L., White, Jaclyn M., Mayer, Kenneth H., & Mimiaga, Matthew J. (2014). Sexual Risk Behaviors and Psychosocial Health Concerns of Female-to-Male Transgender Men Screening for STDs at an Urban Community Health Center. *AIDS Care, 26*(7), 857–864.

Rich, A.C. (2003). Compulsory Heterosexuality and Lesbian Existence (1980). *Journal of Women's History, 15*(3), 11–48. doi.org/10.1353/jowh.2003.0079

Ritter, K., & Terndrup, A. (2002). *Handbook of Affirmative Psychotherapy with Lesbians and Gay Men.* New York, NY: Guilford Press.

Rosario, M., Schrimshaw, E.W., & Hunter, J. (2006). A Model of Sexual Risk Behavior among Young Gay and Bisexual Men: Longitudinal Associations of Mental Health, Substance Abuse, Sexual Abuse, and the Coming-Out Process. *AIDS Education & Prevention, 18*(5), 444–460.

Russel, C.J., & Keel, P.K. (2002). Homosexuality as a Specific Risk Factor for Eating Disorders in Men. *International Journal of Eating Disorders, 31*(3), 300–306.

Schulman, S. (2009). *Ties That Bind: Familial Homophobia and Its Consequences*. New York, NY: New Press.

Shoptaw, S., & Reback, C.J. (2007). Methamphetamine Use and Infectious Disease-Related Behaviors in Men Who Have Sex with Men: Implications for Interventions. *Addiction*, *102*, 130–135.

Skegg, K., Nada-Raja, S., Dickson, N., Paul, C., & Williams, S. (2003). Sexual Orientation and Self-Harm in Men and Women. *American Journal of Psychiatry*, *160*(3), 541–546.

Su, Dejun, Irwin, Jay A., Fisher, Christopher, Ramos, Athena, Kelley, Megan, Mendoza, Diana, Ariss, Rogel, & Coleman, Jason D. (2016). Mental Health Disparities within the LGBT Population: A Comparison between Transgender and Nontransgender Individuals. *Transgender Health*, *1*(1), 12–20.

Virupaksha, H.G., Muralidhar, Daliboyina, & Ramakrishna, Jayashree. (2016). Suicide and Suicidal Behavior among Transgender Persons. *Indian Journal of Psychological Medicine*, *38*(6), 505–509.

Walters, M.L., Chen, J., & Breiding, M.J. (2013). *The National Partner & Sexual Violence Survey: 2010 Findings on Victimization by Sexual Orientation*. Atlanta, GA: National Center for Injury Prevention & Control, Centers for Disease Control & Prevention.

Weinberg, M.S., Williams, C.J., & Pryor, D.W. (2001). Bisexuals at Midlife: Commitment, Salience, and Identity. *Journal of Contemporary Ethnography*, *30*(2), 1808–2208.

Wierzalis, E.A., Barret, B., Pope, M., & Rankins, M. (2006). Gay Men and Aging: Sex and Intimacy. In K. Kimmel, T. Rose, & S. David (Eds.), *Lesbian, Gay, Bisexual, and Transgender Aging* (pp. 91–109). New York, NY: Oxford University Press.

Oppression of the LGBTQ+ Community

6

On June 12, 2016, Pulse, a popular gay dance club in Orlando, Florida, was the site of a mass shooting by one assailant; 49 people were killed, and another 50 were injured, making this hate crime the worst mass shooting in U.S. history. It occurred during LGBT Pride weekend, which was being commemorated throughout numerous communities in the United States as well as internationally (Morris, 2022).

A 1997 survey of 157 lesbians, gays, and bisexuals indicated that 41% reported being the target of physical assaults, verbal harassment, threats, and vandalism of their property as a result of their sexual orientation (Herek et al., 1997). Two decades later, the situation had not improved. According to the Federal Bureau of Investigation (Hauck, 2022), the number of hate crimes based on sexual orientation rose each year from 2014 to 2019, and hate crimes motivated by gender identity bias have risen since 2013. According to experts, the FBI data is likely to dramatically underestimate the true number of hate crimes against the LGBTQ+ community owing to flaws in the data collection process and discrepancies with the much larger number of self-reported incidents. In fact, self-reported data contained in the National Crime Victimization Survey administered by the U.S. Census Bureau reflects more hate crimes than are reflected in the FBI data (Hauck, 2022). Furthermore, it is important to note that people in marginalized communities are less likely to report violence when it occurs (FORGE, 2012).

Hate crimes motivated by bias against sexual orientation and gender identity are illegal under the 2009 Matthew Shepard and James Byrd, Jr., Hate Crimes Prevention Act. Despite this Act, local and state law enforcement

DOI: 10.4324/9780429031397-6

agencies are not required to report this information to the FBI. Further, as of 2020, an estimated 53% of LGBTQ+ adults live in states that don't have hate crime laws covering sexual orientation and gender identity (Hauck, 2022).

According to Ritter and Terndrup (2002), prejudice toward homosexuals began to increase during the fall of the Roman state, during the 3rd century and through to the 6th century. By the 13th and 14th centuries, anti-homosexual attitudes had been integrated into society as well as Christianity and Islam. In fact, the moral and criminal codes of the church and state heavily influenced societal opinion about homosexuality prior to the mid-19th century. However, the social oppression of LGBTQ+ people reached its peak during the McCarthy era of the early 1950s, when homosexuals and communists were the targets of witch hunts (Hooker, 1993). In 1952, homosexuality was officially classified as a mental illness in the first edition of the *Diagnostic and Statistical Manual of Mental Disorders* published by the American Psychiatric Association. Fortunately, Evelyn Hooker's groundbreaking research the following year, which found no differences between heterosexuals and homosexuals in either adjustment or psychopathology, initiated efforts to de-pathologize same-gender attraction and homosexuality.

By the mid-1960s, the gay and lesbian movement was gaining momentum (Thompson, 1994; Alyson Publications, 1993). In 1969, on the heels of the civil rights and feminist movements, the Stonewall Riots sparked the modern lesbian, gay, bisexual, and transgender rights movement (Ciarlante & Fountain, 2010). Since then, LGBTQ+ individuals and communities have become more visible throughout the United States, but continue to experience significant degrees of discrimination and violence, ranging from government-sanctioned discrimination to a wide range of crime victimization, including assault, harassment, stalking, sexual violence, and homicide (Amnesty International, 2010).

During the first 6 months of 2023 alone, over 520 anti-LGBTQ+ bills were introduced in state legislatures across the United States, and 70 had been enacted (HRC, 2023). Of those bills, 220 specifically targeted transgender and non-binary people. Also in 2023, there was an increase in LGBTQ+ erasure bills, which strip away legal protections and rights already established for LGBTQ+ people. States that have been the most aggressive in advancing anti-LGBTQ+ laws include Florida, North Dakota, Tennessee, and Texas (HRC, 2003).

LGBTQ+ people, like members of many other minority groups, are forced to deal with discrimination at home and among family members. Studies show that the victimization of LGBTQ+ people is high when they are in their 20 s and 30 s. (Messinger, 2020). This comes at a time when most are entering into serious romantic relationships. Many of these individuals have not seen healthy same-gender relationships reflected by the media, thereby making it very difficult to identify traits that are inherent in healthy relationships and differentiate them from abusive partnerships, especially if they have been victims of abuse and violence in their families of origin. This is further complicated by pornography that depicts sex between two men, with 10% reflecting coerced sex and 20% reflecting rape, further normalizing IPV (Messinger, 2020).

LGBTQ+ people live within a context of societal discrimination and oppression. *Context* refers to the interrelated conditions in which something exists or occurs (Merriam-Webster, 2021), including surroundings, environment, history, and so on. *Oppression* is the unjust or cruel exercise of authority or power (Merriam-Webster, 2021). Racism, sexism, and anti-LGBTQ+ bias are beliefs that can lead to oppression if they are codified in legislation or become part of a culture. Oppression can be internalized as well as institutionalized, and homophobia, biphobia, transphobia, and heterosexism are components of this oppression. Of primary importance, LGBTQ+ intimate partner violence always occurs within the context of LGBTQ+ oppression, bias, and societal heterosexism, which are very powerful weapons of control. In fact, this context is one of LGBTQ+ IPV's most important and distinguishing characteristics.

As discussed earlier, homophobia and, similarly, biphobia and transphobia (all cultural constructs rather than phobias in the clinical sense) are generally considered to be the irrational fear or hatred of homosexuals, homosexuality, or any behavior or belief that does not conform to rigid sex role stereotypes. The expressions of homophobia/biphobia/transphobia differ depending on the degree and type of prejudice held and range from personal discomfort to outright violence to systematic institutional discrimination against those perceived to be non-heterosexual or defying gender norms (NRCDV, 2007).

According to Herek (1992), heterosexism is the cultural ideology that is defined as a system of beliefs, values, and customs that form the basis for the shared perceptions of social reality of members of a population group. Denial and stigmatization, as well as invisibility and hostility, concerning homosexuality recur repeatedly in our culture. Heterosexism underlies the assumption that everyone is heterosexual and that it is the "correct" or "normal" way to be while it perpetuates the belief that people who are not heterosexual are unnatural, have a lower societal status, and are responsible for their own oppression.

Heterosexism bestows privileges on those assumed to be heterosexual, while rendering invisible or punishing those who are not (NRCDV, 2007). These privileges have included the right to marriage, Social Security survivor benefits, pensions, immigration and taxation benefits, inheritance rights, hospital visitation rights, spousal access to welfare, and so on. In fact, until very recently, over 1,000 federal rights, protections, and benefits afforded to married heterosexual couples were denied to same-sex couples (U.S. General Accounting Office, 2004).

The legalization of same-sex marriage in Canada in 2003, the U.S. Supreme Court's striking down of anti-gay sodomy laws in 13 states, and a court decision in Massachusetts against gay marriage bans produced a major backlash against the LGBTQ+ community. By 2008, fueled by anti-gay rhetoric and political organizing of religious-right groups, at least 40 states and the federal government had adopted constitutional bans on or laws against same-sex marriage (Potok, 2011). In 2008, a ruling by the California Supreme Court made California the second state in the United States to allow same-sex marriage, and these marriages were performed between June 16, 2008 and November 5, 2008. However, the passage of Proposition 8 (an example of institutionalized homophobia) in November of 2008 amended the California constitution to limit marriage to one man and one woman, thereby legalizing discrimination against the gay and lesbian population in California. During the trial challenging Proposition 8, a Columbia University professor, Ilan H. Meyer, an expert in mental health issues among gays, lesbians, and bisexuals, testified that LGB persons were more likely to suffer from mental disorders than heterosexuals *because of discrimination*. According to Meyer, "Proposition 8 sent a message that gay relationships are not respected, that they are of secondary value if they are of any value at all." He further added that the proposition made the public statement that it was acceptable "to designate gay people as a different class of people in terms of their intimate relationships" (Dolan, 2010).

There have been several major legal advances in the United States more recently. One of these was the legalization of same-sex marriage (*Obergefell v. Hodges*) by the Supreme Court in 2015 (Wolf, 2020). Another was the ban on discrimination in employment on the basis of sexual orientation and gender identity (*Bostock v. Clayton County*) in 2020. This decision indicates that LGBTQ people are protected by Title VII of the Civil Rights Act.

As of 2019, however, there were still more than 70 countries in which it was illegal to be LGBT (Wareham, 2020). Some of these nations impose the death penalty for same-sex behavior and relationships. In addition, only 15 countries have legalized same-sex joint adoption, and only 27 nations legally recognize the existence of hate crimes against LGBTQ+ people. This legal discrimination, in addition to discrimination in housing, employment, and other areas, can have significant impact for LGBTQ+ IPV. This is particularly true when these forms of discrimination are coupled with widespread homo/bi/transphobia throughout the world. Victims of LGBTQ+ IPV are frequently reluctant or simply unable to speak out in countries where their relationships are illegal, nor are they able to safely access assistance. In countries where adoption by same-sex couples is illegal, leaving an abuser can mean losing access to a child owing to lack of legal guardianship and the absence of parental rights (Messinger, 2020).

The minority stress that Meyer identifies is a serious problem for many marginalized populations. It is unique because it is an added component to the general stress all people face, and additional adaptation is needed by members of these groups to overcome it. Furthermore, it is chronic and, therefore, associated with, and arising from, institutions and societal norms as opposed to any factors unique to a specific individual. Importantly, it is cumulative as well, so that being a member of more than one minority group escalates stress (Longobardi & Badenes-Ribera, 2017).

Internalized oppression consists of societal beliefs and negative stereotypes that individuals introject or learn to believe about themselves. For example, homosexuality was believed to be a mental illness until 1973, when it was removed from the American Psychiatric Association's classification of mental disorders. An individual who believes that they have mental health problems simply by virtue of being LGBTQ+ has internalized that earlier societal misconception.

Heterosexist stigma creates interrelated challenges that LGBTQ+ people must confront in the course of their psychosocial development, including overcoming internalized homophobia and negotiating the coming out process. Internalized homophobia can lead to self-loathing, low self-esteem, and feelings of inferiority (Weinberg, 1972) and often creates a basic mistrust of one's own sexual and interpersonal identity (Stein & Cohen, 1984) which interferes with the process of identity formation (Malyon, 1982). Importantly, studies have shown that internalized homo/bi/transphobic discrimination can increase the risk of violence within a relationship (Woodyatt & Stephenson, 2016).

In his book entitled, *The Velvet Rage: Overcoming the Pain of Growing Up Gay in a Straight Man's World*, psychologist Alan Downs (2006) discusses the ramifications of societal homophobia for the self. He writes,

> The truth is that we grew up disabled. Not disabled by our homosexuality, but emotionally disabled by an environment that

taught us we were unacceptable, not "real" men and, therefore, shameful ... one cannot be around gay men without noticing that we are a wonderful and wounded lot. Beneath our complex layers lies a deeper secret that covertly corrodes our lives. The seeds of this secret were not planted by us, but by a world that didn't understand us, wanted to change us, and at times, was fiercely hostile to us.

Dr. Downs indicates that one result of this process is rage and stresses that this form of rage is the experience of intense anger that results from the failure to achieve authentic validation. He states,

I often hear it said among psychotherapists who treat gay men that one of the primary problems troubling gay male relationships seeking couple's therapy is this hypersensitivity to invalidation and the ensuing flight into anger ... a verbal slight, an off-hand insult, a glimpse of a disapproving face—any of these things have been known to trigger the "crash and lash" syndrome of rage. The crash occurs when we are overwhelmed with rage and all rational thought comes to an abrupt halt. The emotion seems to erupt within us, consuming us and overloading our brains with thoughts steeped in shame and anger. Then, in a matter of seconds, we lash out at the person who triggered the rage within us.

It is important to understand that this dynamic is not consistent with the dynamics inherent in intimate terrorism that reflect patterns of power and coercive control rather than behaviors that reflect a loss of impulse control, which may be more consistent with the situational or common couple violence described in Chapter 2 (Defining Domestic Violence).

Coming out is a process of reclaiming disowned and devalued parts of the self and developing an identity into which one's sexuality is integrated (Malyon, 1982; Stein & Cohen, 1984). Some writers and clinicians believe that the process of growing up gay in a culture that hates homosexuals is, in and of itself, traumatizing (Rofes, 1996; Brown, 1991; Downs, 2006; Schulman, 2009), and the simple act of living in our homophobic society produces symptoms of post-traumatic stress disorder (Rofes, 1996). Rofes (1996) further argues that the HIV/AIDS epidemic exacerbated the chronic trauma inflicted on LGBTQ+ people by homo/bi/transphobia and anti-LGBTQ+ bias. A later study showed that, over the whole lifetime, the risk of development of PTSD was much higher among those with same-sex partners than it was among the heterosexual reference group. This increased risk was twice as likely with the LGB sample and was largely explained by the greater exposure of sexual orientation minorities to violence, exposure to more potentially traumatic events, and earlier age of trauma exposure (Roberts et al., 2010). The researchers found that this population had greater risk of childhood maltreatment, interpersonal violence, trauma caused by a close friend or relative, and the unexpected death of someone close than did heterosexuals with no same-sex attractions or partners; they concluded that sexual orientation disparities were likely a manifestation of the larger problem of discrimination and bias against LGB people in the United States. The following variables were also cited as contributing factors to these disparities: Nonconformity to gender expectations (Rieger et al., 2008); social isolation and distress resulting from awareness of membership of a stigmatized group (D'Augelli, Pilkington, & Hershberger, 2002; Kelly, Raphael, & Judd, 1998; Radcliffe, Fleisher, & Hawkins, 2007; Meyer, 1995; Gold, Marx, & Lexington, 2007); elevated levels of risk-taking behaviors related to social isolation and psychological distress—especially substance use (Marshal, Friedman, & Stall, 2008; Corliss et al., Austin, 2008), which may exacerbate risk for interpersonal violence; fewer resources to cope with traumatic events such as lower levels of social support (Jorm et al., 2002; Ueno, 2005; Williams et al., 2005); and less access to mental health care (Cochran, 2001; Willging, Salvador, & Kano, 2006; Burgess et al., 2007).

Sexual orientation disparities in exposure to violence over the life course are well documented (Austin, Jun, & Jackson, 2008; Austin, Roberts et al., 2008; Balsam, Rothblum, & Beauchaine, 2005; Corliss, Cochran, & Mays, 2002; Herek, 2009; Herek, Gillis, & Cogan, 1999; Saewyc, Skay, & Pettingell, 2006; Pilkington & D'Augelli, 1995; Tjaden, Thoennes, & Allison, 1999; Whitbeck et al., 2004). LGBTQ+ individuals are more likely to experience violence, including hate crimes, throughout their lives (Herek, 2009; Whitbeck et al., 2004; Garnets et al., 2003; Russell, Franz, & Driscoll, 2001). Furthermore, individuals with minority sexual orientation report elevated frequency, severity, and persistence of physical and sexual abuse in childhood (Austin, Jun, et al., 2008; Balsam et al., 2005; Corliss et al., 2002) and intimate partner violence and sexual assault in adulthood at disproportionate rates (Balsam et al., 2005; Tjaden et al., 1999).

NCAVP data (2012) suggests that people of color, gay men, bisexual persons, young people, and transgender individuals experience more severe and deadly forms of violence while simultaneously having less access to anti-violence services and support. Overall, exposure to childhood violence in the forms of witnessing or experiencing abuse of/by siblings, having parents who experienced child abuse, and witnessing and/or experiencing IPV between parents or caregivers has been positively correlated with increased risk that a sexual minority individual will perpetrate and/or be the victim of domestic violence later in life (Messinger, 2020). The NCAVP (2012) concludes that these communities represent a disproportionate number of reports of violence because of unique intersections of the oppression they experience, how it impacts their relationships, and their access (or lack thereof) to anti-violence prevention programs and anti-violence support.

LGBTQ+ youth are at higher risk for abuse and victimization than LGBTQ+ adults in addition to having higher levels of risk for suicidal ideation, suicide attempts, and suicide completion (Bontempo & D'Augelli, 2002; Cianciotto & Cahill, 2003; Cochran & Mays, 2006; de Graaf, Sandfort, & Tenhave, 2006; Koh & Ross, 2006; Kulkin, Chauvin, & Percle, 2000; Ritter & Terndrup, 2002; Russell, 2006). Harassment and bullying in school have been widely documented as a pervasive problem for LGBTQ+ and gender non-conforming youth across the United States, with serious consequences for their health, mental health, and academic achievement (Human Rights Watch 2001; Kosciw et al., 2010; O'Shaughnessy et al., 2004; Russell et al., 2011). More than 60% of LGBTQ+ students report feeling unsafe at school as a result of their sexual orientation, and almost 40% feel unsafe owing to their gender expression (California Department of Mental Health, 2012). Cianciotto and Cahill (2003) found that 70% of respondents in their study of LGBTQ+ foster youth suffered from physical attacks within their group homes.

According to the *Diagnostic and Statistical Manual of Mental Disorders* published by the American Psychiatric Association (2022), acute stress disorder and post-traumatic stress disorder can result after exposure to actual or threatened death, serious injury, or sexual violation/violence in any of the following ways: Directly experiencing the traumatic event(s); witnessing, in person, the event as it occurred to others; learning that the traumatic events occurred to a close family member or a close friend; or experiencing repeated or extreme exposure to aversive details of the traumatic event(s). The essential features of PTSD include the development of symptoms following exposure to an internal or external stressor that involves a threat to one's physical integrity and/or learning about or witnessing that same threat to others. The response often involves intense fear, helplessness, or terror, as well as re-experiencing the event, avoidance of stimuli associated with it, numbing of general responsiveness, and symptoms of increased arousal such as hypervigilance. Consider the potential trauma to LGBTQ+ persons when they learned of the beating and homicide of Matthew Shepard, a college student who was kidnapped, robbed, pistol-whipped, tied to a fence on a Wyoming ranch in near-freezing temperatures, and left for dead after disclosing to his attackers that he was gay. Shepard was the victim of a hate crime because of his sexual orientation. In addition to the harm done to the individual victim, the impact of hate violence harms members of the victim's community and can leave them feeling isolated, vulnerable, and unprotected by the law (IACP, 1999). Hate crimes such as the Shepard tragedy occur when a perpetrator targets a victim because of their perceived membership of a particular social group.

An attack against an individual or an act of property damage that clearly reflects bias motivation is also an attack against a community and may simultaneously incite community-wide fear and panic as well as frustration and anger. Such attacks send the message that a community, and anyone associated with it, is not safe and raise anxiety and fear for members of the community who may not even have known the victim(s) (Ciarlante & Fountain, 2010). In fact, according to studies by the National Institute of Mental Health, hate crimes based on sexual orientation bias have more serious and long-lasting psychological effects than other crimes because of the link to core aspects of the victim's identity and community (Herek, 1999).

As mentioned previously, gays remain the minority that is most targeted by hate crimes according to the Potok (2011). One study found that 94% of lesbian, gay, and bisexual individuals reported that they had been the victim of at least one hate crime in their lifetime (Herek, Cogan, & Gillis, 2002). In fact, the National Coalition of Anti-Violence Programs reports that anti-LGBTQ+ hate violence increased by 13% from 2009 to 2010, and anti-LGBTQ+ murders increased 23% during the same period—the second highest amount in a decade (NCAVP, 2011). As many as 50.1% of LGBTQ+ survivors did not report the violence to the police, and, when they did, 61% experienced indifferent, abusive, or deterrent police attitudes (NCAVP, 2011). The year 2009 saw the highest rate of LGBTQ+ hate victims of homicide in a decade, with the highest spike in reported incidents in October 2009, which coincided with the passage of the Matthew Shepard and James Byrd, Jr., Hate Crimes Prevention Act (NCAVP, 2010), a correlation that the NCAVP indicates occurred because of increased visibility and targeting of LGBTQ+ persons.

In 2009, the National Center for Victims of Crime and the National Coalition of Anti-Violence Programs found that LGBTQ+ victims of crime did not have consistent access to culturally competent services to prevent and address the violence against them. They further found that mainstream victim assistance agencies could not meet the needs of LGBTQ+ crime victims in culturally sensitive ways, while either LGBTQ-specific anti-violence programs lacked the resources to do so or the resources simply did not exist. They concluded that, without access to culturally competent advocacy, intervention, and other critical services, LGBTQ+ victims will continue to suffer disproportionately from violence and the after-effects of victimization (Ciarlante & Fountain, 2010).

Verbal harassment and intimidation are the most common forms of victimization of LGBTQ+ people, and their psychological consequences may be as severe, and oftentimes more insidious, than those following physical assaults. Anti-gay verbal abuse is one form of violence that is a reminder of other forms of violence, such as physical and sexual assault. It reinforces the victim's sense of being a member of a devalued minority and, hence, a socially acceptable target for violence (Garnets, Herek, & Levy, 1992). When people are attacked because they are perceived to be LGBTQ+, impacts stemming from the victimization align with societal bias, and the victim's sexual orientation is associated with the heightened vulnerability that follows victimization. One's orientation may consequently be experienced as a source of pain rather than of intimacy, love, and community, and the individual may feel punished for being LGBTQ+ (Bard & Sangrey, 1979; Lerner, 1970; Garnets et al., 1992). Further, internalized homophobia may intensify, and feelings of self-blame can lead to depression and helplessness even in individuals who are comfortable with their sexual orientation (Janoff-Bulman, 1979).

There is a dearth of culturally competent victim services for LGBTQ+ victims of crime. Furthermore, many victim-serving agencies are not well trained to work with LGBTQ+ victims of crime, even if the service provider has made efforts to increase its cultural competency (Ciarlante & Fountain, 2010). In fact, many LGBTQ+ victims do not feel that supportive services are readily accessible (Bornstein et al., 2006), and studies have indicated that only one in five survivors of same-gender sexual assault and intimate partner violence received assistance (Ciarlante & Fountain, 2010). Validating this reality, Ciarlante and Fountain (2010) indicate that there are fewer than 40 LGBTQ+-specific anti-violence programs in the country, existing in 20 states, and most are small, staffed largely by volunteers, and generally under-funded and lack the capacity to engage in the outreach, education, and advocacy necessary to raise awareness and increase reporting and help-seeking for crimes against members of the LGBTQ+ community. In addition to their direct service program components being critically understaffed to meet client and community needs, Ciarlante and

Fountain (2010) conclude that more than half of the United States lacks dedicated services for LGBTQ+ victims.

A needs assessment conducted by the Los Angeles LGBT Center in 2017–2018 reflected the lack of progress made nearly a decade later when it found that over two-thirds of needs assessment respondents did not receive any services following a crime, with the most common barriers being (a) fear of retaliation, (b) stigma/bias toward LGBTQ+ persons, (c) the victim's lack of knowledge about the kind of crime they experienced, and (d) inadequate criminal justice response (Whirry & Holt, 2020).

It is within this context of societal oppression, hatred, and fear that LGBTQ+ persons live their lives. Further, they are factors that not only create a fertile climate for domestic violence and abuse but must always be considered when working with persons impacted by LGBTQ+ intimate partner violence.

Continuing Education Questions

1. Which of the following is the assumption that everyone is heterosexual and that it is the "correct" or "normal" way to be, perpetuating the belief that people who are not heterosexual are unnatural or less important and, sometimes, responsible for their own oppression?
   a. Sexism
   b. Racism
   c. Heterosexuality
   d. Heterosexism
2. Victimization of LGBTQ people peaks in their 20 s and 30 s.
   a. True
   b. False
3. How many countries had legally recognized hate crimes against LGBTQ individuals as of 2019?
   a. 12
   b. 27
   c. 65
   d. 108
4. Less than half of LGBTQ students feel unsafe at school owing to their sexual orientation.
   a. True
   b. False

5. Which one of these does *not* describe minority stress, according to Longobardi and Badenes-Ribera (2017)?
    a. Unique
    b. Temporary
    c. Socially based
    d. Cumulative

References

Alyson Publications. (1993). *The Alyson Almanac: The Fact Book of the Lesbian and Gay Community.* Boston, MA: Author.

American Psychiatric Association (APA). (2022). *Diagnostic and Statistical Manual of Mental Disorders* (5th ed., text rev.). doi.org/10.1176/appi.books.9780890425787

Amnesty International. (2010). Stonewalled: Police Abuse and Misconduct against Lesbian, Gay, Bisexual, and Transgender People in the U.S. In *Why It Matters: Rethinking Victim Assistance for Lesbian, Gay, Bisexual, Transgender, and Queer Victims of Hate Violence & Intimate Partner Violence* (pp. 7–8). Washington, DC: National Center for Victims of Crime and the National Coalition of Anti-Violence Programs.

Austin, S.B., Jun, H.J., & Jackson, B. (2008). Disparities in Child Abuse Victimization in Lesbian, Bisexual, and Heterosexual Women in the Nurses' Health Study II. *Journal of Women's Health, 17*(4), 597–606.

Austin, S.B., Roberts, A.L., Corliss, H.L., & Molnar, B.E. (2008). Sexual Violence Victimization History and Sexual Risk Indicators in a Community-Based Urban Cohort of "Mostly Heterosexual" and Heterosexual Young Women. *American Journal of Public Health, 98*(6), 1015–1020.

Balsam, K.F., Rothblum, E.D., & Beauchaine, T.P. (2005). Victimization over the Life Span: A Comparison of Lesbian, Gay, Bisexual, and Heterosexual Siblings. *Journal of Consulting and Clinical Psychology, 73*(3), 477–487.

Bard, M., & Sangrey, D. (1979). *The Crime Victim's Book.* New York: Basic Books.

Bontempo, K.E., & D'Augelli, A.R. (2002). Effects of At-School Victimization and Sexual Orientation on Lesbian, Gay, or Bisexual Youths' Health Risk Behavior. *Journal of Adolescent Health, 30*(5), 364–374.

Bornstein, D.R., Fawcett, J., Senturia, K.D., & Shiu-Thornton, S. (2006). Understanding the Experience of Lesbian, Bisexual, and Trans Survivors of Domestic Violence: A Qualitative Study. *Journal of Homosexuality, 51*(1), 159–181.

Brown, L.S. (1991). Not Outside the Range: One Feminist Perspective on Psychic Trauma. *American Imago, 48*(1), 199–133.

Burgess, D., Lee, T., Tran, A., & Van Ryn, M. (2007). Effects of Perceived Discrimination on Mental Health and Mental Health Services Utilization among Gay, Lesbian, Bisexual, and Transgender Persons. *Journal of LGBTQ Health Resources, 3*(4) 1–14.

California Department of Mental Health. (2012). *First, Do No Harm: Reducing Disparities for Lesbian, Gay, Bisexual, Transgender, Queer and Questioning Populations in California.* Sacramento, CA: Author.

Cianciotto, J., & Cahill, S. (2003). *Education Policy: Issues Affecting Lesbian, Gay, Bisexual, and Transgender Youth*. New York, NY: The National Gay and Lesbian Task Force Policy Institute. Retrieved November, 2, 2007, from thetaskforce.org/downloads/reports/reports/

Ciarlante, M., & Fountain, K. (2010). *Why It Matters: Rethinking Victim Assistance for Lesbian, Gay, Bisexual, Transgender, and Queer Victims of Hate Violence & Intimate Partner Violence*. Washington, DC: National Center for Victims of Crime & the National Coalition of Anti-Violence Programs.

Cochran, S.D. (2001). Emerging Issues in Research on Lesbians' and Gay Men's Mental Health: Does Sexual Orientation Really Matter? *American Psychologist, 56*(11), 931–947.

Cochran, S.D., & Mays, V.M. (2006). Estimating Prevalence of Mental and Substance-Using Disorders among Lesbians and Gay Men from Existing National Health Data. In A.M. Omoto & H.S. Kurtzman (Eds.), *Sexual Orientation and Mental Health* (pp. 143–165). Washington, DC: American Psychological Association.

Corliss, H.L., Cochran, S.D., & Mays, V.M. (2002). Reports of Parental Maltreatment during Childhood in a United States Population-Based Survey of Homosexual, Bisexual, and Heterosexual Adults. *Child Abuse and Neglect, 26*(11), 1165–1178.

Corliss, H.L., Rosario, M., Wypij, D., Fisher, L.B., & Austin, S.B. (2008). Sexual Orientation Disparities in Longitudinal Alcohol Use Patterns among Adolescents: Findings from the Growing Up Today Study. *Archives of Pediatric& Adolescent Medicine, 162*(11), 1071–1078.

D'Augelli, A.R., Pilkington, N.W., & Hershberger, S.L. (2002). Incidence and Mental Health Impact of Sexual Orientation Victimization of Lesbian, Gay, and Bisexual Youths in High School. *School Psychology Quarterly, 17*(2), 148–167.

De Graaf, R., Sandfort, T.G.M., & Tenhave, M. (2006). Suicidality and Sexual Orientation: Differences between Men and Women in a General Population-Based Sample from the Netherlands. *Archives of Sexual Behavior, 35*(3), 253–262.

Dolan, M. (2010). Bias Raises Gays' Risk of Mental Disorders, Witness at Prop. 8 Trial Says. *Los Angeles Times*. Retrieved January 14, 2010, from latimes.com/news/local/la-me-prop8-trial15- 2010jan15,0,3349250.story

Downs, A. (2006). *The Velvet Rage: Overcoming the Pain of Growing Up Gay in a Straight Man's World*. Cambridge, MA: Perseus Books.

FORGE. (2012). Transgender Rates of Violence: Victim Service Providers' Fact Sheet #6. Retrieved from forge-forward.org/resource/rates-of-violence/

Garnets, L.D., Herek, G.M., & Levy, B. (1992). Violence and Victimization of Lesbians and Gay Men: Mental Health Consequences. In G.M. Herek & K.T. Berrill (Eds.), *Hate Crimes: Confronting Violence against Lesbians and Gay Men* (pp. 207–226). Newbury Park, CA: Sage.

Garnets, L.D., Herek, G.M., Levy, B., & Kimmel, D.C. (2003). Violence and Victimization of Lesbians and Gay Men: Mental Health Consequences. In L.D. Garnets & D.C. Kimmel (Eds.), *Psychological Perspectives on Lesbian, Gay, and Bisexual Experiences* (2nd ed.) (pp. 188–206). New York, NY: Columbia University Press.

Gold, S.D., Marx, B.P., & Lexington, J.M. (2007). Gay Male Sexual Assault Survivors: The Relations among Internalized Homophobia, Experiential Avoidance, and Psychological Symptom Severity. *Behavior Research & Therapy, 45*(3), 549–562.

Hauck, G. (2022, Feb. 10). Anti-LGBT Hate Crimes Are Rising, the FBI Says. But It Gets Worse. *USA Today*, Gannett Satellite Information Network. www.usatoday.com/story/news/2019/06/28/anti-gay-hate-crimes-rise-fbi-says-and-they-likely-undercount/1582614001/

Herek, G. (1992). The Social Context of Hate Crimes: Notes on Cultural Heterosexism. In G. Herek & K. Berrill (Eds.), *Hate Crimes: Confronting Violence against Lesbians and Gay Men* (pp. 89–104). Newbury Park, CA: Sage.

Herek, G. (1999). Psychological Sequelae of Hate Crime Victimization among Lesbian, Gay, and Bisexual Adults. *Journal of Consulting and Clinical Psychology*, 67(6), 945–951.

Herek, G.M. (2009). Hate Crimes and Stigma-Related Experiences among Sexual Minority Adults in the United States: Prevalence Estimates from a National Probability Sample. *Journal of Interpersonal Violence*, 24(1), 54–74.

Herek, G.M., Cogan, J.C., & Gillis, J.R. (2002). Victim Experiences in Hate Crimes Based on Sexual Orientation. *Journal of Social Issues*, 58(2), 319–339. doi.org/10.1111/1540-4560.00263

Herek, G.M., Gillis, J.R., & Cogan, J.C. (1999). Psychological Sequelae of Hate-Crime Victimization among Lesbian, Gay, and Bisexual Adults. *Journal of Consulting and Clinical Psychology*, 67(6), 945–951.

Herek, G.M., Gillis, J.R., Cogan, J.C., & Glunt, E.K. (1997). Hate Crime Victimization among Lesbian, Gay, and Bisexual Adults. *Journal of Interpersonal Violence*, 12(2), 195–215. doi.org/10.1177/088626097012002003

Hooker, E. (1993). Reflections of a 40-Year Exploration: A Scientific View on Homosexuality. *American Psychologist*, 48(4), 450–453.

Human Rights Campaign (HRC). (May 23, 2023). Press Release. www.hrc.org/press-release/roundup-of-anti-lgbtq-legislation-advancing-in-states-across-the-country

Human Rights Watch. (2001). *Hatred in the Hallways: Violence and Discrimination against Lesbian, Gay, Bisexual, and Transgender Students in U.S. Schools*. New York, NY: Human Rights Watch.

International Association of Chiefs of Police (IACP). (1999). *Responding to Hate Crimes: A Police Officer's Guide to Investigation and Prevention*. Alexandria, VA: Author.

Janoff-Bulman, R. (1979). Characterological versus Behavioral Self-Blame: Inquiries into Depression and Rape. *Journal of Personality and Social Psychology*, 37, 1798–1809.

Jorm, A.F., Korten, A.E., Rodgers, B., Jacomb, P.A., & Christensen, H. (2002). Sexual Orientation and Mental Health: Results from a Community Survey of Young and Middle-Aged Adults. *British Journal of Psychiatry*, 180(5), 423–427.

Kelly, B., Raphael, B., & Judd, F. (1998). Posttraumatic Stress Disorder in Response to HIV Infection. *General Hospital Psychiatry*, 20(6), 345–352.

Koh, A.S., & Ross, L.K. (2006). Mental Health Issues: A Comparison of Lesbian, Bisexual, and Heterosexual Women. *Journal of Homosexuality*, 51(1), 33–57.

Kosciw, J.G., Greytak, E.A., Diaz, E.M., & Bartkiewicz, M.J. (2010). *The 2009 National School Climate Survey: The Experiences of Lesbian, Gay, Bisexual, and Transgender Youth in Our Nation's Schools [electronic version]*. New York: GLSEN.

Kulkin, H.S., Chauvin, E.A., & Percle, G.A. (2000). Suicide among Gay and Lesbian Adolescents and Young Adults: A Review of the Literature. *Journal of Homosexuality*, 40(1), 1–29.

Lerner, M.J. (1970). The Desire for Justice and Reactions to Victims. In J. Macaulay & J. Berkowitz (Eds.), *Altruism and Helping Behavior* (pp. 205–229). New York: Academic Press.

Longobardi, C., and L. Badenes-Ribera. (2017). Intimate Partner Violence in Same-Sex Relationships and the Role of Sexual Minority Stressors: A Systematic Review of the Past 10 Years. *Journal of Child and Family Studies*, 26(8), 2039–2049. doi:10.1007/s1082 6-017-0734-4

Malyon, A.K. (1982). Psychotherapeutic Implications of Internalized Homophobia in Gay Men. *Journal of Homosexuality*, 7(2/3), 59–69.

Marshal, M.P., Friedman, M.S., & Stall, R. (2008). Sexual Orientation and Adolescent Substance Use: A Meta-analysis and Methodological Review. *Addiction*, 103(4), 546–556.

Merriam-Webster. (2021). Dictionary by Merriam-Webster: America's Most-Trusted Online Dictionary. Merriam-Webster. merriam-webster.com/

Messinger, Adam M. (2020). *LGBTQ Intimate Partner Violence: Lessons for Policy Practice, and Research*. University of California Press.

Meyer, I.H. (1995). Minority Stress and Mental Health in Gay Men. *Journal of Health Social Behavior*, 36(1), 38–56.

Morris, B.J. (2022). *History of Lesbian, Gay, Bisexual and Transgender Social Movements (apa.org)*. American Psychological Association. www.apa.org/pi/lgbt/resources/history

National Coalition of Anti-Violence Programs (NCAVP). (2010). *Lesbian, Gay, Bisexual, Transgender, Queer and HIV-Affected Intimate Partner Violence 2010: A Report from the National Coalition of Anti-Violence Programs*. New York, NY: New York City Gay & Lesbian Anti-Violence Project.

National Coalition of Anti-Violence Programs (NCAVP). (2011). *Hate Violence against Lesbian, Gay, Bisexual, Transgender, Queer and HIV-Affected Communities in the United States in 2010*. New York, NY: New York City Gay & Lesbian Anti-Violence Project.

National Coalition of Anti-Violence Programs (NCAVP). (2012). *Lesbian, Gay, Bisexual, Transgender, Queer, and HIV-Affected Intimate Partner Violence 2011: A Report from the National Coalition of Anti-Violence Programs*. New York, NY: New York City Gay & Lesbian Anti-Violence Project.

National Resource Center on Domestic Violence (NRCDV). (2007). *Lesbian, Gay, Bisexual, and Trans (LGBTQ) Communities and Domestic Violence: Information and Resources*. Harrisburg, PA: Author. Retrieved October 17, 2004, from ncadv.org

O'Shaughnessy, M., Russell, S., Heck, K., Calhoun, C., & Laub, C. (2004). *Safe Place to Learn: Consequences of Harassment Based on Actual or Perceived Sexual Orientation and Gender Nonconformity and Steps for Making Schools Safer*. San Francisco, CA: California Safe Schools Coalition.

Pilkington, N.W., & D'Augelli, A.R. (1995). Victimization of Lesbian, Gay, and Bisexual Youth in Community Settings. *Journal of Community Psychology*, 23(1), 34–56.

Potok, M. (2011). Gays Remain Minority Most Targeted by Hate Crimes. Intelligence Report, February 27.

Radcliffe, J., Fleisher, C.L., & Hawkins, L.A. (2007). Posttraumatic Stress and Trauma History in Adolescents and Young Adults with HIV. *AIDS Patient Care STDS*, 21(7), 501–508.

Rieger, G., Linsenmeier, J.A., Gygax, L., & Bailey, J.M. (2008). Sexual Orientation and Childhood Gender Nonconformity: Evidence from Home Videos. *Developmental Psychology*, 44(1), 46–58.

Ritter, K., & Terndrup, A. (2002). *Handbook of Affirmative Psychotherapy with Lesbians and Gay Men*. New York: Guilford Press.

Roberts, A.L., Austin, S.B., Corliss, H.L., Vandermorris, A.K., & Koenen, K.C. (2010). Pervasive Trauma Exposure among US Sexual Orientation Minority Adults and Risk of Posttraumatic Stress Disorder. *American Journal of Public Health*, *100*(12), 2433–2441.

Rofes, E. (1996). *Reviving the Tribe: Regenerating Gay Men's Sexuality and Culture in the Ongoing Epidemic*. Binghamton, NY: Harrington Park Press.

Russell, S.T. (2006). Substance Use and Abuse and Mental Health among Sexual Minority Youths: Evidence from ADD Health. In A.M. Omoto & H.S. Kurtzman (Eds.), *Sexual Orientation and Mental Health* (pp. 13–35). Washington, DC: American Psychological Association.

Russell, S.T., Franz, B.T., & Driscoll, A.K. (2001). Same-Sex Romantic Attraction and Experiences of Violence in Adolescence. *American Journal of Public Health*, *91*(6), 903–906.

Russell, S.T., Ryan. C., Toomey, R.B., Diaz, R., & Sanchez, J. (2011). Lesbian, Gay, Bisexual, and Transgender Adolescent School Victimization: Implications for Young Adult Health and Adjustment. *Journal of School Health*, *81*, 223–230.

Saewyc, E.M., Skay, C.L., & Pettingell, S.L. (2006). Hazards of Stigma: The Sexual and Physical Abuse of Gay, Lesbian, and Bisexual Adolescents in the United States and Canada. *Child Welfare*, *85*(2), 195–213.

Schulman, S. (2009). *Ties That Bind: Familial Homophobia and Its Consequences*. New York, NY: New Press.

Stein, T.S., & Cohen, C.J. (1984). Psychotherapy with Gay Men and Lesbians: An Examination of Homophobia, Coming Out, and Identity. In E. Hetrick & T. Stein (Eds.), *Innovations in Psychotherapy with Homosexuals* (pp. 60–73). Washington, DC: American Psychiatric Press.

Thompson, M. (Ed.). (1994). *Long Road to Freedom: The Advocate History of the Gay and Lesbian Movement*. New York, NY: St. Martin's Press.

Tjaden, P., Thoennes, N., & Allison, C.J. (1999). Comparing Violence over the Life Span in Samples of Same-Sex and Opposite-Sex Cohabitants. *Violence and Victimization*, *14*(4), 413–425.

U.S. General Accounting Office. (2004). *Defense of Marriage Act: Update to Prior Report*. Washington, DC: Author.

Ueno, K. (2005). Sexual Orientation and Psychological Distress in Adolescence: Examining Interpersonal Stressors and Social Support Processes. *Sociologies & Psychologies*, *68*(3), 258–277.

Wareham, Jamie. (17 May, 2020). Map Shows Where It's Illegal to Be Gay—30 Years since WHO Declassified Homosexuality as Disease. *Forbes Magazine*. forbes.com/sites/jamiewareham/2020/05/17/map-shows-where-its-illegal-to-be-gay--30-years-since-who-declassified-homosexuality-as-disease/#e65134a578aa

Weinberg, G. (1972). *Society and the Healthy Homosexual*. New York, NY: St. Martin's Press.

Whitbeck, L.B., Chen. X., Hoyt, D.R., Tyler, K.A., &. Johnson, K.D. (2004). Mental Disorder, Subsistence Strategies, and Victimization among Gay, Lesbian, and Bisexual Homeless and Runaway Adolescents. *Journal of Sex Research*, *41*(4), 329–342.

Whirry, R., & Holt, S. (2020). *Finding Safety: A Report about LGBTQ Domestic Violence and Sexual Assault*. Los Angeles, CA: Los Angeles LGBT Center.

Willging, C.W., Salvador, M., & Kano, M. (2006). Unequal Treatment: Mental Health Care for Sexual and Gender Minority Groups in a Rural State. *Psychiatric Service*, *57*(6), 867–870.

Williams, T., Connolly, J., Pepler, D., & Craig, W. (2005). Peer Victimization, Social Support, and Psychosocial Adjustment of Sexual Minority Adolescents. *Journal of Youth and Adolescence*, *34*(5), 471–482.

Wolf, R. (June 25, 2020). Supreme Court's Same-Sex Marriage Ruling Turns 5: Acceptance, Advancement, but Opposition Remains. *Des Moines Register*, USA Today. desmoinesregister.com/story/news/politics/2020/06/25/lgbtq-rights-five-years-after-gay-marriage-ruling-battles-continue/3242992001/

Woodyatt, C.R., & Stephenson, R. (2016). Emotional Intimate Partner Violence Experienced by Men in Same-Sex Relationships. *Culture, Health & Sexuality*, *18*(10), pp. 1137–1149. doi:10.1080/13691058.2016.1175027

Psychology and the LGBTQ+ Population

7

The belief that homosexuality is an identity and an inherent part of one's personality is relatively recent (Lev, 2004; Sullivan, 2003). Historically, homosexuality has been theorized to be a problem resulting from pathology, immaturity, a normal variation of nature (Drescher, 2015), as well as abnormal brain functioning, gender confusion, and moral inadequacy. When considered pathological, it was believed to be a disease caused by factors or events such as inadequate parenting, hormonal influences, sexual abuse, and so on; as a problem of immaturity, it was thought to be a developmental arrest that was never outgrown; and, as a normal variation, it was simply conceptualized as a difference that occurred naturally (Drescher, 2015). Homosexuality was also frequently thought to be related to gender—most specifically, the traditional gender binary of two opposites (man/woman). For example, it was believed that a male homosexual's brain most closely resembled the brain of a woman, and vice versa. In fact, Freud theorized that lesbians had a masculine, rather than a feminine, psychology (Freud, 1955/1920, cited in Drescher, 2015). When homosexuality was conceptualized by religion, it was typically considered to be a moral failing or sin. Drescher (2015, p. 568) indicates that, when Western culture shifted its focus from a religious to a secular one, "religious categories such as demonic possession, drunkenness, and sodomy were transformed into scientific categories of insanity, alcoholism, and homosexuality."

Freud's first writings on the subject were published in 1905, although some who theorized about homosexuality and its causes preceded him during the 19th century. Given the historical context in which Freud

DOI: 10.4324/9780429031397-7

practiced, he was generally supportive and affirming of homosexuality (Freud, 1951; Rothblum, 2000). He wrote,

> Homosexuality is assuredly no advantage, but it is nothing to be ashamed of, no vice, no degradation; it cannot be classified as an illness; we consider it to be a variation of the sexual function, produced by a certain arrest of sexual development.
>
> (Freud, 1951, p. 786)

Freud also concluded that attempts to change sexual orientation were likely to be unsuccessful (APA, 2009). Nevertheless, American psychiatry spent much of the 20th century seeking a cure for homosexuality (Bayer, 1987). In fact, Freud's successors persisted in characterizing it as a psychiatric illness that required professional intervention (Sullivan, 2003), while psycho-analytic theory was used to justify conversion and/or reparative therapies (Rothblum, 2000), despite Freud's belief in their ineffectiveness. He wrote, "In general, to undertake to convert a fully developed homosexual into a heterosexual does not offer much more prospect of success than the re-verse, except that for good practical reasons the latter is never attempted" (Freud, 1955/1920, p. 569). However, owing to the dominance of psycho-analysis until the mid-20th century, homosexuality continued to be deemed abnormal and, in many cases, caused by family dynamics (Bieber et al., 1962; Rado, 1940). As a result, substantial numbers of those who came out about their sexual orientation prior to the mid-1970s were often subjected to abusive treatments to change their orientation, including electric shock, induced vomiting, and other traumatic techniques (Krajeski, 1996).

It wasn't until the mid-20th century that there were prominent dis-senting opinions that homosexuality was a pathology (Gonsiorek, 1982; Hooker, 1957). Kinsey's study of human sexuality in the late 1930s found that homosexual behavior was common. His surveys consisted of people who were not psychiatric patients and found that gay men and lesbians made up a significant percentage (10%) of the population (Kenen, 1997; Sullivan, 2003). Further, Kinsey indicated that the percentage of bisexuals was greater than the percentage of persons who were exclusively hetero-sexual or homosexual (Green, Payne, & Green, 2011). In the 1950s, Dr. Evelyn Hooker conducted research that compared the psychological test results of gay and heterosexual men and found that those who were gay had no more indicators of psychological disturbance than did those who were heterosexual. Similar to Kinsey's work, Hooker's work consisted of men who were not psychiatric patients. Widely credited with helping to establish the concept that homosexuality is not a mental illness, Hooker's findings have since been replicated by other investigators using a variety of research methods (Herek, 2009). Despite the groundbreaking work that was done by Kinsey, Hooker, and others, the American Psychiatric Association continued to assert that homosexuality was pathological and classified it as "Sociopathic Personality Disturbance" in the first edition of the *Diagnostic and Statistical Manual of Mental Disorders* (DSM), published in 1952. It was reclassified in 1968 as "Sexual Deviation." In fact, prior to 1970, practically all clinical textbooks defined homosexuality in pathological terms (Hellman & Drescher, 2004).

The efforts of activists during the early days of the gay rights movement were a significant catalyst leading to the removal of homosexuality as a mental disorder from the American Psychiatric Association's DSM (D'Emilio,1983; Kameny, 2009; Drescher, 2015). Following the Stonewall Riots in 1969, LGBTQ+ activists who believed that psychiatric theories were contributing to sexual minority stigma (D'Emilio, 1983; Katz, 1995) disrupted American Psychiatric Association (APA) conventions held in 1970 and 1971. In 1972, gay activists Barbara Gettings and Frank Kameny addressed the APA membership, and John E. Fryer, disguised as Dr. H. Anonymous, illustrated the fear and danger to practitioners of losing their license if their homosexuality was revealed (Ring, 2015). Although a common belief is that homosexuality was removed from the DSM-II in 1973 (Kennedy, 1997; Lev, 2004; Sullivan, 2003; Uldall & Palmer, 2004), the diagnosis was actually replaced with "Ego-Dystonic Homosexuality" in the DSM-III (Lev, 2004) and was characterized by guilt, shame, anxiety, and depression about one's same-sex desires (Sullivan, 2003). Nevertheless, during the same year, the APA's Board of Trustees voted to remove homosexuality from the DSM, but a survey of 2,500 APA members revealed that a majority still considered it to be pathological (Rothblum, 2000). The recommendation to remove it from the DSM was only ratified by 58% of the APA membership (Kennedy, 1997; Drescher, 2015), and the writers of the APA's 1973 position statement emphasized that "by no longer listing it [homosexuality] as a psychiatric disorder, we are not saying that it is 'normal' or as valuable as heterosexuality."

Two years later, in 1975, the American Psychological Association's Council of Representatives adopted the following position:

> Homosexuality per se implies no impairment in judgment, stability, reliability, or general social and vocational capabilities. Further, the American Psychological Association urges all mental health

professionals to take the lead in removing the stigma of mental illness that has long been associated with homosexual orientations.

(Conger, 1975)

However, despite its "removal" in 1973 as a diagnostic category in the American Psychiatric Association's DSM, the stigma associated with homosexuality, as indicated by the APA, actually remained in the DSM for another 14 years. "Sexual Orientation Disturbance" (SOD) replaced "Sexual Deviation" in the DSM-II. SOD regarded homosexuality as an illness if an individual's sexual attractions were distressing to them and they wanted to change their orientation. This diagnostic category was replaced by "Ego Dystonic Homosexuality" in the DSM-III in 1980 and then finally removed from the DSM-III-R in 1987. Although this diagnostic category was not included in the DSM-IV, "Sexual Disorder Not Otherwise Specified" included criteria of persistent and marked distress about sexual orientation (APA, 2000a; Robles-García, Real, & Reed, 2021). The DSM-V and DSM-V-TR have completely removed any diagnostic category for sexual orientation, and so it is fully de-pathologized at this time (Robles-García et al., 2021).

The agreement to remove homosexuality from the DSM was, in essence, a political compromise between those who continued to believe that homosexuality was a pathology and those who saw it as a normal variant of sexuality (Drescher, 2015). However, the "official" stance that lesbians, gay men, and bisexual individuals were not mentally ill allowed for the development of gay and lesbian affirmative counseling at the same time as it bolstered the argument for gay civil rights (Lev, 2005).

Despite the removal of homosexuality from the DSM, the World Health Organization added "Ego Dystonic Sexual Orientation" to the International Classification of Diseases (ICD-10) in 1990 and did not remove it from the ICD-11 until 2019. Ego dystonic sexual orientation was used as a diagnosis when an individual's sexual orientation or attractions conflicted with their self-image and caused anxiety and/or the desire to change their orientation. Unfortunately, both ego dystonic sexual orientation and sexual orientation disturbance essentially paved the way for the practice of reparative therapy (and insurance reimbursement for it), despite the fact that there have been no studies showing that this form of therapy is efficacious. Numerous organizations, including the American Counseling Association, American Psychiatric Association, American Psychological Association, the American Association of Marriage and Family Therapists, American School Counselor Association, American Academy of Pediatrics, National Association of School Psychologists, and the National Association of Social Workers have since all taken the position that homosexuality is not a mental disorder, nor is it a problem that is in need of a cure (Just the Facts Coalition, 2008), and studies indicate that those who have a negative view of homosexuality adhere to outdated theories concluding that sexual orientation is a choice (Sullivan, 2003). Gay and bisexual people follow developmental pathways that are both similar to, and different from, those of heterosexuals (Just the Facts Coalition, 2008). However, LGBTQ+ people cope with prejudice, discrimination, and violence in society and, in some cases, within their own families, schools, and communities because of their sexual orientation and gender identity. According to Frankowski et al. (2004), the etiology of any human sexual orientation or gender identity is unknown, and no scientific evidence exists that indicates that poor parenting, sexual abuse, or other traumatic or adverse life events influence the development of a non-heterosexual orientation (Frankowski et al., 2004; Perrin, 2002). Rather, LGBTQ+ people live their lives within the context of homo/bi/transphobia or anti-LGBTQ bias, and this marginalization negatively affects the health and mental health of those who experience it. Research has found a correlation between LGBT+ status and a higher rate of mental health issues (Cochran, Sullivan, & Mays, 2003; Sandfort et al., 2006) across the life span. LGBTQ+ people experience higher rates of emotional distress, substance use, high-risk sexual behavior (Just the Facts Coalition, 2008), eating disorders, and body image and weight-related problems (Hall, Dawes, & Plocek, 2021). IPV can compound these health disparities because it can lead to increased substance use, HIV and other STI risk, and depression (Goldenberg et al., 2016), among other problems. Resulting manifestations of internalized anti-LGBTQ bias can include low self-esteem, self-hatred, guilt, anxiety, and suicidal ideation, as well as suicide attempts (Boysen et al., 2006; Connolly, 2004; DiPlacido, 1998; Logie, Bridge, & Bridge, 2007; Meyer, 2003; Otis et al., 2006). There is a strong correlation between same-sex attraction and suicidality in adults (de Graaf, Sandfort, & ten Have, 2006), and it has been determined that a greater risk of self-harming behaviors in young adults is comparable to their degree of same-sex attraction (Skegg et al., 2003).

Studies have indicated that LGBTQ+ persons access mental health services at a higher rate than do heterosexuals (Bieschke et al., 2000; Cochran & Mays, 2006; Cochran et al., 2003; Ritter & Terndrup, 2002; Twist et al., 2006). Up to 80% of gay men and lesbians seek counseling (Alexander, 1998; Hughes & Eliason, 2002; Sullivan, 2003; Twist et al., 2006), and the counseling usage rate is two to four times greater compared with heterosexuals (Twist et al., 2006). Lesbians appear to utilize therapy at a higher rate than gay men (Alexander, 1998; Hughes & Eliason, 2002), and usage rates for bisexuals have not been established (Bieschke et al., 2000) because bisexuals are usually classified with gay men and lesbians (Hughes & Eliason, 2002; Miller et al., 2007). Very few studies focus on the non-binary and trans-gender populations, and, in general, many that do exist look at transfeminine individuals who seek hormones and/or surgery (Hughes & Eliason, 2002) rather than mental health counseling.

The California Department of Mental Health (2010) identified the LGBTQ+ population as "unserved, underserved, or inappropriately served" in the mental health system. Mental health providers often receive inadequate education or training regarding the needs of LGBTQ+ individuals, if they receive any at all (Hunter, 2005; Long et al., 2006; Matthews, Lorah, & Fenton, 2006; Morrow, 2000; Ritter & Terndrup, 2002). Furthermore, most therapists are not aware of homo-negative and heterosexist bias inherent in personality theories, therapeutic approaches, and assessment and diagnostic techniques (Morrow, 2000), nor are they necessarily aware of their own biased views, influenced by societal heterosexism, homo/bi/transphobia, and anti-LGBTQ bias. This may, in fact, be particularly true with domestic violence clients and cases, given the dominance of heteronormative and gender-based theories and IPV practices.

Lack of sufficient education and training results in numerous risks to LGBTQ+ clients, including, but not limited to, the failure of therapists to assess the impact of internalized homo/bi/transphobia on clients (LaSala, 2006); misdiagnosing coming out behaviors as indicators of personality disorders (Ritter & Terndrup, 2002); assuming that sexual behavior defines sexual orientation and, thus, arbitrarily defining a client's sexual orientation for them rather than encouraging self-identification; displaying clinical behaviors that perpetuate internalized homo/bi/transphobia with LGBTQ+ clients (Crisp, 2006); pathologizing a client's sexual attractions or gender-variant behavior (Logie et al., 2007); and minimizing or overemphasizing a client's LGBTQ+ status (Berkman & Zinberg, 1997). Therapists who have not received thorough training in obsessive compulsive disorder (OCD) and its numerous variations and subtypes may inadvertently cause harm to clients who present with sexual orientation OCD (formerly homosexual OCD). This disorder occurs when a client has obsessive thoughts and fears that they are of a different sexual orientation (commonly someone who is heterosexual fears that they are homosexual) and believe they will act on this fear. The resulting anxiety has its origins in societal bias, and, in fact, older psychoanalytic therapies may increase the client's anxiety and obsessive thinking (Penzel, 2007) by indicating that the client's thoughts reflect their inner desires. Furthermore, instead of referring the client to a practitioner who specializes in the treatment of OCD, they may attempt to reassure the client about the fallacy of their thoughts, thereby escalating the client's unrealistic fears and level of anxiety unknowingly.

Heterosexism and homo-negative bias within mental health care are blatantly expressed by practitioners who advocate and practice reparative or conversion therapies (Crisp, 2006; Jenkins & Johnston, 2004; Mallon 2001), although there is no empirical research demonstrating that these therapies are effective in changing an individual's sexual orientation (Bieschke et al., 2000; Burack & Josephson, 2005). Condemned by numerous major professional organizations (Crisp, 2006), reparative therapy can cause shame, guilt, and the possibility of irreparable psychological and spiritual damage to LGBTQ+ clients (Jenkins & Johnston, 2004). Conversion/reparative therapy first emerged in the 1800s, and techniques included visits to sex workers, marriage, isolation with a person of the opposite gender, electroshock, lobotomies, and castration (Bieschke et al., 2000).

Despite research that indicates how damaging attempts to change sexual orientation can be to LGBTQ+ clients, as well as the denouncement of such practices by the American Psychological Association, the American Psychiatric Association, the American Association of Marriage and Family Therapists, and various other professional groups, a sizable percentage (12.4%) of pre-test respondents attending training on LGBTQ+ domestic violence in Los Angeles County and surveyed by the L.A. Gay & Lesbian Center's STOP Violence Program in 2005 believed that attempting to help a client change their sexual orientation could be productive. This percentage decreased to 3.5% following training. However, a disturbing 41.1% of respondents stated that they believed their personal biases were irrelevant to their work with LGBTQ+ clients, and an even more disturbing percentage of pre-test respondents (52.7%) claimed to have no bias. Following training, 28.1% stated that they believed their personal biases were irrelevant in their work, and 30.7% claimed to have no bias that would affect their work with LGBTQ+ clients (L.A. Gay & Lesbian Center, 2005).

Even when the actions of mental health practitioners with their LGBTQ+ clients are well-meaning, a number of problems, including lack of education and training, inadequate supervision, heterosexism, religious beliefs, or a combination of any of these, can cause harm to LGBTQ+ clients (Crisp, 2006; Green, 2000, 2004; Guthrie, 2006; Hunter & Hickerson, 2003; Morrow, 2000; Twist et al., 2006; Van Den Bergh & Crisp, 2004; Van Voorhis & Wagner, 2002). Furthermore, LGBTQ+ clients report mixed reviews of their mental health care (Cochran & Mays, 2006; Page, 2004; Ritter & Terndrup, 2002).

Although the sexual or gender minority status of a therapist does not guarantee that they will offer quality or effective mental health care to their LGBTQ+ clients, practitioners who identify as LGBTQ+ themselves tend to receive higher satisfaction scores from LGBTQ+ clients (Hunter & Hickerson, 2003) than do their non-LGBTQ+ counterparts. LGBTQ+ clients can potentially be further harmed by heterosexism within the mental health care system (Berkman & Zinberg, 1997; Crisp, 2006; Logie et al., 2007; Long et al., 2006; Morrow, 2000; Van Den Bergh & Crisp, 2004), and heterosexism in clinical practice can have negative effects on every aspect of practice, including referral, history-taking, assessment, and intervention (Hunter & Hickerson, 2003). Harm can occur in varying degrees, from clients receiving no help at all to their being irreparably damaged psychologically and spiritually (Jenkins & Johnston, 2004).

Institutional heterosexism is manifested in the failure or reluctance to develop LGBTQ+-affirmative programs within mental health agencies. Many clinic administrators and staff fail to recognize the specific needs of LGBTQ+ clients, believing that their needs can be met by existing agency services that focus on, and have been developed for, heterosexual clients (Hunter, 2005; Hunter & Hickerson 2003; Van Voorhis & Wagner, 2002). Alexander (1998) recommends that therapists disclose to their LGBTQ+ clients their professional experience working with other LGBTQ+ clients, even if clients do not ask about it. Because victimization is so pervasive in the lives of LGBTQ+ clients, Alexander argues that LGBTQ+ clients require assurance from therapists that they will not harm or subject them to harm, ridicule them, or violate their personal boundaries.

While all LGBTQ+ individuals are exposed to heterosexism, anti-LGBTQ bias, and prejudice, a majority do not experience major mental health problems (Cochran & Mays, 2006; DiPlacido, 1998; Hall et al., 2021). Despite unfair treatment in society, researchers have found that many LGBTQ+ people are satisfied with their sexual orientation and intimate relationships (Isay, 1989; Miranda & Storms, 1989; Peplau, 1991), and many have actively engaged in the LGBTQ+ civil rights movement dedicated to educating the larger society and changing unfair legal and employment practices. When correlated with positive identity development, LGBTQ+ individuals often display well-being, adaptive social functioning, self-awareness, personal insight, commitment to social justice, and a connection with the LGBTQ+ community, among others (Hall et al., 2021). Further, the LGBTQ+ community offers support in the forms of crisis hotlines, churches, social groups, community centers, and bookstores (Arey, 1995; Butke, 1995), which can increase LGBTQ+ community satisfaction. Social support can mitigate the psychological stress of stigmatization (D'Augelli et al., 2001; Green, 2000), and LGBTQ+ communities may also mirror a positive reflection to the individual, allowing them to compare themselves with peer group members rather than with members of the heterosexist majority (Meyer, 2003). However, LGBTQ+ individuals with otherwise excellent coping skills may be vulnerable when deprived of group support (Meyer, 2003). Psychological adjustment appears to be highest among those who do not attempt to hide their orientation from others (Bell & Weinberg, 1978; Hammersmith & Weinberg, 1973). Further, LGBTQ+ individuals maintain self-esteem most effectively when they identify with and are integrated into the larger LGBTQ+ community (Crocker & Major, 1989). Conversely, those who do not come out, suppress their homoerotic urges, wish they were heterosexual, or are isolated from the LGBTQ+ community may experience significant psychological distress, including impairment in self-esteem (Hodges & Hutter, 1979; Hammersmith & Weinberg, 1973; Malyon, 1982; Bell & Weinberg, 1978; Weinberg & Williams, 1974). This may be especially true for LGBTQ+ IPV survivors who are consistently subjected to isolation as a control tactic, which is typically inherent in domestic violence situations.

In 2000, the American Psychological Association developed and published "Guidelines for Psychotherapy with Lesbian, Gay & Bisexual Clients," which is (1) a frame of reference for affirmative psychological practice and (2) knowledge and referenced scholarship in areas of affirmative practice (APA, 2000b). In 2009, the American Psychological Association's Task Force on Appropriate Therapeutic Responses to Sexual Orientation published its report containing information about the importance of LGBTQ+-affirmative psychotherapy. The Task Force indicated that the multiculturally competent and affirmative approach that it recommended was grounded in an acceptance of five scientific facts, which are discussed in this publication. In 2012, the APA guidelines originally published in 2000 were revised and entitled, "Revised Guidelines for Psychological Practice with Lesbian, Gay and Bisexual Clients," and then, most recently, published as "APA Guidelines for Psychological Practice with Sexual Minority Persons" in 2021 (American Psychological Association, APA Task Force on Psychological Practice with Sexual Minority Persons, 2021). These important guidelines can be found online or by contacting the American Psychological Association in Washington, DC. It is crucial that practitioners not only develop a solid understanding of these concepts and consistently approach their work with members of the LGBTQ+ population within an affirming framework but also recognize that failure to do so with those who are experiencing domestic violence may, at the very least, impede progress and, at worst, cause abuse and violence to escalate.

Continuing Education Questions

1. Which edition of the *Diagnostic and Statistical Manual* (DSM) contained the diagnosis "Ego-Dystonic Homosexuality?"
   a. DSM-II
   b. DSM-III
   c. DSM-IV
   d. DSM-V

2. Research has shown that gay men and lesbians access psychotherapy at higher rates than heterosexuals.
   a. True
   b. False

3. Psychological resilience factors for LGBTQ people include all of the following *except*
   a. Having social support
   b. Embracing and being open about sexual orientation or gender identity
   c. Supressing homoerotic urges
   d. Being integrated and active in the larger LGBTQ community

4. So-called "conversion therapy" is supported by many professional organizations, including the American Psychological Association.
   a. True
   b. False

5. Which one of these is *not* a scientific fact embraced by the American Psychological Association Task Force on Appropriate Therapeutic Responses to Sexual Orientation?
   a. Same-sex attractions, behavior, and orientations per se are normal and positive variants of human sexuality and do not indicate either mental or developmental disorders.
   b. Gay men and lesbians form insecure attachments, and their relationships are not equivalent to heterosexual relationships.
   c. Homosexuality and bisexuality are stigmatized, and this stigma can have a variety of negative consequences throughout the life span.
   d. Some individuals choose to live their lives in accordance with personal or religious values.

References

Alexander, C.J. (1998). Treatment Planning for Gay and Lesbian Clients. *Journal of Gay & Lesbian Social Services, 8*(4), 95–106.

American Psychiatric Association (APA). (2000a). *Diagnostic and Statistical Manual of Mental Disorders* (4th ed., text revision). Washington, DC: American Psychiatric Association.

American Psychological Association. (2000b). Guidelines for Psychotherapy with Lesbian, Gay, and Bisexual Clients. *American Psychologist, 55*(12), 1440–1451.

American Psychological Association, APA Task Force on Psychological Practice with Sexual Minority Persons. (2021). Guidelines for Psychological Practice with Sexual Minority Persons. Retrieved from www.apa.org/about/policy/psychological-practice-sexual-minority-persons.pdf

Arey, D. (1995). Gay Males and Sexual Child Abuse. In L. Fontes (Ed.), *Sexual Abuse in Nine North American Cultures: Treatment and Prevention* (pp. 200–235). Thousand Oaks, CA: Sage.

Bayer, R. (1987). *Homosexuality and American Psychiatry: The Politics of Diagnosis* (2nd ed.). Princeton, NJ: Princeton University Press.

Bell, A.P., & Weinberg, M.S. (1978). *Homosexualities: A Study of Diversity among Men and Women.* New York: Simon & Schuster.

Berkman, C.S., & Zinberg, G. (1997). Homophobia and Heterosexism in Social Workers. *Social Work, 42*(4), 319–332.

Bieber, I., Dain, H.J., Dince, P.R., Drellich, M.G., Grand, H.G., Gundlack, R.H., et al. (1962). *Homosexuality: A Psychoanalytic Study.* New York: Basic Books.

Bieschke, K.J., McClanahan, M., Tozer, E., Grzegorek, J.L., & Park, J. (2000). Programmatic Research on the Treatment of Lesbian, Gay, and Bisexual Clients: The Past, the Present, and the Course for the Future. In R.M. Perez, K.A. DeBord, & K.J. Bieschke (Eds.), *Handbook of Counseling and Psychotherapy with Lesbian, Gay, and Bisexual Clients* (pp. 309–335). Washington, DC: American Psychological Association.

Boysen, G., Vogel, D., Madon, S., & Wester, S.R. (2006). Mental Health Stereotypes about Gay Men. *Sex Roles, 54*(1/2), 69–82.

Burack, C., & Josephson, J.J. (2005). A Report from "Love Won Out: Addressing, Understanding, and Preventing Homosexuality." Retrieved June 18, 2007, from thetaskforce.org/downloads/reports/reports/LoveWonOut.pdf

Butke, M. (1995). Lesbians and Sexual Child Abuse. In L. Fontes (Ed.), *Sexual Abuse in Nine North American Cultures: Treatment and Prevention* (pp. 236–258). Thousand Oaks, CA: Sage.

California Department of Mental Health. (2010). California Reducing Disparities Project [fact sheet]. Retrieved December, 28, 2011, from dmh.ca.gov/Multicultural_Services/CRDP.asp#CRDPDownloads

Cochran, S.D., & Mays, V.M. (2006). Estimating Prevalence of Mental and Substance-Using Disorders among Lesbians and Gay Men from Existing National Health Data. In A.M. Omoto & H.S. Kurtzman (Eds.), *Sexual Orientation and Mental Health* (pp. 143–165). Washington, DC: American Psychological Association.

Cochran, S.D., Sullivan, J.G., & Mays, V.M. (2003). Prevalence of Mental Disorders, Psychological Distress, and Mental Health Services Use among Lesbian, Gay, and Bisexual Adults in the United States. *Journal of Counseling and Clinical Psychology, 71*(1), 53–61.

Conger, J.J. (1975). Proceedings of the American Psychological Association, Incorporated, for the Year 1974: Minutes of the Annual Meeting of the Council of Representatives. *American Psychologist, 30*, 620–651. doi:10.1037/h0078455

Connolly, C.M. (2004). Clinical Issues with Same-Sex Couples: A Review of the Literature. In J.J. Bigner & J.L. Wetchler (Eds.), *Relationship Therapy with Same-Sex Couples* (pp. 3–12). New York, NY: Haworth Press.

Crisp, C. (2006). The Gay Affirmative Practice Scale (GAP): A New Measure for Assessing Cultural Competence and Gay and Lesbian Clients. *Social Work, 51*(2), 115–126.

Crocker, J., & Major, B. (1989). Social Stigma and Self-Esteem: The Self-Protective Properties of Stigma. *Psychological Review, 96*, 608–630.

D'Augelli, A.R., Grossman, A.H., Herschberger, S.L., & O'Connell, T.S. (2001). Aspects of Mental Health among Older Lesbian, Gay, and Bisexual Adults. *Aging & Mental Health, 5*(2), 149–158.

De Graaf, R., Sandfort, T.G.M., & ten Have, M. (2006). Suicidality and Sexual Orientation: Differences between Men and Women in a General Population-Based Sample from the Netherlands. *Archives of Sexual Behavior, 35*(3), 253–262. 10.1007/s1 0508-006-9020-z

D'Emilio, J. (1983). *Sexual Politics, Sexual Communities: The Making of a Homosexual Minority in the United States 1940–1970*. Chicago, IL: University of Chicago Press.

DiPlacido, J. (1998). Minority Stress among Lesbians, Gay Men, and Bisexuals: A Consequence of Heterosexism, Homophobia, and Stigmatization. In G.M. Herek (Ed.), *Psychological Perspectives on Lesbian and Gay Issues: Volume 4: Stigma and Sexual Orientation: Understanding Prejudice against Lesbians, Gay Men, and Bisexuals* (pp. 138–159). Thousand Oaks, CA: Sage.

Drescher, J. (2015). Out of DSM: Depathologizing Homosexuality. National Library of Medicine, PubMed Central, www.ncbi.nlm.nih.gov/pmc/articles/DMC4695779/

Frankowski, B.L., Kaplan, D.W., Diaz, A., Feinstein, R.A., Fisher, M.M., & Klein, J.D. (2004). Sexual Orientation and Adolescents. *Pediatrics, 113*(6), 1827–1832.

Freud, S. (1951). Letter to an American Mother. *The American Journal of Psychiatry, 1*(07), 786–787.

Freud, S. (1955 [1920]). *The Psychogenesis of a Case of Homosexuality in a Woman* (pp. 145–172). London, UK: Hogarth Press. Standard Edition Volume 18.

Goldenberg, T., Stephenson, R., Freeland, R., Finneran, C., & Hadley, C. (2016). "Struggling to Be the Alpha": Sources of Tension and Intimate Partner Violence in Same-Sex Relationships between Men. *Culture, Health & Sexuality, 18*(8), 875–889. doi.org/10.1080/13691058.2016.1144791

Gonsiorek, J.C. (1982). Results of Psychological Testing on Homosexual Populations. *American Behavioral Scientist, 25*, 385–396.

Green, H.B., Payne, N.R., & Green, J. (2011). Working Bi: Preliminary Findings from a Survey on Workplace Experiences of Bisexual People. *Journal of Bisexuality, 1*(11), 300–316.

Green, R.J. (2000). Lesbians, Gay Men, and Their Parents: A Critique of LaSala and the Prevailing Clinical Wisdom. *Family Process, 39*(2), 257–266.

Green, R.J. (2004). Foreword. In J.J. Bigner & J.L. Wetchler (Eds.), *Relationship Therapy with Same-Sex Couples* (pp. xiii–xvii). New York, NY: Haworth Press.

Guthrie, C. (2006). Disclosing the Therapist's Sexual Orientation: The Meaning of Disclosure in Working with Gay, Lesbian, and Bisexual Patients. *Journal of Gay & Lesbian Psychotherapy, 10*(1), 63–77.

Hall, W.J., Dawes, H.C., & Plocek, N. (2021). Sexual Orientation Identity Development Milestones among Lesbian, Gay, Bisexual and Queer People: A Systematic Review and Meta-Analysis. *Frontiers in Psychology, Sec. Gender, Sex and Sexualities, 12,* doi.org/10.3389/fpsyg.2021.753954

Hammersmith, S.K., & Weinberg, M.S. (1973). Homosexual Identity: Commitment, Adjustment, and Significant Others. *Sociometry, 36*(1), 56–79.

Hellman, R.E., & Drescher, J. (2004). Coming Out in the Public Sector: Introduction. In R.E. Hellmen & J. Drescher (Eds.), *Handbook of LGBTQ Issues in Community Mental Health* (p. 19). New York, NY: Haworth Medical Press.

Herek, G.M. (2009). Sexual Stigma and Sexual Prejudice in the United States: A Conceptual Framework. In D. Hope (Ed.), *Nebraska Symposium on Motivation: Contemporary Perspectives on Lesbian, Gay, and Bisexual Identities* (pp. 65–111). New York, NY: Springer.

Hodges, A., & Hutter, D. (1979). *With Downcast Gays: Aspects of Homosexual Self-Oppression* (2nd ed.). Toronto: Pink Triangle.

Hooker, E. (1957). The Adjustment of the Male Overt Homosexual. *Journal of Projective Techniques, 21,* 18–31.

Hughes, T.L., & Eliason, M. (2002). Substance Use and Abuse in Lesbian, Gay, Bisexual and Transgender Populations. *Journal of Primary Prevention, 22*(3), 263–298.

Hunter, S. (2005). *Midlife and Older LGBTQ Adults: Knowledge and Affirmative Practice for the Social Services.* New York, NY: Haworth Press.

Hunter, S., & Hickerson, J.C. (2003). *Affirmative Practice: Understanding and Working with Lesbian, Gay, Bisexual, and Transgender Persons.* Washington, DC: NASW Press.

Isay, R.A. (1989). *Being Homosexual: Gay Men and Their Development.* New York, NY: Avon.

Jenkins, D., & Johnston, L.B. (2004). Unethical Treatment of Gay and Lesbian People with Conversion Therapy. *Families in Society: The Journal of Contemporary Social Services, 85*(4), 557–561.

Just the Facts Coalition. (2008). *Just the Facts about Sexual Orientation and Youth: A Primer for Principals, Educators, and School Personnel.* Washington, DC: American Psychological Association. Retrieved May 20, 2009, from www.apa.org/pi/lgbc/publications/justthefacts.html

Kameny, F. (2009). How It All Started. *Journal of Gay and Lesbian Mental Health, 13,* 76–81.

Katz, J. (1995). *Gay American History: Lesbians and Gay Men in the United States.* New York, NY: Thomas Crowell.

Kenen, S.H. (1997). Who Counts when You're Counting Homosexuals? Hormones and Homosexuality in Mid-Twentieth-Century America. In V.A. Rosario (Ed.), *Science and Homosexualities* (pp. 197–218). New York: Routledge.

Kennedy, H. (1997). Karl Heinrich Ulrichs: First Theorist of Homosexuality. In V.A. Rosario (Ed.), *Science and Homosexualities* (pp. 26–45). New York: Routledge.

Krajeski, J. (1996). Homosexuality and the Mental Health Professions: A Contemporary History. In R. Cabaj & T. Stein (Eds.), *Textbook of Homosexuality and Mental Health* (pp. 17–31). Washington, DC: American Psychiatric Press.

L.A. Gay & Lesbian Center. (2005). *Years 2000–2005: Final Department of Health Services Report*. Los Angeles, CA: STOP Domestic Violence/LAGLC.

LaSala, M.C. (2006). Cognitive and Environmental Interventions for Gay Males: Addressing Stigma and Its Consequences. *Families in Society, 87*(2), 181–189.

Lev, A.I. (2004). *Transgender Emergence: Therapeutic Guidelines for Working with Gender-Variant People and Their Families*. New York, NY: Haworth Clinical Practice Press.

Logie, C., Bridge, T.J., & Bridge, P.D. (2007). Evaluating the Phobias, Attitudes, and Cultural Competence of Master of Social Work Students toward the LGBTQ Populations. *Journal of Homosexuality, 53*(4), 201–221.

Long, J.K., Bonomo, J., Andrews, B.V., & Brown, J.M. (2006). Systemic Therapeutic Approaches with Sexual Minorities and Their Families. In J.J. Bigner & A.R. Gottlieb (Eds.), *Interventions with Families of Gay, Lesbian, Bisexual, and Transgender People: From the Inside Out* (pp. 7–37). New York, NY: Harrington Park Press.

Mallon, G.P. (2001). *Lesbian and Gay Youth Issues: A Practical Guide for Youth Workers*. Washington, DC: CWLA Press.

Malyon, A.K. (1982). Psychotherapeutic Implications of Internalized Homophobia in Gay Men. In J.C. Gonsiorek (Ed.), *Homosexuality and Psychotherapy: A Practitioner's Handbook of Affirmative Models* (pp. 59–69). Binghamton, NY: Haworth Press.

Matthews, C.R., Lorah, P., & Fenton, J. (2006). Treatment Experiences of Gays and Lesbians in Recovery from Addiction: A Qualitative Inquiry. *Journal of Mental Health Counseling, 28*(2), 111–132.

Meyer, I.H. (2003). Prejudice, Social Stress, and Mental Health in Lesbian, Gay, and Bisexual Populations: Conceptual Issues and Research Evidence. *Psychological Bulletin, 129*(5), 674–697.

Miller, M., Andre, A., Ebin, J., & Bessonova, L. (2007). *Bisexual Health: An Introduction and Model Practices for HIV/STI Prevention Programming*. New York, NY: National Gay and Lesbian Task Force Policy Institute, Fenway Institute at Fenway Community Health, and BiNet USA. Retrieved May 28, 2008, from thetaskforce.org/downloads/reports/reports/

Miranda, J., & Storms, M. (1989). Psychological Adjustment of Lesbians and Gay Men. *Journal of Counseling and Development, 68*, 41–45.

Morrow, S.L. (2000). First Do No Harm: Therapist Issues in Psychotherapy with Lesbian, Gay, and Bisexual Clients. In R. Perez, K. DeBord, & Bieschke, K. (Eds.), *Handbook of Counseling and Psychotherapy with Lesbian, Gay, and Bisexual Clients* (pp. 137–156). Washington, DC: American Psychological Association.

Otis, M.D., Rostosky, S.S., Riggle, E.D.B., & Hamrin, R. (2006). Stress and Relationship Quality in Same-Sex Couples. *Journal of Social and Personal Relationships, 23*(1), 81–99.

Page, E.H. (2004). Mental Health Services Experiences of Bisexual Women and Bisexual Men: An Empirical Study. In R.C. Fox (Ed.), *Current Research on Bisexuality* (pp. 137–160). New York, NY: Harrington Park Press.

Penzel, F. (2007). How Do I Know I'm Not Really Gay/Straight? *OCD Newsletter*, Winter. International OCD Foundation, iocdf.org/expert-opinions/sexual-orientation-obsessions

Peplau, L.A. (1991). Lesbian and Gay Relationships. In J. Gonsiorek & J. Enrich (Eds.), *Homosexuality: Implications for Public Policy* (pp. 177–196). Newbury Park, CA: Sage.

Perrin, E.C. (2002). *Sexual Orientation in Child and Adolescent Health Care*. New York, NY: Springer.

Rado, S. (1940). A Critical Examination of the Concept of Bisexuality. *Psychosomatic Medicine, 2,* 459–467.

Ring, T. (August 19, 2015). The Advocate. Storming the Stage: A History of Disruptions to Advance Our Rights. *The Advocate.* advocate.com/politics/2015/08/19/storming-stage-history-disruptions-advance-our-rights

Ritter, K., & Terndrup, A. (2002). *Handbook of Affirmative Psychotherapy with Lesbians and Gay Men.* New York, NY: Guilford Press.

Robles-García, R., Real, T., & Reed, G. M. (2021). Depathologizing Sexual Orientation and Transgender Identities in Psychiatric Classifications. *Consortium Psychiatricum, 2*(2), 45–53. 10.17816/cp61

Rothblum, E.D. (2000). Somewhere in Des Moines or San Antonio: Historical Perspectives on Lesbian, Gay, and Bisexual Mental Health. In R.M. Perez, K.A. DeBord, & K.J. Bieschke (Eds.), *Handbook of Counseling and Psychotherapy with Lesbian, Gay, and Bisexual Clients* (pp. 57–79). Washington, DC: American Psychological Association.

Sandfort, T.G.M., Bakker, F., Schellevis, F.G., & Vanwesenbeeck, I. (2006). Sexual Orientation and Mental and Physical Health Status: Findings from a Dutch Population Survey. *American Journal of Public Health, 96*(6), 1119–1125.

Skegg, K., Nada-Raja, S., Dickson, N., Paul, C., & Williams, S. (2003). Sexual Orientation and Self-Harm in Men and Women. *American Journal of Psychiatry, 160*(3), 541–546.

Sullivan, M.K. (2003). Homophobia, History, and Homosexuality: Trends for Sexual Minorities. In M.K. Sullivan (Ed.), *Sexual Minorities: Discrimination, Challenges, and Development in America* (pp. 1–13). New York, NY: Routledge.

Twist, M., Murphy, M.J., Green, M.S., & Palmanteer, D. (2006). Therapists' Support of Gay and Lesbian *Human Rights. Guidance and Counseling, 21*(2), 107–113.

Uldall, K.K., & Palmer, N.B. (2004). Sexual Minorities and Mental Health: The Need for a Public Health Response. In R.E. Hellman & J. Drescher (Eds.), *Handbook of LGBTQ Issues in Community Mental Health* (pp. 11–24). New York, NY: Haworth Medical Press.

Van Den Bergh, N., & Crisp, C. (2004). Defining Culturally Competent Practice with Sexual Minorities: Implications for Social Work Education and Practice. *Journal of Social Work Education, 40*(2), 221–238.

Van Voorhis, R., & Wagner, M. (2002). Among the Missing: Content on Lesbian and Gay People in Social Work Journals. *Social Work, 47*(4), 345–354.

Weinberg, M.S., & Williams, C.J. (1974). *Male Homosexuals: Their Problems and Adaptations.* New York, NY: Oxford University Press.

LGBTQ+ Domestic/Intimate Partner Violence

8

In this chapter, we will discuss how intimate partner violence applies in general to the collective LGBTQ+ communities. The concepts described herein are crucial to a more specific understanding of LGBTQ+ intimate partner violence—the LGBTQ+ population individually as well as the collective whole—and apply broadly to each LGBTQ+ subpopulation.

As mentioned previously, intimate partner violence occurs when one person in an intimate relationship attempts to gain and/or maintain power and control over an intimate partner by using coercive, abusive, and/or violent tactics and behaviors which can be physical, sexual, psychological, emotional, verbal, and/or financial in nature (NCAVP, 2011, 2012; Peterman & Dixon, 2003; CDC 2006). While LGBTQ+ domestic violence shares some similarities with intimate partner violence in the heterosexual or non-LGBTQ+ community, there are numerous and complex differences that complicate intervention with, and the safety and well-being of, LGBTQ+ individuals (NCAVP, 2009; NRCDV, 2007; Peterman & Dixon, 2003).

Unlike heterosexual battering, LGBTQ+ intimate partner abuse always occurs within the context of societal anti-LGBTQ+ bias, including homo/bi/transphobia—all very powerful and effective weapons of control (Holt, 2002). Just as battered (heterosexual) women experience domestic violence within the context of misogyny and sexism, LGBTQ+ persons experience it within the context of anti-LGBTQ bias and, often, other pertinent factors as well (e.g. racism, sexism, classism, etc.). Context impacts the LGBTQ+ person's experience of domestic violence and how that person copes with it, as well as their ability to access effective assistance. The effectiveness of

DOI: 10.4324/9780429031397-8

assistance received, or lack thereof, generally determines the duration and severity of violence that is experienced.

Members of LGBTQ+ communities live in an environment that renders them vulnerable to covert and overt discrimination and violence. One can ultimately, and with assistance, escape a violent relationship, but it is impossible to escape societal and cultural anti-LGBTQ bias that tends to maintain relative consistency over time. This bias, which is also referred to as institutionalized anti-LGBTQ bias, can be found in all societal institutions with which the LGBTQ+ person comes into contact, including law enforcement agencies and personnel, social welfare organizations, legal assistance providers, as well as the larger legal system, mental health providers, domestic violence organizations, and so on; it frequently exacerbates the situation and provides the abuser with unique and highly effective tactics, including, but not limited to, threats to out the victim, child custody problems, and so on (NRCDV, 2007). It results in what can often be insurmountable obstacles for LGBTQ+ individuals and families throughout the help-seeking and healing process, leaving them isolated and vulnerable to increased levels of violence, injury, and/or death.

When assessing and intervening with individuals who are experiencing IPV, the interface of heterosexism, negative attitudes towards homosexuality and LGBTQ+ people, and prejudice and discrimination based on sexual orientation and/or gender identity must be considered at all levels, from causation through treatment and service provision (APA, 2000). Furthermore, these issues and the overall context are even more complex for LGBTQ+ people of color. Without an understanding of these inherent and complicated differences, intervention is potentially damaging, oftentimes dangerous, and can be lethal.

LGBTQ+ domestic violence shares some similarities with non-LGBTQ intimate partner violence. For example, both LGBTQ+ intimate partner violence and non-LGBTQ domestic violence are fueled by the primary aggressor's desire to achieve and maintain power and control over their intimate partner; both share types of abusive behaviors that are similar in nature (e.g. physical, sexual, emotional, psychological, financial, and environmental); both typically occur in a cycle; many primary aggressors, regardless of sexual orientation or gender identity, were themselves abused as children; in both, violence commonly begins as psychological or emotional abuse and often escalates to physical and/or sexual violence; in both, no race, ethnicity, or socioeconomic status is exempt from violence; and both can be lethal (Center for American Progress, 2011; Whirry & Holt, 2020).

The unique challenges faced by LGBTQ+ individuals, however, create dynamics that are not shared with non-LGBTQ populations. For example, the coming out status of one or both partners can create additional barriers for assistance. For example, it might limit the ability of one or both individuals to seek help as it could reveal their sexual orientation or gender identity. In addition, if one partner is out and the other is not out, this can create a power imbalance in which the "out" partner has a larger support system, and the "in" partner would be unable to seek help from social support (Goldenberg et al., 2016). In fact, outing is such a unique and powerful control tactic that it is often sufficient, in the absence of all other control tactics, to allow the abuser to maintain control of their intimate partner.

Other differences that must be considered include the following:

- LGBTQ+ domestic violence is not believed to be primarily caused by or experienced within the patriarchal structure of society, and IPV in the LGBTQ+ community itself threatens this long-standing popular conceptualization of intimate partner violence.
- The dynamics of LGBTQ+ domestic violence are not primarily based on the gender of the partners.
- The "butch" partner (the partner who is stronger, larger, more masculine) may be as likely to be the victim whereas, in heterosexual relationships, the male partner is usually the aggressor.
- LGBTQ+ primary aggressors have oftentimes been victims of abuse in childhood, frequently having experienced general childhood abuse as well as abuse specific to and because of their sexual orientation or gender identity.
- Significant components of LGBTQ+ domestic violence include internalized as well as institutionalized homo/bi/transphobia.
- The LGBTQ+ cycle of violence is significantly different than the traditional cycle of violence when internalized and institutionalized homo/bi/transphobia are factored into it.
- LGBTQ+ domestic violence is generally invisible and/or rarely acknowledged in either the broad mainstream culture or the LGBTQ+ community.
- Gay and bisexual male victims have a heightened chance of concurrent HIV/AIDS and/or contracting it because of IPV.
- The trauma bond (e.g. "it's me and you against the world") is reinforced by anti-LGBTQ bias in society.
- There is a dearth of research that has studied LGBTQ+ intimate partner violence, and the majority of it looks at prevalence rather than other pertinent factors.

- The help-seeking process is often different because LGBTQ+ individuals tend to consider obtaining assistance primarily from counselors and therapists rather than law enforcement and criminal justice resources, mainstream domestic violence organizations and shelters, and/or clergy.
- LGBTQ+ victims are oftentimes more reluctant to report abuse to authorities, fearing abuse by law enforcement personnel based on sexual orientation and the long history of conflict between police and the community.
- LGBTQ+ people in general are oftentimes less likely to address domestic violence owing to fear of increased bias against the LGBTQ+ community.
- Safety planning can be more challenging owing to the closed and/or insular nature of the LGBTQ+ community.
- Child custody issues are frequently more complicated within LGBTQ+ partnerships.
- The LGBTQ+ community encompasses every culture, race, ethnicity, and so on, thereby heightening the intersectional nature of LGBTQ+ intimate partner violence.
- LGBTQ+ victims are more likely to fight back in self-defense or retaliation than are heterosexual women, thereby increasing the myth of mutual abuse.
- And domestic violence services and resources designed for the LGBTQ+ community are comparatively rare or non-existent (Center for American Progress, 2011; Holt, 2011–2023).

Traditional views of gender roles, heterosexism, negative attitudes towards homosexuality, and prejudice and discrimination based on sexual orientation contribute to the uniqueness of LGBTQ+ intimate partner violence (APA, 1999). Although, in the non-LGBTQ community, it is believed that females are more likely to be victimized by their partners than are men, this is not consistent in the LGBTQ+ community, and surveys indicate that gay men and lesbians, for example, are abused by their partners in relatively equal numbers (NCAVP, 2012). Furthermore, research indicates that LGBTQ+ people are more apt than heterosexuals to fight back in self-defense (Center for American Progress, 2011; Lie et al., 1991; Marrujo & Kreger, 1995) owing to a variety of factors including their perception of equality in terms of size and strength, the lack of LGBTQ+-specific domestic/dating violence services and resources, and problems resulting from internalized homo/bi/transphobia and anti-LGBTQ bias.

Koop (1987) indicated that domestic violence is sufficiently widespread in both heterosexual and LGBTQ+ populations to constitute a public health problem, but few studies, and only a handful of books, have focused specifically on violence within the population, compared with the hundreds of studies, books, and articles that have examined heterosexual domestic violence (NCAVP, 2011, 2012). Although more than a decade has since passed, the field is still lacking sufficient information about the problem. LGBTQ+ intimate partner violence is often not recognized as such because domestic violence has generally been defined and discussed within a heterosexual context and is commonly portrayed as a problem of male violence against women (Lobel, 1986). Many people—non-LGBTQ and LGBTQ+ alike—are apt to minimize the abuse or fail to define it properly. In addition, if the abusive relationship is the first relationship that an individual has had with an LGBTQ+ partner, they may not know what to expect and erroneously see the relationship itself, or the sexual orientation of the partners, as the problem rather than the abuse itself.

Furthermore, anti-LGBTQ bias and societal ignorance about LGBTQ+ persons/issues fuel the numerous misconceptions that exist about intimate partner violence (e.g. men aren't victims, women don't batter, LGBTQ+ domestic violence is mutual, etc.). These misconceptions are underscored by predominant domestic violence theories that are generally dependent on traditional gender-based analyses which tend to exclude the possibility of LGBTQ+ battering. Subsequently, LGBTQ+ domestic violence is frequently invisible, minimized, or not likely to be identified (Friess, 1997; Island & Letellier, 1991; NRCDV, 2007).

In fact, results from a survey conducted by the L.A. Gay & Lesbian Center's STOP Violence Program in 2005 indicated that, while 71% of the respondents knew someone who had experienced LGBTQ+ domestic violence, only 30% thought that the violence was a significant problem. Furthermore, research indicates that the effects of partner violence within ethnic minorities and the LGBTQ+ population is compounded by the fact that these populations often experience a desire to keep their victimization hidden. Some argue that, within minority LGBTQ+ communities, there may be even less acceptance of LGBTQ + orientations than in the broader, non-minority LGBTQ+ community, so that victims may be more reluctant to report their abuse (Barnett, Lee, & Thelen, 1997; Russo, 1999; Sanchez-Hucles & Dutton, 1999; Wiehe, 1998). However, even when LGBTQ+ individuals report their victimization, they often do not receive the legal protections and social services that are afforded their non-LGBTQ+ counterparts (Koss, Ingram, & Pepper, 2000; Leventhal & Lundy, 1999). For example, there are no LGBTQ+-specific domestic violence shelters and less than a handful of LGBTQ+-specific court-approved batterers intervention programs in the United States.

In addition, many LGBTQ+ people fear that acknowledgment of intimate partner violence will further prejudice and misunderstanding of the community itself (NRCDV, 2007; L.A. Gay and Lesbian Center, 2009). In 2008 for example, with the passage of Proposition 8, a ballot referendum that eliminated the previously approved right of same-sex marriage in the state of California, a new barrier to help-seeking and reporting of LGBTQ+ domestic violence was established. When LGBTQ+ people must fight to prove the validity of their relationships, many are not apt to acknowledge the problem itself because it is feared that negative representations of these unions might influence the public and increase anti-LGBTQ bias and discrimination against the LGBTQ+ community, while decreasing chances of winning back the right that was taken away. The subsequent legalization of marriage equality nationwide in 2015 has mitigated this effect, but cultural opposition, particularly among certain populations and in certain areas, still remains (Ofosu et al., 2019).

The causes of LGBTQ+ intimate partner violence include the effects of societal, racial, ethnic, cultural, gender identity, and sexual orientation factors (Harway & O'Neil, 1999; Island & Letellier, 1991; Sanchez-Hucles & Dutton, 1999). Arguably, the most prominent theory for explaining domestic violence is feminist theory, which suggests that partner violence is gender-based (Koss et al., 1994; Bograd, 1988) and caused by the patriarchal structure of our society. This theory is partially responsible for the invisibility of intimate partner violence in the LGBTQ+ population. It also falls short in explaining the cause(s) of LGBTQ+ domestic violence. Our culture, in general, does not dispute that LGBTQ+ people struggle with the same psychiatric disorders, medical conditions, and/or substance use problems as do heterosexuals but rarely considers LGBTQ+ IPV when addressing them. In the LGBTQ+ community specifically, IPV is apt to share the stage, but not the spotlight, with a variety of other important and highly prevalent concerns such as HIV/AIDS and substance abuse. Island and Letellier (1991) argue that domestic violence is not a gender issue. Others have suggested that LGBTQ+ battering has three primary components that lead to it, including learning to abuse, having the opportunity to abuse, and choosing to abuse (Merrill, 1996). Byrne (1996) suggests that sexual orientation, and feelings about it, may contribute to LGBTQ+ domestic violence. Others argue that any analysis of partner violence must consider how personal and institutional oppression (racism, classism, ethnocentrism, homo/bi/transphobia, and heterosexism) contribute to the predisposition to, and the actual triggering of, domestic violence (Kanuha, 1990; O'Neil & Harway, 1999; Waldron, 1996).

Statistics on historically marginalized communities, as well as highly stigmatized forms of violence such as intimate partner violence or violence that relates to personal identity such as hate violence, are underreported (Ciarlante & Fountain, 2010). Furthermore, there are numerous factors that contribute to underreporting in the LGBTQ+ community, including the presence of social stigma against homosexuality, which may prevent some individuals from reporting relational violence (Renzetti, 1997; Russo, 1999; Sanchez-Hucles & Dutton, 1999). For example, national statistics from the FBI's Uniform Crime Reporting (UCR) system suggest that, as of 2016, only 42.1% of all violent crimes were reported to the police, and only just over half of serious violent crime was reported. This is likely to be even lower for LGBTQ+ people for the reasons reported above.

Intimate partner violence is one of the largest and most serious issues confronting LGBTQ+ people (Lobel, 1986). It has significant and serious physical health, mental health, and social consequences for its victims, their families, the LGBTQ+ community, and society at large (Island & Letellier, 1991). Until recently, most studies of intimate partner violence focused almost exclusively on heterosexual partners. However, a number of pre-valence studies that have been conducted since the mid-1980s suggest that LGBTQ+ partner violence is as common as heterosexual domestic violence (Farley, 1996; Renzetti, 1992). Initial prevalence studies that looked at the sexual minority community focused almost exclusively on lesbians. Typically, the research was done with white, middle-class lesbians who were sufficiently open about their orientation to participate in surveys. One early study by Kelly and Warshafsky (1987), however, included 48 lesbians and 50 gay men in the sample and found that lesbians tended to have fewer physically aggressive partners than did gay men, with 95% of their sample using verbally abusive tactics and 47% using physical aggression.

Although the sample sizes and methodologies varied among studies—as well as the wide prevalence range (22–62%) determined by them—relative consistency over time was suggested and reflected an approximate average prevalence rate of 25–33% (Fountain et al., 2009), essentially the same prevalence as in non-LGBTQ populations (Burke & Follingstad, 1999; Coleman, 1991, 1994; NCAVP, 2010). Nevertheless, the wide prevalence range is due to multiple factors, including differences in methodologies; difficulty obtaining representative samples; differing definitions of abuse; lack of differentiation between perpetrators and victims; invisibility of the population; and inclusion and exclusion criteria that restrict studies, overall, to heterosexual samples. Renzetti (1992) has argued that most studies have focused on aggressive behavior per se and have not attempted to classify survey participants as either batterers or victims. She indicates that this approach distorts our understanding of abusive relationships because it assumes that all violence is the same, despite there being important differences between primary aggression, self-defensive behaviors, and retaliatory aggression. When these are not differentiated, Renzetti argues that researchers run the risk of reinforcing the concept of mutual battering.

To date, there are very few studies of intimate partner abuse among transgendered individuals in either heterosexual or same-gender partnerships (APA, 1999). So, while the evolving literature, over time, has suggested that the frequency and severity of LGBTQ+ battering are, in fact, comparable to those in the heterosexual population (Burke & Follingstad, 1999; Coleman, 1991, 1994; NCAVP, 2010), the *true* extent of LGBTQ+ domestic violence remains unknown. In 2009 and 2010, however, there were two studies done (L.A. LGBT Center, 2009; Breiding, Chen, & Black, 2014) that revealed that LGBTQ+ intimate partner violence may, in fact, be more prevalent than what was previously thought based on earlier studies.

Since the Los Angeles Gay & Lesbian Center ("the Center") began collecting and contributing data to the annual national LGBTQ+ Domestic Violence Report, published by the National Coalition of Anti-Violence Programs in the late 1990s, the Center has reported the largest number of cases tracked anywhere in the United States. These numbers were a reflection of the Center's ability to track cases from multiple sources rather than an indication that Los Angeles had more cases of LGBTQ+ intimate partner violence than other regions throughout the United States. In 2008–2009, the Center launched a meta-study that crossed-referenced data via self-reports (i.e. surveys) and through professional assessment by the staff of the Center's STOP and Legal Advocacy Programs. After deducting those cases that did not meet the criteria for IPV (e.g. verbal name-calling, shouting, and/or yelling were not included within the study's parameters), the total case count was 1,483 IPV cases and included members of the transgender and non-binary populations as well as lesbians, gays, and bisexuals. This was believed to be the highest IPV case count with statistically independent data done to date (Jones, 2009). Actual or threatened physical or sexual violence, emotional abuse, and LGBTQ+-related threats (threats to out sexual orientation, gender identity, HIV, or immigration status to cause harm were required for inclusion in the study) were included. The frequency of IPV was 56%. Had verbal aggression such as name-calling been considered, the frequency of IPV would have been 71%. Of the IPV cases, 39% represented the respondent denying having ever experienced domestic violence although the behavior measures (excluding name-calling) indicated either perpetrating or being on the receiving end of violence (L.A. Gay & Lesbian Center, 2009).

The CDC's National Intimate Partner and Sexual Violence Survey (NISVS) was conducted in 2010. The survey did not account for gender identity outside of the traditional binary conceptualization and so it did not include individuals who identified as transgender or non-binary. The survey, which was reported to be the first to provide national data that examined IPV by sexual orientation, found that the lifetime prevalence of physical violence, rape, and/or stalking by an intimate partner was extremely high in the lesbian, gay, and bisexual communities, with bisexual women (61.1%), lesbians (43.8%), bisexual men (37.3%), and gay men (26%) experiencing this violence at higher rates than heterosexual women (35%) and heterosexual men (29%). Upon release of these findings, the CDC director, Dr. Tom Frieden, stated,

> We know that violence affects everyone, regardless of sexual orientation. This report suggests the lesbians, gay men, and bisexuals in this country suffer a heavy toll of sexual violence and stalking committed by an intimate partner. While intervening and providing services are important, prevention is equally critical.

The data compiled by the CDC does not indicate whether violence occurs more frequently in same-sex or opposite-sex couples. Rather, it reflects the lifetime victimization of intimate partner violence, sexual violence, and stalking of respondents who self-identified as lesbian, gay, or bisexual at the time of the survey (CDC, 2013; National LGBTQ Task Force, 2013).

More recently, the Centers for Disease Control released its 2016–2017 Report on Victimization by Sexual Identity in 2023 (Chen et al., 2023). The report, like its predecessor, does not account for IPV prevalence experienced by transgender and non-binary survivors. However, the research reflects higher rates of intimate partner violence experienced by LGBTQ+ people than by the non-LGBTQ+ population owing to the impact of anti-LGBTQ+ bias and oppression. BIPOC LGBTQ+ people and bisexual women are at particularly high risk (Gould, 2023). Fully 56.3% of lesbian women, 47.7% of gay men, 69.3% of bisexual women, 46.1% of bisexual men, 46.3% of heterosexual women, and 44.1% of heterosexual men in the United States experience some form of intimate partner violence during their lifetime. One in two bisexual women reported being stalked, and seven in ten experienced intimate partner sexual violence. Latinx bisexual women experienced the highest rates of any other racial group, with 79.7% of Hispanic bisexual women experiencing intimate partner violence.

Transgender people are at alarmingly high risk for intimate partner violence, crime, and sexual assault. According to the National Center for Transgender Equality, transgender people, and particularly Black and Latina transfeminine individuals, are marginalized, stigmatized, and criminalized. They face violence every day and fear turning to the police for help (Taylor, 2013). Transgender people are 1.9 times more likely to experience physical violence and 3.9 times more likely to experience discrimination than the general population (Durso & Gates, 2012). According to a study of LGBTQ+ crime victims seeking help from IPV victim agencies in the United States and Canada, transgender IPV victims were nearly twice as likely as heterosexual IPV victims to experience physical domestic violence, two and a half times more likely to experience an IPV experience in a public space, and nearly four times more likely to experience discrimination such as verbal abuse by an intimate partner (Messinger, 2020). An analysis by the Williams Institute in 2015 found that between 32% and 50% of all transgender persons experience some form of intimate partner violence in their lifetime, compared with 27% for all U.S. women and 11% for all U.S. men (Brown & Herman, 2015).

Preliminary research also indicates that bisexual women are at extreme risk for IPV, although little data is available in this area. According to the CDC, fully 61% of bisexual women experience rape, physical violence, and/or stalking by an intimate partner in their lifetime, compared with 35% of heterosexual women and 44% of lesbians (NCAVP, 2017). Additionally, one in three bisexual women (37%) has experienced stalking, compared with 16% of heterosexual women, and just under half of all bisexual women (48%) report feeling concerned for their safety versus one-fifth of heterosexual women (20%) and lesbians (22%) (Walters, Chen, & Breiding, 2013).

The prevalence of domestic violence among LGBTQ+ populations is related to the widespread discrimination, hatred, and violence experienced by LGBTQ+ people. An analysis of 164 studies involving over 500,000 LGBTQ+ individuals found that 55% had experienced verbal harassment, 40% had been victims of stalking, 28% had experienced physical assault, and more than one-quarter (27%) had experienced sexual assault at some point in their life (Messinger, 2020). A study of 1,197 LGBTQ+ adults in the United States also found that nearly two in five respondents (39%) reported being rejected by a family member or close friend because of their sexual orientation or gender identity at some point in their life (Walters et al., 2013).

Furthermore, a survey of 354 agencies providing services to homeless youth found that fully 40% of youth who were either without housing or at risk of becoming homeless were LGBTQ+ young people, with family rejection and family abuse serving as key factors in their leaving home (Ibid.). High levels of LGBTQ+ violence and victimization are closely related to internalized and externalized anti-LGBTQ stigma and discrimination. The experience of trauma related to the coming out process is virtually universal in the LGBTQ+ population and is complicated by issues of gender identity, sexual orientation, poor family acceptance, and low socioeconomic status. Many LGBTQ+ persons have been rejected or ostracized by family and community support systems and often receive the majority of their support from abusive partners, making it more difficult for them the leave the relationship (Cohn, 2016).

Given the significant prevalence data that we have about LGBTQ+ domestic violence, coupled with the reality that LGBTQ+ people do not always recognize that what they are experiencing is violent or abusive, owing to domestic violence being commonly defined within a heterosexual framework, it is imperative that therapists and other service providers consistently screen for and identify it in order to increase access by LGBTQ+ victims to appropriate and effective services.

In May of 2009, the National Center for Victims of Crime, together with the National Coalition of Anti-Violence Programs, conducted the first national survey of its kind to assess the state of victim assistance for LGBTQ+ victims and survivors of crime. The large sample of responders (648) included nonprofit domestic violence centers, sexual assault centers, prosecutors' offices, law enforcement agencies, and nonprofit organizations serving child victims. Results indicated that LGBTQ+-focused victim assistance was generally lacking in every survey area, including outreach, cultural competence training, LGBTQ+-specific services, policies, practices, and collaboration with LGBTQ+-specific service providers. The report concluded that these programs were under-resourced, and that these gaps in service compromise the safety of LGBTQ+ individuals, families, and communities (Ciarlante & Fountain, 2010).

In late 2017, the Los Angeles LGBT Center's STOP Violence Program, with a team of independent consultants, conducted a needs assessment throughout Los Angeles. The assessment incorporated data from interviews, focus groups, surveys with survivors as well as community service providers, and discussions with representatives from crime, law enforcement, LGBTQ+ advocacy, women's services, and victim services organizations. It found that the greatest unmet needs of LGBTQ+ victims were for housing and mental health services, and that a particular challenge facing the larger community lay in accessing the information needed to direct these victims to appropriate services and organizations that serve the LGBTQ+ community. The assessment also confirmed that survivors often do not know that support is available to them. Over two-thirds of respondents did not receive any services following a crime, with the most common barriers being (a) fear of retaliation, (b) stigma/bias toward LGBTQ+ persons, (c) the victim's lack of knowledge about the kind of crime they experienced, and (d) inadequate criminal justice response. Both survivors and service providers also identified lack of information about available LGBTQ+ resources and services as a primary barrier to access (Whirry & Holt, 2020). The needs assessment found that there are entrenched and deep distrust on the part of LGBTQ+ communities toward the criminal justice system and its ability to provide needed services, barriers to access for victim support, and therapeutic services that are numerous and complex. There is a lack of knowledge about LGBTQ+ victim resources on the part of all stakeholders, including victims themselves, in response to violent crime; victims usually do not know where to go for support following a crime and do not know if they will be treated well when they arrive; and providers often do not know where to refer LGBTQ+ victims to address their needs, and that capacity is lacking in counseling and treatment, housing and shelter, and supportive services. The situation described in the assessment is one in which

> LGBTQ victims of crime have little knowledge of where they can go for support as victims, feel isolated by their experiences, and face a siloed array of services that lack competence to serve LGBTQ+ persons and are unable to provide a coordinated response that can provide LGBTQ+ victims with access to the full scope of services they may need as victims.
>
> (Los Angeles LGBT Center, 2020, p. 7)

In addition to the information obtained above, thousands of survey respondents have provided the Center with valuable information about the LGBTQ community's perceptions and experiences of domestic violence for the previous two decades. Survey responses have not changed significantly over time, and a composite of those responses is included here. The number of respondents completing the surveys averaged 1,600 annually. Nearly 39% of the respondents indicated that a partner had thrown objects at them or broken objects when angry; 24% had a partner hit, shove, or kick them; 9% had their hair pulled by a partner; 48% had been called names by a partner; 9% had been threatened with outing; 4% had a pet that was harmed by a partner; 14% had exits blocked by a partner; 5% had been subjected to coerced or forced sex by a partner; and 3% had a partner who used a weapon against them.

The majority of respondents (82%) believed that LGBTQ+-specific domestic violence services were important or very important, while only 2% felt differently. When asked what would best help reduce IPV in the LGBTQ+ community, the following was indicated in descending order of importance: Information/education campaigns and workshops (57%); outreach to LGBTQ+ persons at risk for domestic violence (48%); additional LGBTQ+-specific IPV services (44%); and training of mainstream service providers to increase sensitivity to, and understanding of, LGBTQ+ people as well as LGBTQ+ domestic violence (29%). Respondents indicated that they believed the following would be most helpful to LGBTQ+ victims in descending order of importance: Talking to friends (73%), support groups (54%), talking to family members (52%), individual counseling (42%), couples counseling (41%), legal remedies such as restraining orders (31%), soliciting help from a mainstream domestic violence shelter (26%), talking to clergy (16%), staying at a hotel (15%), and staying at a homeless shelter (10%). When asked what they believed would be most helpful to LGBTQ+ persons who were abusing their partners, the responses in descending order of importance included individual counseling (59%), group counseling (52%), talking to friends (49%), couples counseling (42%), talking to family members (38%), soliciting help from law enforcement (28%), legal remedies (26%), and talking to clergy (17%).

While only 20% indicated that they would be likely to call a mainstream domestic violence shelter that was not designed for the LGBTQ+ population, 46% indicated that they would not contact a domestic violence shelter. However, 78% indicated that they would call a domestic violence shelter if the shelter was designed specifically for the LGBTQ+ community. Of those who indicated that they would not contact a shelter, their choices for safe housing in descending order of importance included staying with friends (52%), staying at a LGBTQ+ safe house (36%), staying with family members (29%), staying at a hotel/motel (10%), and staying at a homeless shelter (3%). Four percent indicated that they probably wouldn't leave home, while 7% did not know what they would do if a partner abused them (L.A. Gay & Lesbian Center, 2009).

Nearly half of survey respondents (49.4%) indicated that they believed that awareness of LGBTQ+ domestic violence would increase negative perceptions about the LGBTQ+ community overall.

These responses underscore not only the significant need for sufficient training of service providers but also the great need for information/

education campaigns designed for the LGBTQ+ community and its allies. Friends and family members must share an understanding of LGBTQ+ IPV if they are to be helpful to victims and, in their desire to assist, must not suggest or do anything that inadvertently places them in greater danger. Furthermore, it is imperative that LGBTQ+ victims understand that couples counseling can be dangerous, and that individual counseling for abusers is contraindicated. Because a large majority of respondents favored an LGBTQ+-specific domestic violence shelter and indicated that they would utilize one, it is important to provide the community with information about the current reasons why none exist (i.e. lack of effective assessment practices and accurate differentiation between abuser and victim would compromise the confidentiality of the shelter and, hence, its safety; shelter funding is frequently restricted owing to variables such as the number of shelters in a particular area; etc.).

LGBTQ+ survivors often face enormous challenges, including the response by law enforcement and the criminal justice system to LGBTQ+ domestic violence, accurate assessment of the parties involved in domestic violence cases, and the level of service providers' understanding of the unique differences and complexities of LGBTQ+ domestic violence. A significant number of survivors, defending victims, or secondary aggressors are consistently mandated by the court to attend batterers' (dominant/primary aggressors) treatment, and, despite attempts by a small number of mainstream domestic violence service providers and agencies to be inclusive of the LGBTQ+ community, significant problems are consistently reported by LGBTQ+ survivors and abusers alike. These problems include the high number of agencies that employ exclusionary policies and procedures in relation to gender-variant survivors; the heterosexist language and images used in educational and outreach materials as well as documentation; inconsistent, minimal, or entire lack of training of staff and volunteers on the topic of LGBTQ+ domestic violence; verbal and sexual harassment of LGBTQ+ clients by agency staff or residents; lack of sufficient assessment and training to differentiate between primary victims, defending victims, secondary aggressors, and dominant/primary aggressors, and the subsequent lack of effective intervention; and re-victimization of survivors and/or a substandard level of care by mainstream providers. For example, one mainstream organization that was the recipient of state funding to specifically address LGBTQ+ domestic violence offered a drop-in group for LGBTQ+ survivors of intimate partner violence, a potentially damaging and dangerous modality that is generally not recommended for LGBTQ+ individuals because of the lack of adequate screening of participants. It is imperative that service providers be knowledgeable about, and attempt at all times to provide, a contextualized approach when assessing and intervening in cases of LGBTQ+ intimate partner violence.

Continuing Education Questions

1. What is a difference between LGBTQ IPV and heterosexual, cisgender IPV?
   a. It occurs when one person in an intimate relationship attempts to control, gain, and/or maintain power over an intimate partner by using various abusive and violent tactics and behavior.
   b. The abuse can be physical, sexual, psychological, emotional, verbal, and/or financial.
   c. It is a stigmatized form of violence and is underreported.
   d. The IPV always occurs within the context of societal anti-LGBTQ bias (homophobia, biphobia, and transphobia).
2. In an LGBTQ relationship, one partner being out and one being closeted creates a potential power imbalance.
   a. True
   b. False
3. Which one of these is *not* a reason for the underreporting of LGBTQ IPV?
   a. IPV is a highly stigmatized form of violence.
   b. There is a fear that acknowledgment of intimate partner violence will further prejudice the community itself.
   c. LGBTQ IPV is not that common and tends to be less serious than heterosexual or cisgender IPV.
   d. When LGBTQ people report crime victimization, they often do not receive the legal protections afforded their heterosexual and cisgender counterparts.
4. According to the NCAVP, females are victimized more than males in IPV in the heterosexual community and also in the LGBTQ community.
   a. True
   b. False
5. Which of the following explains the fact that LGBTQ victims of IPV are more likely to fight back in self-defense?
   a. The perception of equality in terms of size and strength.
   b. The lack of LGBTQ-specific domestic/dating violence services and resources.

   c.   The problems resulting from internalized homophobia and anti-LGBTQ bias.

   d.   All of the above.

References

American Psychological Association (APA). (1999). Intimate Partner Abuse and Relationship Violence. Retrieved February 6, 2024, from www.apa.org/about/division/activities/partner-abuse.pdf

American Psychological Association (APA). (2000). Guidelines for Psychotherapy with Lesbian, Gay, and Bisexual Clients. *American Psychologist, 55*(12), 1440–1451. Retrieved October 14, 2003, from apa.org/pi/lgbc/guidelines.html

Barnett, O.W., Lee, C.Y., & Thelen, R.E. (1997). Gender Differences in Attributions of Self-Defense and Control in Inter-partner Aggression. *Violence Against Women, 3,* 462–481.

Bograd, M. (1988). Feminist Perspectives on Wife Abuse: An Introduction. In K. Yllo & M. Bograd (Eds.), *Feminist Perspectives on Wife Abuse* (pp. 11–28). Newbury Park, CA: Sage.

Breiding, M.J., Chen J., & Black, M.C. (2014). *Intimate Partner Violence in the United States—2010.* Atlanta, GA: National Center for Injury Prevention and Control, Centers for Disease Control and Prevention.

Brown, T., & Herman, J.L. (2015). *Intimate Partner Violence and Sexual Abuse among LGBTQ People: A Review of Existing Research.* Los Angeles, CA: Williams Institute.

Burke, L.K., & Follingstad, E.R. (1999). Violence in Lesbian and Gay Relationships: Theory, Prevalence, and Correlational Factors. *Clinical Psychology Review, 5,* 487–512.

Byrne, D. (1996). Clinical Models for the Treatment of Gay Male Perpetrators of Domestic Violence. In C. Renzetti & C. Miley (Eds.), *Violence in Gay and Lesbian Domestic Partnerships* (pp. 107–116). Binghamton, NY: Harrington Park Press.

Center for American Progress. (2011). *Domestic Violence in the LGBT Community: A Fact Sheet.* american.progress.org/article/domestic-violence-in-the-lgbt-community/

Centers for Disease Control. (2006). Understanding Intimate Partner Violence [fact sheet]. Retrieved August 29, 2007, from cdc.gov/ncipc/dvp/ipv_factsheet.pdf

Centers for Disease Control (CDC). (June 25, 2013). CDC Release Data on Interpersonal and Sexual Violence by Sexual Orientation [CDC online newsroom press release]. cdc.gov/media/releases/2013/p0125_nisvs.html#

Chen, J., Khatiwada, S., Chen, M.S., Smith, S.G., Leemis, R.W., Friar, N., Basile, K.C., & Kresnow, M. (2023). *The National Intimate Partner and Sexual Violence Survey (NISVS) 2016/2017: Report on Victimization by Sexual Identity.* Atlanta, GA: National Center for Injury Prevention and Control, Centers for Disease Control and Prevention.

Ciarlante, M., & Fountain, K. (2010). *Why It Matters: Rethinking Victim Assistance for Lesbian, Gay, Bisexual, Transgender, and Queer Victims of Hate Violence & Intimate Partner Violence.* Washington, DC: National Center for Victims of Crime & the National Coalition of Anti-Violence Programs.

Cohn, R. (2016). Senate Health Committee Analysis. Analysis of Assembly Bill 2051. www.leginfo.ca.gov/pub/05-06/bill/asm/ab_2051-2100/ab_2051_cfa_20060621_093713_sen_comm.html

Coleman, V. (1994). Lesbian Battering: The Relationship between Personality and Perpetration of Violence. *Violence and Victims, 9*(2), 139–152.

Coleman, V.E. (1991). Violence in Lesbian Couples: A Between Groups Comparison. [Doctoral dissertation, California School of Professional Psychology, Los Angeles, 1990.] *Dissertation Abstracts International, 51*, 5634B.

Durso, L.E., & Gates. G.J. (2012). *Serving Our Youth: Findings from a National Survey of Services Providers Working with Lesbian, Gay, Bisexual and Transgender Youth Who Are Homeless or at Risk of Being Homeless.* Los Angeles, CA: William's Institute.

Farley, N. (1996). A Survey of Factors Contributing to Gay and Lesbian Domestic Violence. In C. Renzetti & C. Miley (Eds.), *Violence in Gay and Lesbian Domestic Partnerships* (pp. 35–42). Binghamton, NY: Haworth.

Fountain, K., Mitchell-Brody, M, Jones, S.A., and Nicols, K. (2009). *Lesbian, Gay, Bisexual, Transgender and Queer Domestic Violence in the United States in 2008.* New York, NY: National Coalition of Anti-Violence Programs.

Friess, S. (1997). Behind Closed Doors: Domestic Violence. *The Advocate, 748*, 48–52.

Goldenberg, Tamar, Stephenson, Rob, Freeland, Ryan, Finneran, Catherine, & Hadley, Craig. (2016). "Struggling to Be the Alpha": Sources of Tension and Intimate Partner Violence in Same-Sex Relationships between Men. *Culture, Health & Sexuality, 18*(8), 875–889. doi:10.1080/13691058.2016.1144791

Gould, A. (2023). *Insights from CDC's National Intimate Partner and Sexual Violence Survey.* Los Angeles, CA: National LGBTQ Institute Intimate Partner Violence.

Harway, M., & O'Neil, J.M. (1999). *What Causes Men's Violence against Women?* Thousand Oaks, CA: Sage.

Holt, S. (2002). LGBTQ Domestic Violence. *Arise, 5*, 38–40.

Holt, S. (2011–2023). Unpublished lectures, Masters of Arts Program, Antioch University, Los Angeles, California.

Island, D., and Letellier, P. (1991). *Men Who Beat the Men Who Love Them.* Binghamton, NY: Harrington Park Press.

Jones, S.A. (2009). *Lesbian, Gay, Bisexual, Transgender & Queer Domestic Violence in the United States in 2008.* NCAVP Annual Report (2009 release edition). New York, NY.

Kanuha, V. (1990). Compounding the Triple Jeopardy: Battering in Lesbian of Color Relationships. In L. Brown & M. Root (Eds.), *Diversity and Complexity in Feminist Therapy* (pp. 169–184). Binghamton, NY: Harrington Park Press.

Kelly, E.E., & Warshafsky, L. (1987). *Partner Abuse in Gay Male and Lesbian Couples.* Paper presented at the Third National Conference for Family Violence Researchers, Durham, NH.

Koop, C.E. (1987). *Healing Interpersonal Violence: Making Health a Full Partner.* Keynote address at the Surgeon General's Northwest Conference on Interpersonal Violence, Seattle, WA.

Koss, M.P., Goodman, L.A., Browne, A., Fitzgerald, L.F., Keita, G.P., & Russo, N.F. (1994). *No Safe Haven: Male Violence against Women at Home, at Work, and in the Community.* Washington, DC: American Psychological Association.

Koss, M.P., Ingram, M., & Pepper, S. (2000). Male Partner Violence against Women: Medical Impact and the Response of the Health Care System. In A. Baum & T. Reveson (Eds.), *Handbook of Health Psychology* (pp. 541–557). Mahwah, NJ: Lawrence Erlbaum.

L.A. Gay & Lesbian Center. (2009). *Unpublished proposal for funding—Department of Justice.* Los Angeles, CA: STOP Partner Abuse/Domestic Violence Program/LAGLC.

Leventhal, B., & Lundy, S.E. (1999). *Same-Sex Domestic Violence: Strategies for Change.* Thousand Oaks, CA: Sage.

Lie, G., Schilit, R., Bush, J., Montagna, M., & Reyes, L. (1991). Lesbians in Currently Aggressive Relationships: How Frequently Do They Report Aggressive Past Relationships? *Violence and Victims, 6*(2), 121–135.

Lobel, K. (Ed.) (1986). *Naming the Violence: Speaking Out about Lesbian Battering.* Seattle, WA: Seal Press.

Los Angeles LGBT Center. (2020). *Finding Safety: A Report about LGBTQ Domestic Violence and Sexual Assault.* Los Angeles, CA: Los Angeles LGBT Center.

Marrujo, B., & Kreger, M. (1995). Definition of Roles in Abusive Lesbian Relationships. In C.M. Renzetti & C.H. Miley (Eds.), *Violence in Gay and Lesbian Partnerships* (pp. 23–33). Binghamton, NY: Harrington Park Press.

Merrill, G.S. (1996). Ruling the Exceptions: Same Sex Battering and Domestic Violence Theory. In C.M. Renzetti & C.H. Miley (Eds.), *Violence in Gay and Lesbian Domestic Partnerships* (p. 921). Binghamton, NY: Harrington Park Press.

Messinger, A.M. (2020). *LGBTQ Intimate Partner Violence: Lessons for Policy, Practice, and Research.* Oakland, CA: University of California Press.

National Center for Transgender Equality. (2020). *Murders of Transgender People in 2020 Surpassed Total for Last Year in Just Seven Months.* Washington DC, August 7.

National Coalition of Anti-Violence Programs (NCAVP). (2009). *Lesbian, Gay, Bisexual, Transgender & Queer Domestic Violence in the United States in 2008.* NCAVP Annual Report (2009 release edition). New York, NY.

National Coalition of Anti-Violence Programs (NCAVP). (2010). *Lesbian, Gay, Bisexual, Transgender, Queer and HIV-Affected Intimate Partner Violence 2010: A Report from the National Coalition of Anti-Violence Programs.* New York, NY: New York City Gay & Lesbian Anti-Violence Project.

National Coalition of Anti-Violence Programs (NCAVP). (2011). *Hate Violence against Lesbian, Gay, Bisexual, Transgender, Queer and HIV-Affected Communities in the United States in 2010.* New York, NY: New York City Gay & Lesbian Anti-Violence Project.

National Coalition of Anti-Violence Programs (NCAVP). (2012). *Lesbian, Gay, Bisexual, Transgender, Queer, and HIV-Affected Intimate Partner Violence 2011: A Report from the National Coalition of Anti-Violence Programs.* New York, NY: New York City Anti-Violence Project.

National Coalition of Anti-Violence Programs (NCAVP). (2017) *LGBTQ and HIV Affected Intimate Partner Violence in 2016.* New York, NY.

National LGBTQ Task Force. (February 4, 2013). *Bisexual Women Have Increased Risk of Intimate Partner Violence, New CDC Data Shows.* thetaskforce.org/news/bisexual-women-have-increased-risk-of-intimate-partner-violence-new-cdc-data-shows/

National Resource Center on Domestic Violence (NRCDV). (2007). *Lesbian, Gay, Bisexual, and Trans (LGBTQ) Communities and Domestic Violence: Information and Resources.* Harrisburg, PA: Author. Retrieved October 17, 2004, from ncadv.org

O'Neil, J.M., & Harway, M. (1999). Preliminary Multivariate Model Explaining the Causes of Men's Violence against Women. In M. Harway & J.M. O'Neil (Eds.), *What Causes Men's Violence against Women?* (pp. 12–17). Thousand Oaks, CA: Sage.

Ofosu, E.K., Chambers, M.K., Chen, J.M., & Hehman, E. (2019). Same-Sex Marriage Legalization Associated with Reduced Implicit and Explicit Antigay Bias. *Proceedings of the National Academy of Sciences, 116*(18), 8846–8851.

Peterman, L.M., & Dixon, C.G. (2003). Domestic Violence between Same-Sex Partners: Implications for Counseling. *Journal of Counseling and Development, 81,* 40–47.

Renzetti, C. (1992). *Violent Betrayal: Partner Abuse in Lesbian Relationships.* Newbury Park, CA: Sage.

Renzetti, C.M. (1997). Violence in Lesbian and Gay Relationships. In L.L. O'Toole & J.R. Schiffman (Eds.), *Gender Violence: Interdisciplinary Perspectives.* New York, NY: New York University Press.

Russo, A. (1999). Lesbians Organizing Lesbians against Battering. In B. Levanthal & S.E. Lundy (Eds.), *Same Sex Domestic Violence: Strategies for Change* (pp. 83–96). Thousand Oaks, CA: Sage.

Sanchez-Hucles, J., & Dutton, M. (1999). The Interaction between Societal Violence and Domestic Violence: Racial and Cultural Factors. In M. Harway & J.M. O'Neil (Eds.), *What Causes Men's Violence against Women?* Thousand Oaks, CA: Sage.

Taylor, P. (2013). *A Survey of LGBTQ Americans: Attitudes, Experiences, and Values in Changing Times.* Washington DC: Pew Research Center.

Waldron, C.M. (1996). Lesbians of Color and the Domestic Violence Movement. In C.M. Renzetti & C.H. Miley (Eds.), *Violence in Gay and Lesbian Domestic Partnerships* (pp. 43–51). Binghamton, NY: Haworth Press.

Walters, M.L., Chen, J., & Breiding, M.J. (2013). *The National Intimate Partner and Sexual Violence Survey (NISVS): 2010 Findings on Victimization by Sexual Orientation.* National Center for Injury Prevention and Control, US Centers for Disease Control and Prevention.

Whirry, R., & Holt, S. (2020). *Finding Safety: A Report about LGBTQ Domestic Violence and Sexual Assault.* Los Angeles, CA: Los Angeles LGBT Center.

Wiehe, V.R. (1998). *Understanding Family Violence: Treating and Preventing Partner, Child, Sibling, and Elder Abuse.* Thousand Oaks, CA: Sage.

Intimate Partner Violence and the Coming Out Process   9

Based in part on our experience, we have determined that the stages of LGBTQ+ identity development and the coming out processes apply to LGBTQ+ intimate partner violence cases in a unique manner (Holt, 2012). In addition to the dynamics and variables previously described, the reality of oppression informs the LGBTQ+ identity development and coming out process. Domestic violence, in turn, influences the development of identity, and the subsequent coming out process influences how the LGBTQ+ person is apt to experience intimate partner violence and the help-seeking process. In fact, obtaining help for domestic violence is synonymous with coming out, a major life decision for many people.

LGBTQ+ individuals who are experiencing intimate partner violence are confronted with a confusing range of options when considering securing, or attempting to secure, help. There are very few domestic violence services that have been designed specifically for members of the LGBTQ+ community. Traditional IPV services rarely address their unique needs and experiences, which can be potentially harmful and even life-threatening.

There are services and organizations that are *anti-LGBTQ+* and there are those that are *ambivalent* about the LGBTQ+ population and its needs. The former refuse to serve LGBTQ+ individuals and families. The latter will generally not turn LGBTQ+ people away but they also usually do not indicate that LGBTQ+ individuals and families are welcome. Very often, they adopt a "don't ask, don't tell" policy. Clients are usually presumed to be heterosexual, and the problems they bring to counseling are addressed within a heteronormative framework.

DOI: 10.4324/9780429031397-9

Those services and organizations that indicate that they are *LGBTQ+ sensitive* or *friendly* welcome members of the LGBTQ+ community. However, the providers may or may not have received training about the LGBTQ+ population and how varying issues impact the community. If training has been received, it tends to vary widely in applicability, length, focus, and so on. While these services and organizations attempt to be knowledgeable about and affirming of the unique needs and variables impacting their LGBTQ+ clients, they may not have sufficient training to be effective and may inadvertently and/or unknowingly adopt an approach geared to, and developed for, non-LGBTQ clients. Generally, LGBTQ+ sensitive or friendly therapists do not have sufficient training in LGBTQ+ domestic violence, if they have received any training at all on the subject.

LGBT-affirmative therapy honors LGBTQ+ identities and focuses on helping clients develop authenticity and embrace their sexual orientation and/or gender identity. It does not attempt to eliminate, diminish, or change these identities but, rather, celebrates them. It has been endorsed by the American Psychological Association. An LGBTQ+-affirmative therapist may or may not have training and education in LGBTQ+ intimate partner violence. They would, however, typically value the client's identity and work to diminish or eliminate the impact that internalized homophobia/biphobia/transphobia has had on the client and the violence that they have experienced. Depending on their knowledge level and experience working with LGBTQ+ intimate partner violence, they may inadvertently conceptualize the domestic violence within a heteronormative framework.

LGBTQ+-specific services and organizations work primarily with LGBTQ + individuals and families. Providers of these services have received extensive training and education in LGBTQ+ issues and focus on the interplay between societal oppression, its impact on the individual client, and the role that it has played in producing or exacerbating problems that the client may have. Again, an LGBTQ+ therapist may not have had training in LGBTQ+ intimate partner violence, but they would generally attempt to address violence in an LGBTQ+ context which actively incorporates into the overall treatment plan how the individual client, as well as the problem being experienced, has been changed by societal and institutionalized anti-LGBTQ+ bias. LGBTQ+-specific therapists often, but not always, identify as LGBTQ+ themselves or are allies of the community.

According to Mustanski, Kuper, and Greene (2014) and Hall (2019), *sexual orientation* is a multidimensional construct that refers to an individual's positioning within aspects of sexuality, including sexual attraction, behavior, and identity. Hall, Dawes, and Plocek (2021) have defined identity development as the changes, processes, and experiences over time that can involve awareness, exploration, appraisal, commitment, integration, and communication concerning a person's identity as a sexual being, which is based on their patterns of sexual attractions and behaviors. Hall indicates that, while there are commonalities in sexual identity development models, there are diverse trajectories across population groups as well. For example, people in sexual minority groups navigate different tasks and milestones related to their stigmatized orientation than do people who identify as heterosexual.

Coming out refers to the sequence of events through which individuals recognize their sexual orientation (or gender identity) and decide whether or not to disclose it to others. This is a fluid, continuous process that occurs throughout a person's life and generally begins when they first questions feelings that are perceived to be different from what an they witnessed when growing up and have implications for their safety. The coming out process can often be a barrier to seeking and receiving services. Because of the heterosexism and anti-LGBTQ bias that exists in our culture, coming out frequently involves a significant amount of introspection and a relatively healthy sense of self-esteem and acceptance. However, it is a process that always involves risk because it can result in rejection and loss of relationships and employment, as well as harassment and abuse from others, ranging from verbal insults to physical violence and homicide. And, because it occurs on a continuum, outing is frequently used as a control tactic by LGBTQ+ abusers against their victims (NCAVP, 2012).

Research focusing on sexual minority identity during the 1970s, 1980s, and 1990s focused on stage models. Although numerous models of the identity development and subsequent coming out processes have been developed, those developed by Vivienne Cass and Eli Coleman are arguably the two that are most commonly referenced (Falco, 1991; Hall et al., 2021). While these models frequently focus on sexual orientation, components of them are sometimes applied to gender identity as well. Both the Cass and Coleman models are linear and include a self-recognition or identity confusion stage, a disclosure or identity comparison stage, a socialization or identity acceptance stage, a positive self-identification or identity pride stage, and an integration and acceptance or identity synthesis stage. The stage(s) that an individual is in at any given time impacts their experience of domestic violence, and that experience reflects the particular stage.

In the 1990s, 2000s, and 2010s, researchers turned their attention to LGB+ milestone identity development models (Kenneady & Oswalt, 2014; Savin-Williams & Cohen, 2015). These researchers conceptualized milestones as events that mark significant points in human development in terms of life changes or achievements. For LGB + people, these milestones include their first awareness of non-heterosexual desires, self-identification as LGB+, and initially coming out to family and friends. Rather than progressing in stages, milestone models attempt to examine patterns in sexual trajectories among LGB + people and to understand factors that shape the timing and sequence of milestones (Hall et al., 2021). Although the aforementioned models are not the same, the societal context of oppression does not differ, regardless of the identity development lens through which an individual or groups are viewed. Hence, individual experiences in reference to domestic violence are not apt to vary significantly.

According to the Cass and Coleman models, the first stage of the process is, respectively, the self-recognition/identity confusion stage. This stage is characterized by the beginning of awareness and increasing levels of both awareness and acknowledgment of one's sexual orientation or gender identity. This stage may include anxiety, confusion, denial, repression of feelings, and attempts to conceal one's identity. The second stage is the disclosure/identity comparison stage and is characterized by vacillation between denial and acknowledgment of one's identity. During this stage, one's sexual orientation or gender identity is often revealed to someone who is considered "safe," and there are attempts to clarify what it means to be LGBTQ+ (Falco, 1991). In the milestone model, one's first awareness of non-heterosexual desires would be similar, especially if any negative cognitions or feelings are associated with this awareness.

Individuals in the first and second stages of the process are generally not apt to define their problem as one of domestic violence, or they tend to believe that all LGBTQ+ relationships are violent, in part because of the lack of role models for LGBTQ+ people. Outing is an especially effective control tactic during these stages, and LGBTQ+ individuals are often hesitant to seek assistance for intimate partner violence when they define it as such because they are fearful of outing themselves. Many people in these earlier stages may be hesitant to access LGBTQ+-specific programs and/or services but can strongly benefit from referrals to them. It is especially important that service providers working with individuals in these stages be as bias-free as possible and develop a solid understanding of the multiple ramifications of internalized anti-LGBTQ bias as well as the importance of self-acceptance and self-esteem and the roles each play in an individual's ability to maintain safety for themselves.

The third stage of the process is the socialization/identity acceptance stage, which is characterized by increased socialization with LGBTQ+ people as well as the development of self-acceptance. It is followed by the positive self-identification/identity pride stage. During this stage, there is immersion in LGBTQ+ culture and development of pride in one's identity. Individuals in the third and fourth stages of the coming out process are often more apt to seek out and benefit from LGBTQ+-specific programs and/or services. For many, specific services, when available, are invaluable. Those who receive services from mainstream providers may risk damage to their developing self-esteem and, hence, experience increased potential for escalating violence because their unique issues and concerns are rarely addressed sufficiently. In the milestone model, the individual's self-identification as LGB+ and coming out behaviors, as well as the timing of both, would similarly apply.

The final stage of the process is the integration and acceptance/identity synthesis stage. This stage is characterized by the integration of one's sexual orientation or gender identity into one's sense of self. Individuals in the final stage of the process may possibly benefit from both LGBTQ+-sensitive and/or LGBTQ+-affirmative IPV services but can, instead, flourish in LGBTQ+-specific services while not risking that their unique and complex needs will be ignored or ineffectively addressed from services that are merely LGBTQ+-sensitive/affirmative.

Continuing Education Questions

1. The Cass and Coleman models have how many stages of coming out?
   a. 3
   b. 4
   c. 5
   d. 6
2. The socialization/identity acceptance stage is characterized by the beginning of awareness and increasing levels of awareness and acknowledgment of one's sexual orientation or gender identity.
   a. True
   b. False
3. What is true of people in the first and second stages of the coming out process?
   a. They are more apt to define their problem as domestic violence.
   b. They tend to believe all LGBTQ relationships are violent owing to the lack of LGBTQ relationship role models.
   c. Outing is not a powerful tool of IPV used on victims in these stages.
   d. They are more willing to access LGBTQ-specific resources.

4. LGBTQ-specific services are especially sought out and needed by people in the third through fifth stages of the coming out process.
   a. True
   b. False
5. Which of the following features is incorrectly matched with its corresponding coming out stage?
   a. Vacillation between denial and acknowledgement of one's identity: Disclosure/identity comparison stage
   b. Immersion in the LGBTQ culture and development of pride in one's identity: Positive self-identification/identity pride stage
   c. Integration of one's sexual orientation or gender identity into one's sense of self: Acceptance/identity synthesis stage
   d. Hesitancy to access LGBTQ-specific programs but strong benefits can result from referrals to them: Socialization/identity acceptance stage

References

Falco, K.L. (1991). *Psychotherapy with Lesbian Clients: Theory into Practice*. New York, NY: Brunner Mazel.

Hall, W.J. (2019). Sexual Orientation. In C. Franklin (Ed.), *Encyclopedia of Social Work*. United States: National Association of Social Workers Press and Oxford University Press.

Hall, W.J., Dawes, H.C., & Plocek, N. (2021). Sexual Orientation Identity Development Milestones among Lesbian, Gay, Bisexual & Queer People: A Systematic Review and Meta-analysis. In *Frontiers in Psychology, Sec. Gender, Sex & Sexualities, 12*. www.froniiersin.org/articles/10.3389/fpsyg

Holt, S. (2012). LGBTQ Domestic Violence: A Contextual Approach [Dissertation].

Kenneady, D.A., & Oswalt, S.B. (2014). Is Cass's Model of Homosexual Identity Formation Relevant to Today's Society? *American Journal of Sexuality Education, 9*, 229–246. doi:10.1080/15546128.2014.900465

Mustanski, B., Kuper, L., & Greene, G.J. (2014). Development of Sexual Orientation and Identity. In D.L. Tolman & L.M. Diamond (Eds.), *APA Handbook of Sexuality and Psychology, Vol. 1. Person-Based Approaches* (pp. 597–628). Washington, DC: American Psychological Association.

National Coalition of Anti-Violence Programs (NCAVP). (2012). *Lesbian, Gay, Bisexual, Transgender, Queer, and HIV-Affected Intimate Partner Violence 2011: A Report from the National Coalition of Anti-Violence Programs*. New York, NY: New York City Anti-Violence Project.

Savin-Williams, R.C., & Cohen, K.M. (2015). Developmental Trajectories and Milestones of Lesbian, Gay, and Bisexual Young People. *International Review of Psychiatry, 27*, 357–366. doi:10.3109/09540261.2015.1093465

The LGBTQ+ Cycle of Violence **10**

Many domestic violence experts believe that relationship violence generally occurs within a cycle that, without intervention, increases in frequency and severity (see Figure 10.1). According to this theory, the repeating cycle of violence includes three distinct phases:

1. The tension-building phase.
2. The explosion or acute battering incident.
3. The calm, loving respite, remorse, or "honeymoon" phase.

These phases vary in time and intensity between couples and within the same couple. The length of time that a couple remains in a phase varies. While LGBTQ+ persons experience the cycle of violence similarly to heterosexual persons, the LGBTQ+ cycle of violence is exacerbated by internalized and institutionalized anti-LGBTQ bias and heterosexism. These represent additional challenges to safety and help-seeking.

Phase One: The Tension-Building Phase

This phase is characterized by the development of tension within the relationship that includes mild-to-moderate incidents of abuse and violence such as criticism, name-calling, verbal humiliation, gaslighting, and so on, by the abuser. The survivor often feels that they are "walking on eggshells" and behaves in ways that they hope will prevent the escalating tension and

DOI: 10.4324/9780429031397-10

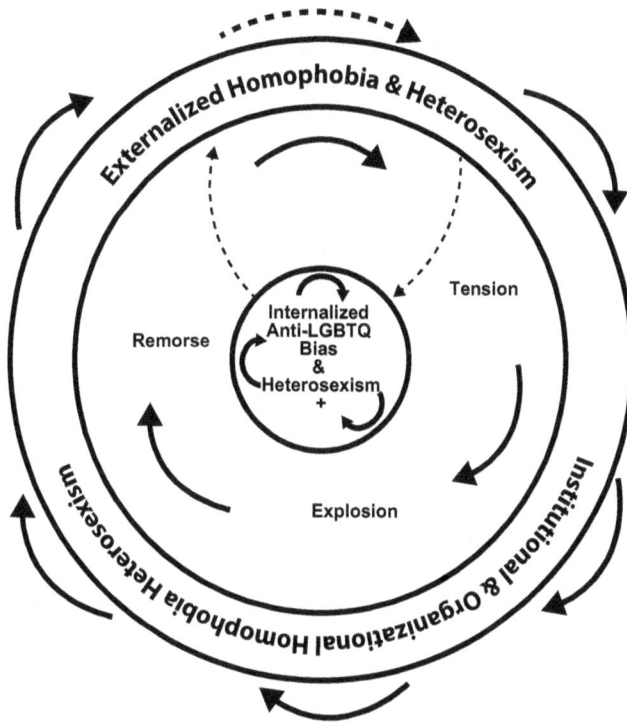

Figure 10.1 LGBTQ+ Cycle of Violence

While LGBTQ+ persons experience the cycle of violence similarly to heterosexual persons, the LGBTQ+ cycle of violence is exacerbated by internalized and institutionalized bias (homo/bi/transphobia) and heterosexism. These present additional challenges to safety and help-seeking.

Source: © 2018 Los Angeles LGBT Center's STOP Violence Program

eventual acute incident of violence. This phase is known for the anticipatory anxiety of the victim and the increasing irritation and anger of the abuser. This phase can be very short in duration or drawn out over weeks, months, or years.

Phase Two: The Explosion or Acute Battering Incident

This phase involves a major act of abuse and violence by the abuser against the victim. This phase is usually shorter than Phase One and Phase Three. During it, the victim may attempt to retreat or act in self-defense or retaliation.

If the police are involved, it is usually during Phase Two. California law mandates that an arrest be made if there is evidence of physical abuse of either of the partners. If neither is arrested, violence may increase when the police leave. Sometimes, both persons will be arrested, or the victim will be arrested instead of the batterer.

Phase Three: The Calm, Loving Respite, Remorse, or "Honeymoon" Phase

During this phase, the abuser frequently feels remorseful about their behavior and acts in an apologetic and loving fashion. This phase often begins with gifts, declarations of love, and lovemaking. The abuser is often fearful that the survivor will leave the relationship and may claim that they will be destroyed if the relationship ends. The survivor often has hope that the abuser will change. The abuser may make promises that they won't be abusive and violent in the future and may seek help for their "anger management problems" or suggest couple counseling. It is rare, however, for abusers to accept help unless the survivor leaves, or threatens to leave, the relationship and they believe that seeing a counselor may help get the partner back, or if the criminal justice system requires the abuser to get help. While the duration of this phase can be of any length, it always reverts to the tension building phase, and the cycle repeats itself.

Typically speaking, the cycle of violence will repeat itself indefinitely until there is effective intervention that eliminates it. Without intervention, however, the cycle will increase its speed and the number of times it repeats itself until there is no honeymoon phase and the cycle is simply alternating between the tension building phase and acute incident. In addition, the survivor may often do something during the tension building phase that they believe will trigger or "provoke" the abuser to initiate the acute incident in an attempt to reduce or alleviate the anticipatory anxiety they are feeling and to move into the honeymoon phase.

Many domestic violence advocates and activists have, since the 1980s, utilized the cycle of violence to understand the cyclical nature of intimate partner violence and the behavioral patterns in abusive relationships. Developed in 1979 by psychologist Lenore Walker, the cycle has, on occasion, been criticized for its simplicity and flaws in research relating to it. However, to more fully understand how context affects intimate personal violence, it is helpful to understand the LGBTQ+ cycle of violence. Often considered to be a theory of domestic violence, explanation of the cycle can be used as a very effective intervention for clients in conjunction with psychoeducation. In particular, clients who minimize the abuse they're experiencing, as well as clients who are in denial that what they are experiencing constitutes "domestic violence," frequently benefit when the cycle is explained to them and/or they see it illustrated on paper.

Although no research has established whether LGBTQ+ persons experience the cycle of violence with the same frequency as do heterosexuals, many LGBTQ+ victims and abusers report a pattern that is similar to the traditional cycle of violence that includes a tension-building stage, acute incident, and honeymoon stage. Extrapolating from the work of Walker (1979), and based in part on our own experience, we have determined that the cycle of violence similarly applies to LGBTQ+ IPV cases, but with some important differences. The LGBTQ+ cycle of violence incorporates internalized and institutionalized anti-LGBTQ bias, as well as an inner core that comprises the LGBTQ+ victim's and/or batterer's internalized homophobia/biphobia/transphobia/anti-LGBTQ bias. Internalized anti-LGBTQ bias produces a heightened sense of shame because of one's sexual orientation or gender identity as well as an internalization of all or most of the cultural and societal messages and misconceptions about LGBTQ+ domestic violence that exist. Once internalized, these messages can lead to heightened traumatic bonding and isolation within the couple as well as increased difficulty in breaking through the cycle itself in order to seek help and assistance.

If either of the individuals is able to break out of the cycle and seek help, they frequently encounter institutionalized anti-LGBTQ bias and heterosexism—both forms of oppression, prejudice, and/or discrimination that encircle the standard cycle and ultimately create a formidable barrier to freedom from abuse. For example, lesbians seeking refuge at a domestic violence shelter may encounter homophobia and bias from other residents or staff members or may simply be confronted with the invisibility of their experience in the form of information and educational materials that only address heterosexual domestic violence; gay men may be ridiculed by court personnel when applying for a restraining order or may instead be granted a mutual restraining order or refused a protective order at all; a transgender person may be consistently referred to by their birth name (or "dead name") and with incorrect gender pronouns; and so on.

After having been re-victimized by the system and society in these and other ways (e.g. LGBTQ+ persons are common victims of anti-LGBTQ bias and hate crimes), the LGBTQ+ person is likely to return to the abusive relationship (which often feels safer than the hostile outside world) and to be more apt to minimize future abusive incidents, and to have heightened difficulty seeking help in the future. Trapped within their abusive relationships, LGBTQ+ victims are exposed to increasing levels of violence and are at proportionately higher risk. Over time, the LGBTQ+ victim may be apt to fight back or retaliate against the abusive partner. One reason for this is the perception of equal size and strength of both individuals; another is the lack of LGBTQ+-specific resources and the prevalence of institutionalized anti-LGBTQ bias.

When internalized anti-LGBTQ bias increases, it heightens the dynamic of traumatic bonding for both victim and abuser, making it more difficult for the victim to seek assistance and easier for the abuser to objectify the victim through projection. Projection is the unconscious act of attributing something inside ourselves to someone else. For example, the LGBTQ+ abuser projects their own feelings of self-hatred (internalized anti-LGBTQ bias) onto the victim, thereby making it easier to objectify the victim, which makes it ultimately easier to abuse them. The victim, in turn, projects their feelings of victimization onto the abuser and subsequently minimizes the abuse while feeling empathic toward the abuser. In some cases, internalized anti-LGBTQ bias and homophobia/biphobia/transphobia (and the projection of it) may be one reason that LGBTQ+ defending victims and secondary aggressors use abuse and violence against their abusers.

Stockholm Syndrome refers to the bonds developed between hostages and their captors and has been used to further understand the experience and behavior of domestic violence victims (Graham & Rawlings, 1991). Similar to the dynamics of Stockholm Syndrome, traumatic bonding describes the strong emotional attachment that develops between victims and their abusers that can occur in relationships where there is a power imbalance (Dutton & Painter, 1981). As a result of the social isolation that exists, victims bond to the positive characteristics of the abuser and experience similar reactions as defined by Walker during the honeymoon stage of the cycle of violence (Walker, 1979). Traumatic bonding is similar to what occurs in LGBTQ+ couples and families who have been rejected by or estranged from other sources of support because of sexual orientation or gender identity, thereby often generating a "me and you against the world" attitude within the couple.

The lack of LGBTQ+-specific services, coupled with these previously discussed dynamics, as well as the lack of LGBTQ+-specific IPV services and resources, creates a situation in which victims frequently either give up altogether or fight back in self-defense or retaliation. However, most providers differentiate between victim and batterer in heterosexual cases based on the gender of the partners and often inadvertently follow the same assessment process with LGBTQ+ individuals and couples. This reality—coupled with the reality of self-defensive or retaliatory behaviors—makes assessment very difficult, even for the most seasoned of domestic violence specialists. However, when providers do not fully understand the dynamics of LGBTQ+ intimate partner violence, or if they rely on a knowledge base that has conceptualized partner abuse as dependent on gender, the results not only are often ineffective but can be potentially dangerous and life-threatening. For example, victims are placed in treatment that is more appropriate for batterers; batterers are given services that are more appropriate for victims; victims are unable to access domestic violence services because they have been inaccurately assessed in the past; victims are arrested and charged with domestic violence; both victim and batterer are arrested; victims are unable to obtain restraining orders, or both parties obtain them; and so on.

Continuing Education Questions

1. The LGBTQ cycle of violence differs from the traditional cycle of violence in what ways?
    a. Internalized homophobia is present
    b. External homophobia is present
    c. There is a tension-building stage, an acute stage, and a honeymoon stage
    d. A and B
2. Internalized anti-LGBTQ bias produces a heightened sense of shame because of one's sexual orientation or gender identity as well as internalization of all or most of the cultural messages and misconceptions about LGBTQ intimate partner violence that exist. Once internalized, these messages can lead to heightened traumatic bonding and isolation within the couple and increased difficulty breaking through the cycle itself.
    a. True
    b. False
3. What are barriers to LGBTQ IPV victims and perpetrators seeking help?
    a. Anti-LGBTQ attitudes in greater society
    b. Internalized homophobia creating shame
    c. Risk of unequal or ineffective treatment by medical and legal resources
    d. All of the above

4. Traumatic bonding can be defined as the strong emotional attachment that develops between victims and their abusers that can occur in relationships where there is a power imbalance.
   a. True
   b. False
5. Which of the following is *not* one of the possible negative outcomes when LGBTQ IPV victims/perpetrators are treated?
   a. Victims are placed in treatment appropriate for victims
   b. Batterers are given services more appropriate for victims
   c. Victims are unable to access domestic violence services because they have been inaccurately assessed in the past
   d. Both victim and batterer are arrested

References

Dutton, D.G., & Painter, S.L. (1981). Traumatic Bonding: The Development of Emotional Attachments in Battered Women and Other Relationships of Intermittent Abuse. *Victimology: An International Journal, 6,* 139–155.

Graham, D.L.R., & Rawlings, E.I. (1991). Bonding with Abusive Dating Partners: Dynamics of the Stockholm Syndrome. In B. Levy (Ed.), *Dating Violence: Young Women in Danger* (pp. 119 015–135). Seattle: Seal Press.

Walker, L. (1979). *The Battered Woman.* New York, NY: Harper & Row.

LGBTQ+ Intimate Partner Violence and Substance Abuse

11

The discussion of substance use and intimate partner violence within the LGBTQ+ community takes place against a backdrop of the known association of these two phenomena in the general population. There is a large body of literature that shows the association between alcohol use diagnoses and recent alcohol use and male-to-female IPV perpetration among heterosexuals. There has been a robust finding of an association between illicit drug use and male-to-female domestic violence as well (however, there is a distinct lack of data for specific substances). These associations, particularly with alcohol, have been shown in both cross-sectional and longitudinal studies (Stuart, O'Farrell, & Temple, 2009), although there is no conclusive evidence of the directionality of this association (i.e. does substance use cause IPV or does IPV cause substance use). However, multiple studies have shown increases in the amount of substance use among men and women arrested for domestic violence or in domestic violence treatment programs. Conversely, studies have shown increased IPV among men and women presenting for inpatient substance use treatment. In many cases, the crossover exceeds 50%, indicating a very strong association. One study concluded that, among heterosexual male IPV perpetrators, there was an 8–19 times higher likelihood of domestic violence occurring on a "heavy drinking" day (Stuart et al., 2009).

There has been relatively little research on this topic that has included LGBTQ+ people. However, research has shown consistently that the LGBTQ+ community uses substances at a higher rate than its heterosexual counterparts. Studies indicate that, when compared with the general

DOI: 10.4324/9780429031397-11

population, LGBTQ+ people are more likely to use alcohol and drugs, have higher rates of substance abuse, are less likely to abstain from substance use, and are more likely to continue heavy drinking into later life (U.S. Department of Health and Human Services, 2019). Estimates of the incidence of addiction in the LGBTQ+ population range between 28% and 35%, compared with 10–12% in the heterosexual community (Cabaj & Klinger, 1996). Furthermore, there are studies that indicate discrepancies in the LGBTQ+ community with cocaine, other illicit substances, marijuana, and binge drinking (Xavier Hall, Newcomb et al., 2022). According to Stults et al. (2015), over 50% of younger men who have sex with men report binge drinking within the previous year, and over 10% report using illicit drugs. Other research confirms that LGBTQ+ youth have a higher prevalence of substance use. For example, 95% have tried an illicit substance, which is higher than the general population. In particular, bisexuals and lesbians have four times the rate of substance use than do their heterosexual counterparts (Garofalo et al., 1999). As has already been shown, there is also a greater lifetime prevalence rate of IPV in the LGBTQ+ community, making IPV and substance use an important area for future research.

From these studies and others, it has been well established that LGBTQ+ persons use and abuse alcohol as well as all other types of drugs. However, certain drugs have gained more popularity than others in the LGBTQ+ community. One large disparity that has been shown in the literature is the increased use of alcohol by lesbians when compared with heterosexual women. Lesbians are twice as likely to have used alcohol in the previous month, four times more likely to get intoxicated every week, and five times more likely to drink daily (U.S. Department of Health and Human Services, 2019). However, this does not diminish that the majority of studies show that gay and bisexual men as well as transgender persons also use alcohol at a higher rate than the general population. In many studies, bisexuals had the highest rate of alcohol use of all LGBTQ+ subgroups (Keuroghlian et al., 2015; King et al., 2008).

Another major disparity in the literature is related to the use of party drugs, including MDMA, Special K (ketamine), and GHB (gamma hydroxybutyrate), especially by GBTQ+ men. The use of methamphetamine by these groups has also increased dramatically throughout the years (Drug Abuse Warning Network, 1998; Derlet & Heischober, 1990; Morgan et al, 1993; NIDA, 1994), and HIV and hepatitis C infections are linked with its use (CDC, 1995). Studies show that men who have sex with men (MSM) in particular have 27 times the rate of methamphetamine use as their heterosexual counterparts (Xavier Hall, Newcomb et al., 2022). Methamphetamine (commonly known as *meth* or *crystal meth*) is a highly addictive and powerful central nervous system stimulant. A Schedule II drug with little medical use but a high potential for abuse, the drug works directly on the brain and spinal cord by interfering with normal neurotransmission (Rizzo, 2011). The use of meth has increased in areas with high LGBTQ+ populations (St. John, 2012).

Meth floods the brain with dopamine, which results in a powerful sense of well-being (St. John, 2012), and many GBTQ+ men use meth as they struggle to reduce or eliminate feelings of shame or guilt or those associated with family rejection, as well as minority stress and societal trauma. However, it can also cause "crystal dick," a term indicating an increase in sexual desire at the same time as the drug takes away the ability to perform (St. John, 2012). According to Gelles (1993), amphetamines may be the only drugs that cause violent behavior. Amphetamines heighten excitability and muscle tension and may lead to impulsive acts. The behavior that follows amphetamine use is related to both the dosage and the personality of the user prior to taking the drug. In fact, high-dosage users who already have aggressive personalities are likely to become more aggressive when using amphetamines (Taylor & Leonard, 1983). This is obviously relevant when discussing IPV.

Some meth users have sex only when they are high, which can cause sex and meth to become strongly linked in the brain, a state that often leads to unsafe sex and an increased risk for HIV infection (St. John, 2012) and other sexually transmitted infections. Sex-related substance abuse, also known as "chemsex," involves other substances, such as nitrite inhalants and GHB, and is associated with group sex and riskier sexual behavior (e.g. less use of condoms). This has been called a "syndemic" in the literature owing to the link between childhood sexual abuse, substance abuse, depression, IPV, and HIV/AIDS infection (Miltz et al., 2019). Because so much research focusing on the LGBTQ+ population has yet to be done, including the link between LGBTQ+ domestic violence and substance use, there is still much we don't know. Currently, the majority of our knowledge about substance use within LGBTQ+ populations is limited to self-identified white gay men and lesbians with higher levels of education (Hughes & Eliason, 2002).

Historically, entrance into the LGBTQ+ community was (and still often is) through LGBTQ+ bars and clubs since they were frequently the only location for meeting and socializing with other LGBTQ+ people. The mixing of alcohol, drugs, and social gatherings can put many at risk (D'Augelli et al., 2001; Matthews & Selvidge 2005; Matthews, Lorah, & Fenton, 2006). Furthermore, LGBTQ+ individuals experiencing external stigma, internalized LGBTQ+ homo/bi/transphobia, isolation, family rejection, minority stressors, and societal trauma may use alcohol or drugs as a coping mechanism (D'Augelli et al., 2001; Matthews & Selvidge, 2005; Matthews et al., 2006). Participants in a study of gay men and lesbians in recovery revealed that conflict related to sexual orientation was a major contributing factor to their alcoholism (Matthews et al., 2006). Further, substance use may allow an individual to act on their "tabooed" desires while helping them with the emotional or psychological aftermath of such actions (California Department of Mental Health, 2012). Support in the form of LGBTQ+-specific recovery programs or meetings, as well as connections with clean and sober LGBTQ+ individuals, has been found to facilitate recovery (Matthews et al., 2006). However, these facilities and programs have been very limited in number and reach, so that many LGBTQ+ people are left without culturally competent treatment (U.S. Department of Health and Human Services, 2019).

A review of the heterosexual, cisgender literature such as that indicated earlier in this chapter indicates a clear association between domestic violence and substance use. The research focusing on LGBTQ+ people is much more limited, but similar results have been found thus far. Studies show that 25–67% of sexual minority abusers are under the influence of a substance at the time of the perpetration of IPV. Studies also show that, in intimate partner homicides, alcohol and drugs are found in the systems of both LGBTQ+ victims and perpetrators more frequently than with heterosexual, cisgender couples (Messinger, 2020). The two most common substances that have been studied in the limited literature on LGBTQ+ IPV are alcohol and methamphetamine. Given the discrepancies in use within this community, it makes sense to focus on these. There is little research regarding other substances.

Alcohol has been studied most extensively. It is clear from the heterosexual, cisgender literature that it is the most prevalent abused substance in the context of IPV (Stuart et al., 2009). Similarly, rates of substance use within the LGBTQ+ community show that alcohol is a highly abused substance in this community as well. A Canadian study found that "problematic alcohol use" and illicit drug use by gay and bisexual male adults in the previous 6 months was associated with roughly 1.5 times the risk of lifetime bidirectional IPV (reporting both victimization and perpetration, which was much more common than reporting either victimization or perpetration alone in the sample; Kirschbaum et al., 2023). Davis et al. (2015) also found that alcohol use was associated with both victimization and perpetration of IPV in same-sex male couples. In Black men who have sex with men, studies have similarly found that heavy drinking is associated with victimization and perpetration of IPV over the course of the relationship and in the previous 30 days (Wu et al., 2014). When looking at lesbian relationships, much has been made of the distinction between shared drinking between the couple (light drinking involving both members of a couple in a shared experience) and discrepant drinking (large differences in drinking between couple members and often done apart from the other partner; Lewis et al., 2018). In heterosexual, cisgender couples, it has been shown that shared drinking can be healthy for a relationship, whereas discrepant drinking is highly associated with IPV and general relationship conflict (Fischer & Wiersma, 2012). As mentioned previously, lesbians have a particularly high risk of alcohol abuse. Coleman (1990) found that 71% of violent lesbian couples reported using alcohol or drugs, compared with 29.4% of lesbian couples considered to be non-violent. Studies show that discrepant drinking in lesbians is linked to higher psychological and physical aggression in IPV. It is also linked to lower relationship satisfaction in lesbian couples. There has been speculation that drinking discrepancy creates conflict in a relationship which progresses to IPV or that partners are drinking either to cope with negative emotions which independently lead to IPV and/ or to cope with the IPV itself. As with other studies, it is difficult to pinpoint a causal relationship (Lewis et al., 2018). There are very few studies that focus on bisexual men and women, as this group is largely included in studies with the associated gender (e.g. "gay and bisexual men") and not studied independently. That is a direction for future research. Transgender people have also not been studied extensively, and so more research is needed. Similar trends have emerged with youth, although much of the focus continues to be on young MSM. Among MSM, those reporting IPV were one to two times as likely to engage in two or more instances of alcohol consumption in the last month and more than five times as likely to have used any drugs in the previous 30 days. Substance use was associated with IPV as well as with at-school victimization, homelessness, and/or suicidality (Stults et al., 2015). A more recent study included transgender women with GBTQ+ men and found that IPV was associated with higher use of alcohol as well as other substances (Xavier Hall, Newcomb et al., 2022).

The second large disparity that has been the topic of more focus has been the use of methamphetamine and "party drugs," mainly by gay and bisexual men. In heterosexual, cisgender male-to-female IPV, meth has been shown to subjectively increase aggression, sex drive, and the need to procure more substance. Male meth users indicated that these factors led them to be more likely to commit IPV (Watt, 2017). In gay and bisexual men, studies have found that meth and drugs of abuse, such as ketamine and GHB, have been linked to IPV. In the PROUD study in the United Kingdom by Miltz et al., they specifically looked at "chemsex," which has been linked to group sex, anonymous sex, and riskier sexual behaviors. They found that it is also significantly related to IPV. Another study showed that injecting amphetamines in the previous year was significantly associated with IPV victimization (Miltz et al., 2019). For youth, MSM reporting IPV were twice as likely to have used stimulants in general and twice as likely to have used them in the previous month (Stults et al., 2015). Studies show that methamphetamine is linked to IPV in gay and bisexual youth, with some studies including all of those assigned male at birth (Xavier Hall, Javanbakht et al., 2022; Xavier Hall, Newcomb et al., 2022).

In reference to other substances, there is limited evidence for substance-specific data. In heterosexual, cisgender couples, marijuana abuse has been linked to IPV in cross-sectional and longitudinal studies. However, the relationship between marijuana and aggression is mixed. Similarly, with cocaine, the relationship with aggression has shown mixed results in studies, but there is a strong relationship between cocaine use and IPV perpetration in male–female couples (Stuart et al., 2009). Very few studies have focused on these substances with LGBTQ+ people, primarily youth. However, those have found a significant relationship between marijuana and cocaine and IPV (Stults et al., 2015; Xavier Hall, Newcomb et al., 2022).

Clearly, there is much need for additional research. Substances that are commonly used change in terms of prevalence. For example, psychedelics are currently being used more widely. One of these is ayahuasca, which is a plant-based psychedelic which promotes dissociation and hallucinations. Usually taken in liquid form, it leads to a "trip" which can be pleasant but can also cause anxiety, confusion, and paranoia if it goes badly. The active chemical is DMT (dimethyltryptamine) (Alcohol and Drug Foundation, n.d.a). A similar substance is psilocybin, found in "magic" mushrooms, which is another hallucinogenic which causes a "trip." This is also ingested orally and can cause euphoria, but also paranoia as well as side effects such as nausea and dizziness (Alcohol and Drug Foundation, n.d.c). The other psychedelic for which there has been a resurgence in popularity is LSD (lysergic acid diethylamide), which was developed in the 1930s as a semi-synthetic compound. It was developed from a fungus that infects grain and it is consumed orally in crystalline form. It can also lead to a negative "trip" and can worsen psychosis (Alcohol and Drug Foundation, n.d.b). All of these substances are being investigated for mental health uses, but none has been approved (Multidisciplinary Association for Psychedelic Studies, 2023).

As previously stated, studies have not been able to conclusively determine a causal relationship between substance use and IPV, but the association is very clear. Gondolf (1994) argues that three theories may explain the connection between substance abuse and domestic violence: The disinhibition theory states that drinking breaks down inhibitions and leads to antisocial behavior; the disavowal theory emphasizes the role of social learning in the user's violent relationships and contributes to the use of rationalizations, or excuses, for abusive behavior; and the interaction theory suggests that the interaction of various physiological, psychological, and social factors explains the connection. Others have proposed an explanation that distal factors (hostility, aggression, antisocial traits, gender roles) interact with proximal factors (acute intoxication, situational cues, etc.) to result in IPV (Stuart et al., 2009).

Gondolf (1994) suggests that alcohol abuse and domestic violence may be caused by underlying needs for power and control associated with distorted perceptions of masculinity. This heteronormative theory was conceived in part because women drink for different reasons than men, and their drinking is more commonly related to depression and to sedate the emotional trauma associated with battering (Lisansky-Gomberg, 1981). Even with methamphetamine, a recent study from South Africa indicated that male methamphetamine users with negative attitudes toward women were much more likely to perpetrate IPV (Watt, 2018). In fact, the APA indicates that the presence of abuse in a woman's past is the greatest predictor of alcohol or drug abuse (APA, 1996). Additional studies also show that women who have been previously abused are at the highest risk for IPV victimization in a form of revictimization (Watt, 2018). For LGBTQ+ populations in particular, all of these factors exist as well (gender roles still being important, though they may play out differently). In addition, there are other, unique factors that are independently associated with both substance use and IPV. These include internalized homophobia, minority stress, and a disproportionate experience of traumatic events such as childhood sexual abuse (Xavier Hall, Newcomb et al., 2022; Miltz et al., 2019). These concepts and their relationship to IPV are explored in more detail in other sections of the book.

Overall, substances are typically considered to be co-factors for domestic violence rather than its cause, and it is imperative that both be addressed concurrently. A common mistake made by many clinicians includes focusing on the client's substance abuse problem(s) first and/or primarily while delaying or ignoring the violence until the client has decreased or eliminated their use of substances. Not only is this dangerous and can increase the incidence and severity of violence, but elimination of substances will do little, if anything at all, to alleviate coercive, abusive, and controlling behaviors on the part of abusive clients. The best outcomes result from effective intervention and treatment of both problems simultaneously, by providers who are specialists in each.

Continuing Education Questions

1. Which of the following is true about methamphetamine?
   a. It is used by heterosexual men at the same rate as MSM
   b. It is natural and derived from plants
   c. It is used to enhance sexual experiences and is linked to HIV infection
   d. It is decreasing in use within the LGBTQ+ community
2. The interaction theory states that drinking breaks down inhibitions and leads to antisocial behavior
   a. True
   b. False
3. Which one of these is false regarding LGBTQ substance use?
   a. It is associated with LGBTQ IPV
   b. The rates are higher than those for heterosexuals in most studies
   c. Most studies have focused on African American LGBTQ people so far
   d. Club/party drug use has increased within the LGBTQ community
   e. All of the above
4. There is a positive association between methamphetamine use, HIV positivity, and IPV within the LGBTQ community
   a. True
   b. False
5. What percentage of sexual minority abusers are under the influence at the time of the abuse, according to Messinger (2020)?
   a. 1–15%
   b. 21–48%
   c. 25–67%
   d. 85–97%

References

American Psychological Association (APA). (1996). *Violence and the Family: Report of the American Psychological Association Presidential Task Force on Violence and the Family.* Washington, DC: American Psychological Association.

Alcohol and Drug Foundation. (n.d.a). Ayahuasca. https://adf.org.au/drug-facts/ayahuasca/

Alcohol and Drug Foundation. (n.d.b). LSD. https://adf.org.au/drug-facts/lsd/#wheel

Alcohol and Drug Foundation. (n.d.c). Psilocybin. https://adf.org.au/drug-facts/psilocybin/#wheel

Cabaj, R.P., & Klinger, R.L. (1996). Psychotherapeutic Interventions with Lesbians and Gay Couples. In R. Cabaj & T. Stein (Eds.), *Textbook of Homosexuality and Mental Health* (pp. 485–501). Washington, DC: American Psychiatric Press.

California Department of Mental Health. (2012). *First, Do No Harm: Reducing Disparities for Lesbian, Gay, Bisexual, Transgender, Queer and Questioning Populations in California.* Sacramento, CA: Author.

Centers for Disease Control and Prevention (CDC). (1995). Increasing Morbidity and Mortality Associated with Abuse of Methamphetamine—United States, 1991–1994. *Morbidity and Mortality Weekly Report, 44*(47), 882–886.

Coleman, V.E. (1990). Violence between Lesbian Couples: A between Groups Comparison [Unpublished doctoral dissertation. University Microfilms International, 9109022].

D'Augelli, A.R., Grossman, A.H., Herschberger, S.L., & O'Connell, T.S. (2001). Aspects of Mental Health among Older Lesbian, Gay, and Bisexual Adults. *Aging & Mental Health, 5*(2), 149–158.

Davis, A., Kaighobadi, F., Stephenson, R., Rael, C. T., & Sandfort, T. (2016). Associations between Alcohol Use and Intimate Partner Violence among Men Who Have Sex with Men. *LGBT Health, 3*(6), 400–406. 10.1089/lgbt.2016.0057

Derlet, R.B., & Heischober, B. (1990). Methamphetamine: Stimulant of the 1990s? *Western Journal of Medicine, 153*, 625–628.

Drug Abuse Warning Network. (1998). *Data from the Drug Abuse Warning Network, ADAM.* Rockville, MD: Substance Abuse and Mental Health Services Administration.

Fischer J.L., & Wiersma, J.D. (2012). Romantic Relationships and Alcohol Use. *Current Drug Abuse Reviews, 5*, 98–116.

Garofalo, R., Wolf, R., Wissow, L.S., Woods, E.R., & Goodman, E. (1999). Sexual Orientation and Risk of Suicide Attempts among a Representative Sample Of Youth. *Archives of Pediatrics & Adolescent Medicine, 153*(5). 10.1001/archpedi.153.5.487

Gelles, R.J. (1993). Alcohol and Other Drugs Are Associated with Violence—They Are Not the Cause. In R.J. Gelles & D.R. Loseke (Eds.), *Current Controversies on Family Violence* (p. 184). Newbury Park, CA: Sage.

Gondolf, E.W. (1994). Alcohol Abuse, Wife Assault and Power Needs. In *The Relationship between Substance Abuse and Domestic Violence.* Austin, TX: Texas Council on Family Violence.

Hughes, T.L., & Eliason, M. (2002). Substance Use and Abuse in Lesbian, Gay, Bisexual and Transgender Populations. *Journal of Primary Prevention, 22*(3), 263–298.

Keuroghlian, A.S., Reisner, S.L., White, J.M., & Weiss, R.D. (2015). Substance Use and Treatment of Substance Use Disorders in a Community Sample of Transgender Adults. *Drug and Alcohol Dependence, 152*, 139–146. 10.1016/j.drugalcdep.2015.04.008

King, M., Semlyen, J., Tai, S.S., Killaspy, H., Osborn, D., Popelyuk, D., & Nazareth, I. (2008). A Systematic Review of Mental Disorder, Suicide, and Deliberate Self Harm in Lesbian, Gay and Bisexual People. *BMC Psychiatry, 8*(1). 10.1186/1471-244x-8-70

Kirschbaum, A.L., Metheny, N., Skakoon-Sparling, S., Grace, D., Yakubovich, A.R., Cox, J., Palachi, A., Sang, J.M., O'Campo, P., Tan, D.H.S., & Hart, T.A. (2023). Syndemic Factors and Lifetime Bidirectional Intimate Partner Violence among Gay, Bisexual, and Other Sexual Minority Men. *LGBT Health, 10*(S1), S89–S97. 10.1089/lgbt.2023.0117

Lewis, R.J., Winstead, B.A., Braitman, A.L., & Hitson, P.T. (2018). Discrepant Drinking and Partner Violence Perpetration over Time in Lesbians' Relationships. *Violence Against Women, 24*(10), 1149–1165. 10.1177/1077801218781925

Lisansky-Gomberg, E.S. (1981). Learned Helplessness, Depression and Alcohol Problems of Women. In P. Russianoff (Ed.), *Women in Crisis* (pp. 41–42). New York: Human Science Press.

Matthews, C.R., & Selvidge, M.M.D. (2005). Lesbian, Gay, and Bisexual Clients' Experiences in Treatment for Addiction. In E. Ettorre (Ed.), *Making Lesbians Visible in the Substance Use Field* (pp. 79–90). New York, NY: Harrington Park Press.

Matthews, C.R., Lorah, P., & Fenton, J. (2006). Treatment Experiences of Gays and Lesbians in Recovery from Addiction: A Qualitative Inquiry. *Journal of Mental Health Counseling, 28*(2), 111–132.

Messinger, A.M. (2020). *LGBTQ Intimate Partner Violence: Lessons for Policy, Practice, and Research.* University of California Press.

Miltz, A.R., Lampe, F.C., Bacchus, L.J., McCormack, S., Dunn, D., White, E., Rodger, A., Phillips, A.N., Sherr, L., Clarke, A., McOwan, A., Sullivan, A., & Gafos, M. (2019). Intimate Partner Violence, Depression, and Sexual Behaviour among Gay, Bisexual and Other Men Who Have Sex with Men in the PROUD Trial. *BMC Public Health, 19*(1), 431. 10.1186/s12889-019-6757-6

Morgan, P., McDonnell, D., Beck, J., Joe, K., & Gutierrez, R. (1993). Ice and Methamphetamine Use: Preliminary Findings from Three Sites. In S. Sowder & G. Beschner (Eds.), *Methamphetamine: An Illicit Drug with High Abuse Potential.* Rockville, MD: Head.

National Institute on Drug Abuse (NIDA). (1994). *Community Epidemiology Work Group. Epidemiology Trends in Drug Abuse [fact sheet].* Rockville, MD: Author.

Multidisciplinary Association for Psychedelic Studies. (January 10, 2023). Our Research. maps.org/our-research/

Rizzo, M. (2011). The Perfect Storm: Crystal Meth, Dopamine, and LGBTQ Domestic Violence. Unpublished paper.

U.S. Department of Health and Human Services. (2019). *A Provider's Introduction to Substance Abuse Treatment for Lesbian, Gay, Bisexual, and Transgender Individuals.* Lulu.com

St. John, S. (2012). Out of the Darkness: Beating Crystal Meth Addiction, *Vanguard, 12*(4), 4–5.

Stuart, G.L., O'Farrell, T.J., & Temple, J. (2009). Review of the Association between Treatment for Substance Misuse and Reductions in Intimate Partner Violence. *Substance Use & Misuse, 44*(9–10), 1298–1317. 10.1080/10826080902961385

Stults, C.B., Javdani, S., Greenbaum, C.A., Kapadia, F., & Halkitis, P.N. (2015). Intimate Partner Violence and Substance Use Risk among Young Men Who Have Sex with Men: The P18 Cohort Study. *Drug and Alcohol Dependence, 154*, 54–62. 10.1016/j.drugalcdep.2015.06.008

Taylor, S., & Leonard, K.E. (1983). Alcohol and Human Physical Aggression. In R. Green & E. Donnerstein (Eds.), *Aggression: Theoretical and Empirical Reviews* (vol. 2; pp. 77–11). New York: Academic Press.

Watt, M.H., Guidera, K.E., Hobkirk, A.L., Skinner, D., & Meade, C.S. (2017). Intimate Partner Violence among Men and Women Who Use Methamphetamine: A Mixed-Methods Study in South Africa. *Drug and Alcohol Review, 36*(1), 97–106. 10.1111/dar.12420

Wu, E., El-Bassel, N., McVinney, L.D., Hess, L., Fopeano, M.V., Hwang, H.G., Charania, M.R., & Mansergh, G. (2014). The Association between Substance Use and Intimate Partner Violence within Black Male Same-Sex Relationships. *Journal of Interpersonal Violence, 30*(5), 762–781. 10.1177/0886260514536277

Xavier Hall, C.D., Javanbakht, M., Iyer, C., Costales, C., Napolitano, J.C., Johnson, T., Castro, C.F., Newcomb, M.E., Kipke, M.D., Shoptaw, S., Gorbach, P.M., & Mustanski, B. (2022). Examining the Impact of Social Distancing and Methamphetamine Use on Sexual Risk and Intimate Partner Violence in Sexual and Gender Minority Young Adults during the COVID-19 Pandemic. *Drug and Alcohol Dependence, 232*, 109231. 10.1016/j.drugalcdep.2021.109231

Xavier Hall, C.D., Newcomb, M.E., Dyar, C., & Mustanski, B. (2022). Patterns of Polyvictimization Predict Stimulant Use, Alcohol and Marijuana Problems in a Large Cohort of Sexual Minority and Gender Minority Youth Assigned Male at Birth. *Psychology of Addictive Behaviors: Journal of the Society of Psychologists in Addictive Behaviors, 36*(2), 186–196. 10.1037/adb0000751

LGBTQ+-Affirmative Intimate Partner Violence Intervention and Advocacy

12

As indicated previously, LGBTQ+ domestic violence has been relatively invisible and has been the focus of very little theoretical and empirical attention. A thorough understanding of intimate partner violence and the interventions and treatment for it in general can only be considered a starting point when conceptualizing and working with LGBTQ+ domestic violence. LGBTQ+ affirming advocates and counselors should be knowledgeable about LGBTQ+ domestic violence and its similarities to and differences from non-LGBTQ intimate partner violence, as well as relevant issues pertinent to the LGBTQ+ population. These include LGBTQ+ identity development formation and the coming out process, societal responses to the LGBTQ+ population, internalized and institutionalized anti-LGBTQ bias and stigma, and the diverse differences within the broader LGBTQ+ community and its various subpopulations. It is of the utmost importance that providers identify, explore, and challenge their own biases about LGBTQ+ individuals and LGBTQ+ intimate partner violence. Furthermore, there is an important distinction between services that are LGBTQ+-sensitive and LGBTQ+-affirmative and those that are LGBTQ+-specific, and these differences should be understood and addressed with the client.

Between July 2003 and June 2005, the L.A. Gay & Lesbian Center's STOP Violence Program distributed 129 pre-tests and 114 post-tests to staff members of domestic violence service organizations, social service agencies, HIV/AIDS organizations, and legal advocacy programs who were assembled to participate in 3-hour training courses on LGBTQ+ intimate

DOI: 10.4324/9780429031397-12

partner violence. Although 24% of the pre-test respondents indicated that they had worked with members of the LGBTQ+ community, only 16.3% indicated that they had received previous training in the subject. The majority (82.2%) had not received any training in either the LGBTQ+ community in general or LGBTQ+ domestic violence. Slightly more than 74.4% were either unaware of having worked with LGBTQ+ persons in the past or had no experience with the LGBTQ+ population. (Holt, 2005). More than one in ten (10.9%) of pre-test respondents incorrectly believed that domestic violence was more common in heterosexual relationships than LGBTQ+ relationships, and 5.4% were unsure. Post-tests revealed that 10.5% still believed, after training, that domestic violence was more common in heterosexual partnerships. This very slight decrease may reflect the inability of the respondents to alter their stereotypes of LGBTQ+ persons and their relationships without extensive training.

Some 69.8% of pre-test respondents were unable to identify basic misconceptions about LGBTQ+ domestic violence that should be addressed with LGBTQ+ clients (men can be victims of domestic violence, women can abuse their partners, etc.), but this percentage decreased following training to 51.8%. While 58.1% of pre-test respondents were able to identify one way in which anti-LGBTQ+ bias or homophobia impacts LGBTQ+ persons experiencing domestic violence by indicating the lack of LGBTQ+-sensitive and LGBTQ+-specific resources, 78.1% of post-test respondents were able to identify how anti-LGBTQ+ bias could affect their LGBTQ+ clients. The majority of pre-test respondents were unclear about what the greatest factor was for potential lethality of LGBTQ+ persons impacted by domestic violence, with 31% indicating that the disclosure of sexual orientation could be deadly and 40.3% indicating that lack of services would be to blame.

A substantial majority of pre-test respondents (75.9%) were unable to list even one difference between domestic violence in non-LGBTQ and LGBTQ+ relationships, but this percentage decreased to 30.7% following training. A sizable 27.9% of pre-test respondents revealed stereotypical thinking processes when incorrectly indicating that it is often true that a "femme" partner is more frequently the victim of LGBTQ+ domestic violence while a "butch" partner is more frequently the batterer, and 12.4% were unsure. This erroneous assumption can have very dangerous consequences for LGBTQ+ victims, abusers, and service providers alike and is the reason why LGBTQ+ victims are often arrested and mandated to batterers' treatment and LGBTQ+ batterers are housed in the same shelter as their victims or allowed to attend the same drop-in support groups.

Following training, only 3.5% still maintained this stereotype, and the percentage of those who were unsure dropped by 8 points (LAGLC, 2005). As many as 89.8% of pre-test respondents were unable to identify any stage of the coming out process and how it might impact LGBTQ+ clients experiencing domestic violence, but this percentage decreased to 56.1% following training (LAGLC, 2005). Pre- and post-training tests distributed consistently to subsequent training participants over the years have yielded only minor improvements.

Clearly, service providers need significantly more than 3 hours of training on the subject of LGBTQ+ domestic violence before they are able to sufficiently and effectively respond to LGBTQ+ survivors and those who abuse. Rather, multiple hours of in-depth training in both LGBTQ+ issues and LGBTQ+ domestic violence are needed before they are capable of providing LGBTQ+-affirmative therapy. Recent surveys conducted with Master's-level students who completed 16 hours of non-LGBTQ+ domestic violence training at two institutions of higher education in Southern California, spanning more than a decade (2010–2023), yielded a similar, yet even more disappointing, outcome. While the vast majority of students gained sufficient knowledge of the subject matter to intervene in a safe, although basic, manner with all domestic violence clients—regardless of sexual orientation or gender identity—they consistently minimized the dynamics of a case of LGBTQ+ domestic violence presented to them and subsequently failed to apply appropriate interventions to the case in a manner consistent with their response to non-LGBTQ IPV cases presented to them. There continues to be a lack of education specific to LGBTQ+ IPV, and this is pervasive across time and many educational levels and institutions. In fact, research by Brown and Herman in 2015 has shown that service providers often do not take LGBTQ+ domestic violence as seriously as heterosexual IPV. In a survey of 120 staff members of domestic violence agencies, LGBTQ+ IPV was judged as both less serious and less likely to worsen over time compared with heterosexual IPV, and domestic violence staff were significantly less likely to recommend that victims consider leaving the abuser if the victim and abuser were of the same gender. Furthermore, a study of 171 university students who were provided with identical IPV scenarios with only the sexual orientation changed found that participants (a) considered same-gender domestic violence to be less serious than male against female abuse, (b) were more likely to recommend that the victim press charges in male against female abuse than in same-gender domestic abuse, and (c) perceived same-gender victims to be less believable than heterosexual victims (National Center for Transgender Equality (2020).

In another survey, approximately 70% of clients who reported that they had sought some form of service or help had experienced prejudice and/or negative responses to their gender or sexuality, ranging from service providers dismissing it altogether to shaming the client (Whirry & Holt, 2020).

"LGBTQ+-affirmative psychotherapy" (also known as "gay-affirmative therapy", "gay & lesbian-affirmative therapy", and "queer-affirmative therapy") is a term that was coined and defined by Alan K. Malyon in 1982. Among other accomplishments, Dr. Malyon was the founder and president elect of the Society for the Psychological Study of Lesbian and Gay Issues, which became Division 44 of the American Psychological Association (Ybarra, M.J., 1988), an APA division that focuses on the diversity of sexual orientations. In contrast to a modality or specific set of interventions and practices, LGBTQ+-affirmative therapy counters therapeutic approaches that view homosexuality within a pathological context. Instead, this approach maintains a positive view of LGBTQ+ identities and relationships and addresses the negative and harmful influences that societal homophobia/biphobia/transphobia and heterosexism have on LGBTQ+ individuals and communities and the symptoms that these often create, including anxiety, depression, and shame-based syndromes (Weinraub, 2021). There is a strong focus on the therapeutic alliance, and the therapist serves as an advocate for the client and acknowledges the sociopolitical reality of LGBTQ+ persons that those who are heterosexual do not have (APA, 2012).

Kingdon (1979) developed seven principles for lesbian-affirmative therapy that can be extended to include members of the GBT population and suggests that therapists (1) know the definition, prevalence, theories, and myths about the LGBTQ+ community; (2) are familiar with community resources; (3) have skills to help the client explore and determine their sexuality; (4) have assessment skills to determine whether a problem is due to internal dynamics or society's reaction to sexual orientation; (5) have group therapy skills, since LGBTQ+ groups can help alleviate isolation; (6) believe that society, as well as the individual, needs to change; and (7) evaluate personal homophobia/biphobia/transphobia and heterosexism.

According to Skinner and Otis (1996), programs that specialize in working with the LGBTQ+ population provide a safe place for LGBTQ+ persons to talk about all aspects of their lives without fear of criticism or judgment, which can be a liberating experience. In addition, they offer the opportunity to address issues that would be overlooked in a mainstream program, including socialization skills, dating and intimacy issues, aspects of grief and loss, issues related to HIV/AIDS, coming out, internalized homophobia/biphobia/transphobia, spirituality, the use of recreational drugs, and so on. In addition, they are sensitive to the damage experienced by LGBTQ+ persons in our culture (Hicks, 2000). However, LGBTQ+-affirmative therapy and programs focused on LGBTQ+ communities are a relatively recent phenomenon. Hicks (2000) indicates that, although there are not enough controlled studies to demonstrate effectiveness, it is clear to many who work in these programs that they seem to be powerful in helping patients achieve recovery and healing.

Proujansky and Pachankis (2014) reviewed eight potential LGB-affirmative psychotherapy principles for improving minority stress-coping among sexual minority clients in an attempt to create and test the efficacy of treatment utilizing these principles in an ongoing randomized controlled trial. The principles included (1) normalizing the mental health impact of minority stress; (2) facilitating emotion awareness, regulation, and acceptance; (3) decreasing avoidance; (4) restructuring minority stress cognitions; (5) empowering sexual minority clients to communicate assertively; (6) validating sexual minority individuals' unique strengths; (7) building supportive relationships; and (8) affirming healthy, rewarding expressions of sexuality.

As previously defined in this book, "minority stress refers to the sexual (orientation) stigma manifested as prejudice and discrimination directed at non-heterosexual persons and the excess stress to which individuals from stigmatized social categories are exposed" (American Psychological Association Task Force on Appropriate Therapeutic Responses to Sexual Orientation, 2009; Meyer, 2003). When excess stressors combine with general life stressors, Hatzenbuehler (2009) asserts that they "get under the skin" of sexual minority individuals to jeopardize mental health and, therefore, represent potential treatment targets when psychotherapy is conducted with sexual minority clients. Proujansky and Pachankis indicate that there are multiple individual negative ramifications that can result from this process, including, among others, low self-worth (Wichstrøm & Hegna, 2003), chronic expectations of rejection (Pachankis, Goldfried, & Ramrattan, 2008), poor emotional awareness (Hatzenbuehler, McLaughlin, & Nolen-Hoeksema, 2008), emotional suppression (Matthews et al., 2002), achievement-contingent self-worth (Pachankis & Hatzenbuehler, 2013), hopelessness (Plöderl, & Fartaćek, 2005), shame (Newcomb & Mustanski, 2010), and internalized negative societal attitudes about LGBTQ+ people (Newcomb & Mustanski, 2010).

High levels of LGBTQ+ violence and crime victimization are closely related to internalized and externalized anti-LGBTQ stigma and discrimination. The experience of trauma related to the coming out process is virtually universal with the LGBTQ+ population and is complicated by issues of gender orientation, poor family acceptance, and low socio-economic status. Many LGBTQ+ persons have been rejected or ostracized by family and community support systems and often receive the majority of their support from abusive partners, making it more difficult for them to leave violent relationships (Cohn, 2016).

The following LGBTQ+-affirming premises for intervention serve as a primer for advocates, counselors, and a variety of other diverse services providers that can be easily used in a variety of settings. (*Note*: Counselors and therapists who work within a LGBTQ+-affirmative model are generally educators and advocates for their clients first and foremost and often make referrals to providers with specialized training and expertise in the subject of LGBTQ+ intimate partner violence for more extensive psychotherapy, if such providers are available in the area.)

- It is imperative that service providers examine their own attitudes and feelings about LGBTQ+ persons before working with the population. Identify internalized versions of homophobia/biphobia/transphobia, heterosexism, and other forms of bias that have been incorporated into your belief system. Consider the origin of these beliefs and challenge them before intervening with members of the LGBTQ+ community. Similarly, identify and examine all myths and misconceptions about LGBTQ+ intimate partner violence that you have internalized. Also consider their origins and challenge them before intervening with LGBTQ+ clients.

Once this has been done:

- Let your community know that you are supportive of LGBTQ+ people.
- Create a safe environment for LGBTQ+ individuals by using inclusive forms, informational materials, brochures, pamphlets, posters, and so on.
- If you provide informational materials about intimate partner violence for your clients, make sure that they include information about LGBTQ+ domestic violence. If they do not include information about it, secure materials that either focus on this issue or have significant information about it in them.
- Respect your client's anxieties about disclosure of sexual orientation or gender identity. They are frequently based on real fears of bias and discrimination and the subsequent effects on child custody, family

support, job and financial security, immigration status/deportation, and so on.

- Don't make assumptions about anyone's sexual orientation or gender identity until it is disclosed.
- Never force disclosure of sexual orientation or gender identity. This should always be left up to the client. Replace heteronormative language with gender-neutral language until the gender of the client's partner or spouse is disclosed.
- Establish your acceptance of human diversity and let the client know that you have not made assumptions about it or them. For example, you might ask the individual if they are involved in a relationship and then follow up with a question asking whether the relationship partner identifies as male, female, non-binary, transfeminine or transmasculine, and so on. By making this question routine, you indicate that you are aware of human diversity and its importance.
- Once sexual orientation or gender identity has been disclosed, ascertain to whom and when the client is comfortable disclosing it and/or what name and gender pronouns they prefer.
- If you are unable to communicate your acceptance of diversity, refer the client to another service provider.
- Be aware that survivors of LGBTQ+ domestic violence may question their sexuality or gender identity because of the trauma they have experienced. While it is appropriate to acknowledge their doubts, it is not appropriate or helpful to label sexual orientation as the reason for the trauma or indicate in any way that sexual orientation and gender identity are deviant and can be changed. Helping the survivor explore their feelings and identify their sexual orientation or gender identity is the most appropriate response, provided that you explain clearly that sexual orientation and gender identity do not cause domestic violence, and that it occurs in all populations.
- Use the LGBTQ+ person's language. Respect the client's discomfort with terms such as "domestic violence." Terms such as "conflict resolution," "healthy relationships," and "communication skills," while not a substitute for terms describing abusive relationships, may more easily prompt a discussion about abuse when it is present.
- Clients who have been abused by same-gender partners may be hesitant to trust a professional of the same gender. Respect the client's preferences and honor them whenever possible.
- Do not assume that LGBTQ+ clients will believe that what they've experienced is abusive. Because of the invisibility of LGBTQ+ intimate

partner violence within society and the numerous myths and misconceptions that surround it, LGBTQ+ individuals may not be aware that they are experiencing abuse, even when it is severe. Additional education about the dynamics of abuse and its prevalence in the LGBTQ+ community should be provided to them.

- Do not believe the misconceptions associated with LGBTQ+ domestic violence. While it may be easy to reject the more traditional myths about heterosexual domestic violence, you may not as easily notice or dismiss those associated with LGBTQ+ domestic violence. Determine what misconceptions the client has about LGBTQ+ intimate partner violence and challenge the misconceptions while providing education about the realities of it.

- Remember that, while members of the larger LGBTQ+ community affected by domestic violence experience certain commonalities, LGBTQ+ domestic violence is different for lesbians than it is for gay men; different for bisexuals than it is for gays and lesbians; and different for transgender individuals than it is for gays, lesbians, and bisexuals. For example, women experience intimate partner violence within a misogynist and sexist culture as well as an anti-LGBTQ environment, and LGBTQ+ people of color experience multiple layers of oppression, including racism. In the broader LGBTQ+ community itself, those who identify as bisexual or transgender are sometimes marginalized and/or misunderstood. Furthermore, males and females are socialized differently, which may impact how they conceptualize and experience domestic violence. Although some theorists have attempted to do so, LGBTQ+ domestic violence cannot be entirely explained with a traditional male-to-female model. When working with LGBTQ+ clients, it can be helpful to ascertain how the client views their gender, if they see an intersection between their gender or gender role and the abuse, which parent or caregiver tended to be the client's primary role model in childhood, and so on.

- Learn about your state's statutes and laws relating to the rights of LGBTQ+ people regarding partnerships, children, anti-discrimination protections, immigration relief, and so on, as well as those that pertain to protective and restraining orders and domestic violence legislation in general. Domestic violence laws often contain heteronormative and opposite-gender terms and language, which can exclude LGBTQ+ people from protections. While some states include gender-neutral language in their domestic violence legislation, the application and enforcement of it is dependent on a variety of factors, including the level of knowledge, training, and bias that criminal justice and other responders have about it.

- Be knowledgeable about the stages of the coming out process and utilize this knowledge when conceptualizing and developing your interventions. Assist LGBTQ+ people in identifying preferences and options for LGBTQ+-specific or LGBTQ+-sensitive/affirmative service and refer when necessary.

- Be realistic about referrals. Identify expectations and potential challenges for the referral in addition to discussing with the LGBTQ+ individual how these challenges can be handled should they arise. For example, if you refer a client to a shelter, be honest with them about the possibility that other residents may be biased. Discuss the possibility that they will experience additional challenges to ongoing safety when they leave the shelter because of the insular nature of the LGBTQ+ community and assist with individualized safety planning. Appropriate preparation of the client for the referral can improve the outcome.

- Understand how internalized anti-LGBTQ bias contributes to LGBTQ+ domestic violence. Anti-LGBTQ bias is an irrational fear of or disdain for homosexuality or refers to prejudices based on stereotypes and myths. Anti-LGBTQ bias may come from the abuser (even if they are LGBTQ+), law enforcement officials, health and mental health professionals, as well as the victim. When people see themselves or others as second-class citizens, they may strike out at their partners, refuse assistance, or believe that they deserve the abuse.

- Do not expect your LGBTQ+ clients to educate you about sexual orientation, gender identity, the LGBTQ+ community, LGBTQ+ domestic violence, or anti-LGBTQ bias. LGBTQ+ clients who are experiencing intimate partner violence need all of their internal resources to focus on obtaining and maintaining safety and eliminating violence from their lives. It is the responsibility of the service provider to educate themselves about how to work appropriately and effectively with their clients. It is important to have an understanding of how cultural and societal factors impact, and are impacted by, domestic violence. An in-depth understanding of these factors underscores the importance of understanding different populations within their cultural context. Providers are then more apt to provide effective intervention, regardless of whether they define themselves and their services as "LGBTQ-sensitive/affirmative" or "LGBTQ-specific."

- Learn about the resources in your local LGBTQ+ community and utilize them. The National Coalition of Anti-Violence Programs (www. ncavp.org) and the National LGBTQ+ Institute on Intimate Partner

Violence (lgbtqipvinstitute.org) maintain a listing of LGBTQ+-specific anti-violence programs and LGBTQ+ IPV programs in the United States.

- Assist LGBTQ+ clients in identifying which domestic violence services that are offered in your region feel safe and potentially free from anti-LGBTQ bias. For example, LGBTQ+ individuals may have had anti-LGBTQ experiences with law enforcement in the past and may be averse to utilizing them for help.

- Collaborate with LGBTQ+ organizations and coordinate care of LGBTQ+ individuals. Do not hesitate to consult LGBTQ+ domestic violence specialists and organizations.

- Ask about children. Given the oftentimes precarious rights of LGBTQ+ parents, many clients may be frightened to discuss situations that could be perceived as harmful to their children and thus jeopardize their custody rights. Make sure you normalize their fears while you provide extensive information about the effect of domestic violence on children.

- Although substance abuse may be a symptom of domestic violence or even appear to be the reason that domestic violence is present, substance use does not cause violence. Rather, it is a co-factor for it. If substances are being abused, the person engaged in the substance use has another problem to overcome in addition to intimate partner violence. Because domestic violence is an intervention priority, substance abuse and domestic violence should be treated concurrently. Generally speaking, and while popularity of substances may vary regionally, drugs such as crystal meth, poppers, ecstasy, GHB, K (Special K), anabolic steroids, heroine, Viagra, and Cialis are popular in the gay and bisexual men's community; alcohol tends to be popular in the lesbian and bisexual women's community; and Xanax, Valium, and alcohol tend to be popular in the broader LGBTQ+ community. While these drugs are abused in the heterosexual community as well, LGBTQ+ substance users may have the added incentive to escape the pressures of coping in a world where they are stigmatized and, thus, more easily turn to substances. Furthermore, in some areas, bars and clubs may be the only locations where LGBTQ+ people can congregate and socialize with other LGBTQ+ people.

- Be willing to advocate for LGBTQ+ individuals. It may not be easy to challenge criminal justice personnel who neglect to identify domestic violence or health and mental health care professionals who fail to properly assist your client. While you may do everything in your power to help your LGBTQ+ clients, others may fail. It is important for you to recognize these injustices so you can help your client overcome shortcomings in the system and counsel and support them through negative outcomes, however unjust.

- Be cautious about offering drop-in support groups to LGBTQ+ clients or referring them to mediation for legal problems. Be hesitant about placing LGBTQ+ individuals in groups designed for heterosexuals unless the group facilitator has received training in LGBTQ+ domestic violence, has experience working with LGBTQ+ clients, and there are other LGBTQ+ clients in the group. If an LGBTQ+-specific group is not available, consider utilizing individual counseling. Intervention with primary victims should be focused on crisis intervention, safety planning, and providing information and education about LGBTQ+ domestic violence. Intervention with defending victims is similar to intervention with primary victims and should include education about healthy communication, conflict resolution, and anger management techniques. The focus of anger management should be framed within the context of safety planning. Intervention with secondary aggressors should be focused primarily on anger management techniques and safety planning, combined with a strong educational component that focuses on domestic violence in the LGBTQ+ community. Intervention with primary aggressors should focus on all aspects of domestic violence in the LGBTQ+ community, with consistent focus on the dynamics of power and control. Group counseling is the modality of choice for primary aggressors, and individual counseling can be contraindicated unless the individual counselor has received extensive training in LGBTQ+ domestic violence and/or specializes in it. If an LGBTQ+-specific group is not available, individual counseling can be utilized with extreme caution. Anger management is only a small part of the overall curriculum when working with batterers, so an anger management group should not suffice in the absence of a group for primary aggressors.
- Acknowledge limitations with services and the service delivery system because of anti-LGBTQ bias while communicating to clients that these limitations should not be seen as barriers to a life free from abuse.

The recommendations listed above are only a starting point for affirmative practice for service providers working with LGBTQ+ clients who are experiencing intimate partner violence; they are not meant to replace LGBTQ+-specific intervention and treatment when it is appropriate, indicated, and available. While all of these recommendations are included as part of LGBTQ+-specific intervention and treatment for domestic violence, LGBTQ+-specific intervention and treatment encompass numerous other approaches and issues pertinent to the LGBTQ+ population, as well as interventions specifically tailored to address the complexity and uniqueness of LGBTQ+ intimate partner violence. For example, there is an LGBTQ+-specific batterers' intervention group curriculum that was approved by the L.A. County Probation Department and contains informational and educational components that must be addressed with LGBTQ+ abusers if treatment is to be effective but would not be utilized by a mainstream program. The curriculum includes information about

- Abuse and violence within and directed against the LGBTQ+ community.
- Sociological ramifications of violence for the general community and the LGBTQ+ community in particular.
- The role of the LGBTQ+ community in the battered women's movement.
- An overview of LGBTQ+ domestic violence.
- Differences and similarities between LGBTQ+ domestic violence and heterosexual violence.
- Myths and misconceptions about domestic violence.
- The impact of socialization on gender roles, gender-role variations, and their interconnectivity with domestic violence.
- Forms of oppression and its connection to violence.
- The impact of anti-LGBTQ bias on members of the LGBTQ+ community.
- What internalized homophobia/biphobia/transphobia and anti-LGBTQ bias are, how they are internalized, their effects on LGBTQ + individuals, and so on.
- The dynamics of power and control tactics that are LGBTQ+-specific.
- The LGBTQ+ cycle of violence.
- Legal ramifications of violent behavior for LGBTQ+ individuals.
- Substance abuse in the LGBTQ+ community and the role of substances in domestic violence.
- The unique psychosocial and intergenerational concerns of LGBTQ+ families when domestic violence is present.
- How HIV/AIDS impacts, and is impacted by, intimate partner violence.
- Existing resources in the LGBTQ+ community.

This is not an exhaustive listing of the curriculum and does not list informational and educational components that are more general in nature such as anger management skills and techniques, healthy expressions of anger, the dynamics of power and control, differences between emotions and behavior, affect regulation, self-esteem, communication skills, conflict resolution skills, problem-solving skills, stress management, and so on.

LGBTQ+ respondents to a 2018 needs assessment survey conducted by the Los Angeles LGBT Center had a wide range of suggestions regarding how to improve services for individuals who have experienced and/or are experiencing intimate partner violence. The most frequent suggestion involved the need for specialized provider training across the spectrum of service providers, from police and hospital personnel to mental health and school counselors. Across these sectors, LGBTQ+ sensitivity, respect, and understanding were seen as being sorely lacking, and violence was all too often minimized, not taken seriously, or not addressed. Respondents also noted the need for greater awareness of LGBTQ+ domestic violence and how to prevent it, particularly owing to the misconception that domestic violence is primarily a heterosexual issue involving heterosexual men's violence against their female partners (Whirry & Holt, 2020).

Note

If you are interested in training and/or consultation regarding LGBTQ+ intimate partner violence, contact the National LGBTQ+ Institute on Intimate Partner Violence (lgbtqipvinstitute.org).

Continuing Education Questions

1. In the 2003–2005 LGBT Center STOP Violence Program LGBTQ IPV training courses, approximately what percentage of participants could not even identify one difference between LGBTQ IPV and heterosexual IPV in the pre-test?
    a.   25
    b.   50
    c.   75
    d.   100
2. According to Skinner and Otis (1996), specialized treatment programs targeting LGBTQ IPV offer no advantage over standard programs.
    a.   True
    b.   False

3. All of these are best practices when treating LGBTQ IPV except:
   a. Be aware of the stages of the coming out process and where someone falls in that process
   b. Use neutral language such as "spouse" and "partner" until someone is ready to self-disclose orientation and gender identity
   c. Help patients to change their sexual orientation or gender identity if they feel conflicted about these after trauma
   d. Ask about children and whether or not children are in the home or affected by the IPV

4. There are no differences in the patterns of substance use between heterosexual, cisgender people and members of the LGBTQ community.
   a. True
   b. False

5. Group counseling is the modality of choice for
   a. Primary aggressors
   b. Secondary aggressors
   c. Victims
   d. Innocent bystanders

References

America Psychological Association (APA). (2012). *Affirmative Psychotherapy with Gay Clients (with Kathleen J. Bieschke)*. apa.org/pubs/videos/4310898

American Psychological Association Task Force on Appropriate Therapeutic Responses to Sexual Orientation. (2009). *Report of the Task Force on Appropriate Therapeutic Responses to Sexual Orientation*. Washington, DC: American Psychological Association.

Brown, T., & Herman, J.L. (November 2015). *Intimate Partner Violence and Sexual Abuse among LGBTQ People: A Review of Existing Research*. Los Angeles, CA: Williams Institute.

Cohn, R. (2016). Senate Health Committee Analysis. Analysis of Assembly Bill 2051. Available from www.leginfoca.gov/pub/05-06/bill/asm/ab ... 2051-2100/ab_2051_cfa_20060621_093713_sen_comm.html

Hatzenbuehler, M.L. (2009). How Does Sexual Minority Stigma "Get under the Skin"? A Psychological Mediation Framework. *Psychological Bulletin, 135*(5), 707–730. 10.1037/a0016441

Hatzenbuehler, M.L., McLaughlin, K.A., & Nolen-Hoeksema, S. (2008). Emotion Regulation and Internalizing Symptoms in a Longitudinal Study of Sexual Minority and Heterosexual Adolescents. *Journal of Child Psychology and Psychiatry, 49*(12), 1270–1278. 10.1111/j.1469-7610.2008.01924.x

Hicks, D. (2000). The Importance of Specialized Treatment Programs for Lesbians and Gay Patients. *Journal of Gay & Lesbian Psychotherapy, 3*(3/4), 81–94.

Holt, S. (2005). *Final Report: California Department of Health Services, Maternal & Child Health Branch Prevention Funding Accomplishments 2000–2005*. Los Angeles Gay & Lesbian Center. Unpublished.

Kingdon, M.A. (1979). Lesbians. *The Counseling Psychologist, 8*(1), 44–45.

Matthews, A.K., Hughes, T.L., Johnson, T.P., Razzano, L.A., & Cassidy, R. (2002). Prediction of Depressive Distress in a Community Sample of Women: The Role of Sexual Orientation. *American Journal of Public Health, 92*(7), 1131–1139. 10.2105/ajph.92.7.1131

Meyer, I.H. (2003). Prejudice, Social Stress, and Mental Health in Lesbian, Gay, and Bisexual Populations: Conceptual Issues and Research Evidence. *Psychological Bulletin, 129*(5), 674–697.

National Center for Transgender Equality. (August 7, 2020). *Murders of Transgender People in 2020 Surpasses Total for Last Year in Just Seven Months*. https://transequality.org/blog/murders-of-transgender-people-in-2020-surpasses-total-for-last-year-in-just-seven-months

Newcomb, M.E., & Mustanski, B. (2010). Internalized Homophobia and Internalizing Mental Health Problems: A Meta-analytic Review. *Clinical Psychology Review, 30*(8), 1019–1029. 10.1016/j.cpr.2010.07.003

Pachankis, J.E., Goldfried, M.R., & Ramrattan, M.E. (2008). Extension of the Rejection Sensitivity Construct to the Interpersonal Functioning of Gay Men. *Journal of Consulting and Clinical Psychology, 76*(2), 306–317. 10.1037/0022-006x.76.2.306

Pachankis, J.E., & Hatzenbuehler, M.L. (2013). The Social Development of Contingent Self-Worth in Sexual Minority Young Men: An Empirical Investigation of the "Best Little Boy in the World" Hypothesis. *Basic and Applied Social Psychology, 35*(2), 176–190. 10.1080/01973533.2013.764304

Plöderl, M., & Fartaček, R. (2005). Suicidality and Associated Risk Factors among Lesbian, Gay, and Bisexual Compared to Heterosexual Austrian Adults. *Suicide and Life Threatening Behavior, 35*(6), 661–670. 10.1521/suli.2005.35.6.661

Proujansky, R.A., & Pachankis, J.E. (2014). Toward Formulating Evidence-Based Principles of LGB-Affirmative Psychotherapy. *Pragmatic Case Studies in Psychotherapy, 10*(2), 15. 10.14713/pcsp.v10i2.1854

Skinner, W.F., & Otis, M.D. (1996). Drug and Alcohol Use among Lesbian and Gay People in a Southern U.S. Sample: Epidemiological, Comparative, and Methodological Findings from the Trilogy Project. *Journal of Homosexuality, 30*(3), 59–62.

Weinraub, J. (October 19, 2021). *What Is Queer Affirmative Therapy?* wellsanfrancisco.com/what-is-queer-affirmative-therapy/

Whirry, R., & Holt, S. (2020). *Finding Safety: A Report about LGBTQ Domestic Violence and Sexual Assault*. Los Angeles, CA: Los Angeles LGBT Center.

Wichstrøm, L., & Hegna, K. (2003). Sexual Orientation and Suicide Attempt: A Longitudinal Study of the General Norwegian Adolescent Population. *Journal of Abnormal Psychology, 112*(1), 144–151. 10.1037/0021-843x.112.1.144

Ybarra, M.J. (December 31, 1988). Alan Kent Malyon; Noted Psychologist. *Los Angeles Times*. www.latimes.com/archives/la-xpm-1988

Mental Health Approaches to LGBTQ+ Intimate Partner Violence

13

Domestic violence shelters, criminal justice responses, and batterers' intervention programs are the primary services offered to those who experience intimate partner violence (Hamby, 1998). However, evidence exists to support the lack of effectiveness of many mainstream and widespread interventions within these services and organizations (Goodman & Epstein, 2008). Furthermore, many domestic violence victims, for a variety of reasons, have little access to or use for the services that exist (Goodman & Epstein, 2008). This is especially true of members of the LGBTQ+ population (Los Angeles LGBT Center, 2018). Furthermore, when LGBTQ+ people utilize these services, they often encounter providers who lack training to address their unique needs (Ford et al., 2012).

During the early days of the battered women's movement, services were provided almost exclusively by shelters (Goodman & Epstein, 2008), and shelters remain a primary service still offered today to populations victimized by domestic violence. Shelters provide life-saving services and typically offer a broad range of assistance, including emergency housing, counseling, crisis hotlines, support groups, legal help, community education, transportation, children's services, and transitional living programs (Gondolf & Fischer, 1988; Koss et al., 1994). Shelters, however, may offer limited access to those who are differently abled and/or older in age, as well as certain populations including male victims or female victims with male children over a particular age, those with chronic physical or psychiatric illness, transgender and non-binary victims, and others. Critics of shelter services have primarily focused on their inability to address the needs of women from diverse ethnic, national, racial, and religious

DOI: 10.4324/9780429031397-13

backgrounds as well women who identify as LBT (Koss et al., 1994; Timmins, 1995). Others have found that over 60% of the women who are housed in domestic violence shelters return to their abusive partners within 2 months of leaving the shelter (Campbell, Sullivan, & Davidson, 1995; Campbell et al., 1998; Strube & Barbour, 1984). This can be particularly problematic for those survivors because abuse is often more frequent and severe among women (survivors) who have separated from their partners (Anderson, 2003; Campbell et al., 2003; Johnson & Hotton, 2003; Rennison & Welchans, 2000).

Despite the main role that shelters have played in the response to domestic violence, the subject is not new to the profession of psychology. Although intimate partner violence was rarely considered by health and mental health practitioners prior to the 1970s, psychological researchers and theorists in the 1960s and 1970s described battered women as masochistic and presumed that they unconsciously enjoyed being abused and periodically provoked the abuser's violent behavior (Schechter, 1982; Snell, Rosenwald, & Robey, 1964). However, domestic violence was thought to be a private family matter. Victims rarely revealed the source of their injuries to healthcare professionals, and healthcare professionals generally did not ask questions. If abuse was revealed, the provider typically recommended that the victim leave the violent relationship—despite the increased risk of danger and lethality when doing so—and the potential obstacles inherent in leaving were not addressed (Dobash & Dobash, 1979), nor were safety plans developed and implemented.

By the early 1980s, professionals began to view the mental health issues and behaviors of battered women as a response to the violence itself rather than its cause (Goodman & Epstein, 2008). Psychologist Lenore Walker developed the concept of battered woman syndrome and argued that abuse victims were trapped in violent relationships because of (1) learned helplessness as well as (2) the cycle of violence (Walker, 1979, 1984a, 1984b). Activists and mental health professionals were among the first to recognize that many victims of domestic violence were suffering from psychological symptoms that were similar to those observed in soldiers after combat. As a result, advocates and therapists joined the veterans' movement to fight for official recognition of post-traumatic stress disorder as a diagnosis (Herman, 1992). As a direct result of these efforts, PTSD was added to the third edition of the DSM in 1980.

In addition to symptoms related to PTSD, domestic violence creates numerous serious and long-lasting psychological and emotional injuries to those who experience it. Victims often struggle with low self-esteem, social isolation, feelings of despair, distrust, hopelessness, and anger (Follingstad et al., 1991; Koss et al., 1994; Riger, Raja, & Camacho, 2002; Sackett & Saunders, 1999). On average, half of domestic violence victims suffer from depression, and 20% struggle with suicidal thoughts and feelings (Golding, 1999). Many victims of battering attempt to self-medicate the psychological pain of abuse and PTSD-related symptoms through alcohol and drug abuse (Clark & Foy, 2000; Hien & Hien, 1998; Lemon, Verhock-Oftedahl, & Donnelly, 2002). Walker (1993) indicates that individuals who have been exposed to intimate partner violence develop symptoms that can resemble those of individuals with personality disorders. In fact, when children are living in families in which domestic violence is occurring, their physical safety and psychological well-being are compromised. The younger the child, the more severe the impact of witnessing violence, and, when children are exposed to domestic violence as they are developing initial beliefs about the world, safety, and their caregivers, it can damage their core sense of self and of others (Chemtob & Carlson, 2004; Margolin, 2005; Wolfe et al., 2003).

Lay advocates and paraprofessionals, primarily in shelters, have historically provided counseling rooted in feminist empowerment concepts within the modalities of short-term crisis counseling, support groups, and informational sessions, as well as on hotlines (Lundy & Grossman, 2001). Efforts to help abused women cope with psychological and emotional distress have often been political in nature and have focused on the common experiences shared by victims as well as the external societal forces that contribute to its occurrence. Counseling has typically included helping women address and overcome the practical obstacles they face in leaving their abusive partners, such as lack of safe housing, childcare, and employment opportunities (Goodman & Epstein, 2008). Others advocated addressing violence by medicating the victim to obtain symptom reduction and/or emphasized the importance of maintaining family stability no matter how great the costs (Dobash & Dobash, 1979). Over time, psychological theories of domestic violence became less sexist in conceptualization but still continued to place responsibility for the violence primarily on survivors and believed its cause resulted from provocation and/or demands for equality in intimate relationships by the person being victimized (Koss et al., 1994; Schechter, 1982).

Over time, increasing numbers of advocates with mental health training joined the shelters. Because their training was primarily rooted in the medical model, they tended to utilize internally focused practical solutions rather than addressing the broader political issues that underscore domestic violence (Chalk & King, 1998; Lundy & Grossman, 2001; Schechter, 1982).

As a result, tensions arose between those utilizing a traditional shelter-based approach and those who utilized more traditional psychotherapeutic approaches (Goodman & Epstein, 2008). These differences resulted in few collaborative efforts or integrative theoretical models (Gomez & Yassen, 2007), as well as increased tension. This tension has been exacerbated by short-term treatment approaches and reimbursement policies driven by the insurance industry, the dominance of evidence-based therapies for which indicators of success can be counterproductive for domestic violence victims and abusers, and the overall lack of sufficient training of service providers (Goodman & Epstein, 2008). Other contributors to this tension between an advocacy-based approach and a mental health approach are the practical experience of advocates with mental health practitioners (which is often negative) and reports from survivors who have had uninformed interventions and treatment from them.

The overall lack of provider training in intimate partner violence presents a significant problem for traditional domestic violence organizations as well as mental health practitioners, in addition to survivors, abusers, and their families. Despite increased efforts in recent years to address intimate partner violence in graduate and training programs for psychologists, marriage and family therapists, professional counselors, and social workers in the United States, many mental health practitioners are poorly trained—if they are trained at all—to assess for and effectively intervene in cases of intimate partner violence (Goodman & Epstein, 2008; Hansen & Harway, 1993). A tragic example of this lack of training was illustrated in 2003:

> In December 2003, a man shot and stabbed his wife to death during a couples counseling session then fatally shot himself. According to the story in the *Los Angeles Times*, he became infuriated during the therapy session because his wife indicated that she wanted a divorce. He shot her with a semiautomatic pistol and then stabbed her several times. According to the psychologist who was treating the couple, they were "having troubles typical in a marriage."
>
> (Thermos, 2003)

This was not the result of "troubles typical in a marriage." Rather, this was the outcome of inadequate assessment and unknowledgeable treatment planning, both most probably the result of insufficient training of the therapist.

Furthermore, mental health practitioners often have the same misconceptions about intimate partner abuse as does the general public. Studies done by Gondolf (1992) suggest that psychiatrists and mental health professionals typically minimize violence and rarely address it with their clients, instead focusing on symptoms and diagnoses. Similarly, research by Hansen, Harway, and Cervantes (1991) focused on the ability of mental health providers to accurately perceive violence within couples presenting for therapy and to appropriately intervene. Not only did fully 40% of their sample fail to identify the presence of domestic violence, but none predicted lethality when it was present; they concluded that mental health practitioners who were members of both the American Association of Marriage and Family Therapists (AAMFT) and the American Psychological Association (APA) discounted the seriousness of domestic violence and focused instead on other clinical issues and concerns. Over a decade later, the study was replicated, and, although the researchers determined that therapists had improved somewhat in their ability to identify IPV, only one therapist in the sample accurately predicted lethality (Dudley, McCloskey, & Kustron, 2008). These studies, as well as surveys by others (Whirry & Holt, 2020), suggest that mental health professionals, regardless of discipline, often lack education about domestic violence and are subsequently limited in their ability to effectively intervene. In fact, Hamby (1998) argues that responding to IPV, for many mental health providers, is more complicated than responding to other problems because of the criminal aspects of domestic violence, legal system involvement, and the reality that one person can at least appear to be both perpetrator and victim in some circumstances.

Battered women who present in mental health settings with a wide range of problems and disorders are often reluctant to disclose, or fail to mention altogether, that they are experiencing domestic violence, and, in turn, therapists frequently fail to assess for intimate partner violence (Agar & Read, 2002; Harway & Hansen, 1993) or utilize ineffective and oftentimes dangerous interventions (Harway & Hansen, 1993). Unfortunately, misguided, though well-intended, interventions may exacerbate trauma and enhance the dangerousness of the situation (Bograd & Mederos, 1999; Geller, 1998; Hansen & Goldenberg, 1993). Many practitioners also commonly overlook or disregard male survivors of intimate partner violence as well as female perpetrators of violence (New York City Mayor's Office to Combat Domestic Violence, 2009), in addition to the broad spectrum of LGBTQ+ victims and perpetrators. Despite the fact that identification of domestic violence is imperative in order to facilitate appropriate referral and effective intervention and treatment, numerous barriers have been identified. Common barriers include lack of training, time constraints, limited resources for referrals, and fear of offending the client (HRSA, 2002). Furthermore, screening for depression, substance abuse, and other mental health problems will not necessarily identify clients with histories of trauma or domestic violence, despite their high comorbidity with intimate partner violence and PTSD (Baty, 2008).

Few mental health training programs require domestic violence training (Chalk & King, 1998), despite the fact that many students believe they should offer it (Kelly, 1997). Furthermore, few states require training of either their future mental health practitioners or those already licensed and in practice. California is one exception. Senate Bill 564 (Speier) mandates 15 hours of training in spousal or partner abuse for future mental health practitioners in graduate programs and continuing education for licensed practitioners (Senate Bill 564, 2002). Effective in 2004, this bill requires information and education about assessment, detection, and intervention strategies, including knowledge of community resources, cultural factors, and same-gender abuse dynamics. A partner with Senator Jackie Speier's office on the development of Senate Bill 564, the Los Angeles LGBT Center has surveyed existing graduate programs throughout California regarding their implementation of the bill's requirements and has learned that few have actually implemented this requirement or have instead included information about domestic violence in classes focusing on child abuse. Discussions about LGBTQ+ domestic violence are rarely included in these courses and, when they are, they are usually limited to discussions about the similarities LGBTQ+IPV shares with heterosexual domestic violence.

In a survey given to 18 mental health interns at the Los Angeles LGBT Center in September of 2005, 50% indicated that they had received no training/education about (heterosexual) domestic violence, and another 22.2% had only received 1–3 hours of training in it. Prior to being placed at the Center, the majority had not received any training in LGBTQ+ issues, or the training they had received had not been sufficient to work effectively with the general population, much less those members of the population impacted by IPV. Nearly 15 years later, nothing had substantially changed. In 2019, the Los Angeles LGBT Center conducted interviews with licensed mental health therapists, many of whom had been providing services for 20 years or longer. Surveys were also conducted with pre-licensed mental health practitioners. None of the providers had received any significant training during their education related to either general or LGBTQ+-specific intimate partner violence, although some had received training through the Los Angeles Center in conjunction with an internship or supervisory role there. Even those who had received some domestic violence training as part of their education had not received any LGBTQ +-specific IPV training. Of the students interviewed, none had any knowledge of key issues in either LGBTQ+-specific or non-LGBTQ domestic violence. This lack of knowledge included understanding of the origins and manifestations of violence; the process of differentiating abusers and victims; the fact that victims who have left a violent relationship return many times before leaving permanently; and basic facts such as that the most dangerous time between intimate partners in an abusive relationship is when the victim leaves the relationship or develops autonomy (Whirry & Holt, 2020).

In her role as manager of clinical training and education at the Los Angeles LGBT Center and its mental health internship program for 30 years, as well as the founder and director of the Center's STOP Violence Program, Dr. Susan Holt, one of this book's authors, has had the opportunity to train and provide consultation to hundreds of interns and mental health professionals on the topic of domestic violence throughout the years and has found that counselors tend to make one or more of the following mistakes when working with victims or perpetrators of IPV:

1. They believe that traditional clinical approaches can be effective and safe when domestic violence is present (for example, conceptualizing the case exclusively from a psychodynamic orientation).
2. They view domestic violence within an inappropriate context (for example, family systems theory).
3. They believe that domestic violence *always* involves direct physical abuse.
4. They fail to assess or *adequately* assess domestic violence.
5. They utilize an inappropriate treatment modality—generally either individual counseling or anger management for primary aggressors.
6. They incorrectly prioritize presenting issues and/or underestimate the seriousness of the abuse and violence.
7. They provide couples' or family therapy when domestic violence is present without a comprehensive risk assessment before selecting a modality.
8. They encourage victims to leave violent relationships without having realistic and solid safety plans in place.
9. When substance abuse is present, they treat it first or they treat it instead of the domestic violence.
10. When a psychological disorder is present, they focus on it and ignore the violence.
11. They fail to incorporate questions about domestic violence as part of a standardized individual or couples intake process and instead rely on prior experience and a more general client assessment to "get a sense" whether or not IPV exists.

12. They do not consider the complexities and unique challenges involved in safety planning with LGBTQ+ victims.
13. They are not familiar with or know of resources for domestic violence and when or how to make a referral.
14. They lack complete or comprehensive knowledge of mandated reporting issues as they pertain to intimate partner violence.
15. They focus on the client's childhood experiences or other similar variables prior to ensuring that the survivor has been stabilized and has access to basic necessities such as safe housing, food, and so on.
16. And they are unable to accurately differentiate abuser from victim, particularly in LGBTQ+ cases. In total, many clinicians simply don't know what they don't know.

Kantor and Jasinski (1998) indicate that, because more severe and injurious abuse is likely to be associated with numerous psychological problems and with alcohol or other substance abuse problems, specialized clinical skills are required. Hamby (1998) further argues that achieving expertise in intimate partner violence intervention requires specialized education, and Goodman and Epstein (2008) suggest that graduate programs in psychiatry, psychology, and social work institute mandatory training in partner abuse screening and therapy. Furthermore, advocates (Goodman & Epstein, 2008) stipulate that new and additional interventions specifically target diverse survivor populations, including immigrants; ethnic, racial, and religious minorities who were born in the United States; economically disenfranchised individuals; and LGBTQ+ populations. The overarching goal for intervention with both victims and abusers is the promotion of their health and welfare (APA, 1991) and must be based on an understanding of the broader sociocultural context in which intimate partner violence is both permitted and perpetuated (Bograd, 1999; Crowell & Burgess, 1996; Harway & O'Neil, 1999; Jenkins & Davidson, 1999; Koss et al., 1994; Lundy & Grossman, 2001; Wiehe, 1998) and the intersection of complex factors such as gender, race, class, and sexual orientation (Ritchie, 1996). The primary goal of treatment with victims is to increase safety (Hamby, 1998; Harway & Hansen, 1994). With aggressors, the primary goal includes decreasing and ultimately eliminating violent and abusive behaviors and the acceptance of responsibility for thoughts, feelings, and behaviors, as well as the consequences of them.

Crisis intervention is commonly the first modality that is utilized with survivors and generally includes the development of a safety plan as well as attention to practical issues such as housing, finances, legal assistance, and so on (Hart & Stuehling, 1992; Dutton, 1992; Harway & Hansen, 1994).

Dutton (1992) argues that it is also important to assist victims to recognize cues regarding impending danger. Harway and Hansen's (1994) model includes assessment for the existence of violence, assessment of danger, education about domestic violence, and development and practice of a safety plan. A high-risk period for individuals in violent relationships occurs when they consider leaving the relationship (Ellis, 1987; Feld & Straus, 1990), and lethal violence is greatest when victims attempt to leave (Browne, 1987; Wilbanks, 1983; Wilson, Daly, & Wright, 1993), and so it can be dangerous to encourage a victim to leave a violent relationship without a solid safety plan. Once the immediate crisis has been stabilized, short-term therapy can be utilized to help the victim identify the impact of violence on their emotional functioning. During this phase of treatment, the therapist should work on empowerment issues, assist the client in developing independent living skills and attitudes, and help the client grieve the loss of an idealized relationship with the abuser. If the client wishes to remain in treatment, long-term counseling can help the client heal the past, develop trust, and address traumatic responses (Harway & Hansen, 1994).

Using a combination of individual or group therapy, wellness programming, and psychotropic medication, Cobb (2008) recommends the provision of psychoeducation about healthy relationships and the utilization of Socratic questioning to help the client explore how violence is hindering their goals. Mary Ann Dutton's (1992) treatment philosophy is similar and focuses on three major goals, including (1) protection, (2) enhanced choice-making and problem-solving, and (3) healing post-traumatic reactions. She utilizes cognitive behavioral and supportive techniques to achieve these goals. Lenore Walker (1994b) follows a trauma recovery model while using cognitive behavioral therapy and focuses on empowerment, validation, and strengths. Walker also advocates support and treatment groups to reduce isolation, shame, and guilt while they potentially increase social skills and trust. Whalen's (1996) empowerment counseling model is based on the principles of individual choice and self-determination. Within this model, the therapist's role is to provide support, identify resources, supply information, and serve as an advocate for abused clients. Techniques include fostering anger, support system development, and helping the client identify the societal sources of the problem, which, in turn, ideally lead to social action.

Lundy and Grossman (2001) and Abel (2000) argue that there are numerous approaches to address trauma, including those that are psychodynamic, psychoeducational, and cognitive behavioral. These can also be integrated or used singularly. Psychodynamic approaches focus on helping the client gain insight into underlying and possibly unconscious psychological conflicts that shape their response to abuse, while psychoeducational approaches focus on teaching clients coping strategies for dealing with the psychological consequences of abuse (Lundy & Grossman, 2001). Cognitive behavioral approaches focus on the ways in which trauma disrupts positive cognitions about the self and the environment and assists the client in replacing maladaptive beliefs with adaptive beliefs (Hembree & Foa, 2003; Kubany, Hill, & Owens, 2003; Resick & Schnicke, 1992).

Because of the high prevalence of PTSD among domestic violence survivors, it should be assessed and, when present, addressed. Gore-Felton, DiMarco, and Anderson (2007) argue that therapy for PTSD must focus on addressing trauma-related symptoms associated with abuse experiences, and that clients need help identifying triggers; reducing isolation; developing coping skills; and focusing on developing healthy lifestyle choices such as diet, exercise, regular sleep, and relaxation. In addition to cognitive behavioral therapy, treatment for PTSD may also include pharmacotherapy with medications such as sertraline, paroxetine, or other selective serotonin reuptake inhibitors (SSRIs) and antidepressants (Jeffreys, 2009). Goodman and Epstein (2008), however, argue that, while these approaches are valuable, none incorporate the social conditions that cause and maintain domestic violence and other forms of oppression in people's lives and, therefore, fail to address the full range of needs that survivors have. They insist that treatment models must focus attention on major external challenges faced by victims, including ongoing violence, economic dependence, homelessness, unemployment, and isolation from family and community.

Phyllis Chesler (1972) criticized the ways in which psychiatry and traditional therapeutic approaches reinforced the oppression of women and subsequently paved the way for alternative approaches to helping them. Feminist therapy was developed, and its philosophy of treatment was based on a political understanding of the oppression of women and the ways in which that oppression manifested materially and psychologically (Sturdivant, 1980). According to Gilbert (1980), feminist therapy was initially based on two principles, which were (1) the personal is political and (2) the therapist–client relationship is egalitarian. These principles led therapists practicing within this framework to emphasize change over adjustment, demystify the process of therapy, develop willingness to self-disclose, and model nontraditional behaviors for women such as the expression of anger. According to Goodman and Epstein (2008), feminist therapy offers a set of principles that attempts to integrate the internal and external difficulties that survivors face and has been historically used effectively in cases of intimate partner violence.

Walker (1994b) argues that support and treatment groups can be useful to survivors because they can reduce isolation and eliminate shame and guilt, in addition to providing a forum for practicing social skills and developing interpersonal trust. However, she acknowledges that groups can also present problems with confidentiality while making it difficult to tailor treatment to an individual's specific needs. Because empowerment is a primary goal when working with survivors of intimate partner violence, it can be useful to enable the survivor to determine what modality of treatment they prefer. Couples' therapy is highly controversial and can jeopardize the safety of the victim and make it impossible for them to participate in therapy without fear of repercussions. Critics (Bograd, 1984; Hansen & Goldenberg, 1993; Walker, 1994b) argue that a systemic framework involves allocating responsibility and blame among all parties instead of assigning responsibility to the violent partner and is contraindicated. However, some recommend the cautious use of couples' therapy when the safety of victims can be ensured and the perpetrator has successfully participated in a batterers' intervention program (Edleson & Tolman, 1992). According to Fox (1999), lesbians entering therapy are desperate to have their relationships recognized as legitimate, and the therapist's refusal to conduct conjoint sessions may mean that the client(s) will transfer to a therapist ignorant of domestic violence issues. Conversely, in their discussion of gay male battering, Island and Letellier (1991) argue that couples' counseling is never appropriate. Despite these differences, Holtzworth-Munroe, Beatty, and Anglin (1995) indicate that couples' therapy may offer several benefits over individual treatment and argue that it may give the therapist a more accurate picture of the violence because it is not based solely on the abuser's report; it allows for techniques and information to be given to both partners; and it can focus on better communication patterns that could ultimately prevent situations in which the abuser is prone to lose self-control. However, couples' counseling, if undertaken, should only be conducted with a domestic violence specialist.

Abusers typically present on a continuum, with those with impulse control problems and lower-level abuse at one end and perpetrators who display antisocial traits with severely violent behaviors at the opposite end. Those who present with traits consistent with personality disorders are typically in the middle of the continuum (Holt, 2020). Common interaction dynamics among abusers can include violence as a response to loss of control, unmet dependency needs, fears, anxiety, frustrations, and threats to self-esteem. Extreme, severe, and intermittent episodes of rage with no apparent stimulus may be associated with personality disorders (Kantor &

Jasinski, 1998). While individual therapy might be useful to abusers who present with co-occurring psychiatric disorders and/or substance abuse, individual therapy with abusers is generally contraindicated unless the therapist has received specialized or extensive training in intimate partner violence (Holt, 2020). Because abusers are often not accountable for their thoughts, feelings, actions, or the consequences of these, minimize the violence they perpetrate (Holtzworth-Munroe, Beatty, & Anglin, 1995), and frequently feel victimized in their relationships, even the most seasoned psychotherapists often inadvertently collude with them, thereby increasing their lack of accountability while increasing the potential for abuse and violence. Participation in a batterers' intervention program which focuses on group therapy can be most helpful to those who harm their partners.

While the approaches and formats of batterers' intervention programs vary widely throughout the United States, the curricula tend to utilize cognitive behavioral and psychoeducational techniques that focus on violence management, skill-building, and resocialization (Sonkin, Martin, & Auerbach-Walker, 1985). Batterers' intervention programs were established in the mid-1990s and were developed for cisgender heterosexual men who abuse their female partners. While a limited number of programs provide services for women who abuse their male partners, there is a dearth of programs serving LGBTQ+ clients (Adams, 2003). Adams (2003) contends that, while a trend in batterers' treatment is to make programs more accessible and relevant to underserved populations of abusers, most researchers and service agencies do not collect sexual orientation data from men and their partners but simply presume that they are working primarily with heterosexual abusers (Aldarondo, 2009). Furthermore, abusers in same-sex relationships are likely to feel that a curriculum that is heavily geared toward opposite-gender relationships is not relevant to them (Adams, 2003). Of significant concern are the lack of assessment of LGBTQ+ abusers who have been referred by the court or probation department to court-approved batterers' intervention programs, the assumption by program personnel that the initial law enforcement or court assessment was accurate, and when the alleged abuser is actually the victim.

Many of the batterers' intervention programs for court-referred abusers adhere to state and/or county standards. While standards vary by state, they generally pertain to program philosophy and protocol, victim contact, staff ethics and qualifications, fees, intake procedures, intervention standards (e.g. group is the preferred format, couples' counseling is inappropriate, etc.), and discharge criteria (Austin & Dankwort, 1999). Men who attend these programs are nearly always court-referred or court-mandated, although the proportion of court-referred and self-referred clients varies from program to program. Certified batterer intervention programs have a fairly broad range of minimum program durations, ranging from 12 sessions to 52, with the average duration being 24–26 weekly sessions (Adams, 2003), depending on the state and its penal code.

Batterers' programs utilize a wide variety of techniques that include didactic education, group participatory exercises, structured feedback, self-evaluation, role-plays, skills training and practice, homework assignments, positive reinforcement, and cognitive behavioral techniques. Group is the modality of choice for numerous reasons, including the promotion of accountability, opportunities for social reinforcement and peer support of nonviolence, and facilitation of education. The group format also serves to counter the common perception that violence is a private matter (Adams, 2003). The primary goals in most batterers' intervention programs include assisting the client(s) to overcome denial by broadening their understanding of what constitutes violence and abuse, promoting responsibility for abusive behavior and its consequences, decreasing and ultimately eliminating abusive behavior, helping clients learn alternatives to abuse, and supporting gender equality (Adams, 2003). Harway and Hansen (1994) adhere to a batterers' treatment model that follows a phased approach consisting of crisis intervention, short-term counseling, and long-term therapy. The crisis phase generally focuses on educating about violence, helping with the identification of feelings, teaching socially acceptable channeling of feelings, and developing a danger-management plan. The short-term counseling phase addresses patterns of power and control, feelings of shame and guilt, and dealing with fears of abandonment. Long-term treatment often focuses on attachment issues. A main treatment focus throughout counseling is the development of client responsibility for their thoughts, feelings, and behaviors and the consequences of them.

To date, no studies have looked at the efficacy of LGBTQ+-specific domestic violence treatment.

Continuing Education Questions

1. Our experience at the Los Angeles LGBT Center's SVP showed that counselors often make which of the following mistakes when treating LGBTQ IPV?
   a. They view domestic violence within an inappropriate context (for example, family systems theory)

    b. They fail to assess or adequately assess domestic violence

    c. They provide couples' or family therapy when domestic violence is present without a comprehensive risk assessment before selecting a modality

    d. When substance abuse is present, they treat it first or they treat it instead of the domestic violence

    e. All of the above

2. Screening for depression and substance abuse will identify patients with histories of trauma because of their high comorbidity with intimate partner violence and PTSD

    a. True

    b. False

3. Mary Ann Dutton's treatment philosophy focuses on all of these priorities *except*

    a. Leaving an abusive relationship

    b. Protection

    c. Enhanced choice-making and problem-solving

    d. Healing post-traumatic reactions

4. Because of the high prevalence of PTSD among domestic violence survivors, a component of addressing it might also include treating PTSD

    a. True

    b. False

5. Which of the following is a concern when utilizing couples' therapy to treat LGBTQ IPV?

    a. Allocating responsibility and blame between both parties instead of assigning responsibility to the violent partner

    b. Preventing accurate monitoring of abuse potential owing to the victim's inability to report honestly and the abuser's reluctance to do so

    c. Causing increased violence and abuse following therapy owing to the discussion of difficult issues or the victim's statements or requests during therapy

    d. All of the above

References

Abel, E.M. (2000). Psychosocial Treatments for Battered Women: A Review of Empirical Research. *Research on Social Work Practice*, 10(1), 55–77.

Adams, D. (2003). Treatment Programs for Batterers. *Clinics in Family Practice*, 5(1), 159–176.

Agar, K., & Read, J. (2002). What Happens When People Disclose Sexual or Physical Abuse to Staff at a Community Mental Health Centre. *International Journal of Mental Health Nursing, 11*, 70–79.

Aldarondo, E. (2009) *Assessing the Efficacy of Batterer Intervention Programs in Context.* Position paper presented at the Policy Symposium Batterer Intervention: Doing the Work and Measuring the Progress. Sponsored by the National Institute of Justice and Family Violence Prevention Fund, Bethesda, MD, December 3–4, 2009. Retrieved on October 8, 2015, from: www.futureswithoutviolence.org/userfiles/file/Children_ and_Families/Assessing%20the%20Efficacy%20of%20Batterer%20Intervention %20Programs%20in%20 Context.pdf

American Psychological Association (APA). (1991). Avoiding Heterosexual Bias in Language. *American Psychologist, 46*(9), 973–974.

Anderson, D.J. (2003). The Impact on Subsequent Violence of Returning to an Abusive Partner. *Journal of Comparative Family Studies, 34*, 93–112.

Austin, J.B., & Dankwort, J. (1999). Standards for Batterer Programs: A Review and Analysis. *Journal of Interpersonal Violence, 14*(2), 152–168. 10.1177/088626099014002004

Baty, M.L. (2008). The Intersection of HIV and Intimate Partner Violence: Considerations, Concerns, and Policy Implications. *Prevention and Health Practice.* Retrieved January 21, 2009, from http://endabuse.forumone.com/health/ejournal/ archive/1-7/hiv_ipv.php

Bograd, M. (1984). Family System Approaches to Wife Battering. *American Journal of Orthopsychiatry, 54*(4), 558–568.

Bograd, M. (1999). Strengthening Domestic Violence Theories: Intersections of Race, Class, Sexual Orientation, and Gender. *Journal of Marital and Family Therapy, 25*, 275–289.

Bograd, M., & Mederos, F. (1999). Battering and Couples Therapy: Universal Screening and Selection of Treatment Modality. *Journal of Marital and Family Therapy, 25*, 291–312.

Browne, A. (1987). *When Battered Women Kill.* New York, NY: Macmillan Free Press.

Campbell, J., Rose, L., Kub, J., & Nedd, D. (1998). Voices of Strength and Resistance: A Contextual and Longitudinal Analysis of Women's Responses to Battering. *Journal of Interpersonal Violence, 13*, 743–762.

Campbell, J.C., Sullivan, C.M., & Davidson, W.S. (1995). Depression in Women Who Use Domestic Violence Shelters: A Longitudinal Analysis. *Psychology of Women Quarterly, 19*, 237–255.

Campbell, J.C., Webster, D., Koziol-McLain, J., Block, C., Campbell, D., Curry, M.A., et al. (2003). Risk Factors for Femicide in Abusive Relationships: Results from a Multisite Case Control Study. *American Journal of Public Health, 93*, 1089–1097.

Chalk, R., & King, P.A. (1998). *Violence in Families: Assessing Prevention and Treatment Programs.* Washington, DC: National Academy Press.

Chemtob, C.M., & Carlson, J.G. (2004). Psychological Effects of Domestic Violence on Children and Their Mothers. *International Journal of Stress Management, 11*, 209–226.

Chesler, P. (1972). *Women and Madness.* Garden City, NY: Doubleday.

Clark, A.H., & Foy, D.W. (2000). Trauma Exposure and Alcohol Use in Battered Women. *Violence Against Women, 6*, 37–48.

Cobb, A.J. (2008). *The Intersection: HIV/AIDS and Intimate Partner Violence.* Paper presented at Ryan White All-Grantee Meeting, August 25–28, Washington, DC.

Crowell, N.A., & Burgess, A.W. (1996). *Understanding Violence against Women.* Washington, DC: National Academy of Sciences Press.

Dudley, D.R., McCloskey, K., & Kustron, D.A. (2008). Therapist Perspectives of Intimate Partner Violence: A Replication of Harway & Hansen's Study after More than a Decade. *Journal of Aggression, Maltreatment & Trauma, 17*(1), 80–102. doi:10.1080/ 10926770802251031

Dutton, M.A. (1992). *Empowering and Healing the Battered Woman: A Model of Assessment and Intervention.* New York, NY: Springer.

Edleson J.L., & Tolman, R.M. (1992). *Intervention for Men Who Batter: An Ecological Approach.* Thousand Oaks, CA: Sage.

Ellis, D. (1987). Post-Separation Woman Abuse: The Contribution of Lawyers as "Barracudas," "Advocates," and "Counsellors." *International Journal of Law and Psychiatry, 10,* 401–410.

Feld, S.L., & Straus, M.A. (1990). Escalation and Desistance from Wife Assault in Marriage. In M. Straus & R. Gelles (Eds.). *Physical Violence in American Families: Risk Factors and Adaptations to Violence in 8,145 Families* (pp. 489–505). New Brunswick, NJ: Transaction.

Follingstad, D.R., Brennan, A.F., Hause, E.S., Polek, D.S., & Rutledge, L.L. (1991). Factors Moderating Physical and Psychological Symptoms of Battered Women. *Journal of Family Violence, 6,* 81–95.

Ford, C.L., Slavin, T., Hilton, K.L., & Holt, S.L. (2012). Intimate Partner Violence Prevention Services and Resources in Los Angeles: Issues, Needs, and Challenges for Assisting Lesbian, Gay, Bisexual and Transgender Clients. *Health Promotion Practice, 14*(6), 841–849.

Fox, L.J. (1999). Couples Therapy for Gay and Lesbian Couples with a History of Domestic Violence. In J. McClennan & J. Gunther (Eds.), *Same-Gender Partner Abuse: A Professional Guide to Practice Intervention* (pp. 105–124). Lewiston, NY: Edwin Mellen.

Geller, J. (1998). Conjoint Therapy for the Treatment of Partner Abuse: Indications and Contraindications. In A. Roberts (Ed.), *Battered Women and Their Families: Intervention Strategies and Treatment Programs* (2nd ed.; pp. 76–97). New York, NY: Springer.

Gilbert, L.A. (1980). Feminist Therapy. In A. Brodsky & R. Hare-Mustin (Eds.), *Women and Psychotherapy* (pp. 245–265). New York, NY: Guilford.

Golding, J.M. (1999). Intimate Partner Violence as a Risk Factor for Mental Disorders: A Meta-analysis. *Journal of Family Violence, 14,* 99–132.

Gomez, C., & Yassen, J. (2007). Revolutionizing the Clinical Frame: Individual and Social Advocacy Practice on Behalf of Trauma Survivors. *Journal of Aggression, Maltreatment & Trauma, 14,* 245–263.

Gondolf, E.W. (1992). Discussion of Violence in Psychiatric Evaluations. *Journal of Interpersonal Violence, 7,* 334–349.

Gondolf, E.W., & Fisher, E.R. (1988). *Battered Women as Survivors: An Alternative to Treating Learned Helplessness.* Lexington, MA: Lexington.

Goodman, L.A., & Epstein, D. (2008). *Listening to Battered Women: A Survivor-Centered Approach to Advocacy, Mental Health, and Justice.* Washington, DC: American Psychological Association.

Dobash, R.P., & Dobash, R.E. (1979). *Violence against Wives: A Case against the Patriarchy.* New York: The Free Press.

Gore-Felton, C., DiMarco, M., & Anderson, J. (2007). Brief Summary of Behavioral and Social Science Research Related to Women, Violence, Trauma, and HIV/AIDS. In *Trauma and HIV/AIDS: A Summary of Research Results*. Washington, DC: American Psychological Association/Office of International Affairs. Retrieved October 27, 2008, from www.apa.org/international/hiv-aids.pdf

Hamby, S.L. (1998). Partner Violence: Prevention and Intervention. In J.L. Jasinski & L.M. Williams (Eds.), *Partner Violence: A Comprehensive Review of 20 Years of Research*. Thousand Oaks, CA: Sage.

Hansen, M., & Goldenberg, I. (1993). Conjoint Therapy with Violent Couples: Some Valid Considerations. In M. Hansen & M. Harway (Eds.), *Battering and Family Therapy: A Feminist Perspective* (pp. 82–92). Newbury Park, CA: Sage.

Hansen, M., Harway, M., & Cervantes, N. (1991). Therapists' Perceptions of Severity in Cases of Family Violence. *Violence and Victims*, 6(3), 225–235.

Hart, B.J., & Stuehling, J. (1992). *Personalized Safety Plan*. Retrieved May 10, 2004, from www.justpro@aol.com

Harway, M., & Hansen, M. (1993). Therapist Perceptions of Family Violence. In M. Hansen & M. Harway (Eds.), *Battering and Family Therapy: A Feminist Perspective* (pp. 42–53). Newbury Park, CA: Sage.

Harway, M., & Hansen, M. (1994). *Spouse Abuse: Assessing and Treating Battered Women, Batterers, and Their Children*. Sarasota, FL: Professional Resource Press.

Harway, M., & O'Neil, J.M. (1999). *What Causes Men's Violence against Women?* Thousand Oaks, CA: Sage.

Health Resources and Services Administration (HRSA). (2002). *Healing Shattered Lives: An Assessment of Selected Domestic Violence Programs in Primary Care Settings*. Retrieved May 9, 2010, from ftp://ftp.hrsa.gov/bphc/pdf/omwh/domesticviolence.pdf

Hembree, E., & Foa, E. (2003). Interventions for Trauma-Related Emotional Disturbances in Adult Victims of Crime. *Journal of Traumatic Stress*, 16, 187–199.

Herman, J.L. (1992). *Trauma and Recovery: The Aftermath of Violence from Domestic Abuse to Political Terror*. New York, NY: Basic Books.

Hien, D., & Hien, N.M. (1998). Women, Violence with Intimates, and Substance Abuse: Relevant Theory, Empirical Findings, and Recommendations for Future Research. *American Journal of Drug and Alcohol Abuse*, 24, 419–438.

Holt, S. (2020). *Can Domestic Violence Abusers Benefit from Individual Therapy?* Lecture, Domestic Violence Courses, Antioch University, Los Angeles, CA.

Holtzworth-Munroe, A., Beatty, S.B., & Anglin, K. (1995). The Assessment and Treatment of Marital Violence: An Introduction for the Marital Therapist. In N.S. Jacobson & A.S. Gurman (Eds.), *Clinical Handbook of Couple Therapy* (pp. 317–339). Guilford Press.

Island, D., & Letellier, P. (1991). *Men Who Beat the Men Who Love Them*. Binghamton, NY: Harrington Park Press.

Jeffreys, Matt. (July 1, 2009). *Clinician's Guide to Medications for PTSD*. National Center for PTSD. www.ptsd.va.gov/professional/treat/txessentials/clinician_guide_meds.asp

Jenkins, P., & Davidson, B. (1999). Consensus and Contradictions in Understanding Domestic Violence: Implications for Policy and Model Programs. In T. Gullotta & S. McElhaney (Eds.), *Children Exposed to Marital Violence: Theory, Research, and Applied Issues* (pp. 371–408). Washington, DC: American Psychological Association.

Johnson, H., & Hotton, T. (2003). Losing Control: Homicide Risk in Estranged and Intact Intimate Relationships. *Homicide Studies*, 7, 58–84.

Kantor, G.K., & Jasinski, J.L. (1998). Partner Violence: A Comprehensive Review of 20 Years of Research. In J.L. Jasinski & L.M. Williams (Eds.), *Partner Violence: A Comprehensive Review of 20 Years of Research*. Sage. Retrieved May 29, 2008, from www.sagepub.com

Kelly, V. (1997). Interpersonal Violence Education of Mental Health Professionals: Survey and Curriculum. *Dissertation Abstracts International, 58*, 2683.

Koss, M.P., Goodman, L.A., Browne, A., Fitzgerald, L.F., Keita, G.P., & Russo, N.F. (1994). *No Safe Haven: Male Violence against Women at Home, at Work, and in the Community*. Washington, DC: American Psychological Association.

Kubany, E.S., Hill, E.E., & Owens, J.A. (2003). Cognitive Trauma Therapy for Battered Women with PTSD: Preliminary Findings. *Journal of Traumatic Stress, 16*, 81–91.

Los Angeles LGBT Center. (2018). *Report on Needs Assessment Findings: LGBT Victims of Violent Crime in the City of Los Angeles*. Los Angeles, CA: Author.

Lemon, S.C., Verhoek-Oftedahl, W., & Donnelly, E.F. (2002). Preventive Healthcare Use, Smoking, and Alcohol Use among Rhode Island Women Experiencing Intimate Partner Violence. *Journal of Women's Health and Gender-Based Medicine, 11*, 555–562.

Lundy, M., & Grossman, S. (2001). Clinical Research and Practice with Battered Women: What We Know, What We Need to Know. *Trauma, Violence & Abuse, 2*, 120–141.

Margolin, G. (2005). Children's Exposure to Violence: Exploring Developmental Pathways to Diverse Outcomes. *Journal of Interpersonal Violence, 20*, 72–81.

New York City Mayor's Office to Combat Domestic Violence. (2009). *Special Issues: Lesbian, Gay, Bi, and Transgender*. Retrieved February, 6, 2009, from www.ci.nyc.cy.us/html/ocdv/html/issues/lesbian.shtml

Rennison, C.M., & Welchans, S. (2000). *Intimate Partner Violence*. Washington, DC: U.S. Department of Justice.

Resick, P.A., & Schnicke, M.K. (1992). Cognitive Processing Therapy for Sexual Assault Victims. *Journal of Consulting and Clinical Psychology, 60*, 748–756.

Riger, S., Raja, S., & Camacho, J. (2002). The Radiating Impact of Intimate Partner Violence. *Journal of Interpersonal Violence, 17*, 184–205.

Ritchie, B. (1996). *Compelled to Crime: The Gender Entrapment of Black Battered Women*. New York, NY: Routledge.

Sackett, L.A., & Saunders, D.G. (1999). The Impact of Different Forms of Psychological Abuse on Battered Women. *Violence and Victims, 14*, 105–117.

Schechter, S. (1982). *Women and Male Violence: The Visions and Struggles of the Battered Women's Movement*. Boston, MA: South End Press.

Senate Bill 564. (2002). Retrieved November, 9, 2012, from www.leginfo.ca.gov/pub/0002/bill/sen/sb_0551-0600/sb_564_bill_20020912_cjapt

Snell, J.E., Rosenwald, R., & Robey, A. (1964). The Wifebeater's Wife: A Study of Family Interaction. *Archives of General Psychiatry, 11*, 107–112.

Sonkin, D., Martin, D., & Auerbach-Walker, L. (1985). *The Male Batterer: A Treatment Approach*. New York, NY: Springer.

Strube, M.J., & Barbour, L.S. (1984). Factors Related to the Decision to Leave an Abusive Relationship. *Journal of Marriage and Family, 46*, 837–844.

Sturdivant, S. (1980). *Therapy with Women: A Feminist Philosophy of Treatment*. New York, NY: Springer.

Thermos, W. (2003) *Man Kills His Wife, Self During Counseling*. Retrieved September 1, 2022, from latimes.com/archives/la-xpm-2003-dec-03-me-husband3-story.html

Timmins, L. (Ed.) (1995). *Listening to the Thunder: Advocates Talk about the Battered Women's Movement.* Vancouver, Canada: Women's Research Centre.

Walker, L. (1979). *The Battered Woman.* New York, NY: Harper & Row.

Walker, L. (1984a). Battered Women, Psychology, and Public Policy. *American Psychologist, 39,* 1178–1182.

Walker, L. (1984b). *The Battered Woman Syndrome.* New York, NY: Springer.

Walker, L.E. (1993). The Battered Woman Syndrome Is a Psychological Consequence of Abuse. In R. Gelles & D. Loseke (Eds.), *Current Controversies on Family Violence* (pp. 133–153). Newbury Park, CA: Sage.

Walker, L.E. (1994). *Abused Women and Survivor Therapy: A Practical Guide for the Psychotherapist.* Washington, DC: American Psychological Association.

Whalen, M. (1996). *Counseling to End Violence against Women: A Subversive Model.* Thousand Oaks, CA: Sage.

Whirry, R., & Holt, S. (2020). *Finding Safety: A Report about LGBTQ Domestic Violence and Sexual Assault.* Los Angeles, CA: LGBT Center.

Wiehe, V.R. (1998). *Understanding Family Violence: Treating and Preventing Partner, Child, Sibling, and Elder Abuse.* Thousand Oaks, CA: Sage.

Wilbanks, W. (1983). The Female Homicide Offender in Dade County, Florida. *Criminal Justice Review, 8,* 9–14.

Wilson, M., Daly, M., & Wright, C. (1993). Uxorcide in Canada: Demographic Risk Patterns. *Canadian Journal of Criminology, 35,* 265–291.

Wolfe, D.A., Crooks, C.V., Lee, V., McIntyre-Smith, A., & Jaffe, P.G. (2003). The Effects of Children's Exposure to Domestic Violence: A Meta-analysis and Critique. *Clinical Child and Family Practice, 6,* 171–187.

LGBTQ+ Intimate Partner Violence Assessment and Diagnosis   **14**

The American Psychological Association (1996) recommends that routine screening for a history of victimization be included in standard medical and psychological examinations and be considered in the development of individual treatment plans. However, Gondolf (1992) found inconsistent documentation of violence issues in psychiatric evaluations. According to Aldarondo and Straus (1994), screening for partner abuse is the most basic intervention skill that any provider should possess. Jordan and Walker (1994) warn that the lack of detection of a client's history of abuse may have significant implications for clinicians who may treat symptoms without addressing one of the major causes of the individual's emotional problems. Lack of detection may also have significant ramifications for the client as well, including the development of an ineffective treatment plan and risk to the client and their family members of increased violence, injury, and even death. Aldarondo and Straus (1994) assert that screening for partner abuse is relatively rare, although research has substantiated that many victims of domestic violence will not return for a second visit if violence is not addressed (Goodstein & Page, 1981). The Los Angeles LGBT Center found that the majority of mental health providers do not incorporate a specific domestic violence intake or assessment as part of their standardized individual or couples intake and screening process. Instead, most therapists indicated that they rely on prior experience and a more general client assessment process to "get a sense" for whether or not intimate partner violence is present. Some therapists stated that abuse and violence issues can sometimes reveal themselves later in the course of individual or couples

DOI: 10.4324/9780429031397-14

counseling (Whirry & Holt, 2020). Although it cannot always be avoided, discovering the existence of domestic violence later in the course of treatment can be a reflection of poor assessment and treatment planning and, at worst, involves the significant possibility of harm and/or danger for the client(s). In addition, studies have shown that screening for IPV during every healthcare visit was desired by 92% of sexual minority men, and 96% felt that a provider's inquiry about IPV showed that the provider cared.

According to experts (Harway & Hansen, 1994; Aldarondo and Straus, 1994), clients experiencing domestic violence are unlikely to specifically address the violence as a presenting issue or primary problem. They argue that, in addition to maintaining substantial denial and resistance to the label of abuse, it is rare for clients to present information about violence during an intake, even if the clinician asks directly about it. Ferraro and Johnson (1983) indicate that many clients will complete the intake convincing the therapist that they have not experienced violence because they have acquired characteristics that serve to protect them and keep them in their abusive relationships. Because domestic violence is commonly defined within a heteronormative framework, LGBTQ+ people do not always recognize that what they are experiencing is violent or abusive, even when the battering is severe. In fact, it is common for battered LGBTQ+ victims to see their sexual orientation or gender identity as the problem, rather than the violence itself (Katz-Wise & Hyde, 2012; Whirry & Holt, 2020). Harway and Hansen (1994) encourage clinicians to persevere and ask follow-up questions, even when clients deny violence. In addition, Helton (1986) indicates that assessment should involve more than one question regarding abuse.

While Aldarondo and Straus (1994) argue that the most important aspect of screening is asking directly about domestic violence, Harway and Hansen (1994) maintain that direct questions about violence may not yield helpful information and recommend a series of questions directed at the couple's style of conflict resolution. Similarly, Schechter (1987) recommends that clinicians should routinely ask general questions such as "What happens when your partner does not get their way?" and "How do you and your partner resolve conflict?" as well as questions that are more specific such as "Does your partner ever threaten you?" and "Is your partner highly jealous or do they watch your every move?" While batterers' programs often suggest that clinicians ask concrete questions such as "What happens when you lose your temper?", "Have you ever hit your partner?", and "Have you ever pushed or shoved your partner?" (Kantor & Jasinski, 1998), Aldarondo (1998) cautions that abusive men may not consider pushing and shoving to be violent, and so the therapist should avoid using these terms. Whirry and

Holt (2020) found that the presence of the word "violence" in the phrases "domestic violence" and "intimate partner violence" may contribute to an assumption among therapists and other service providers that physical violence must be involved in order for true domestic violence to be taking place. Some mental health providers recommended using words such as "abuse" and "control" as a way to better define behavior along the full continuum of domestic violence. According to Whirry and Holt (2022), mental health providers hold differing views of what defines LGBTQ+ domestic violence. While some therapists believe that abusive behaviors take place along a continuum that includes emotional, financial, verbal, psychological, and physical abuse, other therapists defined intimate partner violence as primarily involving direct physical violence. Therapists who took a continuum-oriented view believed that defining domestic violence primarily in terms of physical violence could cause therapists to not recognize or treat violence in other forms or stages. One therapist noted that, in her experience, 90% of abusive relationships do not involve physical violence but instead center around psychological dominance and control, which is the hallmark of the vast majority of domestic violence situations. Yet another therapist, Mary Fox, PhD, stated

> I'm more apt to use the word "abuse" than I am "violence" because violence is a physical attack that's damaging and that's the end of the story for me. This enters the territory of law. Abuse is a wider construct. It can include the emotional embattlement, the emotional punishment, the verbal lashing out, the fear. By defining abuse like that, I think I see it more easily and more readily and I do see a lot of abuse.
>
> (Whirry & Holt, 2020, p. 22)

It may be more useful to ask questions that do not rely on the gender of the client, such as "Do either you or your partner have difficulty managing your anger?" and "Have either you or your partner either hit, shoved, pushed, kicked, or slapped the other?" Harway and Hansen (1994) indicate that alternative approaches, such as assessing for characteristics and symptoms that victims of trauma commonly share, can be utilized if persistent inquiry fails to inform the clinician of violence in the client's relationship. Affirmative responses to threats of violence, destruction of property, and/or abuse of pets are signs of potentially lethal violence, and immediate intervention may be necessary (Kantor & Jasinski, 1998.) When conducting assessments with couples, Kantor and Jasinski (1998) recommend that the partners be interviewed separately so that each can speak openly about their relationship.

Mainstream domestic violence services and providers have relied on our culture's binary conceptualization of gender to determine which partner is being victimized (the female) and which partner is battering (the male) (House, 2006). In fact, even the APA (1996) has asserted that the strongest risk factor for being a victim of partner violence is being female. It is easy to see how this dominant theory came to be. The battered women's movement grew out of the women's movement. Feminists such as Pharr (1988) reasoned that patriarchy and sexism caused violence against women. Hence, patriarchy has been conceptualized by the battered women's movement and some researchers as the primary reason for domestic abuse (Dobash & Dobash, 1979; Yllo & Straus, 1990), but, while some studies of battered women have identified conservative gender attitudes among violent husbands (Coleman, Weinman, & Hsi, 1980; Rosenbaum & O'Leary, 1981), others (Neidig, Friedman, & Collins, 1986) have found no such link. However, House (2006) argues that most battered women use force at some point during their abusive relationship, and that there are female batterers. Others indicate that men and women assault one another at approximately equal rates (Archer, 2000; Hamel, 2007). However, many in the domestic violence field believe that women use violence in self-defense or in order to escape or to retaliate for a history of abuse by abusive male partners (Dobash & Dobash, 1988).

The gender symmetry debate began with the publication of the controversial National Family Violence Survey in 1980 (Straus, Gelles, & Steinmetz, 1980). The survey indicated that rates of wife-to-husband assault were slightly higher than rates of husband-to-wife assault. These findings were essentially confirmed by the second National Family Violence Survey in 1990 (Straus, 1990). Later studies confirmed these results, while others indicated that men were disproportionately likely to be perpetrators and women were disproportionately likely to be victims (Tjaden & Thoennes, 2000). This debate was further fueled by research indicating that lesbian couples also experience domestic violence, giving support to the view of women as perpetrators as well as victims (Merrill & Wolfe, 2000; Renzetti, 1992). (At that point in time, GBT male victims were not even considered to be viable victims because of their gender and so were not considered within the debate.)

Citing studies by Dutton (1994) and Yllo (1993) that indicated that most men are neither physically assaultive nor controlling, Hamel (2007) argues that patriarchal explanations are contradicted by research. Hamel bolsters his argument by indicating that women are as victimized in same-sex relationships, where patriarchal structures should not exist, as in heterosexual ones

(Coleman, 1994; Lie et al., 1991), and that violent lesbians include "feminine" as well as "butch" types (Renzetti, 1992). However, the patriarchal structures that exist in LGBTQ+ relationships are different than those that tend to exist in opposite-gender relationships. In fact, Pence (1987) has argued that patriarchy is not only a gender issue but a form of domination and control that permeates the thinking of all human beings subjected to a patriarchal environment, thereby making the patriarchy–domestic violence link more complicated than it often appears, particularly as it applies to LGBTQ+ domestic violence.

According to Cope and Darke (1999), patriarchy is essentially a set of interlocking power structures and practices, including heterosexism, homophobia, transphobia, racism, classism, sexism, ageism, and ableism, all forms of oppression that are hierarchical in nature and are based on the unequal distribution of wealth, privilege, and access in society used by the group in power to maintain its position. Homophobia is described as an irrational fear of homosexuality (Bhugra, 1987) as well as an intolerance of any sexual differences from an established norm (Gramick, 1983). Further, in samples of the general population, men consistently tend to express more hostility and negative affect than do women toward sexual minorities in general and gay men in particular (Herek, 1988; Kite, 1992; Kurdek, 1988; Whitley, 1988).

Core male gender identity, male role, or heterosexual masculinity is threatened by gender nonconformity in other men (Herek, 1986b; Kerns & Fine, 1994; Pleck, Sonenstein, & Ku, 1994; Reiter, 1991), and Herek (1986a) contends that men affirm their heterosexual masculinity by expressing who they are not and/or defining themselves in opposition to gay males. Importantly, gender non-conformity is devalued more in men than in women (Page & Yee, 1985). Gay men are deprecated on the basis of a cultural association between male homosexuality and femininity. Lesbians, on the other hand, are stereotyped as being masculine. Gender role stereotypes are an important component of patriarchy and underscore heterosexism and homophobia, both components of patriarchy and primary beliefs used to enforce culturally idealized gender roles (NRCDV, 2007). The result is an idealization of masculinity that is directly linked to the prevalence of domestic violence, and so, in part, homophobia is a variation of sexism which often underscores domestic violence and is often a primary force in LGBTQ+ intimate partner abuse.

The majority of gays and lesbians, however, actively reject heterosexual gender roles as models for their own relationships (Peplau, 1991). Furthermore, according to Goodman and Epstein (2008), the impact of gender is modulated by its interaction with other self- and socially defining characteristics such as ethnicity, culture, class, age, ability, immigration status, personal history, and sexual orientation. Even when traditional gender roles are utilized by LGBTQ+ people, they do not predict which partner is, or will be, abusive. In fact, it is not unusual for a "femme" partner to be abusive or a "butch" partner to be victimized. Furthermore, research suggests that the roles of batterer and victim often alternate between same-gender partners over time (Miller, Bobner, & Zarski, 2000). However, an argument can be made that this conclusion may be the result of insufficient assessment. In fact, research has indicated that lesbians are more apt than heterosexual women to fight back (Walker, 1986) in self-defense and retaliation, and that they are consistently assessed inaccurately when they do.

When heterosexual women use violence against their intimate partners, it happens within the context of societal sexism, is shaped by gender roles, and manifests differently than the violence perpetrated by men. In addition, claims that men are battered as often as women generally do not take into account that women's use of violence is often preceded by severe acts of violence (AHR, 2010). Further, Avalon (1999) argues that heterosexual women generally do not use violence to obtain a desired result. The use of violence also has different consequences for men and women. According to Advocates for Human Rights (2010), women more often recognize violence as contrary to their socially prescribed gender roles and more readily admit to using violence. Men typically minimize or deny the violence, reflecting a greater feeling of entitlement to use violence.

According to Dasgupta (2001), reports of violence against men are often exaggerated, and men accused of domestic violence often minimize and deny their partner's claims by arguing that the abuse was mutual or that they were the victims. Furthermore, women's and men's uses of force also have different physical manifestations. A batterer's use of force is often controlled, and batterers may consciously choose to inflict injuries where they are not visible or in areas that the victim may feel uncomfortable revealing to others such as police. However, when women use force, the physical injuries are frequently visible because they are generally self-defensive wounds (e g. scratching, biting vs. strangling, actions that create bruises, etc.) (House, 2006).

Therefore, it is not effective to rely on gender when attempting to differentiate an LGBTQ+ victim from an LGBTQ+ abuser, and doing so can be dangerous. For example, survivors rather than batterers have been arrested, incarcerated, charged with domestic violence, mandated to pay a fine, and required to attend a specific number of batterers' treatment sessions as required by a court. Furthermore, batterers have been inadvertently sheltered with their victims or allowed to attend the same drop-in support groups; both partners have been arrested; victims have been subject to restraining orders or unable to obtain them; batterers are mandated to attend an arbitrary number of anger management sessions rather than the standard weeks of batterers' treatment mandated by various penal codes and, in so doing, increase their ability to manipulate the system while making no significant changes; batterers are assessed to be victims and treated as such, which can validate and increase the abuser's feelings of victimization and, hence, abusive behaviors; batterer and victim are seen together in couples' counseling, which can exacerbate the violence; and so on.

Many therapists expressed the view that the pervading overlay of traditional heterosexual gender roles can complicate the ability of providers to adequately recognize and respond to LGBTQ+ domestic violence. This includes a standardized image of intimate partner violence as nearly always involving a larger heterosexual man abusing a smaller heterosexual woman. While this is, of course, an accurate image in many IPV cases, this standard heteronormative image can never be effectively or realistically applied to intimate LGBTQ+ relationships. The Los Angeles LGBT Center's assessment model explores the dynamics of each intimate relationship based on the unique characteristics, behaviors, and beliefs of the two individuals involved, with no preconceptions or prior constructs involved. The resulting safety or treatment plan draws from a range of intervention and treatment modalities to provide the best and most effective plan for each victim or both members of a partnership (Whirry & Holt, 2020).

Marrujo and Kreger (1996) argue that we cannot rely upon gender to define the roles in an abusive relationship, especially in cases of lesbian battering when both women report using violence to resolve conflict. House (2006) substantiates this point by arguing that it is a significant error to rely on gender when screening for service eligibility, because lesbians and gay men look to domestic violence agencies for assistance. This can be further complicated by the basic stance of many mainstream programs that the person presenting for services is the victim and that "her" story should be believed (Whalen, 1996) and taken at face value. House (2006) recommends that providers conduct thorough assessments with all individuals who request services so that they will not be thrown off guard when conducting assessments with males in mixed-gender relationships and with individuals in same-gender relationships.

Accurate assessment with heterosexuals and LGBTQ+ people alike can be challenging, because batterers often believe they are being victimized. Further, victims are more apt to take responsibility for the abuse (House, 2006), often believing they are to blame and that their behaviors are provocative and abusive. In addition, as a way of lessening their anticipatory anxiety during the cycle of violence, domestic violence victims may behave in ways they believe will "provoke" the abuser's abusive behavior to reduce the duration of the tension-building stage and move more rapidly into the honeymoon stage of the cycle. House (2006) recommends obtaining a detailed description of a recent incident of abuse and argues that survivors are more apt to provide specific details about the event, while batterers may not present a clear picture of it, may be vague, may avoid answering questions, may be quick to change the subject, and so on. She further indicates that it is common for many survivors to go over the incident repeatedly in an attempt to make sense of it.

Sullivan and Laughlin (1999) discuss the importance of differentiating the victim from the perpetrator in cases of same-sex violence. Margolies and Leeder (1995) distinguish victim characteristics from those of abusers and indicate that victim characteristics include low self-esteem, internalized feelings, rare difficulty managing anger, infrequent jealousy, assumption of too much responsibility, feelings of inadequacy within the relationship, tendency to manipulate the environment to maintain safety, and feelings of fear or a fight-or-flight alertness after episodes of partner violence. They further indicate that perpetrator characteristics include pathological jealousy; problems controlling anger; refusal to accept responsibility for their behavior; being controlling, manipulative of the partner's activities and relationships, and disrespectful of the partner's boundaries; blaming the victim; a history of being abused as a child; and feeling "high" after an episode of violence.

When working with members of the LGBTQ+ community, it can be helpful to think about assessment on a continuum, with primary victims at one end of the continuum and those who developed an established pattern of fighting back and/or appear to possess elements of both aggressor and victim (defending victims and secondary aggressors) along the continuum. Historically, the terms "self-defending victim" and "mutual combatant" have been used to define women who use violence in relationships (Steinmetz, 1977–1978; Straus, 1980; Straus et al., 1980). The mutual combatant has been defined as the woman who fights back and may at times initiate the violence, whereas the self-defending woman may use physical aggression to prevent further injury (Marrujo & Kreger 1996).

Saunders (1988) proposed that these terms were not mutually exclusive when applied to heterosexual victims, because many victims report a retaliatory anger at the time of the self-defensive act of physical aggression, and concluded that abused women who use violence can most clearly be defined as self-defending victims. However, Renzetti (1992) stressed that not all violent acts are the same, and that there is a difference between initiating an act of violence and using violence as self-defense or retaliation and that severity of injuries and determining who used the violence in self-defense are important. In her study of lesbians, 78% reported that they had either defended themselves or fought back against an abusive partner. Further, in their sample of lesbians who reported being both victims and perpetrators of violence, Lie et al. (1991) indicated that 30.3% perceived their aggression as self-defensive, and 39.4% viewed it as "mutual aggression."

In their research with lesbians, Marrujo and Kreger (1996) found that 34% reported a pattern of fighting back, which they define as a repeated pattern of physical and/or emotional aggression in response to the partner's aggressive act and is distinguished from self-defense owing to the fact that it became an established pattern of response and is not confined to an isolated incident. Further, the motivation was to hurt, injure, or get even with the initiating partner. Twenty-seven percent of Marrujo and Kreger's sample had many of the psychological characteristics commonly used to describe male heterosexual perpetrators, and 39% exhibited psychological characteristics most often used to describe heterosexual victims. To allow more flexibility in treatment, the authors defined three distinct roles: Primary aggressor, participant, and primary victim. In this model, primary aggressor and victim are comparable to heterosexual batterers and victims, while the participant is a role that contains elements of both roles. Marrujo and Kreger (1996) also proposed that primary aggressors were initiators and were interested in escalating the conflict and violence, while the primary victim was interested in disengaging from the conflict, deescalating the violence, and securing personal safety. The participant, in contrast, fought back for the duration of the conflict once it had been initiated by the partner and was not interested in disengaging.

We have found this model to be very useful when assessing and intervening in LGBTQ+ intimate partner violence but have also found that it is not fully sufficient. In 2000, expanded it further to include four distinct roles while eliminating the term "participant." In this model, the primary aggressor is the primary initiator of abuse and violence and is motivated by the desire to gain and/or maintain power and control over their intimate partner or to punish the partner for resisting control; the primary victim is not apt to initiate violence or fight back, although they may express anger directly or passive-aggressively. Their primary motivation is the attainment of safety, and their primary objective, once conflict begins, is to disengage as quickly as possible. Defending victims share similarities with primary victims and will generally not initiate violence. However, they are not as apt as primary victims to avoid conflict. They will fight back to defend themselves but will generally disengage as soon as possible in an effort to attain safety. Disengagement occurs once they sense that they have achieved a degree of safety that wasn't present when the conflict began. In contrast, secondary aggressors appear to share more similarities with primary aggressors, although their response is a result of the victimization they have experienced. They may initiate violence in retaliation or in self-defense but will not do so as frequently or consistently as primary aggressors, although, in some cases, they appear to initiate in equal amounts to the partner. However, with thorough assessment, they do not share all of the characteristics or behaviors of primary aggressors. Once engaged, secondary aggressors generally have no interest in disengaging, and their motivation is commonly to express anger at and retaliation for their partner's aggression while obtaining some degree of safety for themselves. This is the category that is most confusing for law enforcement officers, criminal justice personnel, and shelter staff. In fact, when service providers have not received training in differentiating victims from abusers, violence in a situation with a defending victim or secondary aggressor often appears to be "mutual." However, primary victims, defending victims, and secondary aggressors are all victims who are expressing their responses to that victimization differently. People who are being victimized may become defending victims or secondary aggressors simply because of context, because of the perception of equality in size and strength, or because of the dearth of resources that are LGBTQ+-specific. "When there are fewer resources, victims are often placed in a position in which they feel that the only thing they can really do is fight back" (Hough, 2017).

According to Devika Shankar, a domestic violence advocate and trainer,

> Holt's four categories encompass the diversity of relationships. Traditionally, in this kind of work, we've looked at it as binary—as victim and abuser—but when it comes to domestic violence and people experiencing trauma, things are so much more complex than that.
>
> (Holt, cited in Guzik, 2017)

Shankar, who has nearly a decade of work in domestic violence shelters, indicates that

> it was only when I learned this model that things started falling into place. I would see clients who were being victimized but were acting out in ways that we couldn't understand or that felt problematic in a certain way. By not understanding these dynamics, we weren't really

providing the best services that we could to the other people that didn't fall into these categories.

(Holt, cited in Guzik, 2017)

According to Jacquie Marroquin of the California Partnership to End Domestic Violence (Guzik, 2017), the state's largest coalition of domestic violence programs and advocates, "There is a growing awareness that a one size fits all approach to services is not effective for different communities."

There are a number of variables that, when assessed, can assist with differentiation between victim and abuser. For example, determine if clients have chronic mental and physical health problems. Individuals who have been battered are more likely to experience chronic health conditions, including anxiety and depression, symptoms consistent with PTSD, substance use, suicidality, lower back pain, headaches, difficult sleeping, diabetes, asthma, digestive and gastrointestinal disorders, sexually transmitted infections, and brain injuries (Coker et al., 2002). Increased cortisol levels resulting from domestic violence stressors can lead to hypertension, stroke, and heart disease (Pico-Alfonso et al., 2004). However, while 92% of all women felt that screening for IPV is important, 75% indicated that they have never been screened for IPV by a doctor or nurse, while only 6% with a chronic health condition indicated that their doctors ever made the connection between the two (Verizon Foundation, 2013).

Variables initially defined by Tara Hardy of AABL (Advocates for Abused and Battered Lesbians) in Seattle, WA, can be helpful during assessment. In this model, context, intent, and effect are assessed for a full range of abusive incidents. The context is defined as the meaning a certain behavior gives to the overall context of the situation and relationship, the intent identifies the primary goal or motivation of the behavior, and the effect concludes who was physically or emotionally hurt as a result of the behavior.

While these categories facilitate increased accuracy in assessment as well as enhanced and more appropriate treatment planning, there is no simple formula for assessment. We have found from experience that it is often a process of discovery that may take time. However, there are some factors to keep in mind when assessing LGBTQ+ clients:

1. Determine the context in which the abusive incident(s) occurred.
2. Determine which partner tends to place blame on others and/or is slow to take responsibility for their actions, beliefs, emotions, and so on.
3. Does the client, upon presentation, focus on their victimization by others?

4.   Determine which partner acts out of fear or self-protection more consistently.
5.   Determine if the client is attempting to systematically assert power and control over their partner or whether they are attempting to regain personal power.

Diagnosis

The *Diagnostic and Statistical Manual of Mental Disorders* (DSM), published by the American Psychiatric Association (APA), is a consistently evolving publication that changes in response to research and clinical data as well as advocacy and political pressure. As previously discussed, the APA deleted homosexuality as a disorder from the DSM as a result of advocacy and political pressure from the gay rights movement (Island & Letellier, 1991; Silverstein, 1991; Bayer, 1981). However, Island and Letellier (1991) argue that the DSM and its publishers are "dangerously out of touch with reality" when considering domestic violence and criticize that the publication lacks diagnostic categories that illustrate and categorize the problem. Others with similar concerns include Lenore Walker and Judith Herman, who have both proposed modifications to the DSM criteria for post-traumatic stress disorder (PTSD) in an effort to ensure that the diagnosis more accurately reflects the effects of domestic violence victimization (Harway & Hansen, 1994; Herman, 1992). Some see diagnosis as a bind since it imposes a pathologizing label on struggling victimized clients, while the label itself may be the only way the client can obtain the assistance they need (Goodman & Epstein, 2008).

By the early 1990s, PTSD had become the predominant framework for understanding the psychological responses of victims to domestic violence. Golding (1999) concluded that 64% of battered (heterosexual) women displayed symptoms of PTSD. However, the DSM's criteria for this diagnostic category are stated in the past tense, and domestic violence, while it can continue after the intimate relationship with the victimized partner has ended, is commonly a current and ongoing series of traumatic events that occur whether or not the abusive relationship is current or past (APA, 2000). The category of acute stress disorder (308.3) is no more applicable than PTSD to the nature of domestic abuse because its pattern of symptoms typically occurs within a prescribed period of time. An important consideration that has not been incorporated into the DSM is complex post-traumatic stress disorder, or C-PTSD (also referred to as complex trauma). First described in 1992 by Judith Herman in her book *Trauma & Recovery*, C-PTSD categorizes psychological injuries that result from protracted exposure to prolonged social and/or interpersonal trauma in the context of either captivity or entrapment. This diagnosis is distinct from PTSD, and forms of trauma associated with C-PTSD include sexual abuse, physical abuse, emotional abuse, domestic violence, and torture.

The only DSM section that includes categories that are applicable to domestic violence is the section entitled, "Other Conditions That May Be a Focus of Clinical Attention." There are three "Spouse or Partner Violence" categories, separated from one another depending upon the type of violent behavior used (i.e. physical, sexual, or psychological), with each category specifying confirmed or suspected violence or other circumstances related to it. Of course, a significant problem with existing DSM categories that apply to domestic violence is their Z code status and subsequent typical exclusion from insurance reimbursement (Wylie, 1995).

Island and Letellier (1991) make a strong argument for the development and inclusion of more appropriate categories pertinent to domestic violence in the DSM. Despite the advocacy of Lenore Walker, Judith Herman, and Island and Letellier about this issue, it appears to remain unresolved. There do not appear to be any new or revised diagnostic categories that would appropriately apply to perpetrators of domestic violence either (APA, 2012). Island and Letellier (1991) indicate that the diagnostic criteria for intermittent explosive disorder (312.34) is too general to account for the more specific and patterned behavior attributable to batterers. Further, they indicate that most clinicians do not believe that impulse control is a problem of batterers, given that they are rational and aware that they use abuse to gain and maintain power and control over their partners.

DSM coding for LGBTQ+ intimate partner violence is currently insufficient and problematic. Problems and patterns related to abuse and domestic violence, in particular, are not classified on a continuum and do not allow for variations such as the defending victim, secondary aggressor, and primary aggressor categories that increase the efficacy of treatment planning. Furthermore, these extremes do not allow for different types of domestic violence (i.e. "situational violence," "common couple violence," and "intimate terrorism").

Continuing Education Questions

1. Studies show that what percentage of sexual minority men want to be screened for IPV on every visit?
   a. 14
   b. 45

    c. 75

    d. 92

2. Asking about LGBTQ IPV directly always results in an honest and clear answer.

    a. True

    b. False

3. Which one of these is *not* a challenge when assessing for LGBTQ IPV?

    a. You cannot rely on gender identity to know who is the victim and who is the perpetrator

    b. LGBTQ IPV is usually not that severe and does not rise to the level of clinical intervention or treatment

    c. Victims are more likely to take responsibility than perpetrators

    d. Applying usual heterosexual models of LGBTQ IPV does not always translate effectively

4. The LGBTQ IPV model developed by the authors of this book includes four categories.

    a. True

    b. False

5. What is the most likely diagnosis given to victims of LGBTQ IPV by providers?

    a. Intermittent explosive disorder

    b. Obsessive compulsive disorder

    c. Post-traumatic stress disorder

    d. Binge-eating disorder

References

Advocates for Human Rights (AHR). (2010). Women's Use of Violence in Intimate Relationships. Retrieved August 1, 2012, from www.stopvaw.org/women_s_use_of_violence_in_intimate_relationships

Aldarondo, E. (1998). Perpetrators of Domestic Violence. In A. Bellack & M. Hersen (Eds.), *Comprehensive Clinical Psychology*. New York: Pergamon.

Aldarondo, E., & Straus, M.A. (1994). Screening for Physical Violence in Couple Therapy: Methodological, Practical, and Ethical Considerations. *Family Process, 33,* 425–439.

American Psychiatric Association (APA). (2000). *Diagnostic and Statistical Manual of Mental Disorders* (4th ed., text revision). Washington, DC: American Psychiatric Association.

American Psychiatric Association (APA). (2012). DSM-5 Development. Retrieved October 29, 2012, from http://www.dsm5.org

American Psychological Association (APA). (1996). *Violence and the Family: Report of the American Psychological Association Presidential Task Force on Violence and the Family.* Washington, DC: American Psychological Association.

Archer, J. (2000). Sex Differences in Aggression between Heterosexual Partners: A Meta-analytic Review. *Psychological Bulletin, 126,* 651–680.

Avalon, S. (1999). Advocacy and the Battered Women's Movement: Advocates for Human Rights. Retrieved August 1, 2012, from www.stopvaw.org/women_s_use_of_violence_in_intimate_relationships

Bayer, R. (1981). *Homosexuality and American Psychiatry.* New York: Basic Books.

Bhugra, D. (1987). Homophobia: A Review of the Literature. *Sexual and Marital Therapy, 2*(2), 169–177.

Coker, A.L., David, K.E., Arios, I., Desai, S., Sanderson, M., & Brandt, H.M. (2002). Physical and Mental Health Effects of Intimate Partner Violence for Men and Women. *American Journal of Preventive Medicine, 23,* 260–268. doi:10.1016/50749-3797(02)00514-7

Coleman, K., Weisman, M., & His, B. (1980). Factors Affecting Conjugal Violence. *Journal of Psychology, 105,* 197–202.

Coleman, V. (1994). Lesbian Battering: The Relationship between Personality and Perpetration of Violence. *Violence and Victims, 9*(2), 139–152.

Cope, A., & Darke, J. (1999). *Trans Accessibility Project: Making Women's Shelters Accessible to Transgendered Women [fact sheet].* Washington, DC: National Resource Council on Domestic Violence/LGBTQ Communities and Domestic Violence.

Dasgupta, S.D. (2001). Towards an Understanding of Women's Use of Non-lethal Violence in Intimate Heterosexual Relationships. Retrieved August 1, 2012, from http://www.stopvaw.org/women_s_use_of_violence_in_intimate_relationships

Dobash, R.E., & Dobash, R. (1979). *Violence against Wives.* New York: Free Press.

Dobash, R.E., & Dobash, R. (1988). Research as Social Action: The Struggle for Battered Women. In K. Yllo & M. Bograd (Eds.), *Feminist Perspectives on Wife Abuse* (pp. 51–74). Thousand Oaks, CA: Sage.

Dutton, D. (1994). Patriarchy and Wife Assault: The Ecological Fallacy. *Violence and Victims, 9,* 67–182.

Ferraro, K.J., & Johnson, J.M. (1983). How Women Experience Battering: The Process of Victimization. *Social Problems, 30,* 325–339.

Golding, J.M. (1999). Intimate Partner Violence as a Risk Factor for Mental Disorders: A Meta-analysis. *Journal of Family Violence, 14,* 99–132.

Gondolf, E.W. (1992). Discussion of Violence in Psychiatric Evaluations. *Journal of Interpersonal Violence, 7,* 334–349.

Goodman, L.A., & Epstein, D. (2008). *Listening to Battered Women: A Survivor-Centered Approach to Advocacy, Mental Health, and Justice.* Washington, DC: American Psychological Association.

Goodstein, R.K., & Page, A.W. (1981). Battered Wife Syndrome: Overview of Dynamics and Treatment. *American Journal of Psychiatry, 138*(8), 1036–1044.

Gramick, J. (1983). Homophobia: A New Challenge. *Social Work, 28,* 137–141.

Guzik, H. (June 21, 2017). *In a Push for Fair Treatment, Los Angeles LGBT Center Creates New Categories for Relationship Violence.* California Health Report.

Hamel, J. (2007). Toward a Gender-Inclusive Conception of Intimate Partner Violence Research and Theory: Part 1—Traditional Perspectives. *International Journal of Men's Health, 6*(1), 26–53.

Harway, M., & Hansen, M. (1994). *Spouse Abuse: Assessing and Treating Battered Women, Batterers, and Their Children.* Sarasota, FL: Professional Resource Press.

Helton, A.M. (1986). The Pregnant Battered Woman. *Response to Victimization of Women and Children, 9*(1), 22–23.

Herek, G.M. (1986a). On Heterosexual Masculinity: Some Psychical Consequences of the Social Construction of Gender and Sexuality. *American Behavioral Scientist, 29,* 563–577.

Herek, G.M. (1986b). The Social Psychology of Homophobia: Toward a Practical Theory. *Review of Law and Social Change, 14*(4), 923–934.

Herek, G.M. (1988). Heterosexuals' Attitudes toward Lesbians and Gay Men: Correlates and Gender Differences. *Journal of Sex Research, 25*(4), 451–477.

Herman, J.L. (1992). *Trauma and Recovery: The Aftermath of Violence from Domestic Abuse to Political Terror.* New York, NY: Basic Books.

Hough, S. (June 21, 2017). *In a Push for Fair Treatment, Los Angeles LGBT Center Creates New Categories for Relationship Violence.* California Health Report.

House, E.R. (2006). When Women Use Force: An Advocacy Guide to Understanding This Issue and Conducting an Assessment with Individuals Who Have Used Force to Determine Their Eligibility for Services from a Domestic Violence Agency. Retrieved August 1, 2012, from www.stopvaw.org/women_s_use_of_violence_in_intimate_relationships

Island, D., & Letellier, P. (1991). *Men Who Beat the Men Who Love Them.* Binghamton, NY: Harrington Park Press.

Jordan, C.E., & Walker, R. (1994). Guidelines for Handling Domestic Violence Cases in Community Mental Health Centers. *Hospital and Community Psychiatry, 45*(2), 147–151.

Kantor, G.K., & Jasinski, J.L. (1998). Partner Violence: A Comprehensive Review of 20 Years of Research. In J.L. Jasinski & L.M. Williams (Eds.), *Partner Violence: A Comprehensive Review of 20 Years of Research.* Sage. Retrieved May 29, 2008, from www.sagepub.com

Katz-Wise, S.L., & Hyde, J.S. (2012). Victimization Experiences of Lesbian, Gay, and Bisexual Individuals: A Meta-analysis. *Journal of Sex Research, 49*(2–3), 142–167.

Kerns, J.G., & Fine, M.A. (1994). The Relation between Gender and Negative Attitudes toward Gay Men and Lesbians: Do Gender Role Attitudes Mediate This Relation? *Sex Roles, 31*(5–6), 297–307.

Kite, M.E. (1992). Individual Differences in Males' Reactions to Gay Males and Lesbians. *Journal of Applied Social Psychology, 22*(15), 1222–1239.

Kurdek, L.A. (1988). Correlates of Negative Attitudes toward Homosexuals in Heterosexual College Students. *Sex Roles, 18*(11–12), 727–738.

Lie, G.Y., Schilit, R., Bush, J., Montagne, M., & Reyes, L. (1991). Lesbians in Currently Aggressive Relationships: How Frequently Do They Report Aggressive Past Relationships? *Violence and Victims, 6*(2), 121–135.

Margolies, L., & Leeder, E. (1995). Violence at the Door: Treatment of Lesbian Batterers. *Violence Against Women, 1,* 139–157.

Marrujo, B., & Kreger, M. (1996). Definition of Roles in Abusive Lesbian Relationships. In C. Renzetti & C. Miley (Eds.), *Violence in Gay and Lesbian Domestic Partnerships* (pp. 23–33). New York, NY: Harrington Park Press.

Merrill, G., & Wolfe, V. (2000). Battered Men: An Exploration of Abuse, Help Seeking and Why They Stay. *Journal of Homosexuality, 39*(2), 1–30.

Miller, A.J., Bobner, R.F., & Zarski, J.J. (2000). Sexual Identity Development: A Base for Work with Same Sex Couple Partner Abuse. *Contemporary Family Therapy, 22,* 189–200.

National Resource Center on Domestic Violence (NRCDV). (2007). *Lesbian, Gay, Bisexual, and Trans (LGBTQ) Communities and Domestic Violence: Information and Resources.* Harrisburg,˙ PA: Author. Retrieved October 17, 2004, from www.ncadv.org

Neidig, P., Friedman, D., &.Collins, B. (1986). Attitudinal Characteristics of Males Who Have Engaged in Spouse Abuse. *Journal of Family Violence, 1,* 223–233.

Page, S., & Yee, M. (1985). Conception of Male and Female Homosexual Stereotypes among University Undergraduates. *Journal of Homosexuality, 12*(1), 109–118.

Pico-Alfonso, M.A., Garcia-Linares, M. Isabel, Celda-Navarro, Nuria, Herbert, Joe, & Martinez, Manuela. (2004). Changes in Cortisol and Dehydroepiandrosterone in Women Victims of Physical and Psychological Intimate Partner Violence. *Biological Psychiatry, 56*(4), 233–240. doi:10.1016/j.biopsych.2004.06.001

Pence, E. (1987). In Our Best Interest: A Process for Personal and Social Change. In NRCDV (Ed.), *LGBTQ Communities and Domestic Violence.* Duluth, MN: NRCDV.

Peplau, L.A. (1991). Lesbian and Gay Relationships. In J. Gonsiorek & J. Enrich (Eds.), *Homosexuality: Implications for Public Policy* (pp. 177–196). Newbury Park, CA: Sage.

Pharr, S. (1988). *Homophobia: A Weapon of Sexism.* Inverness, CA: Chardon Press.

Pleck, J.H., Sonenstein, F.L., & Ku, L.A. (1994). Attitudes toward Male Roles among Adolescent Males: A Discriminant Validity Analysis. *Sex Roles, 30*(7–8), 481–501.

Reiter, L. (1991). Developmental Origins of Anti-homosexual Prejudice in Heterosexual Men and Women. *Clinical Social Work Journal, 19*(2), 163–175.

Renzetti, C. (1992). *Violent Betrayal: Partner Abuse in Lesbian Relationships.* Newbury Park, CA: Sage.

Rosenbaum, A., & O'Leary, D. (1981). Marital Violence: Characteristics of Abusive Couples. *Journal of Consulting and Clinical Psychology, 49,* 63–71.

Saunders, D.G. (1988). Wife Abuse, Husband Abuse, or Mutual Combat? A Feminist Perspective on the Empirical Findings. In K. Yllo & M. Bograd (Eds.), *Feminist Perspectives on Wife Abuse* (pp. 90–113). Newbury Park, CA: Sage.

Schechter, S. (1987). Empowering Interventions with Battered Women. In S. Schechter (Ed.), *Guidelines for Mental Health Professionals* (pp. 9–13). Washington, DC: National Coalition Against Domestic Violence.

Silverstein, C. (1991). Psychological and Medical Treatments of Homosexuality. In. J. Gonsiorek & J. Enrich (Eds.), *Homosexuality: Research Implications for Public Policy* (pp. 101–114). Newbury Park, CA: Sage.

Steinmetz, S.K. (1977–1978). The Battered Husband Syndrome. *Victimology: An International Journal, 2,* 499–509.

Straus, M.A. (1980). Victims and Aggressors in Marital Violence. *American Behavioral Scientist, 23,* 681–704.

Straus, M.A. (1990). Injury and Frequency of Assault and the Representative Sample Fallacy in Measuring Wife Beating and Child Abuse. In M. Straus & R. Gelles (Eds.), *Physical Violence in American Families: Risk Factors and Adaptations to Violence in 8,145 Families* (pp. 75–91). New Brunswick, NJ: Transaction.

Straus, M.A., Gelles, R.J., & Steinmetz, S.K. (1980). *Behind Closed Doors: Violence in the American Family.* Garden City, NY: Doubleday/Anchor.

Sullivan, J.S., & Laughlin, L.R. (1999). Identification and Treatment Modalities for Victims of Same-Sex Partner Abuse. In J. McLennan & J. Gunther (Eds.), *Same-Gender Partner Abuse: A Professional's Guide to Practice Intervention* (pp. 93–104). Lewiston, NY: Edwin Mellen.

Tjaden, P., & Thoennes, N. (2000). *Extent, Nature, and Consequences of Intimate Partner Violence: Findings from the National Violence Against Women Survey.* Washington, DC: U.S. Department of Justice. Retrieved May 19, 2009, from www.ojp.usdoj.gov/nij/pubs-sum/181867.htm

Verizon Foundation. (2013). *Exploring the Relationship between Domestic Violence and Chronic Health Conditions.* www.ncdsv.org/Verizon-More_exploring-the-Relationship-Between-DV-and-Chronic-Health-Conditions-survey-summary_10-2013pdf

Walker, L. (1986). Battered Women's Shelters and Work with Battered Lesbians. In K. Lobel (Ed.), *Naming the Violence* (pp. 73–76). Seattle, WA: Seal Press.

Whalen, M. (1996). *Counseling to End Violence against Women: A Subversive Model.* Thousand Oaks, CA: Sage.

Whirry, R., & Holt, S. (2020). *Finding Safety: A Report about LGBTQ Domestic Violence and Sexual Assault.* Los Angeles, CA: Los Angeles LGBT Center.

Whitley, B.E. (1988). Sex Differences in Heterosexuals' Attitudes toward Homosexuals: It Depends upon What You Ask. *Journal of Sex Research, 24,* 287–291.

Wylie, M.S. (1995). Diagnosing for Dollars? *The Family Therapy Networker, 19*(3), 22–69.

Yllo, K. (1993). Through a Feminist Lens: Gender Power and Violence. In R. Gelles & D. Loseke (Eds.), *Current Controversies in Family Violence* (pp. 47–62). Thousand Oaks, CA: Sage.

Yllo, K., & Straus, M. (1990). Patriarchy and Violence against Wives: The Impact of Structural and Normative Factors. In M. Straus & R. Gelles (Eds.), *Physical Violence in American Families* (pp. 383–399). New Brunswick, NJ: Transaction.

LGBTQ+ Intimate Partner Violence Intervention and Treatment

15

The assessment and treatment of LGBTQ+ domestic violence are inherently challenging. While it shares some similarities with partner violence in non-LGBTQ persons, differences between the two are numerous and complex. If these differences are not known, understood, acknowledged, and addressed by the therapist, intervention is potentially dangerous and can be life-threatening. The following case illustrates the challenges as well as the benefits of assessing and intervening in LGBTQ+ domestic violence, utilizing a LGBTQ+-affirmative and LGBTQ+-specific approach.

Assessment of intimate partner violence, regardless of the sexual orientation of the parties, is challenging and complicated by the dynamics of domestic violence itself: Abusers commonly feel victimized, and victims often believe they are responsible for the abuse—especially if they have fought back in self-defense or retaliation or did something to provoke their partner's abuse in an effort to shorten the tension-building stage of the cycle of violence and move more quickly into the honeymoon stage. Furthermore, behaviors that are often self-defensive (pushing the partner away, holding the partner's arms or wrists to keep from being hit, scratching, blocking punches) are often viewed to be abusive by the abuser and victim as well as service providers involved with the case. Because of these confusing variables, when providers attempt to intervene, for example, they often revert to stereotypes or stay within the traditional gender-based and heteronormative context of domestic violence theory, which can result in an inaccurate assessment and potentially ineffective or harmful treatment plan.

DOI: 10.4324/9780429031397-15

Therefore, when conducting an assessment, it is crucial to distinguish between the initiation of violence, the motivation for its initiation, and the types of behaviors used during the conflict (i.e. self-defending, retaliatory). Many mental health professionals fail to distinguish between these categories when they conduct an assessment of intimate partner abuse. Furthermore, their assessments rarely contain information that is sufficient to make an accurate or adequate evaluation of the violence and distinguish between victim and abuser—especially in LGBTQ+ cases.

The client, whom we will call "Stephen," is a 36-year-old cisgender gay white male (pronouns: he/his) mandated by the court to batterers' treatment following a domestic violence arrest and charge. He reports that his neighbors called the police in response to a "loud argument" that he had with his male partner ("Allen") 2 weeks earlier. The client states that arguments between him and his partner are common. He indicates that he feels resentful about his arrest and subsequent court requirement to attend treatment. He reports that, while his eating and sleeping patterns are stable, he has difficulty concentrating and fears that he might lose his job as a manager at a printing company because of this problem.

Stephen reports that his parents sent him to therapy at age 15 when he disclosed to them that he was gay. He states that the therapist focused on attempting to change his sexual orientation rather than the "real issues," and he is now reluctant to trust mental health professionals. He reports that he attempted to kill himself at age 13 when he realized he was gay by consuming a handful of his mother's sleeping pills (Ativan). He states, "It didn't really hurt me. I just slept a lot for a couple of days. No one even realized what I'd done." There have been no psychiatric hospitalizations. The client has never taken psychotropic medication and is reluctant to consider it at this time. He reports that he thinks about suicide periodically but has no current intent, plan, or means. No past or current homicidal ideation is present.

The client reports that his partner of 14 years is his primary source of emotional support and states, "I can't imagine being with anyone but him." He and his partner have lived together for 13 of their 14 years as a couple, got married in 2015, and recently purchased a house together. They have no children but recently considered adopting a child. The client reports that they have few friends, and, when they socialize, it is generally for work-related events. None of his or his partner's co-workers are aware of the problems within their relationship. Neither the client nor his partner is close to their family of origin. The client reports that he has never been close to his parents ("They don't respect me") or his only sibling, an older brother who lives in New York.

Stephen reports that he occasionally uses alcohol and crystal methamphetamine. He indicates that his substance use is limited to weekends. The client states that he rarely has more than two drinks at a time (usually wine with dinner) and uses meth roughly one or two weekends each month. He reports no significant consequences of use, although he admits that both he and his partner have difficulty managing anger during and following crystal use. The client's family has a history of alcoholism (both parents and brother). During Stephen's teen years, his mother consistently used Ativan for anxiety and sleep. There have been no previous or current recovery attempts. The client denies sexually compulsive/addictive behaviors. He reports concerns about body image but does not appear to have symptoms consistent with an active eating disorder.

Stephen states that both he and his partner have explosive tempers and difficulty managing anger. He also reports that both he and his partner tend to have a "jealous nature" and have periodically interrogated each other about outside interests and activities. He states that he periodically feels restricted because of his partner's HIV status. He reports a history of name-calling and insults by both him and his partner when angry and states that his partner threatened to "out" him to his employer several years ago but did not follow through with the threat. The client reports that there have been numerous incidents of hitting and shoving during his 14-year relationship, and that both partners have thrown objects and slammed doors when angry.

The initial intake interviewer (a general clinician) determined from the information gathered that the abuse between the client, Stephen, and his partner, Allen, was "mutually abusive," and that the client should be placed in an anger management group. Upon review of the intake, however, the LGBTQ+ domestic violence specialist (Dr. Green, also reviewed to as "they" throughout the case illustration) reviewing it determined that further assessment with Stephen was necessary. While domestic violence commonly appears to be "mutual" in LGBTQ+ relationships, mutual abuse/combat is, in reality, very rare, and a primary aggressor can usually be identified with thorough and comprehensive evaluation by a domestic violence specialist. Although Stephen initially appeared to be the partner that was more prone to primary aggression, Dr. Green also wanted additional information, prior to placement in treatment, about the client's difficulties with concentration, periodic suicidal ideation, substance use, body image, and restrictions imposed on the relationship because of Allen's HIV status. Furthermore, they wanted details of Stephen and Allen's conflicts and abusive and violent incidents to determine if the abuse was the result of "common couple violence" or "intimate partner terrorism." Therefore, an appointment was scheduled with Stephen for a comprehensive intimate partner violence evaluation.

The primary assessment goal with Stephen was to determine if he was, in fact, the primary aggressor in his relationship with Allen, and, if not, what assessment category was most appropriate. An additional goal was to determine what, if any, other difficulties or problems were exacerbating the abuse and violence. To accomplish this, Dr. Green planned to determine if there was a pattern of power and control in the relationship, and, if so, which partner appeared to gain and maintain the majority of power and control. The clinician began by assessing if Stephen was in crisis and needed immediate crisis intervention or stabilization. He denied being suicidal or homicidal, but Dr. Green, nevertheless, did a full suicide assessment because of Stephen's history and ruled out an immediate crisis. Once it was determined that the assessment could safely proceed, Dr. Green discussed the limits of confidentiality with Stephen and provided him with information about informed consent (this was also initially provided to him in writing prior to the start of the session), discussed his rights and responsibilities as a client, gave him information about the Health Insurance Portability and Accountability Act (HIPAA) as well as information about fees, and then provided him with information about their qualifications, education, and experience in the domestic violence field. Dr. Green also discussed the purpose and importance of the assessment, differentiated for Stephen how an assessment session differed from a therapy session, explained the risks and benefits of treatment, and provided information about how treatment would proceed following the assessment.

Because Stephen appeared to be anxious, Dr. Green normalized his anxiety and asked if he had any initial questions or requests. They provided him with basic information about LGBTQ+ domestic violence, including how prevalent it is in the LGBTQ+ community, and then continued by asking how he and Allen resolved conflicts in their relationship and what they usually argued about. Dr. Green asked him to describe the history of his relationship, including the circumstances of how he and Allen met, good times in the partnership, periods of separation, the reason for and number of separations, and so on. They also questioned him about his past relationships, asked if there was abuse in these relationships, and inquired about how he and his former partners resolved conflict.

During this process, Stephen and Dr. Green were slowly building rapport. As a result, and as they progressed, Stephen became increasingly more apt to describe the qualities of his relationship with Allen, the first abusive incident(s) that occurred in the relationship, and how frequently subsequent incidents had occurred, the duration of each, and the details of the most abusive incident(s). Dr. Green attempted to determine if Stephen felt he could live without Allen (and, if not, the level of his possessiveness); if he was afraid of Allen; if he believed Allen was afraid of him; if he or Allen had ever required medical treatment as a result of the abuse in the relationship; if weapons were ever involved in the abuse; if Stephen was aware of physical/emotional/environmental cues preceding the abuse; if he had difficulties managing his anger outside the home; and if he saw himself as the victim, abuser, or as mutually abusive. Stephen indicated that, because of his angry outbursts, he was abusive and, that, overall, the violence in his relationship with Allen was mutual.

To further inform the assessment, Dr. Green also attempted to determine if Stephen had been involved in any situations outside the home that included violence (gangs, cults, rivalries, etc.); if he had ever been abusive to himself in any way (cutting, burning, head banging, and other forms of self-destructive or self-mutilating behaviors, etc.); if he had been the victim of other types of violence (stranger sexual assault, physical assault, mugging, etc.); if there were any experiences of discrimination or bias that he may have suffered; and if he had ever been harassed and/or the recipient of bias or hate violence. He reported that he had been the victim of a gay bashing several years earlier and he remained frightened of how others would treat him if they learned of his sexual orientation, but Dr. Green ruled out symptoms consistent with a PTSD diagnosis.

Having obtained specific information about the abuse and violence in Stephen's relationship, Dr. Green proceeded to do a more general psychosocial assessment that would further inform the overall evaluation (and treatment) process. They first obtained additional information about Stephen's use of substances and learned that he preferred alcohol to crystal methamphetamine, which was Allen's drug of choice. Dr. Green also learned that Stephen consumed more alcohol than he had initially reported to the initial intake interviewer and regularly had several drinks after dinner as well as one-to-two glasses of wine prior to dinner each day, which was more than he generally intended. Although no one in Stephen's life had ever expressed concern about his use of alcohol, he appeared to be embarrassed and ashamed when discussing it. Exploration of his affect revealed that he drank primarily to decrease anxiety about his relationship with Allen and had a desire to decrease his use but felt unable to do so. In fact, when Stephen was intoxicated, Allen was actually less likely to pressure him into using crystal meth with him, a drug that heightened and sustained Allen's sexual pleasure but increased his level of sexual aggressiveness toward Stephen. Further discussion revealed that Stephen was frightened by his partner's sexual aggressiveness because, when high, Allen usually refused to practice safer sex, and Stephen feared that he might contract HIV or another sexually transmitted disease. Stephen's pattern of methamphetamine use did not meet the DSM criteria for stimulant use disorder. Rather, Dr. Green determined that his methamphetamine use was mild and infrequent and generally occurred because of coercion on the part of Allen. However, he believed that Stephen's use of alcohol was associated more closely with the violence in his relationship and was becoming increasingly problematic in his life. Additional assessment of other compulsive or addictive behaviors revealed nothing significant, and Dr. Green concurred with the initial interviewer's assessment that no active eating disorders were present. Rather, Stephen's concerns about body image appeared to be mild and related to his belief that others only valued him based on qualities such as physical attractiveness and youth.

Stephen was oriented to person, place, time, situation, familiar objects, and others. His attention and concentration appeared to be normal, and he was able to filter out irrelevant stimuli during the interview. However, he complained that he was often unable to focus and felt periodically distracted when thinking about Allen and their relationship, although this was not evident during the evaluation session. Stephen's comprehension of language was excellent, and his affect was appropriately expressive. He reported no problems with recent memory, recent past memory, or remote memory, and his short-term retention appeared to be normal. His coordination and perceptual abilities appeared to be average. However, Stephen's self-image was poor, and his social judgment and decision-making capabilities were slightly impaired. He also appeared to lack sufficient insight into his presenting problems.

Dr. Green found no evidence of attention deficit disorder, bipolar disorder, antisocial personality disorder, narcissistic personality disorder, or borderline personality disorder. All of these are sometimes compatible with perpetration of domestic violence. In addition, Dr. Green did not detect enough characteristics to diagnose intermittent explosive disorder or posttraumatic stress disorder, the latter being common with victims of intimate partner violence. However, further assessment of Stephen's anxiety revealed traits consistent with panic disorder. Because Stephen's physical health was excellent, the panic attacks did not appear to be due to a medical condition or another mental disorder, although it was possible that they may have been induced by Stephen's periodic use of methamphetamine.

Dr. Green still planned to refer Stephen to a physician for a physical evaluation prior to treatment to rule out any medical problems, internal injuries, and head trauma since there had been physical violence in the relationship.

Dr. Green also learned that Stephen felt periodically depressed, but the level of his depression was mild, and he had no incidents of major depression. Although he disclosed that he occasionally felt that it would be relieving to simply "fade away," he reported that he would never take his own life, and that the incident at age 13 when he consumed his mother's sleeping pills had frightened him. His appetite, eating and sleeping patterns, as well as his energy levels were normal. He denied feelings of hopelessness. Further assessment of suicidality revealed no current intent, plan, or means. The clinician ruled out persistent depressive disorder (dysthymia) because Stephen's depression was not consistently present or present for more days than not. The difficulty that he had concentrating at work seemed to be related to the domestic violence because it only occurred when Stephen was thinking of his conflicts and/or relationship with Allen and his recent arrest. Further questioning revealed that he was not at risk for losing his job as stated in the initial intake, and that he had, in fact, recently received an excellent performance evaluation. His reduced self-esteem also seemed to be related to the intimate partner violence as well as internalized homophobia.

Since Stephen identified as a gay man, it was important to determine where he was in the coming out and identity formation process. The Cass model was used. Stephen did not have any of the characteristics of the first stage (confusion, denial and repression of same-gender feelings, attempts to pass as heterosexual, etc.), but, because he had only come out to a limited number of people, the clinician surmised that he may be in the midst of the second stage. If this was true, it indicated that Stephen might be highly vulnerable. His self-esteem could either be heightened or diminished based on experiences with others. In fact, when domestic violence is present, there is greater risk that the behavior of others perceived by the client to be judgmental or negative will increase the isolation already inherent in the abusive relationship as he and Allen develop a "me and you against the world" attitude—an attitude that is further increased by the dynamic of traumatic bonding resulting from the relationship violence.

Dr. Green easily ruled out the presence of situational violence. It was more challenging, however, to identify if Stephen's was a problem of common couple violence or intimate terrorism. Furthermore, because the overwhelming majority of LGBTQ+ individuals are raised in heterosexual homes and because violence is generally learned, they sometimes adopt the behaviors and cognitions associated with male privilege and entitlement regardless of their gender identity or expression.

Ultimately, however, Dr. Green suspected that this was a case of intimate terrorism because there appeared to be a pattern of coercive control by Allen whenever he felt threatened by Stephen's autonomy and attempts to be self-sufficient.

Because Stephen believed that he and Allen were mutually abusive, the clinician asked him to talk in detail about three incidents of violence in their partnership. Had the duration of Stephen and Allen's relationship been briefer, Dr. Green would have also obtained detailed information about incidents of abuse in Stephen's past relationships as well. The incidents he discussed helped him identify, as best as possible, the behaviors for which he was responsible as well as behaviors that he attributed to Allen. Dr. Green then helped him define the context of the incident(s), his intent and motivating factors during them, and the ultimate effect(s) of his behavior. For example, Stephen reported an incident of reckless driving several days earlier while he and Allen were in the car together. He stated that they were on their way to a restaurant, and he was driving. He and Allen began arguing about who would pay for the meal. Tempers flared, and Allen called Stephen derogatory names while pounding the dashboard with his fist. In response, Stephen began driving faster as his anger at, and fear of, Allen increased. When Allen grabbed Stephen's wallet and began throwing money out the window, Stephen made an illegal U-turn in the middle of the road and sped recklessly toward home. After yelling at Stephen to "slow down," Allen's anger decreased, and he sat in sullen silence the remainder of the way home. Neither Stephen nor Allen spoke to one another for the remainder of the evening, and Stephen reported that he felt relieved by their lack of communication. Stephen also reported that similar incidents in the car had occurred with some regularity. He identified that, during the incident, his intent was to get home as quickly as possible where he felt safer and better able to put some distance between him and Allen. He denied feeling motivated to frighten Allen with his reckless driving or retaliate against him. His secondary intent was to bring outside attention to him and Allen in hopes that Allen's behavior would subsequently decrease or stop altogether.

After exploring two other incidents of abuse in Stephen's relationship with Allen that produced similar results, Dr. Green conducted a lethality assessment (Harway & Hansen, 1994). For this portion of the assessment, Dr. Green attempted to determine additional information about any of the following factors previously assessed, as well as if any of the following remaining factors were present and to what degree. These factors included objectification of the partner; blaming the partner for perceived injuries to self; ability to be separate from the partner; obsession with partner; extreme dependence on partner; consistent feelings of rage toward or betrayal by the partner; feelings of abandonment by the partner; acute depression, hopelessness, and/or despair; extreme jealousy; perpetration of previous incidents of physical and/or sexual violence; current or past abuse of children; current or past pet abuse; threats; suicide attempts; prior arrests for violence against strangers; prior arrests for domestic violence; access to the partner; access to weapons; increases in the frequency and severity of abusive behaviors; amphetamine abuse; desire to stop violent and controlling behaviors; and the degree to which either partner was closeted about sexual orientation and willing to risk this to maintain control of the partner.

Without an evaluation similar to the one described above, it would be difficult to determine with certainty that Stephen was the primary aggressor in his relationship with Allen. He had traits that were consistent with those commonly presented by primary aggressors including resentment about his arrest and requirement to attend batterers' intervention and treatment, social isolation, dependency on his partner and their relationship, substance abuse, anger management problems, and abusive and violent behaviors. However, Stephen also utilized numerous self-defensive behaviors and was frightened of Allen's rage, took responsibility for the majority of his abusive behaviors and the consequences of them, displayed a significant amount of remorse about his abusive behaviors, and tended to internalize rather than externalize blame for his circumstances. Furthermore, Stephen's degree of jealousy was moderate rather than pathological; he maintained selective rather than total control; he tended to manipulate his environment or situation to maintain safety; he was intrusive regarding his partner's activities only on occasion; he had rare anger management problems outside the home; he expressed retaliating anger toward his partner or internalized his anger rather than maintaining a high level of generalized anger and rage in the relationship; he displayed a fluid identify that was not male-identified; he did not display a sense of entitlement; he vacillated between being self- and other-focused; and he had a general sense of respect for the boundaries of others. In addition, Stephen was generally not the initiator when he fought with Allen but would participate in the fighting once it began. Furthermore, he had a tendency to fight back for the duration of the conflict but was generally not fully engaged in the fighting and, although he was not interested in escalating conflict, he would generally not attempt to disengage from it.

Dr. Green assessed that the ongoing risk for violence was relatively high because it appeared to be more severe and consistent than the types defined as situational violence or common couple violence. Further, because it was not frequently limited to particular recurring topics and was more global in nature, Dr. Green categorized it as intimate terrorism. The results of the lethality assessment, while serious, did not indicate that homicidal ideation was present or imminent. In Dr. Green's opinion, Stephen was clearly not the primary aggressor, but he was not a primary or defending victim either. Rather, Dr. Green assessed Stephen to be a secondary aggressor.

Per the DSM-V (APA, 2013), Stephen's primary diagnosis was included as an "Other Condition That May Be a Focus of Clinical Attention." It did not meet the criteria for Z63.0 ("Relationship Distress with Spouse or Intimate Partner") because this category excludes clinical encounters for Z.69.1 ("Spouse or Partner Abuse").

Dr. Green diagnosed Stephen as follows:

1. Primary diagnosis:
    a. Z69.11 "Encounter for Mental Health Services for Victim of Spouse or Partner Psychological Abuse"
    b. Z69.11 "Encounter for Mental Health Services for Victim of Spouse or Partner Violence, Physical"
2. Secondary diagnosis:
    a. 300.01 "Panic Disorder"
    b. 305.00 "Alcohol Use Disorder"

As explained earlier in this text, DSM coding for domestic violence is currently insufficient and, oftentimes, problematic. Problems related to abuse and domestic violence, in particular, are not classified on a continuum but in oppositional categories only (abuser vs. victim). These extremes do not allow for variations in assessment categories or different types of violence. While Stephen's problems due to panic disorder and to substances were both significant, Dr. Green prioritized panic disorder before substance abuse because the panic was severe enough to warrant immediate and focused attention and had the potential to impact Stephen's ability to participate in group therapy (and, if it escalated, could potentially affect his ability to participate in individual treatment as well), the modality of choice for clients experiencing intimate partner violence. Dr. Green determined that Stephen's abuse of alcohol must be treated concurrently with the primary problem of domestic violence. Because domestic violence, however, is always the treatment priority, Dr. Green planned to discuss with Stephen how it would be treated first and foremost. In this case, there is nothing that requires a mandated report for child abuse, elder, or dependent adult abuse, nor is there a duty to protect (*Tarasoff*, 1976).

Whether working with abuser or victim, survivor safety is crucial and the guiding force for all intervention and treatment planning. Group is generally the treatment modality of choice for both survivors and abusers. Individual counseling is contraindicated when working with batterers since the counselor will often inadvertently collude with the client and their feelings of blame of and anger toward the victim and subsequently increase the potential for abuse. Couples' counseling is generally contraindicated because it is not safe for the survivor to talk honestly or freely about the abuse in front of the abusive partner, and because domestic violence is not a relationship problem. In addition, abusive behaviors could be triggered by the session itself and generally occur after the couple leave the therapist's office.

Were Stephen to go to a batterers' intervention program designed primarily for heterosexuals, chances are high that his unique needs as a gay man would not be addressed. Furthermore, he would most surely be assessed as a primary aggressor rather than an aggressive victim or secondary aggressor. In addition, his safety in a mainstream group could not necessarily be guaranteed, or he may be told by the group facilitator(s) that it is too dangerous to disclose his sexual orientation to the other group members. The facilitator might also suggest that his presence in the group will give the heterosexual group members an excellent opportunity to learn more about the LGBTQ+ community, which is not Stephen's responsibility and uses energy that he needs for healing.

In addition, the curriculum of the group will most likely not address any issues or topics specific to LGBTQ+ domestic violence and will presumably focus exclusively on domestic violence within a heterosexual context (which would not be useful to Stephen). However, in a LGBTQ+-specific program, the group curriculum includes not only basic information about domestic violence in general but also information about misconceptions of LGBTQ+ abuse, the impact of internalized and institutionalized homo/bi/transphobia on LGBTQ+ domestic violence, the unique aspects of the LGBTQ+ cycle of violence, projection by the partner(s) and its impact, LGBTQ+-specific power and control tactics, substance abuse in the LGBTQ+ community, LGBTQ+ partners and families, the effect of HIV and AIDS on domestic violence, and support systems in the LGBTQ+ community. The overall context is, at the very least, LGBTQ+-affirmative and is preferably LGBTQ+-specific.

The intimate partner violence with which Stephen presented is the treatment priority and needs to be addressed within a treatment group specifically designed for members of the LGBTQ+ community that are not primary aggressors. Because Stephen lives in a very large urban area (Los Angeles), there is a group available that has been designed for secondary aggressors. However, if this was not the case, an anger management group (sensitive to the needs of LGBTQ+ clients) in conjunction with individual therapy for victims would be indicated. If no LGBTQ+-affirmative anger management group exists, the incorporation of anger management techniques within individual therapy would be indicated. Group membership will consist of other LGBTQ+ individuals who have been assessed as secondary aggressors. The group will meet once a week for 2 hours and will include a psychoeducational component as well as group process work. Because Stephen is a court-mandated client, he may remain in the group for 52 weeks, as required by California's penal code, if the court does not revise this requirement of the domestic violence charge against him.

Because Stephen is a secondary aggressor, facets of his treatment will include a mixture of interventions designed for LGBTQ+ domestic violence victims and those for LGBTQ+ individuals who use aggressive behaviors in self-defense and retaliation for their victimization.

Substantial focus during treatment will be on the development of a realistic safety and danger management plan. There will be more focus on domestic violence prevention and anger management techniques than is commonly found in groups designed for primary aggressors. These techniques include the utilization of time-outs; identification of psychological, behavioral, and environmental cues preceding violence; iceberging (assisting clients in identifying vulnerable emotions that frequently co-occur with anger and are often unacknowledged or expressed); journaling; and the identification of anger-escalating self-talk and the modification of it. In addition, Stephen will be helped to identify misconceptions about LGBTQ+ domestic violence that he has learned. Once these misconceptions are identified, Stephen will be helped to challenge, modify, and replace them with accurate information about LGBTQ+ intimate partner abuse.

Prior to Stephen's placement in group, Dr. Green will contact the court and/or probation department on his behalf and inform them of the results of their evaluation. They will also conduct any additional advocacy that is needed to ensure that Stephen's records accurately reflect his status as a secondary aggressor rather than a primary aggressor. This is vitally important for Stephen's future safety. When the arrest record for LGBTQ+ clients is not corrected, primary aggressors have even more power and control in the relationship, and clients such as Stephen are generally denied future assistance from domestic violence organizations.

Dr. Green will also consider Stephen's diagnosis of panic disorder to be a treatment priority secondary to intimate partner violence. Although individual therapy is generally contraindicated for people with abusive behaviors, Dr. Green believed that Stephen's participation in a group might eventually be compromised if his panic disorder remains untreated, and so they planned to address it in concurrent individual therapy. In addition, Dr. Green must also pay attention to Stephen's victimization, and so group and individual therapy together are ideal. If the panic disorder does not respond to treatment and/or if it escalates or seriously impedes Stephen's ability to participate in group or his ability to even come in for treatment, the clinician will advocate again with the court/probation department on Stephen's behalf and request that the remainder of Stephen's court requirement (group therapy) be completed in individual treatment. If approved, Dr. Green will increase the number of individual sessions per week, and the intimate partner violence and panic disorder will both be addressed in individual treatment. While this is not ideal, they believe that it will be preferable to and safer than ineffective treatment or no treatment.

Another focus in Stephen's individual and group therapy will be on the development of social support systems. Other issues to be addressed include Stephen's internalized homophobia and plans to carefully monitor his progression through the tasks and stages of the coming out and identity formation process, address the interaction between his development in this regard and the domestic violence, and then tailor interventions accordingly. Dr. Green will also determine family-of-origin trauma that Stephen may have experienced and incorporate these aspects into the individual treatment plan. Family-of-origin trauma at this point in treatment will be addressed utilizing cognitive behavioral techniques, because abusive and violent behaviors must substantially decrease or be eliminated before dynamic emotional processing of the trauma should occur. Consistently throughout the treatment, Dr. Green will also be monitoring Stephen's safety plan and helping him revise it for optimal effectiveness as necessary. Overall, treatment will be conducted within an LGBTQ+-specific, trauma-informed framework.

Another focus in therapy will be on the development of safer sex practices within the overall context of safety planning. The HIV status of one or both partners creates additional obstacles for the victim and may aggravate the consequences of the abuse. Allen's sexual practices and their impact on Stephen need to be factored into all discussions about the intimate partner violence.

Stephen's abuse of alcohol also needs to be addressed in concurrent substance abuse treatment. If Stephen's panic disorder does not impede his ability to participate in group treatment, then Dr. Green plans to refer him to an early recovery group for gay substance users. Referral to an LGBTQ+ 12-step group might also be a possibility. As the treatment of Stephen's substance use progresses, the members of the treatment team overseeing his case will be better able to assess if his alcohol use has been triggering and/or exacerbating his panic attacks. The interplay and connection between substance use and domestic violence will also be an issue that is addressed in Stephen's domestic violence group. If, however, Stephen's panic disorder impacts his ability to participate in group treatment, the substance use will be treated in individual therapy until Stephen is able to join a group.

Throughout treatment, Dr. Green will monitor where Stephen's and Allen's relationship is in the LGBTQ+ cycle of violence. If, at any point, the violence in Stephen's relationship increases, Dr. Green will help him explore options for safer housing and other basic necessities that he might need. While it is unlikely that a traditional domestic violence shelter will house Stephen, a non-shelter-based intimate partner violence program may be able to assist Stephen in finding temporary living accommodations in a hotel, transitional or shared housing facility, or with friends.

A treatment team approach is the most effective way to address a complicated case like this one. In addition to increasing the potential for a positive outcome, members of the team will provide valuable support to one another while decreasing the isolation that can often develop for solo practitioners. Working with LGBTQ+ domestic violence can be frustrating and incredibly challenging. Limitations with the system because of homophobia/biphobia/transphobia, heterosexism, and anti-LGBTQ+ bias should always be acknowledged but not seen as insurmountable barriers to the ability of clients to live lives free of abuse and violence.

Continuing Education Questions

1. Which one of these is *not* a risk factor for LGBTQ IPV in Stephen's history?
    a. Suicide attempt
    b. Alcohol and crystal meth use
    c. Explosive temper on the part of him and his partner
    d. Absence of current major depressive episodes
2. When assessing for LGBTQ IPV, it is important to interview the partners together.
    a. True
    b. False

3. Which of the following is part of a lethality assessment?
   a. Objectification of partner
   b. Obsession with partner
   c. Consistent feelings of rage toward or betrayal by partner
   d. Current or past pet abuse, threats
   e. All of the above
4. Treatment for LGBTQ IPV should wait until all mental health issues are resolved.
   a. True
   b. False
5. Which of the following is false?
   a. LGBTQ IPV is not common, and so it is difficult to find any cases of it
   b. Victims often feel responsible, and perpetrators can feel victimized, making these determinations difficult
   c. Applying usual heterosexual models of LGBTQ IPV does not always translate effectively
   d. None of the above

References

American Psychiatric Association (APA). (2013). *Diagnostic and Statistical Manual of Mental Disorders* (5th ed.). Washington, DC: American Psychiatric Association.

Harway, M., & Hansen, M. (1994). *Spouse Abuse: Assessing and Treating Battered Women, Batterers, and Their Children*. Sarasota, FL: Professional Resource Press.

Tarasoff v. Regents of the University of California, 131 Cal. Rptr. 14 (Cal. 1976).

Legal and Ethical Issues 16
Pertinent to LGBTQ+
Intimate Partner
Violence

Domestic violence cases typically involve a wide spectrum of disorders (Jordan & Walker, 1994), and the serious psychological and physical impacts of violence have been well documented in the literature (Walker, 1994; Carmen, Rieker, & Mills, 1984; Rose, Peabody, & Stratigeas, 1991; Post, Willett, & Franks, 1980; Gondolf, 1985; Sonkin, Martin, & Auerbach-Walker, 1985; Hotaling & Sugarman, 1986; Coleman & Strauss, 1979; Hamberger & Hastings, 1988). Seventy-five percent of spousal assaults occur at the point of separation or divorce (Bureau of Justice Statistics 1988), a time when family members often seek assistance from mental health providers or are mandated by a court to participate in treatment (Jordan & Walker, 1994). It is imperative that clinicians be alert to the possibility that the person seeking assistance may be in danger or may present a danger to others (Jordan & Walker, 1994). Clinicians are also exposed to liability if they fail to inquire about the existence of violence (McNeill, 1987). Furthermore, clinicians must be knowledgeable about the various effects of intimate partner violence and subsequent referral sources that are equipped to assist.

Legal issues include criminal and civil laws that govern and/or impact the practice of mental health counseling and therapy. Laws governing mental health professionals are specifically articulated in licensing laws such as the prohibition of sex with clients, misleading or false advertising, and so on. Ethical issues, on the other hand, are ethical standards that create a model code of conduct to ensure the protection of patient rights. Ethical codes are frequently adopted or used to provide guidance by state licensing boards and national and state mental health associations to set forth

DOI: 10.4324/9780429031397-16

minimum standards of practice (Sonkin, Rosenberg, & Liebert, 2012). According to Sonkin et al. (2012), the most common areas in which mental health professionals encounter difficult legal and ethical decisions in treating populations experiencing domestic violence include (1) informed consent and other issues related to client safety, (2) confidentiality and privilege, (3) scope of competence and license, (4) financial issues, and (5) advertising.

Mental health professionals who work with victims and perpetrators of domestic violence are frequently faced with reporting child, dependent adult, and elder abuse. The specifics of mandatory reporting laws vary by region and state, and so it is best to check with your specific licensing board or professional membership organization for the requirements in your area. In California, the law indicates that a therapist must contact the appropriate social service agency immediately, or as soon as is practically possible, and follow up with a written report once the reporting threshold standard has been met for abuse of another and/or imminent threats of abuse. The time frame for this may vary with the agency to which the report needs to be made. In California, an elder is considered to be a person 60 years or older. A dependent adult is defined as any person between the ages of 18 and 59 who has a physical or mental limitation that restricts their ability to carry out normal activities or to protect their rights, including, but not limited to, persons who have physical or mental disabilities or whose physical or mental abilities have diminished because of age (Sonkin et al., 2000). According to Sonkin et al. (2000), California once considered using the dependent adult abuse law to justify the reporting of domestic violence. It was argued that some abused women may be so psychologically impaired owing to depression and/or post-traumatic stress disorder as a direct result of their victimization that they would qualify as suffering from a mental limitation restricting their ability to carry out normal activities or protect their rights. However, mental health practitioners are *not* mandated reporters of domestic violence, and, if it is reported, it is a breach of confidentiality. However, if the victim of domestic violence is a minor, elder, or dependent adult, reporting is mandatory, but, in such cases, the report is required owing to the abuse of the protected class rather than the domestic violence itself (Association for Advanced Training in the Behavioral Sciences, 2010).

In the past, when a child was not the direct victim of abuse but was a witness to domestic violence between adults, mental health providers were not necessarily mandated reporters because domestic violence had occurred or because the minor witnessed domestic violence. A report was mandatory depending upon the effect on the minor. If the clinician determined that, in witnessing the violence, the minor had unjustifiable mental suffering or if the child or their health was placed in a situation such that their person or health was endangered, Penal Code 11165.3 required a report (Association for Advanced Training in the Behavioral Sciences, 2010). The practice of this is currently in transition, and, in most counties in California, for example, if a child resides in a residence where domestic violence is occurring, this is reportable.

Of women who report their physical or mental health to be poor, three times as many have a history of domestic violence compared with those who do not have IPV in their background (Rivara et al., 2019). In addition to a long list of mental health problems that are either caused or exacerbated by domestic violence, there are a broad array of medical problems that can also result from or worsen because of violence, including cardiovascular disease, hypertension, concussions, asthma, gastrointestinal disorders, frequent headaches, chronic pain, sexually transmitted infections, mobility and activity limitations, among others (Rivara et al., 2019). In addition, domestic violence is more common than any other health problem during pregnancy (UCSF, 2023). Furthermore, violence may start or escalate during pregnancy, and pregnant women who experience domestic violence have been found to have a 37% higher risk of obstetric complications (Cook & Bewley, 2008). Furthermore, homicide is the leading cause of death among pregnant women in the United States (Krulewitch, et al., 2001). Furthermore, fully 40% of women and 15% of men report injuries to the head, neck, or face from domestic violence (Smith et al., 2018; Black et al., 2011). Research indicates that survivors of abuse can sustain head trauma more often than football players, but they are almost never diagnosed (Hillstrom, 2022). In fact, 75% of a cohort of 99 women from a domestic violence shelter study had sustained at least one brain injury (Hillstrom, 2022) To effectively treat domestic violence and its victims, it is imperative that clinicians have knowledge of the full range of physical and mental health consequences, including hidden wounds such as traumatic brain injury (Iverson, Dardis, & Pogidas, 2017), and be able to appropriately refer to practitioners who can address these problems. Sections 11160–11163.5 of California's penal code require mandatory reporting by any health practitioner who provides medical services for a physical condition that they suspect is the result of an injury due to a firearm or assaultive or abusive conduct which may be the result of domestic violence. Although this law is directed to physicians and other medical providers, mental health professionals who work within a medical setting may be required to report abuse disclosed by victims seeking medical services (Sonkin et al., 2012).

According to Jordan and Walker, given the breadth of clinical disorders encountered by domestic violence service providers, the inherent liability in treating dangerous persons and/or those in danger, the stresses experienced by domestic violence program staff members, and the complexity of domestic violence itself, in combination with the comparative lack of training in the subject of intimate partner violence in mental health graduate programs, a solid argument can be made that the provision of domestic violence services constitutes a mental health speciality (Jordan & Walker, 1994). For these reasons, Jordan and Walker (1994) and others (Sonkin et al., 2012; Goodman & Epstein, 2008) argue that domestic violence programs should be managed by well-trained, experienced clinicians with advanced degrees, and that providers of domestic violence services should receive comprehensive initial training and continuing education in intimate partner violence, as well as in related fields such as trauma and substance abuse/chemical dependency, and consistent case-oriented supervision. To date, California is one state in the United States that requires that mental health practitioners receive training in domestic violence prior to licensure (Senate Bill 564, 2004) and as a condition of licensure.

Furthermore, Jordan and Walker (1994) recommend that community clinics establish formal protocols for addressing domestic violence, rather than relying on the judgment of individual clinicians. In our experience, this is especially pertinent, because traditional therapeutic approaches may not be effective, depending on the clinician's expertise in domestic violence, and clinicians who do not specialize in domestic violence, even with training, can inadvertently utilize interventions and modalities that can increase risk. For example, if treatment is not focused sufficiently on power and control dynamics and/or attending attachment issues or if treatment is focused primarily on anger management instead of coercive control problems, the abuser may simply learn the language of change but may not be, in reality, ready for or capable of change.

Therapists who have not received sufficient training in domestic violence may inadvertently collude with the abuser in an attempt to be neutral and/or supportive. In worst-case scenarios, therapists may validate the client's anger and/or rage against their partner. If abusive tactics are not concurrently addressed, the client will frequently use the content of the session and the supportive or validating stance of the therapist to justify the use of abusive and violent behavior. In turn, the abusive behavior is apt to increase, thereby offsetting progress made by the client. Individual therapy should only be recommended when concurrent issues that preclude the individual's ability to successfully participate in an aggressors' group are present. For example, concurrent substance abuse treatment is indicated in cases of alcohol and drug abuse/dependence, and individual counseling may be indicated in cases in which a diagnosis is present and disabling, such as panic disorder. However, individual treatment should focus on alleviating the panic disorder, while the aggressive behaviors should be addressed in a group within the larger framework of a treatment team.

Clinicians who were trained as marriage and family therapists and/or those who practice from a family systems orientation should exercise caution when working with families and/or couples. The therapist's responsibility to protect the welfare of their clients is complicated in situations that involve intimate partner abuse, because the best interests of individual family members are often contradictory. Many therapists attempt to resolve this dilemma by viewing the entire family or partnership as the "client" and, therefore, base their decisions and interventions on the best interests of the family system, rather than on the best interests of individual family members. When domestic violence is present, this approach has significant disadvantages (Association for Advanced Training in the Behavioral Sciences, 2010) and may produce effects not expected by family members or the therapist if the family as a whole is given priority, rather than the family members who are at risk for victimization.

Arguably, one of the most significant court rulings impacting mental health practitioners was the case of *Tarasoff v. the Board of Regents of the University of California* (1976), technically the "duty to protect" but commonly known as the "duty to warn." Depending on the locale or jurisdiction where a mental health practitioner resides or conducts business, the duty to protect is often interpreted differently (Welfel, Werth, & Benjamin, 2009), thereby imposing what Herbert (2002) refers to as a "substantial burden of guesswork on clinicians." One cannot fully understand the duty to warn without also understanding the duty to protect. According to Welfel et al. (2009), the duty to warn applies to those circumstances where case law or statute requires the mental health professional to make a reasonable effort to contact the identified victim of a client's serious threats of harm and to notify law enforcement of the threat. The duty to protect applies to situations where the mental health professional has a legal obligation to protect an identified third party who is being threatened. While the duty to protect provides ways of maintaining the client's confidentiality and can be accomplished with clinical interventions, such as the utilization of or change in medication, referral to specialists, increasing the number and frequency of therapy sessions, close monitoring, hospitalization, and so on, the duty to warn requires a disclosure of confidential information to the person who is being threatened. *Tarasoff* clarified that client confidentiality can be compromised since "the protective privilege ends where the public peril begins" (Perlin, 1997).

It is interesting to note that *Tarasoff* was, in actuality, a case of intimate partner violence. According to accounts by Herbert (2002) and Buckner and Firestone (2000), Prosenjit Poddar was born in India and attended the University of California at Berkeley, where he studied graduate electronics and naval architecture. In the fall of 1968, he met Tatiana Tarasoff at folk dancing classes, and they dated throughout the season. Poddar interpreted a kiss they shared on New Year's Eve as evidence of a serious relationship and proposed marriage, which Tatiana rejected. In response, Poddar underwent an emotional crisis and became seriously depressed. He confided in a friend and co-workers that he had thoughts of killing Tatiana by blowing up her home. His roommate eventually persuaded him to seek mental health assistance, and he confided to Dr. Lawrence Moore that he intended to kill an unnamed woman with whom he was obsessed. After eight sessions during which Poddar repeatedly confessed his homicidal ideation, Dr. Moore told him that he would take steps to restrain him if the threats continued. Poddar stopped treatment, and the doctor conferred about the case and then notified campus police of the events. During their interview with Poddar, he acknowledged having a troubled relationship with Tatiana but denied any death threats. The police officers found him to be rational and released him. Shortly thereafter, Poddar purchased a gun and proceeded to stalk Tatiana. One evening, on finding her at home alone, he stabbed her to death and then called the police and waited to be arrested. A psychiatric examination indicated that he was suffering from paranoid schizophrenia. He was convicted of murder in the second degree and appealed the decision on multiple grounds. His conviction was reduced to manslaughter. Two years later, the California Supreme Court vacated the judgment of the appeals court and remanded the case for retrial. However, Poddar was not retried. Instead, the state released him on the condition that he immediately leave the United States. He returned to India and is reportedly married (Merton, 1982).

Since the Tarasoff case, California and other states have legislated and/or expanded guidelines for therapists dealing with clients who present a serious danger of violence to another. Several of those most commonly cited situations have also arisen from cases of family or intimate partner violence. In the case of *Hedlund v. Superior Court of Orange County* (1983), a client made a specific threat to harm his wife while talking to his therapist. The therapist failed to communicate this threat, and the client subsequently assaulted the victim while she and her 3-year-old were in their car (Sonkin et al., 2012). In *Bradley Center v. Wessner* (1982), a hospitalized patient who was upset over his wife's extramarital affair repeatedly threatened to kill her and her lover. Even though the treating therapist was aware that the patient was carrying a weapon in his car for that purpose, he was given an unrestricted weekend pass to visit his children, who were living with his wife. While at the wife's home, he shot and killed both the wife and her lover. The Georgia Supreme Court ruled that a physician has a duty to take reasonable care to prevent a potentially dangerous patient from inflicting harm (Laughran & Bakken, 1984). *Jablonski v. the United States* (1983) widened *Tarasoff* to include the protection of intended victims of violence in the absence of a direct threat. A psychiatric patient with a history of violence toward women killed his wife although he had made no specific threats toward her. The court ruled that the psychiatrist should have known that the patient was likely to commit violence toward his wife because of the patient's history of violence and reasoned that the psychiatrist, therefore, had a duty to protect her by informing her of the danger her husband posed to her (Sonkin et al., 2012). Conversely, a more recent case in Pennsylvania came to a different conclusion. In *Leonard v. Latrobe Area Hospital* (1993), a psychiatrist was found not to have a duty to warn the spouse of his hospitalized patient if no specific threats were made during the hospitalization. The patient shot and killed his spouse 2 months after being discharged (Buckner & Firestone, 2000). A Vermont case extended the duty to warn to property. In *Peck v. Counseling Service of Addison County*, a case in which a counselor was told by his client that he intended to burn down another person's barn, the court determined that mental health professionals had a duty to protect not only threatened victims but their property as well (Buckner & Firestone, 2000). In July of 2004, a California appeals court extended the interpretation of *Tarasoff* in *Ewing v. Goldstein* to include the practitioner's duty to warn when a family member of a client communicates to the practitioner that the client poses a risk of grave bodily injury to another person (Jensen, 2005).

Principle A of the APA Ethics Code, "Beneficence and Nonmaleficence," establishes that psychologists aspire to provide services that maximize benefit and minimize harm (APA, 2002). Further, many consider the avoidance of harm to be the priority of modern healthcare and ethics (Beauchamp & Childress, 2008; Herek, 2003; Morrow, 2000).

We will now illustrate and discuss numerous common ethical and legal issues in an LGBTQ+ domestic violence case:

The client, we will call Melody, is a 38-year-old Caucasian cisgender lesbian (pronouns: she/her) who is mandated by the court to attend batterers' treatment following an abusive incident with her partner, Jennifer. During the incident, neighbors called the police, and Melody, the larger and more masculine-appearing of the two women, was arrested and charged with domestic violence. Because Melody had no previous arrests, the charge was reduced to a misdemeanor. In addition to spending the night in jail, Melody was mandated to pay a fine and attend 52 weeks of batterers' treatment in a court-approved program. When reviewing the listing of court-approved programs in Los Angeles County, Melody noticed that there was only one program that was listed as "LGBTQ specific" but there were several others that indicated that they were "LGBTQ sensitive." Assuming that there were essentially no differences between specific and sensitive programs, she called a "sensitive" program that was close to her home rather than the "specific" program that was over 52 miles away. During the initial intake, Therapist A did not address Melody's sexual orientation other than to advise her not to disclose it to the other group members. No information about domestic violence or clinic procedures and policies was discussed or given to her. Based on Therapist A's recommendation, Melody referred to Jennifer as "Jim" for the first 5 weeks that she was in group. However, during the sixth session, Melody referred to Jennifer by her accurate name and was questioned by the group about it. When she disclosed that she was a lesbian and that Jennifer was her intimate partner, several members made derogatory and judgmental comments about her sexual orientation. One member told Melody that she was no longer welcome in the group, and another member with a history of severe violence perpetration threatened, while making a physically aggressive gesture, to set her "straight" after an upcoming group in the "next few weeks." The group facilitator, Therapist B, did not intervene or address the incident in any way. Throughout the following weeks, the majority of the group members refused to acknowledge or talk to Melody until, one evening following group, 2 weeks after she had been threatened in group, Melody was assaulted by two of the group members when walking to her car. Although her injuries were relatively minor, she called the group facilitator to report the incident and was told that nothing could be done since the incident happened off-site.

Melody immediately called the "LGBTQ specific" program that was included on the court listing of approved programs and set up an appointment for an intake. At its onset, Therapist C provided basic information to Melody about the limits of confidentiality, fees, LGBTQ+ domestic violence, how it is generally treated, and what the potential risks and benefits of treatment included. Therapist C also advised her that the material they discussed would be presented in a program meeting consisting of three to five other domestic violence specialists who would review the case together, discuss, then decide on treatment recommendations. After obtaining Melody's written consent for this, the therapist proceeded to ask Melody a lengthy series of questions about the abuse in her relationship as well as her sexual orientation while providing additional information to her about domestic violence in LGBTQ+ relationships, including information about how it differed from intimate abuse in heterosexual relationships. Therapist C also assessed if Melody was in crisis or immediate danger and, after discovering that she was not in crisis, discussed safety planning and danger management options with her. In addition, Therapist C provided her with informed consent information, information about her rights as a patient, the limitations of confidentiality, and information about HIPAA. Therapist C also provided Melody with information about her qualifications, education, and experience working with domestic violence cases. Two days after the initial assessment, Melody received a call from Therapist C who told her that her case had been reviewed and it had been determined that she was not a primary aggressor and, as such, was more appropriately suited for a group comprised of women who were victims of domestic violence. Therapist C assured Melody that the program would advocate on her behalf with the court and probation department and attempt to obtain approval for her participation in the more appropriate group for victims of LGBTQ+ domestic violence. Therapist C also referred her to a legal specialist within the program who advised her of her legal rights and options. To address Melody's acute symptoms resulting from her victimization, Therapist C made arrangements for Melody's immediate placement in individual therapy after determining that Melody was interested in both individual and group modalities.

Cases such as Melody's are as common as they are complex. Because it can be challenging for law enforcement officers to accurately differentiate between abuser and victim in LGBTQ+ domestic violence cases in the relatively short amount of time they have for assessment, either both parties are arrested, neither party is arrested, or victims are arrested, charged, and required to attend batterers' intervention. However, because LGBTQ+ domestic violence has been relatively invisible within the larger domestic violence movement, LGBTQ+-specific resources are scarce or nonexistent in most areas, and members of the public rarely know the differences between LGBTQ +-sensitive/friendly/affirmative and LGBTQ+-specific psychotherapy. To date, there are less than a handful of LGBTQ+-specific batterers' intervention programs that are court-approved in the United States.

The ethics codes of the American Psychological Association, the ACA (American Counseling Association), and other professional mental health associations clearly state that discrimination on the basis of minority status—be it race, ethnicity, gender, or sexual orientation—is unethical and unacceptable. Still, some therapists practice reparative or conversion therapy with LGBTQ+ people; others hold erroneous perceptions of the population; and others have values that they impose—either consciously or unconsciously—on their clients.

The treatment of individuals who have experienced violence presents two general ethical dilemmas. First, therapists may often treat beyond their level of competence with the LGBTQ+ population as well as with domestic violence, and, second, certain modalities and forms of treatment may not be appropriate for victims of violence or abusers, respectively.

Melody's case illustrates several ethical and legal dilemmas. First, there is an ethical problem with the advertising of services. In the domestic violence field, there has been an indiscriminate use of the term "LGBTQ-sensitive/friendly/affirmative" which implies some degree of understanding of the LGBTQ+ population as well as the ability to work with LGBTQ+ clients. Therapists A and B not only lacked understanding of and sensitivity to LGBTQ+ persons but had no understanding or training in LGBTQ+ domestic violence. Because the general public is not necessarily aware of the important distinctions between LGBTQ+-sensitive/friendly/affirmative treatment and LGBTQ+-specific treatment, it is the responsibility of service providers to explain it and disclose their level of training and experience to the client. Furthermore, California law prohibits any advertising that is false, misleading, or deceptive.

Therapists A and B, and presumably their employer, advertised that they were LGBTQ-sensitive but failed to provide LGBTQ-sensitive services. Melody received no information from Therapists A or B that enabled her to make an informed choice about the service or service provider(s) she initially selected. Rather, she was given misleading information. Had she been honestly informed of the limitations of the providers and the services they provided, and had she acted on that information by selecting a provider who was more equipped to work appropriately with her situation, it is probable that she wouldn't have been revictimized.

Another dilemma illustrated by Melody's case is scope of competence and scope of practice. Therapists should only provide services that they are competent to perform as a result of education, training, and experience. Those who perform beyond their competence fall below the accepted standard of care, resulting in potential harm to clients, and may incur civil law suits based on malpractice and negligence. According to the California Code of Regulations 1845, it is unprofessional conduct for a therapist to perform, or hold themselves out as able to perform, professional services beyond their field or fields of competence as established by the therapist's education, training, and/or experience. In contrast, the scope of practice is determined for the entire profession. Every professional activity that therapists undertake must be within both scope of practice and scope of competence.

Although Therapists A and B were not necessarily acting outside of their scope of practice (although this could be argued based simply on the fact that Therapist B failed to intervene or address the discriminatory and abusive incident that occurred in group), they did act outside their scope of competence in this case. Furthermore, it could be argued that they also acted outside their scope of practice. The American Psychological Association developed and published 21 speciality guidelines for psychotherapy with lesbian, gay, and bisexual clients that prohibit unfair discrimination based on sexual orientation. The guidelines not only affirm that a psychologist's role is to acknowledge how societal stigma affects clients but also address attitudes toward LGB people and sexual orientation issues, relationships and family concerns, diversity within the LGB community, and training and education needed to work with the LGB population. Although these guidelines cannot be considered to be standards per se because they are not mandatory, no actual standards exist to date for working with members of the LGBTQ+ community. In the general law of negligence, the standard of care is that degree of care which a reasonably prudent person should exercise in same or similar circumstances. If a person's conduct falls below this standard, they may be liable to pay damages for injuries or damages resulting from their conduct. The therapist must exercise the average degree of skill and care exercised by other members of the profession practicing with similar qualifications, education, and locality. Therapists A and B violated all of the APA guidelines for psychotherapy with lesbian, gay, and bisexual clients when assessing and intervening with Melody and were, therefore, arguably working outside their scope of practice.

In terms of these therapists working outside of their scope of competence, it was harmful to place Melody in a group with heterosexual female batterers. A comprehensive assessment would have revealed that Melody was incorrectly evaluated and could be harmed by the treatment that was selected. Furthermore, Therapist A presumably knew of the potential risk to Melody when they encouraged her not to disclose her sexual orientation to the other group members. Unethical as this was in and of itself, it was also negligent and a gross failure to provide informed consent. Therapist A should have discussed the nature of the treatment, the potential risks and benefits associated with it, alternatives to treatment (including the alternative of no treatment), and any other information that would be required by the standard of care in a specific case (for example, information about domestic violence and its treatment). Any treatment that takes place without informed consent falls below the standard of care and may subject the therapist to civil liability.

Assuming that Therapist A believed Melody to be a primary aggressor and that her placement in a batterers' group was appropriate, Therapists A and B should have either obtained consultation, education, and training about LGBTQ+ domestic violence or referred Melody to a LGBTQ+-specific domestic violence program or specialist. Therapist B acted unethically when they allowed the group members to make derogatory comments to Melody and failed to take seriously the threat that was made to "set her straight." It was Therapist B's responsibility not only to set limits with this behavior but to immediately conduct a risk assessment, provide safety and danger management planning, and notify the police as well as the court and probation department of the offending member's behavior. Therapist B had a duty to warn because one group member communicated a serious threat of violence against an identifiable victim that, for all intents and purposes, appeared to be imminent. Following this, it was the therapist's obligation to provide education to the group about LGBTQ+ persons and LGBTQ+ domestic violence while promoting tolerance for all minority populations and helping group members see how oppression of any population is connected to domestic violence and the power and control tactics that are a significant part of it. It was also Therapist B's responsibility to refer Melody to another service provider when group members subsequently refused to acknowledge or talk to her. It was also Therapist B's responsibility to set limits on this behavior while, again, connecting it to the tactics of domestic violence. When Therapist B was informed by Melody of her assault by another group member, they should have referred her for medical attention and reported the incident to the court and probation department. Therapist B should have also provided Melody with appropriate legal options.

Fortunately, Melody found her way to Therapist C, who provided her with ethical and legally sound treatment. As a result of LGBTQ+-specific treatment, Melody not only left the abusive relationship with Jennifer but resolved the majority of problems that were related to her victimization in the first group she attended and the revictimization that occurred.

Continuing Education Questions

1. Seventy-five percent of spousal assaults occur at the:
   a. Beginning of the relationship
   b. Point of separation or divorce
   c. Middle of the relationship
   d. None of the above

2. Mental health providers are mandated reporters of intimate partner violence
   a. True
   b. False

3. According to Sonkin et al. (2012), the most common areas where mental health professionals encounter difficult legal and ethical decisions in treating populations experiencing domestic violence include
   a. Informed consent and other issues related to client safety
   b. Scope of competence and license
   c. Financial issues
   d. All of the above

4. In terms of LGBTQ IPV, the legal and ethical rules are the same.
   a. True
   b. False

5. Which case extended the *Tarasoff* ruling of "duty to warn" to include property?
   a. *Hedlund v. Superior Court of Orange County*
   b. *Bradley Center v. Wessner*
   c. *Peck v. Counseling Service of Addison County*
   d. *Jablonski v. the United States*

References

American Psychological Association (APA). (2002). Ethical Principles of Psychologists and Code of Conduct. *American Psychologist, 57*, 1060–1073. Retrieved November 13, 2008, from apa.org/ethics/code2002.html

Association for Advanced Training in the Behavioral Sciences. (2010). *Marriage & Family Therapy*. Ventura, CA: Author.

Beauchamp, T.L., & Childress, J. (2008). *Principles of Biomedical Ethics* (6th ed.). New York. NY: Oxford University Press.

Black, M.C., Basile, K.C., Breiding, M.J., Smith, S.G., Walters, M.L., Merrick, M.T., Chen, J., & Stevens, M.R. (2011). *National Intimate Partner and Sexual Violence Survey: 2010 Summary Report [Internet]*. Atlanta, GA: Centers for Disease Control and Prevention. www.cdc.gov/violenceprevention/pdf/nisvs_report2010-a.pdf

Buckner, F., & Firestone, M. (2000). "Where the Public Peril Begins": 25 Years after *Tarasoff*. *Journal of Legal Medicine, 21*(2), 187–222. 10.1080/01947640050074698

Bureau of Justice Statistics. (1988). *National Crime Survey Report to the Nation* (2nd ed.). Washington, DC: US Department of Justice, Bureau of Justice Statistics.

Carmen, E.H., Rieker, P.P., & Mills, T. (1984). Victims of Violence and Psychiatric Illness. *American Journal of Psychiatry, 141*, 378–383.

Coleman, D.H., & Strauss, M.A. (1979). *Alcohol Abuse and Family Violence*. Durham NH: University of New Hampshire, Family Violence Program.

Cook, J., & Bewley, S. (2008). Acknowledging a Persistent Truth: Domestic Violence in Pregnancy. *Journal of the Royal Society of Medicine, 101*(7). 10.1258/jrsm. 2008.080002

Gondolf, E.W. (1985). Fighting for Control: A Clinical Assessment of Men Who Batter. *Social Caseworker, 66*, 48–54.

Goodman, L.A., & Epstein, D. (2008). *Listening to Battered Women: A Survivor-Centered Approach to Advocacy, Mental Health, and Justice*. Washington, DC: American Psychological Association.

Hamberger, L.K., & Hastings, J. (1988). Characteristics of Male Spouse Abusers Consistent with Personality Disorders. *Hospital and Community Psychiatry, 39*, 763–770.

Herbert, P.B. (2002). The Duty to Warn: A Reconsideration and Critique. *Journal of the American Academy of Psychiatry and the Law, 30*, 417–424.

Herek, G.M. (2003). Evaluating Interventions to Alter Sexual Orientation: Methodological and Ethical Considerations. *Archives of Sexual Behavior, 32*, 438–439.

Hillstrom, C. (March 1, 2022). The Hidden Epidemic of Brain Injuries from Domestic Violence. *New York Times Magazine*.

Hotaling, G., & Sugarman, D. (1986). An Analysis of Risk Markers in Husband to Wife Violence: The Current State of Knowledge. *Violence and Victims, 1*, 101–124.

Iverson, K.M., Dardis, L.M., & Pogidas, T.K. (2017). Traumatic Brain Injury and PTSD Symptoms as a Consequence of IPV. *Comprehensive Psychiatry, 74*, 80–87. doi10:1016/comppsych.2017.01.007

Jensen, D.G. (2005). The Two *Ewing* Cases and *Tarasoff*. *The Therapist, 17*(2), 31–37.

Jordan, C.E., & Walker, R. (1994). Guidelines for Handling Domestic Violence Cases in Community Mental Health Centers. *Hospital and Community Psychiatry, 45*(2), 147–151.

Krulewitch, C., Pierre-Louis, M.L., deLeon, G.R., Guy, R., & Green, R. (2001). Hidden from View: Violent Deaths among Pregnant Women in the District of Columbia, 1988–1996. *Journal of Midwifery & Women's Health, 46*, 4–10.

Laughran, W., & Bakken, G.M. (1984). The Psychotherapist's Responsibility toward Third Parties under Current California Law. *Western State University Law Review, 12*(1), 1–33.

McNeill, M. (1987). Domestic Violence: The Skeleton in Tarasoff's Closet. In D.J. Sonkin (Ed.), *Domestic Violence on Trial: Psychological and Legal Dimensions of Family Violence*. New York: Springer.

Merton, V. (1982) Confidentiality and the Dangerous Patient: Implications of *Tarasoff* for Psychiatrists and Lawyers. *Emory Law Journal, 31*, 263.

Morrow, S.L. (2000). First Do No Harm: Therapist Issues in Psychotherapy with Lesbian, Gay, and Bisexual Clients. In R.M. Perez, K.A. DeBord, & K.J. Bieschke (Eds.), *Handbook of Counseling and Psychotherapy with Lesbian, Gay, and Bisexual Clients* (pp. 137–156). Washington, DC: American Psychological Association.

Perlin, M.L. (1997). The Duty to Protect Others from Violence. In *Hatherleigh Guide to Ethics Therapy* (pp. 127–146). New York: Hatherleigh Press.

Post, R.C., Willett A.B., & Franks, R.D. (1980). A Preliminary Report on the Prevalence of Domestic Violence among Psychiatric Inpatients. *American Journal of Psychiatry, 137*, 974–975.

Rivara, F., Avanta, A., Lyons, V., Massey, A., Mills, B., Morgan, E., Simckes, M., & Rowhani-Rahbar, A. (2019). The Effects of Violence on Health. *Health Affairs, 38*(10). www.healthaffairs.org/doi/10.1377/hlthaff.2019.00480

Rose, S.M., Peabody, C.G., & Stratigeas, B. (1991). Undetected Abuse among Intensive Case Management Clients. *Hospital and Community Psychiatry, 42*, 499–503.

Senate Bill 564. (2004). Retrieved November, 9, 2012, from leginfo.ca.gov/pub/0002/ bill/sen/sb_0551-0600/sb_564_bill_20020912_cjapt

Smith, S.G., Zhang, X., Basile, K.C., Merrick, M.T., Wang, J., Kresnow, M. et al. (2018). *National Intimate Partner and Sexual Violence Survey: 2015 Data Brief—Updated Release [Internet]*. Atlanta, GA: Centers for Disease Control and Prevention. www.cdc.gov/ violenceprevention/pdf/2015data-brief508.pdfGoogle Scholar

Sonkin, D., Martin, D., & Auerbach-Walker, L. (1985). *The Male Batterer: A Treatment Approach*. New York, NY: Springer.

Sonkin, D.J., Rosenberg, M.S., & Liebert, D.S. (2012). Domestic Violence Treatment: Legal and Ethical Issues. In *Treatment of Intimate Violence: Multidimensional Psychotherapeutic Perspectives*. New York, NY: Haworth Press. Retrieved May 10, 2012, from eurowrc.org/06.contributions/1.contrib_en/15.contrib.en.htm

University of California San Francisco (UCSF). (2023). *Domestic Violence during Pregnancy*. www.ucsfhealth.org/education/domestic-violence-and-pregnancy

Walker, L.E. (1994). *Abused Women and Survivor Therapy: A Practical Guide for the Psychotherapist*. Washington, DC: American Psychological Association.

Welfel, E.R., Werth, J.L., Jr., & Benjamin, G.A.H. (2009). Introduction to the Duty to Protect. In J. Werth Jr., E. Welfel, & G. Benjamin (Eds.), *The Duty to Protect: Ethical, Legal, and Professional Considerations for Mental Health Professionals* (pp. 3–8). Washington, DC: American Psychological Association.

Appendix A
Sample LGBTQ+ IPV Case with Proper Step-Wise Evaluation

The client, who we will call "Luisa" (pronouns: she/her), is a 51-year-old heterosexually identified woman who was assigned male at birth. She presented to the Los Angeles LGBT Center for a mental health evaluation 3 months after being attacked by her partner. The partner, a heterosexual male we will call "John," had been making increasing threats against her in the months leading up to the assault against Luisa. According to Luisa, John was paranoid and increasingly suspicious. He thought people were following him, and this paranoia eventually extended to Luisa. He felt she might be cheating and that she was poisoning his food. This was made worse by his increasing alcoholism. John would drink, leave the house for days, and then return in an angered state. He had threatened her life and pushed her repeatedly. This escalated when he assaulted her with a knife and slashed her face (neighbors heard the commotion and called law enforcement). John was arrested, and Luisa spent 2 weeks in intensive care. Once released from the hospital, she came to the Center for assistance.

During the mental health intake, Luisa reported that she was born in Mexico and was one of ten children. Her mother cleaned houses for a living, and her father was a construction worker. Luisa does not remember having much contact with her parents, who were busy working most of the time. She was raised mainly by older siblings, the oldest being a teenager when she was born. Luisa reported that there were no birth complications when she was born and no developmental delays in her early years. She began school at 5 years of age and reported that it was difficult to concentrate. She did not receive any academic help at home and felt neglected by teachers and other administrators at her school. As a result of this, she quickly lost interest in academics and was, by her own admission, not engaged in schoolwork. Luisa grew up in poverty, and her parents divorced when she was 6 years old. She suffered sexual abuse from a male cousin as well as from her stepfather, and this made her home life very difficult. After years of suffering this abuse in silence, she was forced to leave home at the age of 14 to escape the abuse. After this, she had to stay wherever she could, got odd jobs to survive, and did not attend school consistently.

As mentioned earlier, Luisa was assigned male at birth. From her earliest memories, she remembers feeling "different" from other boys her age. She never felt comfortable in a male body and would frequently wear the clothes of her mother and older sisters when she was at home. She did not disclose this to her parents or siblings. At school, she had to wear a uniform, which caused a lot of distress since she was uncomfortable in boys' clothing and was not allowed to wear a skirt. Luisa says she was frequently isolated because of this as a child and spent a majority of time alone. Gender exploration continued throughout Luisa's childhood but always in secret. On one occasion, her stepfather caught her in a dress and punished her severely. It was soon after this that the sexual abuse began. Luisa recounts that her cousin and stepfather both threatened to tell everyone about her gender identity in order to keep her silent about the abuse. Luisa was understandably frightened of her family members and societal rejection at that young age and, accordingly, kept quiet. However, over the years, the burden increased, and she was no longer able to tolerate it, which prompted her to leave home.

After the age of 14, Luisa lived mainly on the streets and did transactional sex work in order to survive. She reports that this period of her life was very traumatic and extremely stressful owing to her lack of emotional, physical, and financial security. There were many days where she did not know where she would sleep or where her next meal would come from, and she believed that the sex work was a necessary evil to keep her afloat. At times, older men would allow her stay with them for periods of time in exchange for sex, but that was not consistent either. During this period, Luisa was introduced to feminizing hormones by other transgender women that she met on the streets who introduced her to the concept of medical gender transition. Luisa says she tried estrogen pills but could not obtain them consistently and never had a medical provider to monitor them. Socially, however, she was becoming more comfortable being in public in women's clothes and referred to by female pronouns and a female name.

At the age of 19, she met a man who brought her to the United States. Unfortunately, he did not assist her in obtaining documentation, so she was unable to work legally. She worked for cash at a hair salon owned by relatives who were aware of her transgender identity and tolerant of it but not fully accepting. Her goal was to go to cosmetology school, but she was unable to afford it. Soon after coming to the United States, the man who brought her with him decided that he did not want to be with her anymore and kicked her out of his house. Homeless again, she tried to stay with her relatives, but they were not welcoming of her owing to her gender identity. She was forced to stay in and out of shelters until she met John. Their relationship was initially very supportive, although John had a drinking problem even then. His drinking became increasingly regular, and he would often disappear on a binge and return 2–3 days later. Luisa expressed her concern about this, and they had argued, but they had not had a history of other altercations. This changed when John lost his regular job at a convenience store. Over the ensuing months, John became increasingly angry, and his drinking escalated. He shoved and pushed Luisa on several occasions, including once in front of her nephew. His paranoia began several months later, and he started threating Luisa's life.

Initially, Luisa indicated that they communicated effectively and she perceived John to be very loving. They bonded over the trauma both had suffered during childhood. However, it was clear from the beginning that John had the power in the relationship. He was documented, the apartment they shared was in his name, and he maintained a regular job and salary. He became increasingly controlling as the relationship progressed. It started with his being possessive of Luisa, which she perceived to be an indication that he loved and cared about her. Then, he began to control who she spent time with, what she should wear, and what she could eat. Eventually, he kept her hormones away from her and dispensed them while telling her that she was "scatter-brained" and would not remember to take them consistently. He also scrutinized her phone calls and email messages and restricted the time she spent with her family.

Luisa reports that John was initially accepting of her gender identity although he advised her to keep it secret from his family and friends. Luisa was very reluctant about this since she had become accustomed to living her life openly. Ultimately, however, she honored his wishes out of love for him. Luisa reported that she and John talked through their problems when they first met, but this changed when John lost his job. His drinking steadily increased, and he would yell and shout at Luisa when he was intoxicated. He blamed her for his problems and began attacking her appearance, often telling her that she looked like an "unattractive male whore." His negative comments often focused on her ability to "pass" as well as her lack of ability to work or contribute more financially. When the paranoia set in, he refused to obtain mental health treatment and instead became increasingly physically abusive with Luisa. He frequently shoved and pushed her, punched walls, threw household objects, and ultimately assaulted her with a knife. The majority of the violence occurred when John was under the influence of alcohol.

Luisa's symptoms at the time of her intake consisted of depressed mood, anhedonia, very poor sleep, decreased appetite, hypervigilance, and frequent flashbacks of the assault. She had a history of depression as a teenager and in her 20s and 30s but never sought formal treatment. She reported that previous hypervigilance from earlier trauma was relatively mild when compared with her post-assault symptoms. She did not feel safe in the apartment she shared with John and, after his arrest, she became increasingly concerned that, if she returned to the shelter where she had previously lived, he would track her down and kill her. Despite the assault, she missed John and did not want him to be punished because of the trauma he had suffered throughout his life. Nevertheless, John was charged with domestic violence and incarcerated.

This case illustrates many of the concepts that are discussed in this book. These include histories of trauma with victims as well as perpetrators, the common occurrence of lower socioeconomic status in cases of domestic violence, significant patterns of power and control, and sexual/gender minority status.

Based on the Guidelines for Effective Intervention with LGBTQ+ Intimate Partner Violence Cases, this case was assessed and treated in the recommended order.

Step 1: Assess for Suicidality/Homicidality

Luisa presented to the Los Angeles LGBT Center with many symptoms consistent with a major depressive episode. Luisa reported that, although she suffered at times from severe depression, she did not have current or past suicidal ideation. She denied any thoughts of not wanting to live, nor did she have any active thoughts of wanting to hurt herself. She did not have access to weapons, nor did she have a history of attempted or completed suicide of family or friends. Luisa denied a remote or recent history of violent behavior. She denied irritability, verbal or physical outbursts, or wanting to hurt others. Despite the violence she suffered, Luisa had conflicted feelings toward John. She indicated that she still loved him and hoped he would get help.

Step 2: Are There Any Mandated Reporting Obligations?

In this case, there was no child abuse or abuse of an elder or dependent adult. There was also no active threat of violence, and so there was not a duty to protect.

Step 3: Assess Overall State of Basic Functioning and Stabilize as Indicated

When she presented to the clinic, Luisa was struggling with low mood. She was able to brush her teeth, shower, and otherwise take care of herself. However, she did have a decreased appetite and reported 10 lb of unintentional weight loss in the 3 months before her intake. However, she reported problems with sleep since the assault and did not feel safe in the home she shared with John. This caused her a generalized sense of heightened anxiety which affected energy, sleep, concentration, and self-care overall. Owing to these symptoms, Luisa was deemed unable to maintain gainful employment at the time of presentation. She also did not have authorization to work in the United States, which complicated her ability to get a job. These aspects of Luisa's basic functioning were addressed in the treatment plan and attended to immediately.

Step 4: If There Has Been Physical or Sexual Abuse, Refer to a Physician for Evaluation

The Los Angeles LGBT Center has integrated psychiatric and primary care. The patient was initially seen in the mental health department, and referrals were then made to both primary care for a medical assessment and psychiatry for medication management. Luisa was seen for a full physical exam by primary care. The medical team did not find any residual wounds and were able to further tend to the facial laceration that had been treated during Luisa's stay in the hospital. Records from Luisa's hospital stay were obtained, as well as copies of the brain scans that were done to rule out traumatic brain injury. Her blood work was done and was within normal limits.

Step 5: Conduct a Domestic Violence Assessment

A comprehensive domestic violence assessment was done. The intake interviewer determined that Luisa was a primary victim and that John was, most likely, a primary aggressor. The type of violence that Luisa had experienced was intimate terrorism, and there was no evidence of bidirectionality. The evidence for this was the interview and history with Luisa, in which there was a clear narrative of events. There was a pattern of control and abuse on the part of John and it involved multiple areas of Luisa's life. John controlled medications, finances, and socialization, as well as Luisa's gender transition. He was psychologically abusive in his belittling of Luisa which took the form of negative comments about her appearance and her worthiness. He was also physically abusive in the form of pushing and shoving, which escalated into the assault which led to Luisa to the Center.

John's abuse of Luisa followed the typical cycle of violence, with a pattern of tension, acute incident, and remorse. At the time of presentation, the couple had just been through the acute incident. At that point, the cycle was interrupted by the police arresting John and Luisa obtaining medical assistance.

It appeared that Luisa had internalized the belief that the violence she experienced was mutual, and that her gender identity exacerbated John's negative moods. She felt that she was to blame for his arrest and incarceration.

The Cass model was used to determine what stage of the coming out process Luisa was in, and it was determined that she was in the identity acceptance phase. She had been out as transgender in Mexico and the United States until she met John, who forced her back into the closet. However, she was accepting of her gender identity. She was taking hormones and wanted surgeries to complete her transition. John's negative comments and control over the process did not allow Luisa to fully embrace her identity or be as open about it as she wanted to be. Their separation gave her the opportunity to continue the transition and to connect more with the larger transgender and non-binary community in order to move to true identity pride and synthesis.

Step 6: Determine if There Are Any Concurrent Diagnoses

In terms of the psychological assessment, Luisa had clear current and past episodes of major depressive disorder. This was characterized by depressed mood and anhedonia as well as changes in sleep and appetite as well as energy and self-esteem. Attention and concentration were also reportedly affected, but that was not evident in the assessment. Luisa clearly had symptoms of post-traumatic stress disorder from her childhood that had been triggered again and exacerbated by the recent assault by John. These included numbness to her own emotions, flashbacks and re-experiencing of trauma, as well as being on "high alert" at all times. Luisa denied the use of any substances, and there was no evidence of bipolar disorder or psychosis. Luisa did not report any chronic medical problems, and her only medications were hormones.

1. Major depressive disorder, recurrent, severe, without psychotic features (DSM-V code F33.2).
2. Post-traumatic stress disorder, chronic (DSM-V code F43.12).
3. Encounter for mental health services for victim of spouse or partner psychological abuse (DSM-V code V61.11 / ICD-10 code Z69.11).
4. Encounter for mental health services for victim of spouse or partner violence, physical (DSM-V code V61.11 / ICD-10 code Z69.11).

Step 7: Develop Intervention/Treatment Plan Components

This was done in a multidisciplinary fashion and involved a team approach.

Basic Needs

In order to meet Luisa's basic needs, we began with housing assistance. She felt unsafe in her current apartment, and so it was imperative to find her safe housing or shelter. As has been mentioned in this book, there is a lack of LGBTQ+-affirming IPV shelters. Often, shelters lack cultural competence and do not have facilities for transgender men and women. In this case, the Center was able to place Luisa in a transitional/shared housing facility following three nights in a hotel. Gift cards for food and other basic necessities were provided to her. Throughout this process, Luisa was provided with extensive education about LGBTQ+ intimate partner violence and the misconceptions that she had internalized about it, which were challenged and replaced with accurate information. We helped her develop a safety plan and consistently reviewed and updated it as needed.

In addition, we referred her to vocational rehabilitation to obtain work skills to advance her career in hairstyling. Following this process, we were eventually able to assist Luisa with money management and helped her locate an affordable apartment. We also connected her to a legal advocate who was able to provide immigration assistance.

Mental Health Issues

Dealing with Luisa's mental health was the next concern. In order to address the major depressive disorder and PTSD, Luisa was referred to weekly individual therapy with a LGBTQ+ domestic violence specialist to deal with her symptoms and learn healthy coping skills. This was eventually followed by eye movement desensitization and reprocessing (EMDR), a therapy formulated specifically to create new neural connections and heal trauma. Concurrently, Luisa was placed with a psychiatrist and was put on escitalopram (an antidepressant) and prazosin (an anti-anxiety medicine), which allowed her to address her symptoms more easily.

To continue to address the effects of domestic violence, we encouraged Luisa to join our Empowerment Group for Primary Victims. She attended the group for several months and was able to process the trauma with other survivors. She continued to develop coping skills while decreasing the shame she felt about being a victim of IPV.

Medical Issues

At the same time, Luisa was in the process of gender transition and wanted more done in her quest to fully transition. She decided to pursue top surgery, bottom surgery, and facial feminization. We referred her for specific mental health assessment in order to complete referral letters for surgery. We then referred her to surgeons who performed the procedures. In the interim, she was referred to our primary care department during which any existing medical issues were addressed. Her hormone levels were also checked and optimized.

This type of comprehensive care requires a team approach. Many people are involved with cases such as Luisa's. Only with multiple specialists working together can the many facets of a patient be addressed. IPV often occurs in an environment that includes poverty, mental health problems, physical health issues, substance use, and other social stressors. The most successful outcomes have occurred when these variables are all addressed simultaneously. In Luisa's case, she eventually obtained her working permit in the United States, moved into her new home, advanced her career, completed her transition, and is currently stabilized mentally with medications and ongoing psychotherapy.

Appendix B
Sample LGBTQ+ IPV Case 2 with Guided Response

The client we will call Janelli is a 26-year-old cisgender bisexual female of European descent who presents with depression and anxiety resulting from a recent breakup with her male partner, Alex. Alex is a cisgender Black male who is 29 years old. Janelli reports that, although the decision, 2 weeks earlier, to terminate their 3-year relationship following an argument was mutual, she thinks obsessively about Alex and believes she made a "gigantic mistake." Since she and Alex broke up, Janelli has driven past Alex's apartment at least 35 times, has called him at work "more times than I can count," has begged him to reconsider their decision, and has threatened to kill herself when Alex refused to reunite with her.

Further questioning reveals that, during her childhood, Janelli's father frequently abused her mother, her siblings, and the family pet. She denies being abused by her father herself and states that her mother "deserved the abuse" and constantly "provoked" her father to anger.

Janelli reveals that her relationship with Alex has been filled with arguing, name-calling, put-downs, episodes of pulling Alex's hair, and occasional hitting and kicking that she initiated. She indicates that, on one occasion, Alex threw a flower vase at her and shoved her.

During your third session with Janelli, she reports that she and Alex had an argument during the week about her consistent attempts to contact him. She tells you that she initiated the contact and that her motivation was to help Alex understand that she "panics" without him, feels that she cannot live without Alex, and desperately needs to reconcile. She reports that, several years ago, she was diagnosed with panic disorder and generalized anxiety disorder by a former therapist and kept this information from Alex because she was frightened that he wouldn't understand and would subsequently judge and then abandon her because of it.

When Alex told Janelli that he was not interested in reconciling, did not want any future contact with Janelli, and asked that she leave, Janelli refused, insisting that she be able to explain the reasons for her behavior to him. Alex responded by pushing her toward the door. Janelli spit at and slapped Alex in response, left marks on her own face from scratching herself, and then called the police and told them that Alex had physically assaulted her.

The police arrested Alex. Janelli reports that she feels guilty and is now so anxious about Alex's incarceration that she is unable to sleep, eat, or work and cannot get the image of Alex's arrest out of her mind. If/when there is any time when the image of Alex is not uppermost in her mind, she listens to a song that reminds her of Alex. She tells herself repeatedly that Alex will eventually understand that he deserved the abuse for not being more un-derstanding of Janelli's pain and that they will get back together. She also tells you how distraught she was with her 71-year-old mother when her mother confronted her about her behavior and "took Alex's side." In response, Janelli threw a plate of spaghetti in her mother's face and left in anger.

Guided Responses

1.   What is the first concern when you are presented with a case such as this?

Answer: Because safety to self and others is your primary concern, you would first need to further assess Janelli's suicidality and/or homicidality and, if there is imminence, take steps to protect her (and, in the case of homicidality, warn potential victims and the police and then take steps to ensure to the extent possible that she will not harm anyone or their property). Another factor to consider is that this behavior is often consistent with (manipulative) tactics used by primary aggressors and so it is important to factor it into your overall assessment when attempting to determine if Janelli is a primary victim, defending victim, secondary aggressor, or primary aggressor.

2.   Are there any mandated reporting requirements in this case?

Answer: Because Janelli disclosed that she threw a plate of spaghetti in her mother's face (and her mother is over the age of 60), you will need to report this event to Adult Protective Services as soon as possible and follow up with a written elder abuse report within the required time allotted.

3. Now that immediate requirements have been met, what is the next step in evaluation of this case?

Answer: Your next step will be to assess Janelli's overall state of functioning. Incorporating the concepts of Maslow's hierarchy into your assessment, Janelli is unable to sleep, eat, or work because her anxiety is severe, and your immediate goal will be to stabilize her functioning. Because there has been physical violence in her relationship with Alex and because she is having difficulty sleeping and eating, you should consider referring Janelli to a medical doctor for a physical evaluation to rule out any underlying physical or medical conditions that are contributing to these problems. You should also consider referring her to a psychiatrist for psychotropic assistance in her stabilization (assuming that these symptoms are not related to a medical condition).

4. Janelli's functioning has now been assessed, so what should be looked at next?

Answer: You will now want to proceed with a domestic violence assessment. Based on her report, it appears that the type of violence displayed in this case is consistent with intimate terrorism. Note: While it appears that Janelli's distress is specific to her breakup with Alex, she tells you that her relationship with him has been "filled with arguing, name calling, and put downs" which she has initiated and that she has hit, kicked, and punched Alex. This may indicate that the violence is not restricted to one topic area and has happened multiple times, and so it is not consistent with common couple violence or situational violence.

5. Since it has been determined that this is "intimate terrorism," what role in this does Janelli play?

Answer: Additional indications that Janelli's behaviors may be consistent with primary aggression include her daily obsessions that are focused on ignoring the wishes of Alex to end the relationship, the stalking behavior that she is displaying, and the fact that she has initiated many of their arguments that include name-calling and put-downs as well as physical abuse. Further evidence that may indicate that Janelli is a primary aggressor is her history of witnessing violence in her family of origin and her subsequent beliefs that her mother deserved to be abused by her husband and that she was, in fact, to blame for it because she "provoked" the abuse. (Based on Janelli's report of her cognitions and behaviors, the abusive behaviors that Alex has perpetrated appear to have been used in response to Janelli's aggression but nevertheless warrant ongoing assessment before a final conclusion is reached.)

6. In terms of the LGBTQ+ cycle of violence, which stage does this case most likely represent?

Answer: It appears that Janelli is probably in the tension-building stage of the cycle of violence based on her cognitions, coupled with her heightened symptoms of anxiety. Further, she clearly states that Alex "deserved the abuse" that she perpetrated for not being more understanding of her pain.

7. Now that the parameters of the LGBTQ+ IPV have been established, is there anything else going on in terms of mental health?

Answer: Concurrent diagnoses that must be further assessed and/or ruled out include panic disorder, generalized anxiety disorder, obsessive-compulsive disorder, and substance abuse.

8. Finally, the stage is set to put the assessment together. What is the best treatment plan that can be formulated based on the case presentation and evaluation? Remember to keep in mind the biopsychosocial model and address all of the aspects of the case, including social stressors, psychiatric and psychological intervention, and legal and ethical issues.

Answer: Because your final assessment indicates that Janelli is a primary aggressor, your ultimate goal in treatment is to assist her to take responsibility for her actions/thoughts/emotions and their consequences; decrease her abusive behaviors; and, ultimately, eliminate all violent behaviors and power and control patterns.

Referral to a batterers' intervention program (with group treatment for primary aggressors) is the treatment of choice and standard of care. If you determine that Janelli has the criteria to meet the indications for panic disorder, generalized anxiety disorder, obsessive compulsive disorder, or a substance abuse disorder, treatment for them should be initiated simultaneously if you have sufficient training and experience to do so and if the presence of any of them would compromise Janelli's ability to fully participate in group treatment. Otherwise, you should appropriately refer her to someone with sufficient training and experience. If you do work with her on these co-occurring problems, you will want to work as part of a treatment team, which will include having regular conversations about her treatment and progress with the facilitator of the group she attends.

Her aggressive behavior should be treated using a group modality (specifically designed for domestic violence perpetrators), which is the modality of choice, and cognitive behavioral treatment (the treatment of choice), coupled with psychoeducation about LGBTQ+ intimate partner violence. This would include providing Janelli with information about the LGBTQ+ cycle of violence, helping her identify and challenge any myths or misconceptions about IPV that she has internalized, and developing a safety or danger management plan that is consistently discussed and revised as needed for effectiveness; evaluating any internalized homophobia that she may be struggling with and in what stage of the coming out process she is in. Addressing this by using a LGBTQ+-affirmative framework is of primary importance.

In the event that Janelli is experiencing any symptoms consistent with PTSD because of the domestic violence she experienced in her family of origin, focus on stabilizing any symptoms that are interfering with her basic functionality. After she has completed and made progress in primary aggressors' treatment, trauma work can be undertaken.

The primary diagnosis is the V/Z code that most closely describes Janelli's behaviors, followed by any concurrent diagnoses (in this case, specifically panic disorder, generalized anxiety disorder, obsessive-compulsive disorder, and any current substance abuse).

Multicultural aspects of the case include the fact that Alex is Black and Janelli is white, a crucial distinction since Janelli used race, in part, to ensure that it would be likely that Alex would be arrested.

Because the primary goal in treatment is helping Janelli accept responsibility and develop accountability for her actions/cognitions/and emotions, as well as the consequences of them, the group facilitator will need to address her role in having Alex arrested (calling the police, reporting that she was being abused, and scratching herself to underscore that Alex was the abuser) and the subsequent harm she has caused herself, as well as Alex, and the consequences of each. A possible intervention would be to have Janelli contact police and disclose her behavior to them.

In the event that you are unable to locate a batterers' intervention program in your area that is either LGBTQ+-specific or LGBTQ+-affirmative, you may cautiously provide individual therapy to Janelli by following a standard group curriculum while participating in regular consultation with an LGBTQ+ specialist who is trained to work with primary aggressors.

Appendix C
Answer Key

Chapter 1

1. C
2. A
3. D
4. B
5. D

Chapter 2

1. B
2. B
3. C
4. B
5. A

Chapter 3

1. C
2. A
3. E
4. A
5. D

Chapter 4

1. C
2. A
3. D
4. A
5. B

Chapter 5

1. B
2. A
3. B
4. B
5. D

Chapter 6

1. D
2. A
3. B
4. B
5. B

Chapter 7

1. B
2. A
3. C
4. B
5. B

Chapter 8

1. D
2. A
3. C
4. B
5. D

Chapter 9

1. D
2. B
3. B
4. A
5. D

Chapter 10

1. D
2. A
3. D
4. A
5. A

Chapter 11

1. C
2. B
3. C
4. A
5. C

Chapter 12

1. C
2. B
3. C
4. B
5. A

Chapter 13

1. E
2. B
3. A
4. A
5. D

Chapter 14

1. D
2. B
3. B
4. A
5. C

Chapter 15

1. D
2. B
3. E
4. B
5. A

Chapter 16

1. B
2. A
3. D
4. B
5. C

Appendix D
Clinical Guidelines

Guidelines for Effectively Intervening in LGBTQ+ Domestic/Intimate Partner Violence Cases

- Step 1: Assess for suicidal and homicidal ideation. If ideation exists, assess if there is imminence. If there is imminence, intervene appropriately.
- Step 2: Determine if there is anything that is mandatory to report (child abuse, elder abuse, dependent adult abuse, duty to protect/*Tarasoff*).
- Step 3: Assess overall state of basic functioning and stabilize as indicated. (Aspects include sleeping habits, eating habits, ability to work and/or maintain employment, ability to maintain personal hygiene, etc.)
- Step 4: If there has been physical or sexual abuse, refer to a physician for evaluation. (While the presence or consequence of internal injuries should be evaluated and addressed, it is especially important that brain injuries be ruled out if the client has ever sustained physical abuse in the upper portion of the body and/or to the head.)
- Step 5: Conduct a domestic violence assessment (type of violence—intimate terrorism, common couple violence, situational violence); subcategories (psychological abuse, physical abuse, sexual abuse, environmental abuse); assessment categories (primary victim, defending victim, secondary aggressor, primary aggressor); stage of LGBTQ+ cycle of violence; myths/misconceptions about LGBTQ+ IPV the client has internalized; coming out stage the client is in; and client's overall LGBTQ+ identity development.

- Step 6: Determine if there are any concurrent diagnoses that must be addressed immediately. These would include diagnoses that might potentially interfere with any aspects of the treatment plan to address the intimate partner violence.
- Step 7: Develop intervention/treatment plan (note: a safety or danger management plan must always be included).

Guidelines for Assisting Clients and/or Callers Who Are Experiencing a Domestic Violence Crisis

- If a client is contacting you via phone or computer, determine if it is safe for the client to speak with you. If it is not safe, assist the client in identifying if, where, and when they can safely talk with you.
- Determine the client's location and contact information should a wellness/welfare check be necessary.
- As much as possible, and for safety purposes, ask the client *yes* or *no* questions. Determine who is nearby and/or able to hear the conversation.
- If the client has been physically injured, instruct them to call 911 and/or seek immediate medical assistance.
- Never suggest that a client leave an abusive relationship without first having a solid and realistic safety plan in place. Leaving an abusive relationship without a safety plan is dangerous and can increase violence and put the caller's life at risk.
- Do not assume that you are speaking to either a victim or abuser, regardless of how the client identifies. Victims frequently perceive their behaviors to have been abusive and are apt to take responsibility for them, while abusers frequently perceive themselves to be victimized. Validating a client's victimization/victim status based on their self-report can be dangerous and increase violence if you are, in fact, speaking with an abuser. If necessary, refer the client to a domestic violence program for crisis intervention, assessment, and appropriate intervention.
- Before ending the call/session, make sure that an interim safety plan is in place and then refer the client to a domestic violence program for in-depth safety planning. (An interim plan includes immediate steps that an individual can take to reduce the ramifications of abuse and violence. For example, when violence erupts, what parts of a residence are safest for the person? Safe rooms should have easily accessible windows and working door locks and are generally not rooms that contain objects that can easily be used as weapons, such as kitchens and bathrooms. Does the caller have friends and/or family they can call/stay with, etc.? Do they

have their driver's license or other form of identification with them, and do they have cash and/or a credit card available? Do they have medications, important documents, and a change of clothing if they need to leave immediately?)

- If the caller is in need of housing or essential life necessities such as food or clothing, refer them to an anti-violence program that offers these services or a domestic violence shelter that accepts LGBTQ+ clients.
- For additional assistance, refer the client to the National Domestic Violence Hotline (1-800-799-7233).

Guidelines for Assessment of LGBTQ+ Domestic/Intimate Partner Violence

- Because domestic violence is always a treatment priority, screening for and assessment of it should be an integral part of every psychosocial assessment or intake, regardless of the client's presenting issues, and are necessary for the development of an appropriate treatment plan.
- To begin, explain that conflict is periodically present in relationships with others but people don't respond to conflict in the same manner. Therefore, determining how individuals tend to resolve conflict is necessary in order to determine the best placement and treatment plan for the client.
- Begin with general questions, then proceed to more specific questions. For example, general questions would include the following:
  1. Please tell me how you generally respond to conflict with your partner or family members?
  2. Do either you or your partner have difficulty managing anger? Can you provide an example?
  3. When either you or your partner has used substances, do either of you have difficulty managing your anger?

- More specific questions would include the following:
  4. Have you or your partner ever called the other names, intimidated, or threatened the other?
  5. Have you or your partner ever hit, kicked, slapped, or punched the other?
  6. Have you or your partner ever threatened to out the other's sexual orientation or immigration status?

- (Note: Repeat these questions with additional abusive behaviors. If the client has never been hit, kicked, slapped, or punched, or they have not used any of these behaviors specifically, they may answer "no" when asked. Also, keep in mind that pushing, slapping, and scratching are often considered to be defensive, so obtain details about the event during which they were used.)

- Have either you or your partner ever needed medical attention because of aggressive behaviors in your relationship?
- Has law enforcement ever been called because of aggression in your relationship?
- When possible, determine context, intent, and effect of abusive and violent incidents.
- Attempt to determine if there is a pattern of abusive behaviors and/or if the cycle of violence is present. (Note: Domestic violence tends to occur in a pattern. If a pattern does not exist but there have been abusive behaviors, this indicates risk, and IPV interventions are still indicated.)
- Determine what type of violence is present, what stage of the cycle of violence is present, and what stage of the coming out process the client is in.
- Is the client primarily focused on blaming others for their circumstances or is their focus on safety?
- Follow the client's lead when determining what language to use. Because LGBTQ+ clients often don't believe they're experiencing domestic violence, even when it is severe, using the term "violence" may illicit an incorrect response. At this point, it is acceptable to use words that the client can more easily tolerate such as "abuse" or "conflict."
- Be prepared to provide information about LGBTQ+ IPV to clients. For example, explaining the LGBTQ+ cycle of violence to them frequently enables them to see their experience more clearly and "name" it.

Goals and Objectives for Working with LGBTQ+ Intimate Partner Violence Clients and Cases

Goals/Objectives when Working with Primary Victims

- The primary goal when working with primary victims is their empowerment and the development of esteem and autonomy.
- The treatment modality is individual counseling or participation in a survivors' group. While a survivors' group in general is preferred,

whichever modality the client prefers is the one that should initially be utilized. This will help empower the client.

- Initial work with primary victims generally includes crisis intervention and stabilization. Conceptualize Maslow's hierarchy and where the client is on the hierarchy. Consider appropriate referrals (e.g. physicians, psychiatrists, domestic violence community resources and services that may be able to assist).
- Continually assess risk. The severity of domestic violence can change at any moment, and, if/when it does, your treatment plan will need to be revised accordingly.
- If the case involves intimate terrorism in particular, help the client explore options for safe housing. If you refer an LGBTQ+ survivor to a domestic violence shelter, discuss potential challenges such as the shared living environment, homo/bi/transphobia on the part of other residents, and so on. Helping the client prepare for this will help to ensure that they do not leave prematurely.
- Never encourage a victim to leave an abusive relationship without having a realistic safety plan in place. (Note: Safety plans with LGBTQ+ clients can be especially challenging to develop owing to the insular and sometimes smaller nature of the LGBTQ+ community in many locations. This must be taken into account during safety plan development.)
- Be prepared to advocate for your client with law enforcement, the court system, social service providers, and so on.
- Address and include LGBTQ+ factors that affect intimate partner violence (i.e. psychoeducation on LGBTQ+ domestic violence; the coming out process; internalized homophobia/biphobia/transphobia; institutionalized homophobia/biphobia/transphobia; traumas resulting from LGBTQ+ identity, etc.).
- Never refer the client to couples' counseling. If they express an interest in it, explain the reasons why it is contraindicated.
- If the client is a defending victim, incorporate safer disengagement strategies other than self-defense as part of the safety plan in individual counseling.
- If the client is a secondary aggressor, refer the client to an LGBTQ+-affirmative anger management group/program or incorporate anger management techniques into the work done in individual counseling. If a secondary aggressors' group is available, refer the client to it. Anger management techniques should be part of the safety plan.

Goals/Objectives when Working with Primary Aggressors

- The primary goal when working with primary aggressors is increasing their ability to accept accountability/responsibility for their behaviors and the consequences of them and eliminating all patterns of power and control as well as abusive and violent behaviors.
- Individual counseling is contraindicated unless the client has a concurrent mental health disorder that is impacting the intimate partner violence that you are qualified to treat, or the disorder would preclude the client from participating in group treatment.
- Group counseling designed for primary aggressors is the treatment of choice.
- If no LGBTQ+ primary aggressor groups exist in your area, attempt to locate a practitioner who specializes in LGBTQ+ domestic violence and refer your client to that person. If no one with those qualifications is available, proceed to work in close consultation with an LGBTQ+ domestic violence specialist. (Contact the National LGBTQ Institute on Intimate Partner Violence for assistance.)
- If the client is required by the court or probation department to attend individual therapy or anger management counseling, contact the court with the results of your assessment and treatment recommendations.
- Continual assessment of risk is imperative. In the event of escalating abuse/violence, a corresponding change in the treatment plan is crucial.
- Cognitive behavioral therapy is generally the preferred approach when working with aggressors.
- Address and include LGBTQ+ factors that affect intimate partner violence (i.e. psychoeducation on LGBTQ+ domestic violence; the coming out process; internalized homophobia/biphobia/transphobia; institutionalized homophobia/biphobia/transphobia; traumas resulting from LGBTQ+ identity; etc.).

Issues to Consider When Developing an LGBTQ+ Intimate Partner Violence Program

We strongly favor the incorporation of LGBTQ+ intimate partner violence programs into LGBTQ+ mental health programs because (1) LGBTQ+ people experiencing domestic violence are apt when seeking assistance to obtain the help of a mental health professional rather than existing intimate partner violence services and resources; (2) there is a correlation between intimate partner violence and the development and/or exacerbation of mental health problems; and (3) there is a high prevalence of intimate partner violence within the population coupled with a dearth of LGBTQ+-specific domestic violence services.

When developing a program:

- Make sure that mental health staff have the appropriate qualifications to work with intimate partner violence clients. In some states, a domestic violence certification may be required as well as a license, which is generally preferred.
- Regardless of the clinician's certification or license status, ensure that they have received extensive education and training in working with LGBTQ+ clients, as well as within a domestic violence program. The clinician(s) should also have training and education in trauma-informed care as well as LGBTQ+-affirmative counseling.
- Additional and ongoing intimate partner violence continuing education/training should be required of all domestic violence clinicians in the program.
- Clinicians who are not domestic violence specialists within the organization's mental health department should be trained periodically in the subject of IPV to ensure appropriate referrals, maintain standards of care, reduce liability risk, and so on.
- Domestic violence program staff should be professionally engaged with one another and practice as a well-coordinated treatment team.
- Time for consultation, clinical supervision, and lengthier assessment times should be incorporated into staff schedules.
- The ability to have flexibility with client scheduling is often needed to ensure safety.
- Careful planning and coordination must be done if both partners in an abusive relationship are seen within the same program or organization.
- The duration of therapy must be flexible to accommodate changes in the severity and frequency of violence experienced by clients.
- The information in electronic health records must be carefully monitored so that their dissemination is safe.
- The program should have a data system that has preferably been designed to compile and track domestic violence client data.
- The program should understand that a diagnosis of domestic violence is not reimbursable by insurance but must, nevertheless, be used as part of the clinical record.

- The program should partner with a domestic violence shelter and batterers' intervention program if it cannot offer those services itself and should provide training and consultation to the staff of those organizations to ensure LGBTQ+-affirmative care for client referrals.
- The program must be prepared to address secondary victimization/vicarious traumatization among the staff.

Index

Locators in *italic* indicate figures.

abuse history screening 178–179
abuser 13–14; batterer interventions, abuser counselling 114, 169–171; cycle of violence (*see under own heading*); cycle of violence dynamic, victim/abuser 130; differentiation problems (abuser vs. victim) in same-sex violence 165, 166, 183–185, 188, 197, 219; misconceptions 33, 34; presentation continuum 169; prevalence rates 38; self-perception/presentation as victim 184–185, 196; substance abuse–IVP relationship (*see under own heading*)
advocacy, service providers 144–156; allies 7; bias tests and training 145–146; competency demands, educational needs 144–147; Domestic Violence Coalition on Public Policy (1990) 49; legislation influencing 49; LGBTQ+ affirming intervention premises 149–154; National Network to End Domestic Violence (NNEDV) 49; shelters, practical support and advocacy 24, 38, 51, 53, 113–114, 129, 152, 159–160, 161–162; therapeutic alliance 147
AIDS/HIV 9, 39–40, 63, 74, 135, 208

alcohol 134, 136–137, 139, 153; *see also* substance abuse–IVP relationship
Allen, Wanda Jean 3
ally 7; *see also* advocacy
American Association of Marriage and Family Therapists (AAMFT) 89, 92, 163
American Civil Liberties Union (ACLU) 3
amphetamines; *see* methamphetamine
APA (American Psychological Association): Division 44, 147; Ego Dystonic Sexual Orientation as mental disorder, DSM 89; Ethics Code 217, 220; Guidelines for Psychological Practice with Sexual Minority Persons (2021) 94; homosexuality as mental disorder, DSM 88–89; psychotherapy guidelines LGBT+ clients (2000) 94; terminology 7–8
aromantic 2, 8
asexual 2, 8
assessment; *see* intimate partner violence (IPV), assessment and diagnosis

Battered Wives (Martin) 32, 35, 47–48, 51
battered women: childhood, violence exposure 21; movement, advocacy 49,